Routledge Rei

The London and New York Stock Exchanges 1850-1914

First published in 1987, this is a reissue of the first book to offer a detailed comparison of two of the foremost stock exchanges in the world before 1914. It is not only an exercise in comparative economic history but it also relates these institutions to wider world markets, thereby clarifying their functions and how they related to the general financial and economic framework.

Students and researchers in economic and social history will welcome the reissue of this groundbreaking account of two historically important institutions in a crucial period of their development. Financial practitioners and others will also find much of interest here, in terms of both fascinating history and of insights into an era when a global market was rapidly evolving largely free of the twentieth-century distortions and hindrances introduced by wars, interventionist governments and exchange controls.

The London and New York Stock Exchanges 1850-1914

R. C. Michie

Routledge
Taylor & Francis Group

First published in 1987
by Allen & Unwin

This edition first published in 2011 by Routledge
2 Park Square, Milton Park, Abingdon, Oxon, OX14 4RN

Simultaneously published in the USA and Canada
by Routledge
270 Madison Avenue, New York, NY 10016

Routledge is an imprint of the Taylor & Francis Group, an informa business

Publisher's Note
The publisher has gone to great lengths to ensure the quality of this reprint but
points out that some imperfections in the original copies may be apparent.

Disclaimer
The publisher has made every effort to trace copyright holders and welcomes
correspondence from those they have been unable to contact.

A Library of Congress record exists under ISBN: 0043321178

ISBN 13: 978-0-415-66498-1 (hbk)
ISBN 13: 978-0-203-81851-0 (ebk)
ISBN 13: 978-0-415-66502-5 (pbk)

THE LONDON
AND
NEW YORK STOCK EXCHANGES
1850-1914

R. C. MICHIE
University of Durham

London
ALLEN & UNWIN
Boston   Sydney   Wellington

Allen & Unwin, the academic imprint of
Unwin Hyman Ltd
PO Box 18, Park Lane, Hemel Hempstead, Herts HP2 4TE, UK
40 Museum Street, London WC1A 1LU, UK
37/39 Queen Elizabeth Street, London SE1 2QB

Allen & Unwin Inc.,
8 Winchester Place, Winchester, Mass. 01890, USA

Allen & Unwin (Australia) Ltd,
8 Napier Street, North Sydney, NSW 2060, Australia

Allen & Unwin (New Zealand) Ltd in association with the Port
Nicholson Press Ltd,
60 Cambridge, Terrace, Wellington, New Zealand

First published in 1987

British Library Cataloguing in Publication Data

Michie, R.C.
    The London and New York Stock Exchanges,
    1850–1914.
1. Stock Exchange (*London*) – History
2. New York Stock Exchange – History
I. Title
332.64'24212   HG4577
ISBN 0–04–332117–8

Library of Congress Cataloging-in-Publication Data

Michie, R.C., 1949–
    The London and New York stock exchanges, 1850–1914.
Bibliography: p.
Includes index.
1. Stock Exchange (London, England) – History.
2. New York Stock Exchange – History. I. Title.
HG4577.M52   1987   332.64'241   87–1394
ISBN 0–04–332117–8 (alk. paper)

Set in 10 on 12 point Bembo by MCL Computerset Ltd,
Ely, Cambridgeshire
and printed in Great Britain by Billing & Son Ltd, Worcester

Contents

Preface   *page* ix

Introduction   xii

Part One   London   1

1   The London Stock Exchange and the British Securities
     Market   3

2   The London Stock Exchange and the International Securities
     Market I   34

3   The London Stock Exchange and the International Securities
     Market II   64

4   The London Stock Exchange and the Capital Market   99

5   The London Stock Exchange and the Money Market   132

Part Two   New York   165

6   The New York Stock Exchange and the Securities
     Market I   167

7   The New York Stock Exchange and the Securities
     Market II   194

8   The New York Stock Exchange and the US Economy   220

Conclusion   The London and New York Stock Exchanges:
     An Institutional Comparison   249

Bibliography and Sources   285

Index   304

Preface

Both the London and New York Stock Exchanges gave me free access to their archives, and I hope they have nothing to regret from such a decision. They can only become stronger by realizing the role they occupy within a market economy and the requirements it places upon them. The records of the London Stock Exchange are housed in the Guildhall, and I must thank the staff of that institution for their efficiency and hospitality. The New York Stock Exchange has its own archive department, under the control of Deborah Gardner, who made me most welcome, and I cannot thank her enough.

A history of this kind would be a poor one if its sources were confined to the institutions themselves. Consequently, I have to thank numerous other custodians of primary and secondary material, both manuscript and printed, for access to their collections. In London the British Library of Political and Economic Science proved a most valuable source of contemporary printed books, periodicals, journals, etc., supplemented by the holdings of the British Library and Guildhall Library. The Post Office Archives provided important insight into telegraph operations, while the Guildhall Library's holdings of banking, broking and discount records provided flesh to institutional accounts. In New York, the Watson Business Library at Columbia University possesses a large and wonderful, but little used, collection of contemporary books on financial themes rivalling that of the London School of Economics. New York Public Library and New York Historical Society also house important manuscript and printed collections which I was privileged to consult, such as the Annual Reports of the Consolidated Stock Exchange or the records of individual brokers.

Though London and New York provided the bulk of the material used in this study, a perspective on their position was obtained by investigating other stock exchanges in their respective countries. I was already familiar with Scottish operations but I carried this up to 1914 by consulting the archives of the Glasgow Stock Exchange, which was the most important British stock exchange outside London. In the United States more extensive work had to be done, which necessitated visits to Boston, Philadelphia, Chicago, San Francisco and New Orleans. The Boston and Midwest Stock Exchanges allowed me to consult their records, which gave an outsider's view of the New York Stock Exchange, and this was supplemented by the holdings of local and university libraries and historical societies.

All this research and travel required finance, and this was provided from three sources. On the British side grants from the Nuffield Foundation and the Social Science Research Council provided for the work in London, as well as a visit to Glasgow. The United States research was carried out when I was in receipt of a fellowship from the American Council of Learned Societies. Without finance a book of this kind on such a theme would have been impossible for a scholar based in the University of Durham. It was the money that these bodies provided – and I spent – that made this work possible and allowed an idea to be transformed into reality. I am grateful. I would also like to thank the people who made life bearable for me in London and New York when I was in these cities. My brother, Uisdean Michie, and my wife's brother, David Brooks, entertained me while in London; I doubt if I entertained them with my stories about the complexities and consequences of the London Stock Exchange rule book. In New York, I would like to thank Walt Korduba (of A. T. & T. Long Lines) for his generous hospitality to myself and my wife; he put a human face to the most exciting city either of us have ever lived in. On another level, conversation with Michael Edelstein made me realize I was not an economist but a historian.

I would also acknowledge a debt to my father-in-law, Professor J. L. Brooks, a lifelong sceptic of all matters financial. Whatever academic criticism this book receives will be minor in comparison to his dismissal of my whole field of research. In contrast, my mother is ever supportive. I would also like to thank Margaret Hall (the last secretary of the Department of Economic History) and Wendy Duery (of the Department of History) for converting my scrawl into typescript so quickly, efficiently and accurately.

Finally, producing a book of this kind is a lonely task, and I must thank my wife, above all, for the understanding she has shown over the years. It is to her (Dinah Ann Michie) that I dedicate this book.

R. C. Michie,
Department of History,
University of Durham
1986

Introduction

The history of the New York Stock Exchange is not contained
in its archives. From these dry bones and padding a skeleton figure
may be made and stuffed but it will have no true proportion, nor
life, nor footing. For any clear comprehension of the rise of the
Exchange, and its proportionate part in the money market of the
world, it is essential to bring clearly to mind how the institution
originated, how it has multiplied, and what is the basis of its
establishment, its permanence and its service.

(H. G. Hemming, *Hemming's History of the New York Stock
Exchange* (New York, 1905), p. 1)

This book begins where my other (*Money, Mania and Markets*) left
off, for I included in that work a chapter entitled 'London and
Scotland'. In retrospect it is clear that, whereas I knew a great deal
about Scotland, I knew very little about London. Hopefully, I have
rectified that inadequacy; but by adding the dimension of New York
I leave myself open to the charge that I know nothing about the
United States. That is for the reader to judge.

The aim of this book is very simple, for it has been motivated by
a desire to achieve an understanding of the functions occupied by
the London and New York Stock Exchanges, and to explain what
these were, to what extent they changed over time and how they
differed. To obtain this I have to digress from a straightforward
description and analysis of each stock exchange into an examination
of the capital and money markets, the transformation of communications and the workings of the international monetary system.
I hope the reader will regard these as filling a need rather than as
unnecessary irrelevancies, but without them I could not explain how
stock exchanges fitted into economic life. What emerges is that
unless one recognizes the essential connection between the stock
exchange and the money market, the principal role that that
institution occupied is missed altogether. Too many studies have

been obsessed by such themes as the stock exchange and the capital market or the stock exchange and speculation, and too few with accepting the stock exchange at face value and seeing what it actually did. If that is done, the stock exchange emerges as one of the most dynamic institutions of a capitalist economy.

What also emerges from the study is that the superficial similarity of financial institutions is an illusion. The London and New York Stock Exchanges provided the same function through the organization of a market for securities, but the way they did this differed substantially, with important consequences both for themselves and for the economies of which they were part. There was nothing inevitable in the way each evolved. At every stage, depending upon which direction was taken, the institutions could become more alike or more dissimilar. The principles of supply and demand will create a market whereby sellers and buyers can have their needs satisfied, but the form of that mechanism is very much a response to historical, social, cultural and other factors. Unless this is recognized, economics will find itself relegated to a position where it only explains long-term trends on a world basis, and is regarded as irrelevant in any examination of national differences and short-run changes. Not everything can be reduced to a model in which every factor is given a weight. At times there is no substitute for detailed investigation and the insight that comes from that knowledge.

The evolution of stock exchanges in the nineteenth century was both conditioned by world forces and modified by national experience, so that growth was not merely a process of repetitive duplication but an arena where institutions vied for primacy within a highly competitive environment, aided or hindered by the attitudes of their own membership and national governments and the openings that were available to them. Within Britain there were a series of simultaneous developments which moulded the securities market into a particular form, allocating specific roles to its distinct components. Britain's place in the expanding world economy helped transform the London Stock Exchange from merely one of the largest in the world into an institution performing a multitude of different functions on an increasingly international basis. Activity on the London Stock Exchange came to involve more and more the buying and selling of overseas securities on behalf of foreign investors by non-British brokers and dealers in response to fluctuations in the international money market. The London Stock Exchange was offering a service to the world which no other centre could match, drawing talent, money and business to it in consequence. Failure to recognize this entrepôt function invalidates any attempt to assess the relative success or failure of the London Stock Exchange in this period.

At the same time the expansion and integration of the British domestic economy underpinned the existence and continued growth of the provincial stock exchanges. These institutions continued to fulfil an important role though less and less as expressions of local or regional investment preferences and more and more as specialized components of the national securities market, providing an easy entry level for smaller enterprises and a trading forum for issues neglected by London or unsuited to its trading mechanisms. Again any study which only examined one component of the securities market, and then criticized it for not undertaking the functions carried out elsewhere, fails to recognize that it does not exist alone but in unison with the others. Would any study of British banking concentrate solely on the Bank of England without considering the contribution made by commercial banks, savings banks and merchant banks? Britain was a country of sophisticated and specialized financial institutions, each making their own particular contributions which have to be assessed before any deficiencies can be highlighted and their significance estimated. The fact that the London Stock Exchange did not fulfil a particular domestic role did not mean that the economy was in any way disadvantaged if that role was undertaken by another institution.

Within the United States similar problems and questions exist. The New York Stock Exchange moved from being a market for New York investors and New York enterprises to one with a national and international dimension. The New York Stock Exchange was the largest market for US securities and this brought it into intimate contact with the vast number of investors who held such securities worldwide and the other exchanges on which such securities were traded. As a result the New York Stock Exchange was given an importance within the US securities market greater than any other institution, for it acted as the point of equilibrium in the continuous ebb and flow of US securities between the US and Western Europe. At the same time regional and specialist markets continued to exist and thrive, responding to the dynamic growth of the US economy in both scale, variety and location. Again, it would be foolish to use the New York Stock Exchange alone as the basis for generalizations about the efficiency and performance of the US securities market.

This book then is an exercise in financial history in which the same institutions – stock exchanges – are compared and contrasted in different countries over the same time period. The focus is primarily the London Stock Exchange, which was the most important in the world at the time, and secondly the New York Stock Exchange, which was to replace London in the course of the twentieth century. In order to understand the significance of such institutions it is necessary to place them in the environment within which they existed and performed. In the course of the nineteenth century that became an increasingly international one. The growth and functioning of an integrated world economy, in which telegraphic communication and steam transport removed barriers to intercourse and large-scale movements of goods, people and capital, established close inter-dependent relationships and created an entirely new economic environment in the second half of the nineteenth century. This was especially so for Britain which was at the very centre of this world economy, and provided many of the services it required in order to function, such as the organization of shipping, trade, insurance and finance. Consequently, it was inevitable that the London Stock Exchange would be both influenced by these changes and orientate to meet the opportunities created. At the same time national economies, such as that of the United States, were being transformed out of all recognition in the course of the nineteenth century. The United States became, for instance, the major industrial nation of the world by 1914.

This study of the London and New York Stock Exchanges is consequently both an exercise in comparative economic history and an attempt to relate an institution to its wider world markets. By using both approaches it should become clear what were the functions of each stock exchange and how this related to the general financial and economic framework. At the same time it should be evident, from the way each responded to opportunities and challenges, that distinctive markets were created, with important implications for each country.

PART ONE

London

1 The London Stock Exchange and the British Securities Market

In 1876 Ellis referred to the London Stock Exchange as 'the most highly organized market in the world' and, as such, it attracted considerable interest and research.[1] Contemporaries wrote extensively about its history, structure and development, while its merits and defects were the subject of controversy and debate, reaching the level of a Royal Commission in 1878. Since then it has continued to attract attention either directly or as an important factor in Britain's economic performance between 1870 and 1914.[2] While this work has produced much information and understanding, it has also created a certain ambiguity concerning the role and importance of the London Stock Exchange. Studies of the London Stock Exchange itself tend to give it the central role in the securities market, but that is contradicted, especially for domestic finance, by work done on the provincial stock exchanges and on the general functioning of the capital market.[3] This conflict of opinion stems largely from the nature of the studies conducted into the London Stock Exchange, for these have concentrated upon its internal history and development to the virtual exclusion of its external relationships.

The London Stock Exchange was not the sole market for securities in Britain during the nineteenth century, but no attempt has been made to assess the relationship between the various British stock exchanges in a systematic way, or to examine the particular position occupied by London.[4] Through the examination of London's involvement with the Scottish securities market, which possessed a distinct regional identity, the growing integration of the national securities market can be traced, and the role played by the London Stock Exchange and its membership examined in detail. What emerges from this inquiry is the need to extend work on the

3

Stock Exchange from the institutional trading floor to the offices of the members, where their connections and business can be studied so that a fuller picture of the operation of the securities market can be obtained.

Until the mid–nineteenth century, the London Stock Exchange was largely occupied in providing a market for government securities, mainly those issued by the British government. There was trading in the stocks and shares issued by numerous joint-stock concerns, such as banks and insurance companies, gas- and waterworks, docks, canals, railways and miscellaneous institutions. However, even as late as 1840 activity in these was completely dwarfed by that in the obligations of the British and foreign governments. For example, of the £1.3 billion securities known in the London market in 1840, only 11 per cent had not been issued by governments, and, of that, much consisted of such quasi-government organizations as the East India Company, the South Sea Company and the Bank of England.[5] To an extent this domination of the London Stock Exchange by government securities reflected the concentration of their ownership in London. However, even those holders of the National Debt who resided far from London, such as the Scottish and Irish banks, channelled most of their buying and selling through members of the London Stock Exchange. This was so even where an alternative and more convenient stock exchange existed, as in the case of Dublin and the Irish banks. It was found that only London could provide a market that was both large enough and sufficiently well organized to cope quickly with substantial purchases and sales without extreme fluctuations in price.[6]

Despite the difficulties of communication in the early nineteenth century, investors outside London could keep in touch with activity on the London Stock Exchange, while London brokers had long-established contacts with country clients for whom they bought and sold government stock. By granting power of attorney, country clients could give their London brokers authority to deal on their behalf, while large investors, such as banks, could appoint agents who would act for them in such matters. Problems of delay and distance could be circumvented reasonably successfully, though it involved an element of trust by non-London investors. As a result, all trading in the National Debt was concentrated on the London Stock Exchange despite the fact that the holders were to be found nationwide.[7]

The securities known in London did not represent all those in existence in Britain. For example, only London-based joint-stock companies had their issues traded on the London Stock Exchange, because concerns begun elsewhere did not look to that institution for a market. Fenn noted in 1837, for instance, that 'the shares in the provincial gas companies are but little known in the London market', and a similar situation existed for all other forms of provincial joint-stock enterprise.[8] One statistical measure of London's involvement with provincial issues is the proportion of Scottish securities traded in the London market. In 1840 the Scottish securities in existence had a paid-up value of £18.6 million, and, of these, 37 per cent were known in London while 63 per cent were unknown (Table 1.1).[9] This percentage significantly overstates London's interest in Scottish securities, for the London Stock Exchange normally copied from the list produced by Edinburgh brokers, and knowledge therefore did not necessarily reflect participation. Generally, it was only the issues of major provincial enterprises, such as important railways, that attracted any attention on the London Stock Exchange.[10]

These non-London issues, however, were not devoid of a market, for there existed reasonably active trading in their securities in the area in which they operated, and in which the majority of their shareholders lived. There was also considerable trading between adjacent centres, especially where concerns such as banks, insurance companies and, later, railways operated outside one area and attracted a wider shareholding. The inter-market activity took place at the level of direct personal contact between individual brokers in each area, with communication being maintained by regular correspondence. Such an arrangement did not imply the existence of regional, let alone national, markets, but merely a willingness by brokers to try to effect a deal elsewhere on behalf of a client, if the local market proved inadequate. If a purchase or sale could not be made, the transaction became void, while it could often take a considerable time to arrange a deal in a specific security at a specific price and for a specific number of shares.[11]

The contrast between London and these provincial markets can be drawn by comparing the business of the London stockbroking firm of Marjoribanks, Capel & Co. in 1830 with that of the Edinburgh firm of John Robertson & Co. in 1833. During 1830 the

Table 1.1   *Scottish Securities in 1840 and 1883*

Category	Paid-up capital 1840	1883	Proportion quoted in London 1840	1883
Local government stock[a]	£0.3m	£2.1m	—	—
Railways[b]	£2.9m	£91.6m	30%	90%
Services[c]	£2.2m	£1.7m	—	19%
Financial[d]	£12.9m	£23.3m	47%	19%
Industrial, commercial, mining, etc.[e]	£0.3m	£8.2m	—	32%
Total	£18.6m	126.9m	37%	71%

Notes

Scottish securities were classified as the issues of local authorities or joint-stock companies domiciled in Scotland *and* known on the Scottish securities market. National concerns which operated in Scotland, and had shareholders there, were excluded.

[a] The great expansion of local authority borrowing did not come until the later 1880s, and much of that found a market in London.

[b] In 1840 about the only Scottish railway known in London was the Edinburgh to Glasgow line.

[c] The 1883 source omitted many of the smaller utilities which proliferated, such as cemetery companies, steam laundries, market halls, etc., while some gas- and waterworks had been taken over by the municipal authorities.

[d] By 1883 the London Stock Exchange had ceased to quote the Scottish banks. The financial concerns it did list were the larger Scottish insurance and investment companies, such as the North British (£625,000), Northern (£300,000), Scottish American (£360,254) and Scottish Australian (£800,000).

[e] By 1883 the larger Scottish industrial and mining enterprises found a market on the London Stock Exchange, such as Nobel's Explosives (£360,000), Young's Paraffin (£586,625) or Tharsis Sulphur (£1,453,960).

Source: C. Fenn, *A Compendium of the English and Foreign Funds* (London, 1840); J. Reid, *A Manual of the Scottish Stocks and British Funds* (Edinburgh, 1841); H. C. Burdett, *Burdett's Official Intelligence* (London, 1884); W. R. Lawson, *The Scottish Investors' Manual* (Edinburgh, 1884).

London firm handled business worth about £17.7 million, or £1.5 million per month, of which 88 per cent was in British government stock, 7 per cent in foreign government stock (mainly of France, Denmark and the United States), 4 per cent in the stock of the East India Company and only 4 per cent in other British and colonial securities. Virtually no business was done in British non-government issues. By contrast, in 1833 the Edinburgh firm handled a total of £152,000 of business, or £13,000 per month, of which 76 per cent was in Scottish banks and insurance companies, 19 per cent in local gas, water and industrial undertakings and 3 per cent in local canals and railways. The only non-local component was a few transactions in East India Company stock, amounting to 2 per cent of the total. Thus, the London broker's turnover was 38 times that of the Edinburgh broker, while the patterns of business were exact opposites, with London trading almost exclusively in government stock and Edinburgh in the issues of local joint-stock enterprise.[12] Therefore, as late as the 1830s there existed a compartmentalized securities market with activity centred on local markets, each with their own separate securities, personnel and institutions, and only limited interconnections between them. Where the London Stock Exchange possessed unique advantages, such as in providing, through trading in the National Debt, the only ready market for securities in Britain, it attracted business from throughout the country. Where it possessed no particular advantages, such as in the stocks and shares of joint-stock companies, it could not monopolize dealings.

In the era of contact by correspondence, activity on distant markets could not disturb the daily routine of business on the London Stock Exchange. There was no possibility of continuous interaction between markets. Even with the shortening of transport times through the introduction of railways, letters remained the only form of communication. The arrival of these letters made a once-and-for-all impact which was dissipated in the course of the day. Only those present on the floor of the exchange, or able to be in direct contact with them, were in a position to have a continuing influence. Conversely, the behaviour of the market during the day could have no influence outside the exchange itself or its immediate vicinity. It was only the transmission of the closing prices to other parts of the country that affected matters there; and again, that was a once-and-for-all impact. The inter-market communication that did exist was sufficient to keep prices roughly in line, with provincial markets taking their lead from London.[13] However, until the telegraph link was established, the provincial markets traded in ignorance of events in London, and could not adjust until the receipt of the London closing prices.

In order to measure the frequency and degree of divergence from London in the pre-telegraph era, the fluctuations in the price of

Caledonian Railway Stock were examined on both the London and Glasgow Stock Exchanges throughout 1846. These two markets were not linked by telegraph until 1847.[14] The Caledonian Railway had been formed in Glasgow in 1844 as one of two main trunk routes between Scotland and England, and its stock was held extensively in both countries. There were three issues in existence, namely, the old and new stock and the stock of the extension line, and all of them were quoted and traded on both the London and Glasgow Stock Exchanges.[15] For every dealing day during 1846 the range of prices realized by each on the London and Glasgow Stock Exchanges was compared. In only 30 per cent of the cases was there a match or even an overlap. During the rest of the time there was a gap between either the lowest price realized on the London Stock Exchange and the highest on the Glasgow Stock Exchange, or the lowest in Glasgow and the highest in London. This divergence between the prices at which the stock was being traded on each exchange averaged 10.5 per cent of the security's value. In 44 per cent of the cases the London prices were higher by a margin averaging 6.9 per cent, while Glasgow prices were higher 56 per cent of the time, with a 14 per cent average margin.[16]

The conclusion that emerges is that while the prices in each market were related, there was a frequent and considerable gap between the range of prices prevailing on each exchange on the same day. It took a substantial gap, existing for some time, before any movement towards equilibrium between markets was initiated.[17] The delays in communication that existed before the introduction of the telegraph, therefore, precluded the creation of an integrated securities market. Without continuous interaction the London Stock Exchange's impact on other domestic securities markets was restricted to a set of guidelines, in the form of closing prices, with the fluctuations in prices and interest in each market being mainly determined by local supply and demand conditions.

The revolution in communications that took place in the second half of the nineteenth century with the introduction of the telegraph and the telephone was to transform the securities market, and to alter fundamentally the role performed by the London Stock Exchange.[18] The first change came with the establishment of public telegraph lines linking London and the major British cities; this took place in the late 1840s, with the Scottish centres being among the last on the mainland to be connected. By virtue of these lines it became possible to communicate between geographically distant centres in minutes, as opposed to hours or days. Contemporaries were immediately aware of the implications of this for the securities market but it was to take a number of years before they could make full use of the new technology.[19] Not only had a public telegraph system to be constructed, and conveniently sited telegraph offices provided, but numerous technical difficulties had to be surmounted. Variations in the weather, for example, produced so many interruptions to the service that brokers were unwilling to rely upon the telegraph for inter-market communications, and so to integrate it into their daily routine of business. Even by the early 1850s, when these difficulties were being overcome, another problem was uncovered in that the capacity on certain routes was frequently insufficient to meet demand.[20] A system of rapid, reliable and continuous communication was required for inter-market contact, and until the telegraph could provide that its ability to integrate markets and encourage change was considerably circumscribed. However, even by the early 1850s, before the system was working perfectly, the telegraph was beginning to make its impact.

For the rest of the century the telegraph was an integral part of stock exchange operations. Special wires were provided to connect the various stock exchanges with each other, while the telegraphic offices were set up either adjacent to or within stock exchanges in order to provide a faster and more convenient service. In London, pneumatic tubes were installed linking the floor of the Exchange with the telegraph office, further reducing delays between deal and communication.[21] Probably the busiest route was that between the London and Glasgow Stock Exchanges, and here the volume of business periodically outran the capacity of the special wires to cope with it, despite the provision of extra facilities.[22] By 1905 it was estimated by the Post Office that the average time of transmission on this route was a mere 2½ minutes; 70 per cent of all telegrams were sent within 5 minutes of receipt, and 97 per cent under 10 minutes. Though delays could, and did, continue to take place 'due either to failing wires or sudden pressure', it was normal to send a message, have the deal done and receive confirmation well within the half-hour, and this had been the case since at least the 1870s.[23]

Between 1870 and 1899 the number of special wires connecting the London Stock Exchange with regional markets rose from 11 to nearly 60, while the number of telegrams sent from the telegraph office in the Stock Exchange increased from a maximum of 2,884 per day to 28,142 per day.[24] During the second half of the nineteenth century regular communication throughout the day between London and the provincial markets became important for the London Stock Exchange, while the provincial exchanges came to depend upon this new connection in order to function.[25]

The change that the telegraph brought to the securities market can be gauged from a comparison of London and Glasgow Stock Exchange prices for 1860, when the system of communications was well established. Two securities, common to both markets, were chosen, namely, Caledonian Railway Stock and the stock of the Grand Trunk Railway of Canada. During 1860 the daily prices achieved for both on each exchange matched or overlapped 78 per cent of the time. In the 22 per cent of cases where a gap did exist, the divergence was a mere 0.7 per cent of the securities' average value, ranging between 0.3 per cent for Caledonian and 1.2 per cent for Grand Trunk. When prices were out of phase London was higher 46 per cent of the time and Glasgow 54 per cent, with London averaging 0.8 per cent higher and Glasgow 0.6 per cent higher.[26] Consequently, the frequency of matching achieved in 1860 was 2.6 times greater than that of 1846, while the degree of divergence in 1860 was only 7 per cent of that experienced in 1846. Clearly, the price ranges within which each market operated throughout the day had become closely aligned, with any divergence being minimal in comparison to what had prevailed in the past. The London–Glasgow comparison testified to the convergence between geographically separate components of the securities market that had taken place as a result of rapid telegraphic communications, with the timing of the change being related to the arrival of the telegraph. For the first time activity on the floor of the London Stock Exchange could influence behaviour in other markets, and in turn be influenced by them when business was in progress. The possibility now existed for the formation of a single market in securities that would respond to national, rather than to local, supply and demand conditions.

The other development which contributed to the integration of the securities market was the creation of securities common to, and actively traded on, more than one market, and this coincided with the telegraph. During the railway mania numerous railway companies had been formed which attracted investors not only from their own locality but also from other areas, if only from the towns and cities served by the line.[27] As a consequence, the stock issued by the major railways was traded in numerous different centres, and as companies grew in size and range their securities were listed on more and more markets. By the end of December 1845, for example, the Glasgow Stock Exchange quoted 110 railway companies, of which 23, or 21 per cent, were also quoted on the London Stock Exchange. As a result of the numerous amalgamations, the Glasgow Stock Exchange quoted only 46 railway companies by the end of December 1860, but 59 per cent of these were also quoted in London.[28] The proportion of securities unique to any one market was falling at the expense of those common to more than one. A measure of the change can be seen from the securities of Scottish companies in existence in 1883. By then the paid-up value of these securities totalled £126.9 million, of which 71 per cent was also quoted on the London Stock Exchange, compared with only 37 per cent in 1840, and this reflected genuine activity in London rather than copying from each other's lists. The change was caused principally by the railway sector, for Scottish concerns such as the North British and the Caledonian were heavily traded on the London Stock Exchange (Table 1.1). The association between stock exchanges through the quoting of common securities grew in the second half of the nineteenth century. By 1910, for example, the proportion of British railway securities quoted on only one stock exchange had become minute in comparison with those quoted on more than one. The London Stock Exchange quoted British railway securities with a paid-up value of £21.2 million that were unique to itself, but shared £1,149.8 million with Liverpool, £1,141.6 million with Glasgow, £1,105.4 million with Manchester and £1,010.6 million with Edinburgh (Table 1.2). Though only a portion of this would be actively traded on every exchange, it did represent securities commanding a national market. Consequently, while the telegraph provided the means by which the isolation of markets was removed, railway securities provided both an incentive to use the new form of communication and a form of currency which could be moved between centres in order to preserve equilibrium nationally. Without common securities, localized imbalances in the

11

Table 1.2 *Association Matrix: British Railway Securities quoted on British Stock Exchanges, 1910 (£m)*

	Lon.	Abd.	Bel.	Bir.	Bra.	Bri.	Car.	Cor.	Dub.	Dun.	Edn.	Gla.	Hal.	Lds.	Liv.	Man.	New.	Shf.	Swa.
London	21.2	424.1	251.6	970.5	412.1	672.8	317.2	69.8	655.5	0.2	1,010.6	1,141.6	382.0	926.3	1,149.8	1,105.4	497.8	989.2	270.1
Aberdeen	424.1	—	136.5	409.7	382.5	339.6	204.1	—	312.1	0.5	424.3	422.8	345.4	404.8	423.9	415.5	350.1	393.0	156.9
Belfast	251.6	136.5	0.1	23.7	136.5	233.7	151.9	24.1	244.8	—	233.7	233.7	136.5	233.7	250.2	247.0	195.5	195.5	151.9
Birmingham	970.5	409.7	23.7	—	404.0	630.1	285.9	—	672.3	—	914.4	988.1	373.7	881.6	1,043.0	1,050.5	470.3	935.3	238.7
Bradford	412.1	382.5	136.5	404.0	—	350.6	204.1	—	294.1	—	403.8	385.3	343.9	403.8	403.8	409.4	331.5	400.1	156.9
Bristol	672.8	339.6	233.7	630.1	350.6	0.3	316.6	—	511.8	—	606.5	628.1	332.6	615.9	642.5	631.5	413.7	620.1	271.8
Cardiff	317.2	204.1	151.9	285.9	204.1	316.6	—	—	259.7	—	268.7	396.3	209.3	278.1	307.7	299.3	221.2	288.6	274.7
Cork	69.8	—	24.1	—	—	—	—	0.2	36.3	0.1	—	0.5	—	—	19.3	13.5	—	—	—
Dublin	655.5	312.1	244.8	672.3	294.1	511.8	259.7	36.3	3.0	0.5	665.3	688.0	257.2	634.9	702.7	699.1	406.7	678.5	212.6
Dundee	0.2	0.5	—	—	—	—	—	0.1	0.5	0.1	0.5	0.5	—	—	—	—	—	—	—
Edinburgh	1,010.6	424.3	233.7	914.4	403.8	606.5	268.7	—	665.3	0.5	3.2	1,012.0	365.9	881.4	1,004.8	982.2	473.9	924.9	221.5
Glasgow	1,141.6	422.8	233.7	988.1	385.3	628.1	396.3	0.5	688.0	0.5	1,012.0	3.2	373.7	915.6	915.6	1,035.7	493.7	983.3	247.0
Halifax	382.0	345.4	136.5	373.7	343.9	332.6	209.3	—	257.2	—	365.9	373.7	—	368.6	373.7	374.5	340.7	370.0	162.1
Leeds	926.3	404.8	233.7	881.6	403.8	615.9	278.1	—	634.9	—	881.4	915.6	368.6	0.3	918.5	947.4	393.6	885.8	230.9
Liverpool	1,149.8	423.9	250.2	1,043.0	403.8	642.5	307.7	19.3	702.7	—	1,004.8	915.6	373.7	918.5	2.1	1,103.6	494.8	984.5	260.5
Manchester	1,105.4	415.5	247.0	1,050.5	409.4	631.5	299.3	13.5	699.1	—	982.2	1,035.7	374.5	947.4	1,103.6	0.7	494.8	1,034.0	252.2
Newcastle	497.8	350.1	195.5	470.3	331.5	413.7	221.2	—	406.7	—	473.9	493.7	340.7	393.6	494.8	494.8	—	497.8	168.9
Sheffield	989.2	393.0	195.5	935.3	400.1	620.1	288.6	—	678.5	—	924.9	983.3	370.0	885.8	984.5	1,034.0	497.8	—	241.5
Swansea	270.1	156.9	151.9	238.7	156.9	271.8	274.7	—	212.6	—	221.5	247.0	162.1	230.9	260.5	252.2	168.9	241.5	0.1

The table shows the railway securities (paid-up value) quoted on British stock exchanges and the degree to which they were quoted on one or more stock exchange. For example, of the British railway securities quoted on the Glasgow Stock Exchange only £3.2m worth were quoted there, while £1,012m were also quoted on the Edinburgh Stock Exchange and £1,141.6m on the London Stock Exchange. Thus, of the British railway securities quoted at Glasgow, only 0.3 per cent was unique to itself, while 99.7 per cent was found on other British stock exchanges.

Source: Stock Exchange Official Intelligence (London, 1911).

supply of, or demand for, stocks and shares would continue to result in dramatic price fluctuations and an inability to meet requirements. With common securities, local price changes would generate an immediate flow from, or to, that centre so that all markets would rise and fall in line. As each separate market was undermined by a simultaneous removal of the barriers of distance and unique securities, they became components of an integrated national market.

Allied to the development of the telegraph were improvements which allowed those buying and selling on the floor to communicate rapidly outside, with either their offices, clients or brokers on provincial markets. A partial solution to this problem appeared in 1867 with the invention of the ticker-tape machine. This device, with its operator and a staff of reporters collecting prices, allowed a continuous record of prices to be relayed from the floor to all who subscribed to the service, within minutes of a change taking place.[29]

Later, with the appearance of the telephone in the late 1870s, a direct two-way instantaneous communication could be opened up between the floor of the exchange and offices outside, and thence to anyone who possessed a telephone.[30] Through the use of the telephone, buying and selling prices quoted on the floor of the exchange could be matched against those obtainable elsewhere, with the result that bargains could be struck outside the exchange. An alternative market could be created through these inter-office telephone links, which was an extension of that existing on the floor of the stock exchange and interacted with it. This market was not confined to those who happened to be present on the floor at any one time, but could involve all those who were known to be interested in any particular security. As a result, a much larger market was created than the confines of the stock exchange allowed, with benefits for closer pricing, stability and liquidity. One indication of the extensive use to which the telephone was put was that, during October 1908, 81,883 outward and 23,916 inward calls were made or received at the stock exchange telephones linked to brokers' offices. In approximate terms, this meant that a telephone call was made every 6 seconds and one received every 21 seconds during the working day, and this excluded all subsequent office calls.[31]

At first, the telephone provided a purely local service, linking subscribers in one town. However, by the mid-1880s it had become technically feasible to communicate over much longer distances, though Britain was slow to exploit this new possibility because of government restrictions and the Post Office's monopoly of telecommunications.[32] Nevertheless, by 1889 a programme was in hand to link the London Stock Exchange with the provincial stock exchanges by means of direct cables, thereby avoiding delays created by routing via local telephone exchanges. This system came into being during the 1890s.[33] Though numerous complaints were made about the quality of the service, it was put to immediate and extensive use. On the London Stock Exchange the congestion around the trunk line telephone was such that members had to book calls in advance, while on the Glasgow Stock Exchange the times when the telephone to London could be used were ballotted for, and each member was limited to one call every six minutes.[34]

However, though the use of the public system continued, it was increasingly bypassed as the main artery of inter-market communication by the private telephone wire, which began to appear around 1900. These wires linked the offices of London Stock Exchange members directly with the offices of provincial brokers. By keeping this line open throughout the day, and allied to each broker's direct telephonic link from his office to his own exchange, a continuous and immediate two-way contact was established between trading in London and activity elsewhere. This facility was superior to that of the public wires, which were soon relegated to handling the less important business.[35] The development and use of the telephone at local and national level finally overcame the separation of markets caused by distance.[36] There was now only one market, though it might operate in more than one location; for no matter the distance involved, direct and immediate voice contact could be established between those trading in each centre, and that was all that physical proximity gave. The confines of the institution no longer determined the parameters of the market and the forces acting upon it.

This revolution in communications, culminating with the telephone, did more than link London with the provincial exchanges; it also altered the relationship between them, the means of doing business and the whole operation of the market. Before the telegraph, each broker had in other markets his contacts – or correspondents – with whom he transacted business which could not be done locally. This type of relationship continued to exist, being especially useful in securities for which the market was limited, and buying and selling was a matter of negotiation.[37] However, in those securities for which an active market with constantly changing prices existed, the telegraph became the means of communication. In addition, the telegraph made 'shunting' a possibility for the first time. Shunting was the name given to the simultaneous buying and selling of the same security on different domestic exchanges.[38] As the time taken to communicate between markets fell, so did the risk attached to buying or selling in one market, in the expectation of selling or buying in another, in order to close the deal and profit from the price differential. The longer a deal was open, the greater the chance that prices would change, resulting in a loss rather than a profit; consequently shunting was discouraged. With the telegraph, prices in more than one market could be monitored almost simultaneously, and when a difference occurred in the price of a security it could be bought in the lower market and sold in the higher one at the same time. By this process not only were markets kept in equilibrium, but a ready market in securities was created. The profits to be made on the fractional differentials that appeared momentarily encouraged the practice to grow. As a result, shunting became a common practice in the 1850s and was widespread in the 1860s. This was despite some initial opposition from the provincial exchanges, which saw the process as diverting business either to London or to each other.[39]

On the provincial stock exchanges brokers dealt directly with each other, while in London brokers normally transacted business through a jobber, who quoted a buying and selling price for the security in question. The jobber earned his income, or obtained his 'turn', from the margin between these prices. Consequently, if the provincial broker could enter into direct contact with the London jobber, he would not have to share any of the profit made on fractional differences between London and other markets with a London broker. The jobber could quote his buying and selling prices to the provincial broker over the telegraph, in the same way as he quoted them on the floor to London brokers on a person-to-person basis. The jobber would still receive his 'turn', with the prospect of increased turnover from this new business, while the provincial broker would have direct access to London, allowing him to trade at better prices in certain securities and to receive all the profit from any differentials between markets. As early as the 1860s London jobbers appear to have established direct links with provincial brokers. London brokers did continue to play an important role in inter-market activity, as they possessed long-established contacts and an ability to roam the market transacting a varied business, while each jobber dealt in a restricted range of stocks. Nevertheless, the consequence of the improved communications was to break down the division within the London Stock Exchange between jobbers, who acted as market intermediaries and traded on their own account, and brokers, who acted for outside clients and did not quote prices. Increasingly, jobbers formed trading contacts with provincial brokers, while London brokers, in order to compete, began to act as dealers for their provincial contacts.[40]

This change was brought to the fore by the introduction of private telephone lines linking London jobbers or brokers with provincial brokers. Each line cost in the region of £2,000 per annum to rent, and few firms were willing to expend that amount of money. However, those that did invest in the new technology possessed a much more rapid and flexible system of communication, and one which was available for their exclusive use without interruption or delays throughout the day. This led to a concentration of shunting in the hands of a few rather than its being shared generally among the membership of the London Stock Exchange. By 1904 there were ten London Stock Exchange firms with direct lines to the provinces, and these were coming to dominate all inter-market trading, apart from the difficult deals involving negotiation. As a consequence, a distinct group appeared on the London Stock Exchange which specialized in shunting securities between London and the provincial markets, almost to the exclusion of the others who had previously participated in the business. Similar specialization also took place on the provincial stock exchanges.[41]

These shunters were not just passive intermediaries between markets, but active participants. Morrison, a dealer in the miscellaneous market, explained in 1906: 'It was not to be expected that his correspondents at the centre where the chief market was would supply him with frequent prices unless they had some prospect of his bringing them business and unless he had constant quotations from the provincial market he could not make prices here [in London] and the whole business would be sent there direct.'[42] Consequently, it became necessary for the London shunters, whether brokers or jobbers, to integrate their provincial contacts fully into their operations. Not only did they quote their bid and sell prices to provincial brokers, but they also offered to divide with them the 'turn' they made on each purchase or sale. Thus, a provincial broker who bought or sold on behalf of a London shunter benefited from the whole profit to be made from buying in one centre and selling in another, and not just from the difference between the provincial prices and the buying *or* selling prices quoted by London dealers.

At the same time, the London shunters sought to become dealers in the securities traded in the provincial exchanges. As business on the provincial exchanges grew in the second half of the nineteenth century, the call-over system of trading twice a day proved increasingly inadequate. The Glasgow Stock Exchange, for example, abandoned the system for actively traded securities in the mining mania of the mid-1890s, banishing them to another room where there was not only no call-over but also no other procedure. Consequently, there was a growing need on the provincial exchanges for dealers who would act as the market in active securities, buying from and selling to brokers. However, no single provincial exchange had sufficient turnover to justify dealers, though together they had.[43] It was the London shunters who were in a unique position to provide this, as they possessed immediate and extensive contacts on all the provincial exchanges. Warren, a London shunter, described their activities in 1908: 'They stood in the market and telephoned to the country the close prices here [London] and their correspondent dealt on those prices: profits and losses on the bargains at each end were divided, as was the cost of the Telephone, but other expenses or bad debts were not divided.'[44]

The London shunters, therefore, came to fulfil a number of important roles. First, they acted as intermediaries between the London and provincial exchanges, buying and selling indiscriminately in each, depending on price fluctuations. Secondly, they acted as intermediaries between different provincial exchanges, buying in one and selling in the other. Morrison, for example, claimed that 'he was often able to make a profit between the Irish

Exchanges and those of Manchester and Glasgow'.[45] Lastly, behind all this was the fact that the London shunters, through their contacts, made the market in a growing range of securities. Their contacts on the provincial exchanges were kept in constant receipt of the London prices and constantly replied with the provincial prices, and were able to act as their agents, quoting buying and selling prices, accepting deals on their behalf and transmitting these to the London dealer who would seek to close the deal elsewhere and adjust his prices accordingly. In the miscellaneous section of the London Stock Exchange, which covered some eight hundred commercial and industrial companies in 1908, the main trading in many of the securities was in the provincial centres, but London dealers were able to quote close prices and to maintain an active market because of their shunting operations.[46] Thus, even in the areas where the London Stock Exchange was not the natural market, such as in provincial issues, London dealers became increasingly important not only because they kept markets in line, but also because they provided the market-making service which was missing on the provincial exchanges and which was becoming a vital necessity if an active market was to be established and maintained.

This did not mean that the provincial exchanges were being eclipsed by London in the second half of the nineteenth century, as has been suggested by both Reed and Anderson. The overall volume of provincial business was growing and becoming more diversified as the nation increasingly held its wealth in the form of transferable securities. On the Aberdeen Stock Exchange, for example, turnover rose from an average of £98,644 per annum in the 1850s to £114,704 in the 1860s, £261,609 in the 1870s and £353,702 in the 1880s, before falling back to £291,105 in the 1890s, when there was a general switch of interest from securities to property. Impressionistic evidence from other provincial exchanges also suggests a steady growth in business after the collapse of the railway mania in the mid-1840s. The London and provincial exchanges could share in a rapidly expanding volume of business and complement each other, rather than compete for what was available. Though London did develop markets in securities which had once been the exclusive field of the provincial exchanges (such as non-London joint-stock enterprise), this helped to create business both for London and the provinces. The London jobbers helped to establish a wide and active

18

market in these securities, which generated increased dealing on the provincial exchanges and attracted the interest of investors at a national level. The provincial stock exchanges gradually lost their position of being self-contained markets in local securities, and gained a place as specialist components of a national market catering for a particular size of issue or type of enterprise. All the exchanges were being absorbed into an integrated market and given new roles to fulfil, and the shunting jobbers and brokers of London were at the very centre of this rearrangement.[47]

The integration of the securities markets encouraged by these technological and organizational changes did not go unchallenged. The London Stock Exchange, in particular, contained powerful vested interests which opposed change. Unlike the other British stock exchanges, which either owned or rented the premises they occupied, the members of the London Stock Exchange did not control the building they used. This was provided by a company that derived its income from the fees paid by the members. Consequently, it was in the interest of the managers of the London Stock Exchange to make it the only market for securities, and so attract a numerous fee-paying membership. Conversely, the members derived their income from buying and selling securities, either on their own behalf or for clients, but that need not necessarily take place on the floor of the exchange. The fear of the managers was that if free access was given to the prices prevailing on the exchange throughout the day, many brokers could deal at market prices without ever becoming members. Thus the management resisted any changes that might lead to business being transacted outside the stock exchange. When a request was made to install an exchange telegraph in 1868, for example, it was turned down by the management.[48] Eventually, pressure from the membership, which desired the convenience of access to market prices while in their offices, forced the managers to give way. However, it was not until November 1872 that a ticker-tape machine was allowed into the stock exchange. Even then, the service was never allowed to operate to its fullest extent. Only members of the exchange were allowed to become subscribers and the prices relayed provided no more than a guide, for the number of operators and reporters was restricted. These restrictions slowed down the collection and transmission of price changes and the frequency with which prices could be sent out.[49] Consequently, the objections of the managers prevented London prices being made continuously available on the provincial markets. This forced provincial brokers to continue to rely on their contacts with members of the London Stock Exchange for such information, with the result that there was a continuous flow of telegrams between individual members of each exchange. This flow would have been necessary anyway to transmit buying and selling orders, so the lack of a constant and accurate ticker-tape service, relaying London Stock Exchange prices, had only a limited effect on inter-market relationships. It denied other exchanges complete and quick access to the London prices, by which their markets were regulated, without restricting the private communication of this information and the buying and selling operations that accompanied it.

With the appearance of the telephone in the late 1870s, the management of the stock exchange faced a new threat; those trading on the floor could now be directly connected with interested parties outside. The first application to introduce a telephone service between the London Stock Exchange and outside subscribers was made in November 1879. It was rejected.[50] It was not until the exchange was enlarged in 1882–3 that a telephone room was provided, and even then the facilities remained inadequate, inconvenient and of limited use.[51] In contrast to the London Stock Exchange, the provincial stock exchanges accepted the telephone almost immediately.[52] Faced with the continued refusal to provide proper facilities for telephones, in July 1888 the members threatened to find an alternative to the facilities provided by the stock exchange unless the managers gave way.[53] The management backed down, putting only minimal obstacles in the way of further expansion; the year 1888 marked the end of any serious resistance by the management to the changes created by the communications revolution.[54]

However, the managers were not the only group opposing the new developments. While the members of the provincial stock exchanges accepted and profited from their new function, many members of the London Stock Exchange came to resent the change and sought to reverse it, especially the many brokers who had lost their provincial trade to the specialist shunting firms. A general feeling arose that buying and selling had been diverted from London to the provinces. The chairman of the London Stock Exchange summarized their case for the benefit of the provincial exchanges in August 1911: 'By direct communication with our Dealers, country brokers were enabled to deal on the London market on as good terms as a London Broker, while evading the heavy expense and responsibility of London membership . . . Our Exchanges are, and must remain, in competition one with the other – each exchange is, for varying reasons, the principal market in certain stocks and shares.'[55] This view, and the reasoning behind it, was beginning to emerge by 1903 because of the concentration of the provincial business in the hands of a few firms with private telephone wires. It led to a sustained attack on the close relationship between the London shunters and the provincial exchanges, and ignored the growing unity of the securities market which was destroying the individuality of each exchange and forcing a readjustment of organization and working practices.[56] There were those who recognized the implications of the new development and the benefits it brought both to the London Stock Exchange and the securities market in general. One such person was Braithwaite, who stated in January 1908 that 'The shunter has made it possible to deal in anything in which there is a market anywhere, often at a moment's notice or within a very short space of time, which is a great advantage to all concerned.'[57] The essential question was whether business was to be attracted to the London Stock Exchange, because of the superior market offered by its membership through contacts on the floor and by telephone; or whether it was to be forced to come, at the expense of the national market, by denying provincial brokers direct access to London dealers. The majority of the membership chose the latter course since they had no direct stake in the former.

The line of attack used was that of dual capacity. The existing rules prevented jobbers from dealing directly with non-members, while brokers were forbidden to buy and sell on their own account. These rulings had fallen into abeyance, but if they could be revived, shunting would be rendered much more difficult and costly. Access to jobbers would be denied to provincial brokers, while London brokers would be prevented from making a market for their provincial contacts.[58] Eventually, after much debate and many changes of opinion, a new rule was passed for implementation on 1 February 1909. By this rule, dual capacity was forbidden, with

21

no broker being allowed to quote prices and no jobber being allowed to deal for non-members. The restoration of single capacity was the ostensible purpose of this rule, but it was designed mainly to restrict shunting between London and the provincial exchanges, for dual capacity was officially recognized for the purposes of arbitrage with foreign exchanges.[59] However, by the simple device of nominally passing provincial business through co-operative brokers at minimal commission rates, this attempt to limit shunting was quickly circumvented. There were no minimum commission rates on the London Stock Exchange, and the charges made by brokers could be so low as to prevent any serious interruption to shunting. Once the ineffectiveness of the dual capacity rule was recognized, moves were made to block the loophole by implementing a minimum set of commission rates. This was finally achieved in June 1912, and did lead to a marked reduction in the level of shunting between London and the provincial stock exchanges, though it is likely that there was considerable evasion of the minimum rate rules.[60]

The problem was that those members of the London Stock Exchange who benefited directly from shunting were a small minority, especially since the introduction of private wires. Consequently, the majority of the membership could introduce changes detrimental to shunting. Provincial brokers were not members of the London Stock Exchange. Although they warned that it would reduce business and impair the efficiency of the market, their views and opinions were largely ignored, both on the issue of dual capacity and on minimum commission rates. The provincial exchanges did attempt to find an alternative to the use of London, through the circulation of lists between themselves and the formation of a central information office in London to communicate buying and selling requirements. Neither tactic met the needs of an active market and both were eventually abandoned, while the plan to set up a rival stock exchange in London, called the United Exchange, was never attempted, though twice suggested. In 1914, when the war closed all the stock exchanges, the provincial exchanges had not yet persuaded the London Stock Exchange to modify its restrictions on shunting.[61] Consequently, from 1909 onwards and particularly in the two years before the First World War, the efficient operation of the national securities market was slowly circumscribed by restrictions imposed by members of the London Stock Exchange.

This limited provincial brokers in their previously open, easy and inexpensive access to the London Stock Exchange and thus restricted the role played by London dealers in creating an active nationwide market in provincial securities. The rules and regulations imposed by the London Stock Exchange upon its membership had implications for the whole securities market because of the links formed and the roles played by London jobbers and brokers.

Before the imposition of these restrictions there had come into existence an integrated national securities market in Britain, which functioned efficiently at all levels. At the lowest level there existed the market for the securities of numerous small concerns, operating in such fields as industry, commerce, finance, mining and services. This market was to be found within each provincial stock exchange or direct broker-to-broker trading in London. Though this market was neither active nor sophisticated, it did provide a means by which purchases and sales could be made without difficulty.[62] At the same time, links between members of different exchanges meant that it was easy for investors to purchase the securities of any non-local concerns which attracted them.[63]

At the next level were to be found the securities of the larger joint-stock concerns, such as railways and, later, many industrial, commercial and mining ventures. As companies grew in size, by either merger or internal expansion, their stocks and shares were to be found throughout the country rather than in one restricted locality.[64] These securites were, therefore, not to be found on any one exchange, though each had its own specialities, such as Sheffield in engineering, Glasgow in iron and coal, Cardiff in shipping and Liverpool in insurance.[65] The location of a specialist market in any security was unimportant because, by means of shunting and the operations of London dealers, an active market was created to which all investors had equal access through their own local broker.

While the London Stock Exchange did not provide the best market for the securities of many types of joint-stock enterprise, it was still quite willing to quote these securities once they reached a size which could generate sufficient business, such as a paid-up capital value of over £100,000. This indicated a willingness to buy and sell, not necessarily in London but wherever the market lay, and the same was true for the provincial exchanges. By the end of 1900, for example, 98.5 per cent of all securities quoted on the Glasgow

Stock Exchange were also to be found quoted on the London Stock Exchange. Even for a very local exchange, such as Aberdeen, the proportion was 96 per cent (see Table 1.3). These included many Scottish-based concerns which had acquired a London quotation because of their size and extensive operations. Consequently, Edelstein's view that 'the bulk of the securities listed on the provincial stock exchanges from the 1870s to World War I were never traded in London' is not really true.[66] Certainly there were numerous smaller joint-stock companies which possessed a purely local quotation (Table 1.3), and it is also true that the London Stock Exchange was not the main market in many branches of joint-stock enterprise.[67] Nevertheless, the members of the London Stock Exchange were instrumental in creating a wider and more active market in domestic joint-stock enterprise through the integration of their own and the provincial exchanges into a national securities market, in which they acted as the central dealers for the whole system because of the rapid and continuous communications available.

The final level of this national securities market concerned the huge consolidated issues of governments, such as the British National Debt. Though this was quoted on other domestic

Table 1.3(a) *London Stock Exchange, 31 December 1900*

Category	Paid-up capital of quoted securities	Per cent quoted in London alone	London and Glasgow	Per cent quoted in London alone	London and Aberdeen
Government	£3.741m	74.2	25.8	100.0	—
British	£912m	18.6	81.4	100.0	—
Foreign	£2.829m	92.2	7.8	100.0	—
Railways	£3,012m	33.2	66.8	87.6	12.4
British	£1,256m	22.0	78.0	62.1	27.9
Foreign	£1,756m	41.2	58.8	98.7	1.3
Services	£186m	79.0	21.0	100.0	—
Financial	£228m	76.8	23.2	97.0	3.0
Industrial, commercial and mining	£443m	79.7	20.3	99.9	0.1
Total	£7,610m	58.5	41.5	95.0	5.0

Table 1.3(b) *Glasgow Stock Exchange, 31 December 1900*

Category	Paid-up capital of quoted securities	Per cent quoted in Glasgow alone	Glasgow and London	Per cent quoted in Glasgow alone	Glasgow and Aberdeen
Government	£966m	0.1	99.9	100.0	—
British	£743m	0.1	99.9	100.0	—
Foreign	£223m	—	100.0	100.0	—
Railways	£2,016m	0.1	99.9	81.5	18.5
British	£983m	0.3	99.7	64.0	36.0
Foreign	£1,033m	—	—	98.0	2.0
Services	£44m	11.4	88.6	99.7	0.3
Financial	£68m	22.1	77.9	79.8	20.2
Industrial, commercial and mining	£113m	20.4	79.6	99.4	0.6
Total	£3,207m	1.5	98.5	87.9	12.1

Table 1.3(c) *Aberdeen Stock Exchange, 31 December 1900*

Category	Paid-up capital of quoted securities	Per cent quoted in Aberdeen alone	Aberdeen and London	Per cent quoted in Aberdeen alone	Aberdeen and Glasgow
Government	—	—	—	—	—
British	—	—	—	—	—
Foreign	—	—	—	—	—
Railways	£373m	—	100.0	—	100.0
British	£351m	—	100.0	—	100.0
Foreign	£22m	—	100.0	—	100.0
Services	£0.2m	100.0	—	24.0	76.0
Financial	£18.1m	62.0	38.0	24.0	76.0
Industrial, commercial and mining	£3.3m	86.0	14.0	81.0	19.0
Total	£394.6m	4.0	96.0	2.0	98.0

Sources: London Stock Exchange Official List, 31 December 1900; Glasgow Stock Exchange Official List, 31 December 1900; Aberdeen Stock Exchange Official List, 31 December 1900; *Stock Exchange Official Intelligence* (London, 1901).

exchanges, the only market was to be found on the London Stock Exchange, to which all orders were directed. Such was the volume of turnover there that no other centre in Britain could rival London's ability to buy and sell immediately any amount of government stock at close to the current price. The London Stock Exchange's success in doing this enabled it to attract all the business in government stock, which gave it the turnover that allowed it to be the unrivalled market in government stock, and so perpetuated its position. Over time the same picture was to emerge in other securities as they gravitated to the most active market, but that had not happened before the First World War. There were trends in that direction in the stock of the larger English railways, but they were being replaced for shunting purposes by the securities of the larger industrial, commercial and mining companies.

As a result of the existence of securities trading at different levels, the unification between exchanges provided by shunting, and the market-making activity of London dealers, an efficient securities market had been provided for the whole of Britain by the early twentieth century. Companies could find an appropriate place in this market and this could easily change over time according to their growth and appeal. In addition, the range of securities for which a ready market existed had been greatly widened by the development of this national market. Even by the late 1850s only the National Debt could be bought and sold without difficulty and delay, and the improvement by the 1870s had been slight. However, by the early twentieth century there were some two hundred active issues which it was easy to buy and sell at close to market prices, and these included the securities of major railways as well as of a number of large industrial and commercial concerns.[68]

It was this market which was undermined by the action taken by members of the London Stock Exchange in banning dual capacity in 1909 and implementing minimum commission rates in 1912. These measures meant that the domestic market for securities was beginning to operate less efficiently, because the unrestricted communication between London dealers and provincial brokers had been replaced by one which had to go through London brokers and bear commission charges. Not only, therefore, did provincial brokers find it more expensive to use the London market, but the provincial exchanges as a whole were discouraged from using the services provided by London dealers which had become such a vital part of their operation. The eventual result for the market was spelled out clearly by a number of dealers, including Morrison, in a circular published in January 1908:

The pre-eminence of London as the money centre of the world and the greatest exchange mart lies in the freedom from restriction in dealing, and any attempt to impose unnecessary restrictions on a commercial community in the conduct of its transactions must lead sooner or later to the loss of business. The present methods of carrying on business in the House have grown up with the expansion of business, and the increased facilities for its transaction throughout the country and the world. Business must inevitably gravitate towards the centre where it can be despatched with the greatest cheapness and facility, and the new Rule will interfere with both.[69]

However, that had hardly come to pass by the First World War, though the omens were clear.

Thus it becomes evident that the London Stock Exchange, when the actions of the membership are examined, did come to play a central role in the British securities market. This was not only at the level of the issues of governments or vast corporations but also throughout the range of securities available. Though located in London offices, a number of London Stock Exchange brokers and jobbers maintained constant and immediate communication with contacts on other exchanges, and acted in concert with them to ensure the existence of a continuous market in a growing volume and variety of stocks and shares. By the early twentieth century the securities market had become complex and sophisticated, offering an opening at the most appropriate place and level to all transferable securities, and providing a facility by which these securities could become known to the entire investing public when their size and nature warranted it. Securities were not an homogeneous good, and the organization of the market in which they were dealt recognized this fact. However, in the few years before the First World War the functioning of this market was being circumscribed because the majority of members of the London Stock Exchange had lost the direct benefits they obtained from external contacts, and had failed to perceive the indirect benefits brought by an open market. As a result, institutional barriers were imposed which sought to reverse the trends produced by improved communications, beginning with the telegraph in the mid-1840s. Outside interests were powerless to halt such actions because they were non-members.

27

Notes

This chapter first appeared as R. C. Michie, 'The London Stock Exchange and the British Securities Market 1850–1914', *Economic History Review*, vol. 38 (1985), pp. 61–82.

1 A. Ellis, *The Rationale of Market Fluctuations* (1876), p. 25.

2 *Royal Commission on the London Stock Exchange, Report and Minutes of Evidence* (British Parliamentary Papers, 1878, XIX). For a bibliography of works on the Stock Exchange, see E. V. Morgan and W. A. Thomas, *The Stock Exchange: Its History and Functions* (London, 1963), pp. 287–90. Of the general works the following are the most relevant: A. K. Cairncross, *Home and Foreign Investment, 1870–1913* (Cambridge, 1953); A. R. Hall, *The London Capital Market and Australia, 1870–1914* (Canberra, 1963); P. Cottrell, *Industrial Finance, 1830–1914* (London, 1980); M. Edelstein, *Overseas Investment in the Age of High Imperialism: The United Kingdom, 1850–1914* (London, 1982); W. P. Kennedy, 'Institutional Response to Economic Growth: Capital Markets in Britain to 1914', in L. Hannah (ed.), *Management Strategy and Business Development* (London, 1976), pp. 155–76.

3 See Morgan and Thomas, *Stock Exchange*, chs. 6–8, for the role of the London Stock Exchange, and the following for an alternative assessment of its importance: Hall, *London Capital Market*, pp. 27, 67–8; Cairncross, *Home and Foreign*, pp. 90, 95; Cottrell, *Industrial Finance*, pp. 146–53; J. B. Jefferys, *Business Organisation in Great Britain, 1856–1911* (New York, 1977), pp. 317–18; W. A. Thomas, *The Provincial Stock Exchanges* (London, 1973), pp. 68, 119; R. C. Michie, *Money, Mania and Markets: Investment, Company Formation and the Stock Exchange in Nineteenth-Century Scotland* (Edinburgh, 1981), pp. 253–61.

4 See Morgan and Thomas, *Stock Exchange*, chs. 5–10.

5 C. Fenn, *A Compendium of the English and Foreign Funds* (London, 1840); L. H. Jenks, *The Migration of British Capital to 1875* (New York, 1927), p. 14; C. Duguid, *The Story of the Stock Exchange* (London, 1901), p. 162; Morgan and Thomas, *Stock Exchange*, p. 79.

6 J. R. Ward, *The Finance of Canal Building in Eighteenth-Century England* (Oxford, 1974), p. 142; J. Lowe, *Present State of England in Regard to Agriculture, Trade and Finance* (London, 1823), p. 364; J. R. Killick and W. A. Thomas, 'The Provincial Stock Exchanges, 1830–1870', *Economic History Review*, vol. 23 (1970), pp. 102, 105; C. W. Munn, 'The Scottish Provincial Banking Companies, 1747–1864' (PhD thesis, Glasgow University, 1976), pp. 183, 207–8, 305–7; *Bankers' Circular*, 27 November 1827; *Report from the Select Committee on Joint Stock Banks* (British Parliamentary Papers, 1837, XIV) Q. 4402–4 and (British Parliamentary Papers, 1838, VII) Q. 1015.

7 R. M. W. Cowan, *The Newspaper in Scotland* (Glasgow, 1946), p. 5; H. Hamilton, *An Inquiry Concerning the Rise and Progress, the Redemption and Present State and Management of the National Debt* (Edinburgh, 1818),

pp. 313–14; *The Calumnious Aspersions Contained in the Report of the Subcommittee of the Stock Exchange Exposed and Refuted* (London, 1814), p. 31; M. C. Reed, *A History of James Capel & Co.* (London, 1975), pp. 5–6; W. Reader, *A House in the City* (London, 1979), p. 38; E. Pinto, *'Ye Outside Fools': Glimpses inside the Stock Exchange* (London, 1877), p. 32; J. Reid, *A Manual of the Scottish Stocks and British Funds* (Edinburgh, 1841), p. 119; *Glasgow Herald*, 4 August 1834.

8   Fenn, *Compendium* (1837 edn), p. 135; cf. Fenn, *Compendium* (1837 and 1840 edns).

9   Comparisons between Fenn, *Compendium* (1840), and Reid, *A Manual*.

10   Michie, *Money, Mania and Markets*, p. 15; M. C. Reed, 'Railways and the Growth of the Capital Market', in M. C. Reed (ed.), *Railways in the Victorian Economy* (Newton Abbot, 1969), pp. 162–3, 172–4.

11   Cf. Watson/Robertson, Correspondence 1834–7 (Glasgow University, Special Collection MS Gen. 531/13); Thomas, *Provincial Stock Exchanges* p. 36; Michie, *Money, Maina and Markets*, pp. 39–46, 66–74; Reed, 'Railways', pp. 162–3.

12   Reed, *James Capel & Co.* pp. 28–30; Michie, *Money, Mania and Markets*, pp. 70–3, 255.

13   Thomas, *Provincial Stock Exchanges*, pp. 35–6, 75; *Scottish Railway Gazette*, 27 September 1845; Circular of Robert Allan, November 1845, March 1843; *Railway Record*, 24 October 1846.

14   *Scottish Railway Gazette*, 11 November 1847.

15   J. Butt and J. T. Ward, 'The Promotion of the Caledonian Railway Company', *Transport History*, vol. 3 (1970), pp. 255–6.

16   The daily lists of both the London and Glasgow Stock Exchanges for 1846 and 1860 are held by the Economic History Archive of Glasgow University.

17   *Scottish Railway Gazette*, 26 December 1846.

18   E. T. Powell, *The Mechanism of the City* (London, 1910), pp. 63–4; Morgan and Thomas, *Stock Exchange*, p. 126.

19   *Edinburgh Weekly Journal*, 5 February 1845; cf. J. L. Kieve, *The Electric Telegraph: A Social and Economic History* (Newton Abbot, 1973), chs. 2–4.

20   Glasgow Stock Exchange, Minutes, 21 December 1847, 19 May 1852.

21   Edinburgh Stock Exchange, Minutes, 6–14 January 1851; Aberdeen Stock Exchange, Minutes, 10 March 1854; cf. Kieve, *Electric Telegraph*, pp. 71, 82–3, 119, 237; Morgan and Thomas, *Stock Exchange*, p. 162; Thomas, *Provincial Stock Exchanges*, pp. 102–3; Agreement between the Stock Exchange and the Electric Telegraph Co., 13 March 1868.

22   Glasgow Stock Exchange, Minutes, 9 and 15 October 1879, 5 October 1880.

23   Glasgow Stock Exchange, Minutes, 27 December 1900, 15 January 1901, 17 December 1901, 21 November 1905, 5 December 1905, 20 December 1905, 4 September 1906, 19 April 1910; London Stock Exchange (LSE): Committee for General Purposes, 21 March 1876.

24 W. E. Hooper (ed.), *The Stock Exchange in the Year 1900* (London, 1900), p. 159; LSE: Trustees and Managers, Minutes, 9 December 1870; General Purposes, 10 March 1881; Commission on London Stock Exchange, Minutes, p. 30; E. Pinto, *'Outside Fools'*, p. 40; *Stock Exchange Investments: Their History, Practice and Results* (5th edn, 1897), p. 172.

25 Aberdeen Stock Exchange, Minutes, 22 December 1897, 19 February 1901; GPO London to Sec., Aberdeen Stock Exchange, 21 December 1897.

26 See note 16.

27 Killick and Thomas, 'Provincial Stock Exchanges', p. 105; E. C. Maddison, *On the Stock Exchange* (London, 1877), p. 159; Michie, *Money, Mania and Markets*, pp. 117–18; J. P. Lee, 'The Provision of Capital for Early Irish Railways, 1830–53', *Irish Historical Studies*, vol. 16 (1968–9), p. 40; *Scottish Railway Gazette*, 28 December 1850, 18 January 1851; Bell, Begg & Cowan, (Stockbrokers, Edinburgh), Monthly Circular, April 1887, May 1891, February 1895.

28 See note 16.

29 A. D. Poley and F. H. Gould, *The History, Law and Practice of the Stock Exchange* (London, 1911), pp. 262–3.

30 J. E. Day, *Stockbrokers' Office Organisation, Management and Accounts* (London, 1911), p. 100.

31 LSE: Gen. Purposes and Trustees and Managers, Co-Joint Committee, 5 November 1908, 8 June 1909.

32 G. R. Porter and F. W. Hirst, *The Progress of the Nation* (London, 1912), pp. 564–6; Kieve, *Electric Telegraph*, pp. 211–14; C. R. Perry, 'The British Experience, 1876–1912: The Impact of the Telephone during the Years of Delay', in I. de S. Pool (ed.), *The Social Impact of the Telephone* (Cambridge, Mass., 1977), pp. 80–1; B. T. Robson, *Urban Growth: An Approach* (London, 1973), pp. 166–71.

33 LSE: Trustees and Managers, 6 March 1889, 4 April 1889, 16 May 1889, 15 October 1889, 15 March 1899; Hooper, *The Stock Exchange*, p. 161.

34 LSE: Gen. Purposes, 15 February 1904, 29 February 1904, 12 October 1904, 6 October 1913; Gen. Purposes Subcommittee to Confer with the Exchange Telegraph Co., 20 December 1902; Gen. Purposes and Trustees and Managers, Co-joint Committee, 4 May 1909; Trustees and Managers Subcommittee on Enlargement of the House, 17 January 1898, 12 February 1900; Glasgow Stock Exchange, Minutes, 3 February 1897, 31 January 1899, 21 February 1899, 26 February 1901, 17 December 1901, 31 May 1904, 11 October 1904, 29 November 1904.

35 LSE: Gen. Purposes, 12 October 1904; Thomas, *Provincial Stock Exchanges*, pp. 104–5.

36 J. F. Wheeler, *The Stock Exchange* (London, 1913), p. 83; C. Duguid, *The Stock Exchange* (London, 1913), pp. 154–5; Day, *Stockbrokers' Office Organisation*, pp. 217–18.

37 Day, *Stockbrokers' Office Organisation*, p. 100; Michie, *Money, Mania and Markets*, pp. 191–3, 198, 202.

38 The motive behind shunting was to profit from the minute and temporary differences in prices that appeared on different markets reflecting variations in local supply and demand conditions.

39 LSE: Gen. Purposes, 13 March 1865, 21 March 1876, 8 December 1891, 18 December 1906, 18 December 1907; Duguid, *Stock Exchange*, pp. 154–5, 158; H. Withers, *The English Banking System* (Washington, 1910), p. 118; Glasgow Stock Exchange, Minutes, 12 February 1856, 25 March 1857; Michie, *Money, Mania and Markets*, p. 201.

40 LSE: Gen. Purposes, 16 December 1903, 18 December 1903; *Phillips' Investors' Manual* (London, 1887), p. 339; Duguid, *Stock Exchange*, p. 350; Memorandum by the Chairman of the Stock Exchange for the Council of Associated Stock Exchanges (Gen. Purposes, 24 July 1911); *Royal Commission on the London Stock Exchange*, p. 115.

41 LSE: Gen. Purposes, 12 February 1902, 4 January 1904, 15 February 1904, 29 February 1904, 4 December 1906, 12 December 1906, 18 December 1906, 3 January 1907, 7 February 1907, 27 January 1908, 23 July 1908, 24 July 1911; *Financial Times*, 27 January 1908; *The Times*, 17 January 1908; *Investor's Review*, 15 February 1908; Thomas, *Provincial Stock Exchanges*, pp. 105, 209.

42 LSE: Gen. Purposes, 18 December 1906.

43 Michie, *Money, Mania and Markets*, p. 205; *Royal Commission on the London Stock Exchange*, p. 9; Glasgow Stock Exchange, Minutes, 5 January 1847, 12 January 1847.

44 LSE: Gen. Purposes, 27 January 1908, 18 December 1907.

45 LSE: Gen. Purposes, 29 January 1908.

46 LSE: Gen. Purposes, 18 February 1903, 27 January 1908, 2 July 1908; *Royal Commission on the London Stock Exchange*, pp. 126–30; *The Economist*, 30 May 1885.

47 LSE: Gen. Purposes, 15 October 1906, 12 November 1906, 28 November 1906, 12 December 1906, 18 December 1906, 3 February 1908; Thomas, *Provincial Stock Exchanges*, pp. 89, 119; Michie, *Money, Mania and Markets*, pp. 226–7 and ch. 16; Reed, 'Railways', pp. 181–2; B. L. Anderson, 'Law, Finance and Economic Growth in England: Some Long-Term Influences', in B. M. Ratcliffe (ed.), *Great Britain and her World, 1750–1914* (Manchester, 1975), p. 116; Hall, *London Capital Market*, p. 40.

48 LSE: Trustees and Managers, 14 October 1891, 7 October 1868.

49 LSE: Trustees and Managers, 5 February 1873; H. Davies, Sec. of Exchange Telegraph Co. to Sec., Com. for Gen. Purposes, 1 October 1872; W. King, Managing Director, Exchange Telegraph Co., to Sec., Com. for Gen. Purposes, 10 April 1907; Com. for Gen. Purposes Subcommittee to Confer with Exchange Telegraph Co., Minutes, 17 December 1886, 29 November 1892, 30 December 1908; Exchange Telegraph Co., List of Subscribers and Instructions, June 1890;

Memorandum on the Exchange Telegraph Co., 7 December 1878; Morgan and Thomas, *Stock Exchange*, p. 163.
50 LSE: Trustees and Managers, 5 November 1879, 29 January 1880.
51 LSE: Trustees and Managers Subcommittee on the Enlargement of the House, 16 January 1882, 9 March 1883.
52 Glasgow Stock Exchange, Minutes, 2 November 1880, 28 February 1882.
53 LSE: Gen. Purposes, Subcommittee appointed to Confer with the Exchange Telegraph Co., Minutes, 16 April 1886, 29 November 1886, 21 February 1887, 19 November 1887, 29 November 1893.
54 LSE: Trustees and Managers, 11 July 1888, 7 November 1888, 2 January 1889, 3 June 1903.
55 LSE: Gen. Purposes, 24 July 1911.
56 LSE: Gen. Purposes, 18 February 1903, 23 April 1903, 21 May 1903, 29 February 1904, 15 October 1906, 28 November 1906, 7 February 1907.
57 LSE: Gen Purposes, 29 January 1908; cf. 18 February 1903, 18 December 1906, 27 January 1908, 2 July 1908.
58 Duguid, *Stock Exchange*, p. 158; F. Cheswell, *Key to the Rules of the Stock Exchange* (London, 1901), p. 350; W. G. Cordingley, *Guide to the Stock Exchange* (London, 1893), p.12.
59 LSE: Gen. Purposes, 23 July 1908; Thomas, *Provincial Stock Exchanges*, p. 90.
60 LSE: Gen. Purposes, 1 June 1909, 13 January 1912, 2 September 1912, 8 July 1914; Gen. Purposes Subcommittee on Commissions, 1 July 1912, 4 July 1912, 30 September 1912, 20 November 1912, 24 January 1913.
61 Glasgow Stock Exchange, 14 January 1908, 21 January 1908, 28 January 1908, 7 July 1908, 25 August 1908, 1 September 1908, 8 September 1908, 15 September 1908, 29 September 1908, 6 October 1908, 13 October 1908, 8 December 1908, 2 March 1909, 23 March 1909, 14 April 1909, 18 May 1909, 8 June 1909, 15 June 1909, 14 December 1909, 20 January 1910, 15 February 1910, 8 March 1910, 23 January 1912, 29 May 1912, 11 June 1912, 29 October 1912, 26 November 1912, 3 December 1912, 28 January 1913, 11 March 1913, 22 April 1913, 14 May 1913, 10 June 1913, 24 June 1913, 1 July 1913, 23 September 1913, 14 October 1913, 18 November 1913, 10 March 1914, 24 March 1914, 26 May 1914, 23 June 1914.
62 T. Skinner, *The Stock Exchange Year-Book* (London, 1874), p. 211; Michie, *Money, Mania and Markets*, chs. 14–17; Day, *Stockbrokers' Office Organisation*, p. 218. Small may be defined as having a capital of under £100,000; see F. Gore-Brown and W. Jordan, *A Handy Book on the Formation, Management and Winding-up of Joint-Stock Companies* (London, 1902), pp. 453–4.
63 Michie, *Money, Mania and Markets*, pp. 191–2.
64 *Stock Exchange Gazette*, 30 March 1901, 21 September 1901, 28

December 1901; *Investors' Monthly Manual*, 31 January 1887; Cottrell, *Industrial Finance*, p. 92; M. A. Utton, 'Some Features of the Early Merger Movements in British Manufacturing Industry', *Business History*, vol. 14 (1972), p. 52; L. Hannah, 'Mergers in British Manufacturing Industry, 1880–1918', *Oxford Economic Papers*, vol. 26 (1974), pp. 7–8, 14, 18; Jeffery, *Business Organisation*, p. 435; J. S. Jeans, *Railway Problems* (London, 1887), pp. 52–3, 105; R. B. Weir, 'The Distilling Industry in Scotland in the Nineteenth and Early Twentieth Centuries' (PhD thesis, Edinburgh University, 1974), pp. 290, 320, 332–5, 568.

65 C. McLaren, 'Prospects of Iron and Steel Investments', *Financial Review of Reviews (FR)*, October 1906, pp. 249–53; A. R. Foster, 'Cotton Spinning Companies', *FR*, February 1907, pp. 249–51; M. M. Mason, 'Dangers of Colliery Investments', *FR*, November 1913, p. 903; G. D. Ingall and G. Withers, *The Stock Exchange* (London, 1904), p. 117; Thomas, *Provincial Stock Exchanges*, pp. 68, 119.

66 Edelstein, *Overseas Investment*, p. 57.

67 Hall, *London Capital Market*, p. 26; Anderson, 'Law, Finance', p. 116; Cairncross, *Home and Foreign*, pp. 95–6; Jefferys, *Business Organization*, pp. 370–1.

68 *Royal Commission on the London Stock Exchange, Minutes*, p. 30; Gresham Omnium, *A Handy Guide to Safe Investments* (London, 1858), p. 95; Investors' Guardian, *Guide to Investments* (London, 1873), p. 7; General Securities Corporation, *The Investors' Handy Book of Active Stocks and Shares* (London, 1912), pp. ix–xi.

69 H. Morrison & Co. *et al.*, Circular, 20 January 1908.

2 The London Stock Exchange and the International Securities Market I

'Great Britain easily leads the world in the volume of her stock exchange business,' reported C. A. Conant, an American, in 1904.[1] He was typical of the many contemporaries who considered the London Stock Exchange to be by far the largest and most important stock exchange in the world, whether measured by the paid-up capital of quoted securities, the size of active membership, or impressions of the volume of turnover.[2] From 1795, when Amsterdam's Bourse lost its premier position with the arrival of French troops, until 1914, with the outbreak of the First World War, London possessed the world's leading stock exchange. The Paris Bourse had posed a strong challenge during the mid-nineteenth century, but never fully recovered from the disruption caused by the Franco-Prussian war of 1870.[3] The only other serious rival was the New York Stock Exchange; but even by 1914, despite rapid growth, one of its own officials – S. F. Streit – estimated that London's turnover was ten times greater than that of New York. It was the First World War that gave the New York Stock Exchange its opportunity to gain pre-eminence among the world's security markets.[4]

The London Stock Exchange was not only the world's largest before 1914, it was also the most international. In 1903, for example, another American, S. S. Pratt, noted that 'The bonds of every Government, the stocks of every country, are traded in London', and drew unfavourable comparisons with New York, where 'Wall Street confines itself to the securities of the United States.' This opinion of London was echoed by other commentators, such as the British expert on stock exchanges, W. J. Greenwood, in 1911.[5] Only Paris could vie with London as an international centre, and then only in an inferior position. Paris tended to quote and trade in the securities of other European or Mediterranean countries, whereas London's interest was worldwide. This interest also reflected the maintenance of active and intimate connections between the London Stock Exchange and foreign financial centres, particularly in the United States, the Empire and continental Europe.[6]

In a general sense, then, the London Stock Exchange, in conjunction with the other institutions of the City of London, occupied a dominant position in the world economy between 1850 and 1914. Also, in contrast to many other sectors of the British economy, the services provided by 'the City' remained strongly competitive over this period, and probably became of even greater importance. The French economic historian, François Crouzet, in his recent survey of the British economy, arrived at this conclusion: 'The multilateral system of payments ... ensured that every thread of the world's commercial and financial networks passed through London, so that it was between 1870 and 1913 that the City was truly the economic heart of the world.'[7] However, there has been no real attempt to explain how and why the London Stock Exchange, let alone the City itself, became so important in the half-century before the First World War, or to examine whether this growth merely reflected the business generated by the British investor or indicated that London occupied a central position in an international securities market.

The London Stock Exchange's international involvement predated the foundation of the exchange itself in 1773, and was thus partly inherited. During the eighteenth century, British securities, such as government issues and the stock of the East India Company and the Bank of England, were held extensively abroad, especially by the Dutch. As a result close links were established between the members of the Amsterdam Bourse and those operating in the London securities market. The regular settlement of deals in London, for example, was timed to coincide with that in Amsterdam, with a delay to accommodate the arrival of the mail packet. Financial conditions in London generally exhibited similar trends to those in Amsterdam, suggesting a degree of contact between the two financial centres.[8] Nevertheless, integration between the London securities market and those abroad was not fully achieved, though purchases and sales were made in London on behalf of overseas contacts. An examination by L. Neal, for

35

instance, of the prices at which the stock of the Bank of England, the East India Company and the South Sea Company was being traded in both London and Amsterdam during the eighteenth century revealed persistent price differentials between the two markets. This suggests the existence of parallel markets, with a degree of interconnection, rather than an integrated international market, setting uniform prices through competitive buying and selling in different regional centres. At the same time it was clear that, in the eighteenth century, it was the Amsterdam Bourse that dominated, with London taking its lead from there.[9]

During the period of prolonged European warfare and economic disruption, beginning with the French Revolution in 1789 and ending with the Battle of Waterloo in 1815, the position of the London Stock Exchange was considerably altered. Foreign holdings of British securities were reduced to small dimensions and continued to fall afterwards, while it was the British investor who was coming to hold foreign securities, especially the stocks and bonds of governments in continental Europe, the United States and South America.[10] By 1840 a total of £1,303 million (nominal values) of securities was known in London, and, of these, £428 million, or 32.8 per cent, were foreign, of which all but 9.3 per cent were government issues.[11] However, these statistics give a completely false impression of London's active involvement with foreign securities. Many of the South American and United States loans had been defaulted on during the 1820s and 1830s respectively, and their securities were of limited current value and little traded.[12]

At the same time, though the national debts of numerous European governments were known in London, most were never dealt in there – or, at best, only specific issues, and then infrequently. As Charles Fenn observed in 1837: 'The business transacted in the Dutch funds, in the English market, is usually in that portion of the debt raised in Holland, which is issued in bonds, principally of 1,000 florins each, and is negotiable here at the fixed exchange of 12 florins per £ sterling.'[13] Therefore, though foreign securities did attract attention from time to time during the first half of the nineteenth century, interest and activity in them on the London Stock Exchange were neither sustained nor substantial, according to contemporary opinion.

During this period, activity on the London Stock Exchange was dominated by dealings in the British National Debt, which had been greatly swollen by the years of war, and there the buying and selling were largely on behalf of domestic clients.[14] What trading in foreign securities there was was largely confined to those which had been specifically issued in Britain and were held largely by British investors, and so did not involve much contact for the London Stock Exchange with the nationals or markets of other countries. Overseas links did exist – with, for instance, some trading in *rentes* between London and Paris – but this appears to have been of little permanent significance within the market as a whole. The same was true for the flurry of interest in French railway stocks shown in the mid-1840s, for most of these returned to France in the 1850s and ceased to be actively dealt in on the London Stock Exchange. Similarly, though there was considerable interest in US securities, especially state and railroad bonds, involvement remained hesitant before 1850, coloured by the lack of success of previous issues.[15]

Altogether, by 1853, when the paid-up capital of securities quoted on the London Stock Exchange was £1,215 million, a total of £101 million, or 8.3 per cent, was foreign, with 70 per cent emanating from governments and 30 per cent from railway companies. This amount excluded securities that had been issued abroad rather than in Britain, many of which would be known in London and, doubtless, some part-held there. Conversely, of those issued in London not all would necessarily be held there.[16] Consequently, this amount and proportion probably reflected the degree of involvement with, and level of interest in, foreign securities shown by the members of the London Stock Exchange at mid-century. This limited commitment is not surprising given the considerable scepticism regarding the safety and stability of foreign securities because of their poor record to date.[17]

A number of these foreign securities were also quoted on stock exchanges abroad, and possessed active markets there. The £3.5 million Austrian loan of 1852, for instance, had been issued simultaneously in London and Frankfurt, and was traded in both these centres as well as in Paris. Similarly, many of the French and United States railway stocks listed in London at mid-century were to be found respectively on the Paris Bourse or the New York Stock Exchange.[18] This meant that there did exist certain securities that not only were common to more than one market but also were being actively traded in more than one centre. They were not numerous but they did exist, and London had its share of them. Consequently, the buying and selling of these on the London Stock Exchange would both be influenced by similar actions elsewhere and influence events in foreign centres, since the securities were identical whatever their location. A growing demand for an international security in one centre would produce a rise in price there, which, in turn, would provoke a similar rise in another centre, where the security could also be bought, for it could be then transferred to the place at which it was required.

If markets were closely in touch, and if these common securities were of sufficient importance to each, fluctuations in their price, reflecting investors' responses to local conditions, would be automatically transmitted from one market to another through trading activity, and would in turn influence the prices of purely local securities. The result would be that these common securities would act as a governor on the fluctuations in each market, keeping them in line through their continued ebb and flow between exchanges as relative prices changed, and allowing business to gravitate to the markets offering the best prices. Under such circumstances an integrated security market for the world could be created in which one exchange could become a dominant force, to which all others had to adjust. This would be very different from the existence of common trends on different exchanges as each responded in a standard fashion to shared economic experience, such as variations in interest rates, but without any significant or direct interconnections between them. The former represented a position where competition could take place, with certain countries, institutions, or individuals gaining and others losing. The latter was a situation of separate markets moving roughly in line as dictated by similar economic forces.

Even by 1850 limitations to international communications continued to pose a considerable impediment both to the creation of an integrated security market and to London playing much more than a local role in the buying and selling of securities. As long as communications were served by physical means, contact between different financial centres remained too slow to cater for the requirements of an active and sensitive security market, where prices could change continuously throughout the day. Even the coming of the railway and steamship, improvements as they were, merely reduced the degree of impediment without eliminating its significance. By mid-century the fastest form of human transport between London and the nearest foreign exchange, Paris, involved hours of travel, with the closing prices of the Paris Bourse not being received at the London Stock Exchange until 10 a.m. the following day.[19]

From an early stage, attempts were made to circumvent these communication difficulties. Carrier pigeons, for example, were used on the London–Paris route; however, their use was possible only in the summer and was too unreliable to be the basis of regular business.[20] As a result of communications that were inadequate for requirements in the securities market, each national exchange operated in ignorance of its foreign neighbour during the working day and, at best, could only make adjustments at the beginning of the next trading session, when information regarding conditions elsewhere had been received. In the case of Austrian bonds in 1851, for example, the members of the London Stock Exchange were making deals based on Amsterdam prices that were four days old. This caused considerable problems in settling bargains, which the London buyer or seller expected to complete by selling or buying abroad, if prices had changed substantially from those current in London at the time the sale or purchase was agreed.[21]

Under these conditions, for any given security the best market lay where the greatest concentration of investors existed, for that was where turnover would be greatest and where the most likely opportunity existed of dealing at the most advantageous price for the appropriate amount. Therefore, each exchange possessed a certain immunity from competition in those securities the investors residing in its vicinity were interested in; for only it would offer an active market in most of them, and, even where it did not, the time involved in communications would restrict the use of another exchange.

It was possible to buy or sell on other markets, even for the purpose of closing deals opened on one exchange by a matching sale or purchase on another. The fortnightly settlement periods on the London Stock Exchange gave time to contact other European centres, for example, while holding a fixed price deal in London. However, because of the delay involved, and the volatile nature of security prices, the risks incurred were substantial, being directly related to the time elapsing between making a deal in one centre and closing it in another. In order to compensate for the large risk, there had to be the promise of great gain. An illustration of the existence of such international trading in securities, and their speculative nature, comes from the correspondence between Kingsmill Davan, a Liverpool merchant, and his Philadelphia associate, Andrew Clow, in October 1791:

> if you could purchase a quantity of 6 pcts [US government bonds] at parr or 21s per £ on a short credit, on our Joint acct. and enclose it to me immediately, I think they would sell at £120 per £100, when they arrived here. I would make sale at London of it and either pay amt. to your Banker or whoever you direct. You might venture to buy one or £2,000 at the above price. 3 pcts or Deferred will be dangerous at present prices, as t'is impossible it can continue – British stocks are fallen . . . I hope you receive this acct. of rise of stocks in time to profit by it.[22]

However, as the Davan/Clow case indicates, it took a differential of over 14 per cent between British and US prices before the risk of buying in one market and selling in another became acceptable, and the whole affair was one of chance rather than a regular component of business. Little had really changed by the mid-nineteenth century.[23]

It was possible to minimize the risk attached to dealing between exchanges, or utilizing distant markets, by purchasing a 'put' or 'call' option or privilege in London. Through such options the purchaser obtained the right to buy or sell a security at a fixed price at a certain date in the future. This allowed the London price to be fixed and gave sufficient time to allow conditions on other markets to be investigated, with the hope of a profit resulting from any differentials that were found to exist. For example, if a put option was held, and the security could be purchased more cheaply elsewhere, then a profit would result by buying abroad and selling in London. The reverse would be the case with a call option. Naturally, however, those guaranteeing to buy or sell at current prices in three or six months' time charged for the privilege they were extending, and these charges could be up to 20 per cent of the market value of the security in question. This made the purchase of an option a costly procedure and limited its use to those securities where or those occasions when large price differentials were assumed to exist.[24]

The difficulties of communication, then, by denying the necessary information to each exchange and its membership, or by making the costs of minimizing it too great, prevented the creation of an international market in securities, even though the appearance of such was heralded by some contemporaries during the railway mania of the mid-1840s. In October 1845, for instance, *The Economist* claimed:

> These shares [of foreign railways], like government stock of different countries, are now general securities, which are equally dealt in on our own Stock Exchange here and on the Continent; and, like government stock, are another measure which the value of money will be equalised in this and other countries.
>
> The chief countries in Europe may be termed one money market, for they all immediately act upon each other. If money be wanted in Paris stock will fall, and if the shares are not sent to London for sale, English or French, or Spanish or some other stocks which pay best, will be sent and sold on our market, and English capital thus abstracted to pay up the calls of French shareholders.[25]

Though all this was true, the statement disregarded the degree to which such movements took place, the time involved before change occurred and the fact that the amounts transferred were not of sufficient importance to make a major impact. A more realistic observation of the contemporary state of affairs came from *The Times* in the same year, when it noted in March 1845 that 'The heaviness of prices on the Paris Bourse has influenced the market here.'[26]

Securities did flow between London and financial centres abroad, and the London Stock Exchange did influence, and was influenced by, activity on other markets, but this did not mean that the London Stock Exchange was either externally orientated or in a premier position among other exchanges. On all exchanges domestic securities and domestic investors dominated business, and problems of communication meant that the London Stock Exchange had neither the opportunity nor the inclination to play a central role in an international securities market that hardly existed. The picture at mid-century was of a series of loosely connected national or even regional securities markets in which trading was largely controlled by local supply and demand conditions, with only the major imbalances modified by inter-market movements. With the growth of common securities both the pre-conditions and the need for an international securities market existed, but the speed of communications remained unsuited for the nature of the business. Under these circumstances the London Stock Exchange was large because local investment and speculation made it so, and its importance was largely confined to Britain.

This state of affairs was transformed by the revolution in international communications that took place in the second half of the nineteenth century. For Britain, this began with the opening of the submarine cable between Dover and Calais in 1851. In conjunction with the internal telegraph system established in each country, this provided a rapid and direct link between London and Paris, and thence to the exchanges in each centre. Under-sea cables were then laid to other European countries, integrating Britain into the telegraph network of continental Europe.[27] By 1889, 3.6 million telegrams a year were being exchanged between Britain and the rest of Europe, and this reached 6.5 million in 1907, or one telegram every five seconds, with transmission times being measured in minutes rather than hours or days. A major element in this traffic was the continuous communication that took place between the different financial centres, especially London, Paris, Amsterdam, Brussels, Berlin and Frankfurt. There were, for example, nine wires between the London and Paris exchanges alone by 1908. Altogether, of the 17,372 telegrams sent to and received from continental centres by the members of the London Stock Exchange between 12 and 17 July 1909, 43.1 per cent were German, 19.7 per cent French, 17.8 per cent Dutch and 8.2 per cent Belgian, leaving only 11.1 per cent for the rest of Europe. This volume of business represented an equivalent of one telegram being received or dispatched every second for an eight-hour working day during a six-day week.[28]

As early as 1859 the management of the London Stock Exchange had become convinced that the telegraphic link between London and

Paris was indispensable for the conduct of business, while the lines to Amsterdam and Vienna were also considered important.[29] For the rest of the century the telegraph system was progressively extended, putting London in almost immediate contact with all the important centres in Europe. In 1908, J. H. Heaton claimed that 'The electric wires ramify all over Europe. Even villages of any size are connected.'[30] At the same time the capacity of the main lines was constantly expanded, both through duplication of wires and through technological developments that provided additional channels and a greater flow of messages.[31]

Nevertheless, there continued to be difficulties which prevented communications being as rapid and efficient as was technically feasible. The main problem lay with the continental land sections, which because of poor maintenance suffered from breaks in the line that could delay, or even interrupt, the service. A lesser though still serious problem was the attitude of the General Post Office, which failed both to comprehend the urgency of much of the stock exchange telegraph business and to respond fully to its particular demands. As a public service the Post Office did not want to be seen to favour one class of customer more than another, and thus all telegrams were dealt with in strict rotation, dependent upon their time of receipt at the telegraph office. During peak periods, such as between eleven o'clock in the morning and one o'clock in the afternoon, this could lead to lengthy delays.

On 18 April 1906 the delay between the handing in and the transmission of a telegram to Amsterdam was measured as 9.9 minutes from the stock exchange foreign market telegraph, 10.1 minutes by private wire and 11 minutes from the Threadneedle Street telegraph office. Despite demand for an express service, and a willingness among stock exchange members to pay extra for it, the Post Office refused to introduce one, since it might be interpreted as a discriminatory act. As a result some security dealers even resorted to the use of transatlantic cables for their continental business. The Anglo-American Telegraph Company maintained direct wires to the Continent for the forwarding and receipt of its US business and made these available before its busy period after three o'clock (Table 2.1). By this means a very much faster service could be obtained than through the government lines, though at twelve times the cost: 2s a word as opposed to 2d.[32] This indicated that speed of service was of far more importance than price, but that did fall dramatically in the second half of the nineteenth century. In 1851 it cost £1.4 (£1 8*s*) to send the minimum message between London and Paris, while by 1906 the charge had fallen to only £0.04 (10*d*) or a decline of 97 per cent.[33]

Table 2.1 *London Stock Exchange Telegraph Traffic, 1908–9*

(a) Telegrams sent and received to and from France and Germany, 5–7 July 1909

Time	France			Germany		
	London out	*London in*	*Total*	*London out*	*London in*	*Total*
Entire day	1,317	787	2,104	2,821	1,573	4,349
9–10 a.m.	2	17	19	11	234	245
10–11 a.m.	34	87	121	109	196	305
11–12 noon	346	121	467	739	281	1,020
12–1 p.m.	334	137	471	630	223	853
1–2 p.m.	174	119	293	348	191	539
2–3 p.m.	134	94	228	245	88	333

Source: Post Office Memorandum, Anglo-Continental Telegraph Service, 11 August 1909

(b) Telegrams sent and received via Anglo-American Telegraph Co., 22–24 September 1908

Time	Out	In	Total
Entire day	2,005	4,111	6,116
3–4 p.m.	457	1,482	1,939
4–5 p.m.	394	1,062	1,456
5–6 p.m.	215	588	803
6–7 p.m.	82	343	425
7–8 p.m.	54	280	334

Source: M. Carson, Manager, Anglo-American Telegraph Co., to F. J. Brown, General Post Office, London, 22 October 1908.

However, as the need for an ever more rapid and reliable service began to expose the deficiencies of the Anglo–continental telegraph network, the telegraph itself became increasingly less important to communications between European financial centres. In 1891 an alternative was provided in the shape of a telephone link, initially to Paris and later to other cities, such as Brussels in 1903. From the outset, stock exchange business dominated the telephone, and two more cables had to be laid between London and Paris in 1897 to cope with demand. With the telephone, the communication gap between the London and Paris exchanges was reduced to a mere five minutes, as the connection was made, while for the duration of the call instant and continuous communication could prevail. This was in contrast to the twenty minutes between the dispatch of a telegram from the floor of the London Stock Exchange to its arrival on the floor of the Paris Bourse, as it passed through pneumatic tubes, handlers and operators. A three-minute call from London to Paris cost £0.4 (8s) or ten times more than a telegram, but it did provide voice-to-voice contact.[34] As a result, there was a general switch away from the telegraph for those centres possessing direct London telephone connections, namely, Paris and Brussels, while the telegraph continued to be central for business with other continental centres, such as Berlin, Frankfurt and Amsterdam (Table 2.1). Thus, in European communications the arrival of the telephone represented the final stage in the removal of all communications barriers, which had been begun by the telegraph.

The revolution in communications was not confined to London's European links. A much more dramatic change came with the successful completion of a cable under the Atlantic, connecting London and New York. After considerable difficulty and failure, this was finally achieved in 1866, and it marked the beginning of an era when London was to be quickly connected by telegraph to all the major financial centres of the world, such as Melbourne in 1872 and Buenos Aires in 1874.[35] By 1880, when there were nine cables across the North Atlantic alone, one contemporary concluded that 'Vast intervening waters between countries are now no obstacle to the transmission of telegraphic intelligence.'[36] Communication between London and New York, which had taken ten days by ship, could now be made in minutes by the telegraph. The service also became progressively quicker as the number of lines increased, the equipment was improved, the methods of working changed and the staff became more proficient. For example, in 1908 an average of thirty-two telegrams a minute were being sent and received over the Anglo-American Company's wires, during the busy period between 3 p.m. and 4 p.m., compared to a maximum of seven when the cable opened in 1866.[37] At the same time the cost of a one-word telegram fell from £20 in 1866 to £1 in 1902, or by 95 per cent; the cost continued to fall as competition grew, to £0.1

(2*s*) by 1906, or by a further 90 per cent. Such was the degree of sophistication and understanding by then that almost all messages consisted of one-word codes, intelligible only to sender and recipient.[38]

Even at the initial expensive rates the transatlantic cable was immediately and extensively utilized. By 1871 New York brokers were already spending \$0.8 million a year on cabling London.[39] Altogether, the volume of telegrams between London and New York using the Anglo-American cables can be estimated to have risen from about 42,000 a year in 1871 to 570,000 in 1908, or by 1,257 per cent. In addition, by the latter date there was another company – Commercial Cable – also operating on the route and doing a similar amount of business, while direct lines had been laid between the Continent and the United States, bypassing Britain. S. S. Huebner suggests a total of over 5,000 cable messages a day between the London and New York Stock Exchanges by the eve of the First World War, or a conservative 1.4 million a year.[40]

The transatlantic cable companies geared themselves to meet the requirements of London dealers for an express service, positioning their offices adjacent to the exchange, installing the most modern equipment and employing and training skilled operators.[41] As a result of these improvements, the time of transmission between London and New York had been reduced to half a minute by the early twentieth century.[42] This type of business relied upon the rapidity of the service provided; the faster the communication, the greater the volume. The London manager of the Anglo-American Telegraph, for example, reported in 1908 that 'we find that 3 minutes delay is sufficient to contract the volume of traffic sent and received'.[43] The transatlantic cable companies consequently prided themselves on providing the most rapid service possible, whereby a message could be sent and a reply received in a period of under two and a half minutes. Such was the competition on this London–New York route that the difference of a second, or even a quarter of a second, in the time taken to transmit a telegram was considered to be of major importance, because either market could have moved in the interim. The consequence was that almost continuous communication existed between the London and New York Stock Exchanges between 3 p.m. and 8 p.m., with only one minute separating them – compared to the ten days, or 14,400 minutes, of 1866.[44] This transformation was important, with C. Duguid reporting in 1913, regarding the London Stock Exchange: 'the great event of the afternoon is the reception of opening prices from the New York Stock Exchange'.[45] Though the most rapid long-distance telegraphic communications existed between the London Stock Exchange and New York, similar links were forged throughout the world through a web of submarine and land lines. The spatial and temporal barriers that had divided London from other securities markets had been virtually removed through the introduction of the telegraph and telephone and their progressive refinement.

Developments such as these completely altered the environment with which the London Stock Exchange operated. 'Communications between London, Paris, Shanghai, Johannesburg and other great cities is undertaken to-day with greater ease and rapidity than formerly attended the transmission of a message from London to Bath' was one observer's conclusion in 1908, echoed by many others.[46] The conditions for an international market in securities now existed.

One measure of the change that took place is an examination of the prevailing prices for the same securities on the London and New York Stock Exchanges before and after the submarine cable was opened in 1866. In a comparison of the London and New York prices for the stock and bonds of the New York Central and Illinois Central railroads during 1860 (258 observations) there was an overlap in the daily range of prices at which they were traded only 8.5 per cent of the time. During the remaining 91.5 per cent of the time prices diverged, with the differential between the two exchanges averaging 4.8 per cent of the average price. The London range of prices was higher 63.6 per cent of the time, with the difference between London's lowest price and New York's highest averaging 5.7 per cent greater than the average price prevailing in New York. When London was lower, which it was 27.9 per cent of the time, the average difference between London's highest and New York's lowest was 2.6 per cent less than the average New York price. These statistics show the existence of parallel markets responding to similar conditions but trading in ignorance of each other, apart from information that was at least a week old.

The same exercise was repeated for 1870, using US government

5/20 (1867) coupon-bonds, which produced a total of 288 observations. In that year the daily range of prices on each stock exchange now overlapped 73.6 per cent of the time. When there was no overlap the average differential was only 0.52 per cent of the average price. When London was higher, which it was 12.5 per cent of the time, the differential was 0.49 per cent, and when lower (13.9 per cent of the time) it was 0.54 per cent. Altogether, between 1860 and 1870 the coincidence of prices had increased by 76.6 per cent, while the differential had fallen by 89 per cent.[47] As communications, contacts and techniques continued to improve, the differential between London and New York prices continued to decline to almost infinitesimal levels. By 1911 the difference between the prices of US railroad stocks and bonds traded on both the London and New York Stock Exchanges was considered by contemporaries to be in the range of 0.125–0.0625 per cent, which was an improvement of 76–88 per cent on the prevailing 1870 level, or 97–99 per cent compared to 1860.[48]

It is also clear from M. Edelstein's correlation analysis of New York and London yields on first-class US railway bonds that trading on the two exchanges was closely integrated over the 1871–1913 period.[49] This represented a significant transformation from mid-century when it would have taken a major discrepancy in price to promote buying and selling operations and accompanying flows of securities. Activity on the floor of the London Stock Exchange no longer reflected merely the sentiments of those who happened to be there, plus their immediate extramural contacts and orders received by post, but was now subjected to constant intercourse with the exchanges in other countries, so that they all became moulded into a single securities market.

Important as the breakthrough in communications was, it required major accompanying developments to ensure the growth of an international market. Prime among these was the expansion in the volume of securities which were common to more than one exchange and more than one country, for it was through these that activity in one centre was automatically transmitted to another. Common securities already existed at mid-century, especially the issues of certain European governments. A number of states at different times found it impossible to finance their own government spending out of revenue, and so borrowed extensively through the issue of negotiable stocks and bonds, some of which came to be held extensively abroad. States such as Russia and Turkey were permanently indebted, with a high proportion of that debt held by the nationals of other European countries. For other states such a position was only a temporary one. After the Franco-Prussian War of 1870, for example, the French were forced to pay reparations to Germany, and did so partly by issuing a large international loan especially in London, which was eventually repatriated.[50] However, as the countries of Europe became more affluent in the course of the nineteenth century, and their finances became better organized, their government securities tended to be either redeemed or held by their own nationals. The massive French debt was almost entirely French owned as early as 1878, and the same was progressively true for other countries such as Italy and Denmark. It was only the government debt of the less developed European nations, such as Turkey, Russia and Sweden, that was to be found scattered among an international investing public, especially in western Europe.[51]

The real growth in internationally held government debt in the second half of the nineteenth century occurred outside Europe. In the areas being settled by Europeans, such as Canada, Brazil, Argentina and Australia, there was a need for funds to finance economic development, especially capital-intensive infrastructure projects, and this led to the raising of large loans by these countries in the markets of western Europe. The federal and state authorities in the United States had long resorted to such measures to finance transport improvements, while the Civil War led to an enormous expansion of debt in general. Public debt in the United States rose from $90.6 million in 1861 to $2.7 billion in 1865, and a substantial proportion of this came to be held by European investors, especially the British, Germans and Dutch. One estimate suggested as much as $1 billion by 1869.[52] Though most of the United States public debt had been either redeemed or repatriated before 1914, and other countries, like Australia, increasingly absorbed their own national debts, there were always yet more governments keen to become extensive borrowers internationally, such as China, Japan and Mexico. Japan's international debt, for instance, rose from *nil* in 1896 to £1.53 billion in 1913. The reasons could range from financial profligacy to rapid economic development requiring state support, but the outcome was an expansion of government debt, much of which continued to be held internationally. Between 1870 and 1913 world national debt rose from about $11.5 billion to $40 billion.[53]

Illustrative of the position was the range of government securities quoted on the London Stock Exchange in 1910. By the end of that year the debts of the various central, state, provincial and city authorities listed totalled £5.6 billion and contained issues from almost every country of the world – certainly from all that were economically important (Table 2.2). Most of these securities were also quoted on foreign stock exchanges and were extensively held abroad. They represented one of the most mobile elements among the world's transferable assets. From an American viewpoint in 1900, the New York bankers and brokers C. W. Morgan & Co. felt that 'Internationally listed stocks are those securities which are also "listed" on the London Stock Exchange.'[54]

It was not necessary for this debt to be extensively held in Britain, or even generally throughout the world, for it to be important. What it indicated was the potential level of common securities that now existed in which the members of the London Stock Exchange were prepared to deal, with market attention switching readily between them depending upon interest. Within this total only a proportion would command an active market on two or more major exchanges. Trading in the debts of countries such as Britain, France, Germany and the United States was almost entirely confined to their own principal exchanges. Consequently, though British consols were quoted in New York and US federal bonds in London, there was little dealing in these at those locations, and little or no flow of either between them, because there was always sufficient national demand to ensure that almost all their own national debt remained at home. Movement and inter-market activity took place in those government securities that did command an international following, such as Argentinian, Japanese and Turkish debt. So adjustments between the major financial centres would not take place through a transfer of consols or *rentes*, for example, but rather of the bonds of some third state which were actively traded in both markets.[55]

Though government issues were the first and most prominent international securities, they were increasingly complemented, and even replaced in certain cases, by corporate stocks and bonds (Tables 2.3 and 2.4). Issues made by continental European railways, especially the French, were actively traded between London and

Table 2.2   *London stock exchange: Government Securities Quoted, 31 December 1910*

Category	Paid-up value	Average size of individual issue
UK total	£1,050,929,844	£4,342,685
Central government	£765,787,050	£76,578,705
Local government	£285,142,794	£1,229,064
Colonial total	£824,695,955	£2,561,168
Canada	£89,479,440	£1,078,066
Australia	£194,506,177	£2,778,660
New Zealand	£65,552,348	£1,311,047
South Africa	£103,720,294	£2,033,731
Egypt	£95,474,200	£19,094,840
India and Ceylon	£250,477,442	£8,637,153
Others	£25,486,054	£749,590
Foreign total	£3,702,452,964	£15,236,431
France	£1,022,274,418	£511,137,209
Germany	£465,674,817	£93,134,963
Italy	£322,670,073	£107,556,690
Russia	£305,067,293	£19,066,705
Spain and Portugal	£192,357,839	£38,471,567
Scandinavia	£37,745,378	£1,509,815
Netherlands, Belgium, Switzerland	£229,987,948	£22,908,795
Austro-Hungary	£482,018,906	£40,168,242
South-eastern Europe	£26,456,650	£3,307,081
Greece and Turkey	£101,904,500	£5,661,361
USA	£40,697,997	£2,713,200
Mexico	£39,288,263	£9,822,066
Brazil	£93,118,240	£3,448,824
Argentina	£111,496,856	£3,596,673
Chile	£25,142,352	£1,795,882
Uruguay and Paraguay	£27,148,197	£4,524,700
Other Latin American	£17,657,495	£1,765,750
China	£49,098,950	£3,776,842
Japan	£135,849,772	£10,449,982
Others	£4,153,670	£1,038,418
World total	£5,578,078,763	£6,912,117

Sources: London Stock Exchange Official List, 31 December 1910; *Stock Exchange Official Intelligence* (London, 1910 and 1911).

Table 2.3 *London Stock Exchange: Securities Quoted (Paid-Up Capital) (£m), 1853–1913*

Category	1853	1863	1873	1883	1893	1903	1913
Total	1,215.2	1,601.4	2,269.1	3,634.3	4,899.2	6.978.3	9,550
Government[a]							
Domestic	853.6	901.9	858.9	914.5	901.7	1,102.2	1,290
Foreign[b]	69.7	171.4	486.5	975.1	1,031.5	1,411.4	2,034
Total	923.3	1,073.3	1,345.4	1,889.6	1,933.2	2,513.6	3,324
Railways							
Domestic	193.7	245.2	374.0	658.1	854.8	1,104.6	1,217
Foreign	31.3	197.7	353.6	817.2	1,564.2	1,977.8	2,929
Total	225.0	442.9	727.6	1,475.3	2,419.0	3,082.4	4,147
Urban Services[c]							
Total	24.5	27.1	32.9	101.8	140.3	200.1	435
Financial Services[d]							
Total	13.1	26.3	121.8[h]	102.2	199.5	440.5	609
Commercial and industrial[e]							
Total	21.9	26.7	32.6	43.0	172.6	690.9	917
Mining[f]							
Domestic	—	1.0	1.3	0.6	0.3	—	—
Foreign	—	4.1	6.4	20.2	32.6	41.1	91
Total	7.4	5.1	7.7	20.8	32.9	41.1	91
Agriculture[g]							
Total							
(All Foreign)	—	—	1.1	1.6	1.7	9.7	24
Domestic	1,114.2	1,228.2	1,421.5	1,820.2	2,269.2	3,538.3	4,469
Foreign[i]	101.0	373.2	847.6	1,814.1	2,263.0	3,440.0	5,080

Notes

a All forms of government securities – central, provincial, state, city, etc.

b Includes only those foreign securities payable in London. The paid-up capital for those quoted and payable abroad could not be accurately calculated before 1883, and so were omitted by the Stock Exchange Official Intelligence. From that date it could be calculated and was included as a separate category, but it has been excluded from the main table for purposes of comparability. The amounts are: 1883, £2,042.m; 1893, £1,661.8m; 1903, £1,855.6m; 1913, £1,712.0m.

c Water, gas and electricity supply and the provision of urban transport and communications.

d Banking, insurance and other financial intermediaries.

e Commercial and industrial enterprise, including shipping.

f All forms of mining, including oil, but British coal-mining companies have been included with e.

g Plantation companies: tea, coffee, rubber, etc.

h Figure given for that year is limited to marine insurance. An estimate for other insurance companies is included to compensate for the omission, based on the 1863–83 levels.

i The 'foreign' amount is based only on the data from government, railways, agriculture and mining. However, foreign securities or the securities of British companies operating abroad were increasingly to be found in *all* the other categories, though they remained overwhelmingly domestic.

Sources: Stock Exchange Official Intelligence (London 1885), p.CXXIV; (1894), p.1730; (1904), p.1926; (1914), p.1707.

Paris in the 1850s, but as they tended to be absorbed by the French investing public, activity in London waned. Of more permanence were US railroad securities. These had long been known in London, where special sterling-denominated issues had been made, and this interest gradually extended to other European countries, such as Holland, Belgium and Germany. However, the real international prominence of US railroad bonds began in the 1870s when the US government began to repay its wartime borrowings. As a result public debt became both a scarcer and less remunerative investment, and foreign investors increasingly switched to the securities of the major trunk railroads as the best available alternative. The US railroads, and their financiers, actively co-operated in stimulating this interest by making their new issues easily available abroad.[56]

When the Atchison, Topeka & Sante Fe railroad made a new issue of $88 million 4 per cent mortgage bonds in 1896 it allocated 22.7 per cent to Amsterdam, 29.5 per cent to London and the remainder to New York. A company such as this, with a track covering 6,481 miles in the south-west of the United States and an issued capital of $251 million, could offer the stability and guarantees that would rival many a small state or local authority.[57] As a consequence, many of the largest US railroads had their stocks and bonds held not only throughout the United States but also throughout the countries of western Europe. These could range from the Louisville & Nashville, with 50 per cent foreign ownership in 1893, to the Pennsylvania, with 13 per cent in 1913.[58] Adler estimated that British investors alone had altogether £600 million invested in US railroad securities by 1910, though this figure is more likely to reflect the level of European holdings in total. Whatever the exact amount, the result was that the stocks and bonds issued by the major US railroads were extensively owned on both sides of the Atlantic, with these securities commanding active markets not only on the New York Stock Exchange but also on the London, Berlin, Frankfurt, Amsterdam and, to a lesser extent, Paris Stock Exchanges throughout the 1870–1914 period.[59]

Table 2.4   *London Stock Exchange: Securities Quoted (Paid-Up Capital) (in Per Cent of Overall and Individual Totals), 1853–1913*

Category	1853 %	1863 %	1873 %	1883 %	1893 %	1903 %	1913 %
Government							
Domestic	92.5	84.0	63.8	48.4	46.6	43.8	38.8
Foreign	7.5	16.0	36.2	51.6	53.4	56.2	61.2
Total	76.0	67.0	59.3	52.0	39.5	36.0	34.8
Railways							
Domestic	86.1	55.4	51.4	44.6	35.3	35.8	29.4
Foreign	13.9	44.6	48.6	55.4	64.7	64.2	70.6
Total	18.5	27.7	32.1	40.6	49.4	44.2	43.4
Urban Services							
Total	2.0	1.7	1.4	2.8	2.9	2.9	4.6
Financial Services							
Total	1.1	1.6	5.4	2.8	4.1	6.3	6.4
Commercial and industrial							
Total	1.8	1.7	1.4	1.2	3.5	9.9	9.6
Mining							
Domestic	—	19.6	16.9	2.9	0.9	—	—
Foreign	—	80.4	83.1	97.1	99.1	100	100
Total	0.6	0.3	0.3	0.6	0.7	0.6	1.0
Agriculture							
Total							
(All foreign)	—	—	0.1	—	—	0.1	0.3
Total (millions)	£1,215.2	£1,601.4	£2,269.1	£3,634.3	£4,899.2	£6,978.3	£9,550.3
Domestic	97.1	76.7	62.6	50.1	46.3	50.7	46.8
Foreign	8.3	23.3	37.4	49.9	53.7	49.3	53.2

If the foreign securities quoted in London but payable abroad are included, the domestic/foreign proportions are as follows:

Domestic	—	—	—	32	35	40	40
Foreign	—	—	—	68	65	60	60

Source: Table 2.3.

The international success of US railroad securities was increasingly emulated by the issues of railway companies from numerous other countries in the late nineteenth century, as they sought to tap foreign finance to fund their expansion. None was probably more successful in this than the Canadian Pacific Railway, which had, by 1910, issued its common stock, totalling $180 million, to 24,000 investors worldwide. Of its total share capital, 65 per cent was held in Britain, 15 per cent in continental Europe, 10 per cent in the USA and 10 per cent in Canada. As a result, the common stock of the Canadian Pacific was regarded at the time as 'one of the most notable instances of an international stock', being most actively traded in and between London, New York and Berlin, as well as to a lesser extent in other centres.[60] It became commonplace for the issue of securities on behalf of the major railway companies outside western Europe and, later, the United States to be spread over a fairly wide investing public in a number of different countries. The £1.5 million loan floated by the Argentine North-Eastern Railway in 1888, for instance, was taken up by 229 individual and institutional investors to the amount of 62.5 per cent in Britain, 19 per cent in France and 18.5 per cent in Germany.[61] Consequently, there was a growing volume of railroad securities which possessed an international market, reflecting the widespread geographical distribution of their stockholders.

International corporate securities were not confined to railroads but increasingly encompassed a growing variety of other enterprises. The development of large-scale metal mining, for instance, created a number of major companies that attracted a multinational following. This took place in a variety of ways. Two British companies, Rio Tinto and Tharsis, were formed in the 1860s and 1870s to exploit Spain's rich copper deposits, and their success attracted substantial French interest, so that their shares came to be actively traded on both the London Stock Exchange and the Paris Bourse. In 1907 K. Robinson referred to the Rio Tinto shares as 'an international counter' as a consequence.[62] Conversely, companies formed in the mining areas, and owned locally, could attract interest from investors abroad, if successful, so that the market for their securities was no longer confined to one country. This happened to such Australian concerns as Broken Hill Proprietary and Mount Morgan Mining from the late 1880s; they had active markets for their shares in both Melbourne and London by 1900.[63] The same happened with the Anaconda Copper Company of the United States, with foreign buying creating an international market for its securities.[64]

The premier example of both the transformation of local into international securities and the formation of corporations attracting widespread investment interest was the gold-mining boom in South

Africa in the 1890s, which excited interest throughout the world, and especially from every country of Europe. At the peak of the boom, the shares of the principal mining companies were feverishly traded on numerous different exchanges, including not only the major ones of London, Paris and Berlin and the local one established in Johannesburg, but also centres such as Vienna, Madrid, Moscow, Constantinople and Cairo. Though both the boom and the intense interest collapsed, they left a legacy whereby the securities of the major and most successful South African gold-mining companies, like Rand Mines and the Central Mining Corporation, continued to command an international market, encompassing all of the major economies of Europe as well as that of South Africa itself.[65]

Major industrial and commercial companies also found themselves with an international following, or deliberately cultivated it, in the late nineteenth and early twentieth centuries. The Nobel Dynamite Trust, for example, with manufacturing subsidiaries in numerous countries, became an international stock, with Glasgow and Hamburg being the principal centres.[66] However, the prime example of an international security among industrial companies was United States Steel. This concern was formed in 1901 as an amalgamation of eight different US steel companies, many of which were themselves formed from previous mergers. It controlled steel production in the United States, and its huge capitalization of $1,154 million reflected its almost monopoly position. When the company had been organized by J. P. Morgan he had enlisted the support of financial contacts throughout Europe and North America in order to ensure that the stocks and bonds created would be easily absorbed. The consequence was that there were about 175,000 US Steel stockholders by 1913, with 18 per cent of the stock being held abroad. This created an active market in US Steel stocks and bonds on both sides of the Atlantic, but especially in London and New York.[67]

These examples illustrate the growing volume and variety of securities that were held internationally and possessed active markets in two or more centres in different countries. As one set of securities was redeemed or repatriated, ceasing to be traded internationally either temporarily or permanently, another set quickly appeared to take its place. Railroad bonds supplemented government stocks and were, in turn, replaced by the issues of mining and industrial companies. The actual location or nature of the particular enterprise was largely irrelevant as long as it was substantial and established, and could attract widespread support. In the late 1880s and early 1890s several Chicago concerns were merged to form much larger corporations, such as the Chicago Brewing & Malting Co., the Milwaukee & Chicago Brewing & Malting Co. and the Chicago Packing & Provision Co. These were then floated in London, though retaining the involvement of local investors. The result was that the securities of the companies then had active markets in both London and Chicago, and were equally traded in both.[68]

Though the expense of issuing securities internationally could be high, there were definite rewards. If a security could command an international following it became more easily marketable at a higher price, being reliant upon not just one restricted group of investors but the investing public of the world. While this was of little importance for wealthy countries with low interest rates and cheap finance, such as Britain and France, it was of major significance for those countries where finance was in short supply and interest rates were high, such as the United States and Russia. Consequently, if the governments and corporations of these latter countries could make their securities appealing to the investors of the former, they could benefit from a cheaper source of finance. It was worth doing this only for large issues, since the expense could not be justified for the small.

There was therefore a constant incentive to create international securities, through which governments and business could obtain all the funds they required and at less cost. At the same time investors in the capital-rich countries were keen to take up these securities, which offered a better rate of return than was available domestically. As Hirst noted in 1910: 'the debt of any important government can usually be bought on all the leading stock exchanges at pretty much the same price'.[69] This was the case even though the prevailing rate of interest in different economies was not identical and remained so for long periods of time. The price of an international security represented an equilibrium price sufficient to encourage the investor to purchase and the borrower to sell; and, as such, it promoted their constant creation, with their form and nature being left to the mood of the times and the opportunities available.

Notes

1 C. A. Conant, *Wall Street and the Country: A Study of Recent Financial Tendencies* (New York, 1904), p. 147.

2 W. C. Van Antwerp, *The Stock Exchange from within* (New York, 1913), p. 407; Financial Times, *Investors' Guide* (London, 1913), p. 13.

3 K. E. Born, *International Banking in the 19th and 20th Centuries* (Leamington Spa, 1983), p. 35; D. C. M. Platt, *Foreign Finance in Continental Europe and the United States, 1815–1870* (London, 1984), p. 127; C. P. Kindleberger, *A Financial History of Western Europe* (London, 1984), p. 267; C. P. Kindleberger, 'Financial Institutions and Economic Development: A Comparison of Great Britain and France in the Eighteenth and Nineteenth Centuries', *Explorations in Economic History*, vol. 21 (1984), p. 119; W. Parker, *The Paris Bourse and French Finance* (New York, 1920), p. 59.

4 S. F. Streit, *Report on European Stock Exchanges* (New York, 1914), pp. 16–17; cf. H. G. S. Noble, *The New York Stock Exchange in the Crisis of 1914* (New York, 1915).

5 S. S. Pratt, *The Work of Wall Street* (New York, 1903), p. 35; W. J. Greenwood, *Foreign Stock Exchange Practice and Company Law* (London, 1911), p. 364.

6 M. G. Myers, *Paris as a Financial Centre* (London, 1936), pp. 174–5; J. A. Hobson, *The Economic Interpretation of Investment* (London, 1911), p. 13; W. R. Lawson, *American Finance* (London, 1906), p. 387; A. R. Hall, *The Stock Exchange of Melbourne and the Victorian Economy, 1852–1900* (Canberra, 1968), p. 233; R. S. Rungta, *Rise of Business Corporations in India 1851–1900* (Cambridge, 1970), p. 211; Greenwood, *Foreign Stock Exchange Practice*, p. 204.

7 F. Crouzet, *The Victorian Economy* (London, 1982), p. 370, cf. pp. 9–10, 334, 371–2, 380–2. See also introduction by P. Mathias to E. Jones, *Accountancy and the British Economy, 1840–1980: The Evolution of Ernst and Whinney* (London, 1981).

8 P. G. M. Dickson, *The Financial Revolution in England: A Study in the Development of Public Credit* (London, 1967), pp. 335, 475, 509–10; J. C. Riley, *International Government Finance and the Amsterdam Capital Market, 1740–1815* (Cambridge, 1980), pp. 29, 33, 85, 280, 291; E. V. Morgan and W. A. Thomas, *The Stock Exchange: Its History and Functions* (London, 1963), p. 52; S. R. Cope, 'The Stock Exchange Revisited: A New Look at the Market in Securities in London in the Eighteenth Century', *Economica*, vol. 45 (1978), p. 16.

9 L. Neal, 'Efficient Markets in the Eighteenth Century: Stock Exchanges in Amsterdam and London', Business History Conference Paper, April 1982, p. 10; R. V. Eagly and G. V. K. Smith, 'Domestic and International Integration of the London Money Market, 1731–1789', *Journal of Economic History*, vol. 36 (1976), pp. 207, 210–11.

10 Morgan and Thomas, *The Stock Exchange*, p. 80; S. Chapman, *The Rise*

of *Merchant Banking* (London, 1984), p. 14; J. E. Hedges, *Commercial Banking and the Stock Market before 1863* (Baltimore, 1938), pp. 46–7.

11 Calculated from the information in C. Fenn, *A Compendium of the English and Foreign Funds* (London, 1840, 2nd edn).

12 *Bankers' Circular* (London), 23 March 1832; D. Greenberg, *Financiers and Railroads, 1869–1889: A Study of Morgan, Bliss & Co.* (Newark, 1980), p. 23.

13 Fenn, *Funds* (London, 1837 edn), pp. 74–5.

14 R. C. Michie, *Money, Mania and Markets: Investment, Company Formation and the Stock Exchange in Nineteenth-Century Scotland* (Edinburgh, 1981), pp. 254–5.

15 Platt, *Foreign Finance*, pp. 19, 31, 159; Hedges, *Commercial Banking*, p. 47; Greenberg, *Financiers*, p. 23; L. H. Jenks, *The Migration of British Capital to 1875* (New York, 1927), pp. 149–50.

16 *Stock Exchange Official Intelligence* (London, 1885), p. 88.

17 *A New Survey of London* (London, 1853), p. 378; Gresham Omnium, *A Handy Guide to Safe Investments* (London, 1858), p. 88.

18 Gresham Omnium, *Handy Guide*, pp. 47, 57, 83; Platt, *Foreign Finance*, p. 19.

19 London Stock Exchange (LSE): Committee for General Purposes, 6 January 1848.

20 C. Duguid, 'The History of the Stock Exchange', in W. E. Hooper (ed.), *The Stock Exchange in the Year 1900* (London, 1900), p. 104; Morgan and Thomas, *The Stock Exchange*, p. 162.

21 LSE: Gen. Purposes, 17 November 1851.

22 Kingsmill Davan to Andrew Clow & Co., 8 October 1791 (Andrew Clow & Co. Correspondence, Harvard Business School, MS 785).

23 S. R. Cope, 'Bird, Savage & Bird of London, Merchants and Bankers 1782–1803', *Guildhall Studies in London History*, vol. 4 (1981), pp. 209–10; cf. Correspondence of Peter Anspach, New York, 1792 (New York Historical Society, MSS 1228).

24 Cope, 'Stock Exchange Revisited', pp. 8, 15, 17; Dickson, *Financial Revolution*, pp. 336, 491, 507–8; Riley, *International Government Finance*, p. 39.

25 *The Economist*, 4 October 1845.

26 *The Times*, 13 March 1845.

27 J. Kieve, *The Electric Telegraph: A Social and Economic History* (Newton Abbot, 1973), p. 103; H. Barty-King, *Girdle round the Earth: The Story of Cable and Wireless and its Predecessors* (London, 1979), p. xv; P. Ripley, *A Short History of Investment* (London, 1934), p. 88.

28 Post Office (PO) Memorandum: Anglo–Continental Telegraph Traffic, 4 September 1907; Anglo–Continental Telegraph Service, 11 August 1909 (GPO Post 30/1988/E 10513/1911).

29 LSE: Trustees and Managers, 3 February 1859; Report of Proceedings of Committee of PO Accommodation, 18 November 1908.

30   J. H. Heaton, 'The World's Cables and Cable Rings', *Financial Review of Reviews (FR)*, May 1908, p. 9.

31   PO Memorandum: Anglo-Continental Traffic, 1907; Barty-King, *Girdle round the Earth*, pp. 10, 15, 19.

32   PO Memorandum: Proposed Direct Stock Exchange Continental Working, 28 April 1906; Anglo-Continental Traffic, 1907; Anglo-Continental Telegraph Service, 11 August 1909, 4 April 1911.

33   LSE: Trustees and Managers, 26 November 1851; *Financial News*, 11 April 1906.

34   PO Memorandum: Anglo-Continental Traffic, 1907; LSE: Trustees and Managers, 23 July 1903, 6 January 1904; Gen. Purposes, 19 October 1908, 26 April 1909; Barty-King, *Girdle round the Earth*, p. 89; Van Antwerp, *The Stock Exchange*, p. 283.

35   Frank Leslie's *Illustrated Newspaper* (New York), 22 March 1879; C. A. Jones, 'British Financial Institutions in Argentina' (PhD thesis, Cambridge University, 1973), p. 65; Kieve, *Electric Telegraph*, pp. 112–3, 116; Barty-King, *Girdle round the Earth*, pp. 22, 393.

36   *New York Saturday Journal*, 3 April 1880.

37   *Bullionist* (London), 28 July 1886; LSE: Gen. Purposes Subcommittee on Rules and Regulations, 30 May 1908; Manager, Anglo-American Telegraph Co., to F. J. Brown, GPO, 22 October 1908; Barty-King, *Girdle round the Earth*, pp. 22, 110, 393.

38   Pratt, *Work of Wall Street*, pp. 141–2; *Financial News*, 11 April 1906.

39   J. K. Medbery, *Old Times in Wall Street: A Study for Today* (New York, 1871), p. 196.

40   Based on figures from Medbery, *Old Times*, p. 196, and Table 2.1, and estimated using a year with 280 working days. S. S. Huebner, *The Stock Market* (New York, 1922), p. 87.

41   *The Empire* (London), 8 May 1901; PO Memorandum: Notes of a Visit to the Anglo-American Company's Stock Exchange Office, 9 February 1909; Pratt, *Work of Wall Street*, p. 147.

42   PO Memorandum: Manager, Anglo-American Telegraph Co., to GPO, 22 October 1908; F. L. Eames, *The New York Stock Exchange* (New York, 1894), p. 90; Greenwood, *Foreign Stock Exchange Practice*, p. 204; Van Antwerp, *The Stock Exchange*, p. 283; Huebner, *The Stock Market*, p. 87.

43   PO Memorandum: M. Carson to F. J. Brown, 22 October 1908.

44   LSE: Gen. Purposes Subcommittee, 30 May 1908; NYSE: Building Committee, Transcripts, 7 April 1903.

45   C. Duguid, *The Stock Exchange* (London 1913, 3rd edn), p. 156.

46   F. Piccinelli, 'Investment Principles in Italy', *FR*, February 1908, p. 49; cf. E. T. Powell, *The Mechanism of the City* (London, 1910), p. 57; F. W. Hirst, *The Credit of Nations* (Washington, 1910), p. 3.

47   Comparison of London and New York security prices was not a simple procedure. Until 1874 the custom on the London Stock Exchange was to assume an exchange rate of $4.44 to the £, rather than the prevailing

rate of $4.87 (i.e. £1 = 4s 6d). Consequently, in both 1860 and 1870 it was necessary to convert the prevailing London price into an internationally comparable one by dividing by 4.44 and multiplying by 4.87. For 1870 the comparison was further complicated by the fact that, in practice, the United States was on a floating exchange rate. The internationally traded dollar retained the same ratio to gold, and did not fluctuate, but security prices on the New York Stock Exchange were denominated in terms of the inconvertible domestic currency, which traded at a discount to gold. It was therefore necessary to convert the currency dollar price of stocks into gold dollars, by deflating the daily dollar price in New York by the daily premium on gold in New York. These procedures gave comparable prices for London and New York.

Daily London prices came from the London Stock Exchange List, 1860 and 1870, while New York prices were obtained from the Daily List of Sales and Prices on the New York Stock Exchange, 1860 and 1870. Other information came from: Belding, Keith & Co., *United States Bonds and Securities* (London, 1867), pp. 6–8, 11; H. Schmidt, *Foreign Banking Arbitration: Its Theory and Practice* (London, 1875); W. L. Fawcett, *Gold and Debt: An American Handbook of Finance* (Chicago, 1877), pp. 25–6; W. C. Mitchell, *Gold, Prices and Wages under the Greenback Standard* (Berkeley, 1908), pp. 249–52, 315; L. E. Davis and J. R. T. Hughes, 'A Dollar–Sterling Exchange, 1803–1895', *Economic History Review*, vol. 13 (1950–1), pp. 52–78.

48 LSE: Gen. Purposes Subcommittee on Readmission, 23 November 1911.

49 M. Edelstein, *Overseas Investment in the Age of High Imperialism: The United Kingdom 1850–1914* (London, 1982), pp. 82, 330.

50 J. W. Angel, *The Theory of International Prices: History, Criticism and Restatement* (Cambridge, 1926), p. 520; O. Haupt, *The London Arbitrageur, or the English Money Market in Connexion with Foreign Bourses* (London, 1870), p. iv; T. Skinner, *The Stock Exchange Year Book and Diary* (London, 1874), pp. iii–iv, 7; Schmidt, *Foreign Banking Arbitration*, pp. 47–262.

51 Investors' Guardian, *Guide to Investments* (London, 1873), p. 26; General Securities Corporation, *The Investors' Handy Book of Active Stocks and Shares* (London, 1912), pp. xiv–xv; H. Lowenfeld, 'The World's Stock Markets', *FR*, October 1907, p. 7.

52 M. G. Myers, *The New York Money Market: Origins and Development* (New York, 1931), Vol. I, pp. 36, 289; J. H. Dunning, *Studies in International Investment* (London, 1970), p. 182; Greenberg, *Financiers and Railroads*, p. 33; Hedges, *Commercial Banking*, pp. 46–7; Investors' Guardian, *Guide*, p. 16; Hall, *Stock Exchange of Melbourne*, p. 37.

53 W. S. and E. S. Woytinsky, *World Commerce and Governments* (New York, 1955), pp. 740–1; A. E. Davies, *Investments Abroad* (Chicago, 1927), p. 93; R. W. Goldsmith, *The Financial Development of Japan,*

1868–1977 (New Haven, 1983), pp. 57–8; Platt, *Foreign Finance*, p. 154; cf. D. C. North, 'International Capital Movements in Historical Perspective', in R. F. Mikesell, *US Private and Government Investment Abroad* (Eugene, 1962).

54 C. W. Morgan & Co., *How to Speculate Successfully in Wall Street* (New York, 1900), p. 48; cf. R. L. Nash, *A Short Inquiry into the Profitable Nature of our Investments* (London, 1881), p. 39; *The Economist*, 24 April 1880.

55 Hirst, *Credit of Nations*, p. 4; General Securities Corporation, *Investors' Handy Book*, pp. xiv–xv.

56 Jenks, *Migration of British Capital*, p. 149; Platt, *Foreign Finance*, p. 31; P. L. Simmonds, *Fenn's Compendium of the English and Foreign Funds* (London, 1860, 7th edn), p. 229; E. C. Maddison, *On the Stock Exchange* (London, 1877), p. 141; Gresham Omnium, *Handy Guide*, p. 95.

57 NYSE Stock List Committee, Company Submissions: Atchison Topeka & Santa Fe.

58 Clapp & Co., *Weekly Market Letters for 1893* (New York, 1894), 30 June 1893, 21 July 1893, Huebner, *Stock Market*, p. 6.

59 D. R. Adler, *British Investments in American Railways, 1834–1898* (Charlottesville, 1970), pp. 24, 42, 143, 152–3; S. F. Van Oss, *American Railroads and British Investors* (London, 1893), pp. 138, 140; C. F. Speare, 'Selling American Bonds in Europe', in W. H. Hull (ed.), *Bonds as Investment Securities* (Philadelphia, 1907), p. 81; Powell, *Mechanism of the City*, p. 65. This figure of $600 million is likely to be revised by D. C. M. Platt.

60 F. W. Field, *Capital Investments in Canada* (Toronto, 1911), p. 84, 88; General Securities Corporation, *Investors' Handy Book*, pp. xviii–xix.

61 Chapman, *Merchant Banking*, pp. 91, 94, 96–7, 158, 160.

62 K. Robinson, *The Mining Market* (London, 1907), p. 15; S. G. Checkland, *The Mines of Tharsis* (London, 1967), p. 154; E. Vidal, *The History and Methods of the Paris Bourse* (Washington, 1910), p. 226; Bell, Begg & Cowan, Stockbrokers, Edinburgh, Monthly List, December 1887.

63 Hall, *Stock Exchange of Melbourne*, pp. 122, 149.

64 General Securities Corporation, *Investors' Handy Book*, p. 140.

65 H. A. Meredith, *The Drama of Money Making* (London, 1931), pp. 179, 188; *The Story of the Johannesburg Stock Exchange, 1887–1947* (Johannesburg, 1948), p. 46; Davies, *Investments Abroad*, p. 10; Vidal, *Paris Bourse*, p. 232; R. V. Kubicek, *Economic Imperialism in Theory and Practice: The Case of South African Gold Mining Finance 1886–1914* (Durham, NC, 1979), pp. 62, 94, 151.

66 Kerr, Anderson, Muir & Mann, Stockbrokers, Glasgow: Correspondence with A. Nobel, 14 February 1889; with M. A. Phillip, 28 November 1887, 29 November 1887; Davies, *Investments Abroad*, p. 93.

67 NYSE: Listing Statements, US Steel, 6 March 1901; NYSE: Stock List Committee, Company Submissions, US Steel; *New York American*, 9 January 1914; Huebner, *Stock Market*, p. 6; Streit, *European Stock Exchanges*, p. 17.
68 I. D. Fleming, *The Chicago Stock Exchange: An Historical Sketch* (Chicago 1894), no pagination.
69 Hirst, *Credit of Nations*, p. 4.

3 The London Stock Exchange and the International Securities Market II

The revolution in communications and the rapid expansion of international securities were not in themselves sufficient to integrate the world securities market. A mechanism was required through which the trading in separate exchanges became intimately linked, and thence transformed into a specialist component of a world market. This required a positive response from individuals and institutions to the new conditions and opportunities that were coming into existence and were fundamentally altering the environment within which individual markets operated. Since this was not an era when governments or international agencies met and formulated policies and practices, it implied initiative from those actually involved in the market-making process, who were being affected by the changes and could foresee the possibilities arising from them.

Links between different financial centres long pre-dated the mid-nineteenth century. So there existed numerous individuals and firms who were in a position to take advantage of, and benefit from, the increased opportunities that international contacts brought. Foremost among these were the merchant bankers, who possessed either branches, partners, agents, or contacts in different centres and were well experienced in a variety of financial affairs, including the issue of securities and the handling of foreign exchange. Of the 111 merchant banks in London in 1914–15, 35 maintained major contacts with the Far East, 31 with Europe, 30 with South America, 26 with North America, 12 with Africa and 4 with Australia and New Zealand. These connections frequently reflected long-standing relationships dating from the early nineteenth century.[1]

A few of these merchant bankers already dealt in securities by mid-century, using their foreign connections for the conduct of an international business, such as Haes & Sons and R. Raphael & Sons. Raphaels, for example, operated as both merchant bankers and stockbrokers/jobbers, maintaining branches in Hamburg and Amsterdam.[2] Long-established and trusted contacts were essential for the buying and selling of securities on more than one exchange. Dealing had frequently to be done before either payment was received or the security for sale was delivered, and thus the operation rested upon mutual faith in the honesty and reliability of the partners to the transaction. This became more acute with the telegraph, which allowed a divorce between communications and transport. Even in 1889 six weeks had to be allowed for the sending of a share certificate from London to New York, having the register of ownership altered and the certificate returned. However, if it was always necessary to possess the certificate of a security being sold or to possess the cash required to pay for a security being purchased, all the benefits brought by improved telegraphic communications would be lost. A web of international contacts had to be established who would be ready to buy and sell on faith, accepting payment and delivery after the event *if* they had managed to complete the deal requested. Consequently, the merchant banks looked set to become the central agents in inter-stock-exchange activity.[3]

Merchant banks also had the added advantage that the nature of their business necessitated them possessing either actual funds in different centres or at least claims on funds, as credits and debits were continually accumulated through trade with different locations. These geographically dispersed funds provided a means by which the finance for or receipts from the sale of securities in foreign centres could be either paid for abroad or remitted home. A merchant bank could receive or make payment through its foreign associate, debiting or crediting its London account accordingly. Therefore, merchant banks possessed not only the required contacts but also the necessary means to deal internationally in securities. However, though merchant banks long retained the money transfer function, and developed it to meet the needs of security transfers with the finance bill, most did not long retain a position in security dealing itself. Established merchant banking firms began to abandon any form of exchange business in the 1860s and 1870s.[4]

65

Increasingly, it was direct contact between members of different stock exchanges that replaced the use of outside intermediaries, such as merchant banks. Behind this development lay a number of reasons. Most merchant banks were not keen to devote themselves to the new business of continuously dealing in securities between markets in different countries. This departure both involved considerable risk, compared to the activities in trade and investment with which they were familiar, and would also be time-consuming, and so the established firms were reluctant to become heavily involved.

During the 1870s, for example, the merchant bankers Richard Irvin & Co. acted in New York for the London stockbroking firm of E. Satterthwaite & Co. They were paid half per cent commission on the money they collected from sales and dividends, and quarter per cent on the sales and purchases they arranged. However, they were unwilling to participate in any closer relationship whereby they would share in any profits or losses arising from regularly buying and selling securities between New York and London. They refused Satterthwaite's attempt to make such an arrangement, preferring to concentrate on the safe commission business. The same attitudes prevailed in another Anglo-American merchant bank, Morton, Bliss & Co.[5]

Merchant bankers preferred to concentrate upon the handling of issues for governments and corporations, the arranging of long-term finance and investments for individual and institutional clients and the organization and finance of trade – rather than become specialists in the trading in securities both within exchanges and between them. Continued growth in all these other activities presented excellent opportunities for such a choice both for the long-established merchant banks, such as Barings and Rothschilds, and for many of the newer ones, such as Kleinworts and Bensons. Thus, though merchant banks possessed the contacts and the means, they lacked the motivation and inclination to enter the field of security trading.[6]

The rules of the London Stock Exchange provided a minor impediment to the merchant banks playing a major role, for that institution increasingly restricted entry to all individuals and firms who had activities outside broking and jobbing. In the days when admission was more lax, certain merchant banks, such as Raphaels, had been allowed to join, and they retained this privilege despite opposition. Consequently, Raphaels developed security dealing as one of its specialities, possessing contacts in other centres, such as Paris, through which to channel deals. Nevertheless, though membership did confer special benefits on Raphaels, the lack of it did not preclude merchant banks from becoming involved in security trading. A few persevered in the business, such as Samuel Montagu & Co., while new firms, especially of German origin, took it up, such as S. Japhet & Co.[7]

This hesitancy on the part of merchant bankers, for whatever reason, to become involved in the new arrangements was not just a sign of conservatism. A number of members of the London Stock Exchange already had overseas contacts, even before the coming of the telegraph, and so did not rely upon merchant banking intermediation. At the same time, this direct contact produced even more rapid communications between markets than routing via third parties, such as bankers. This speed was important, for it was the brokers with the fastest contacts that could benefit most from marginal price differences in common securities between markets, and so came to monopolize dealing in volatile stocks and shares, to the exclusion of others. The telegraph did not merely provide faster contact, for it also changed the nature of relationships – replacing an earlier era when ties of blood and religion were important, and firms conducted a general business, with one in which specialization and professionalism held sway. Those individuals and firms that profited out of the change, whether they were brokers or merchant bankers, were those who concentrated their activities and provided the speed and expertise required. Many of these were German because the creation of a uniform currency in Germany in 1876 destroyed the flourishing inter-German exchange business, leading to many of the experts migrating to London, where they entered the field of inter-market security dealing.[8]

A clear division thus came to exist between international investment, the movement of securities between markets and the money transfers that these necessitated. Bankers continued to control the money flows, while brokers dominated the security flows, with them both sharing the investment. The consequence was that a growing number of London stockbrokers established strong links with brokers on foreign exchanges. Sales and purchases could be made on receipt of direct telegraphic instructions, with delivery or payment being made at regular intervals, usually through a bank that was represented in both centres. Innumerable instances of such links – or correspondent brokers – exist, connecting individual London brokers with one or more foreign centres, such as Simon & Co. with Paris and Cazenove & Co. and J. B. Samuel & Co. with New York.[9] By such means it became an easy matter for an investor to sell or purchase securities in a foreign market. When, for example, Earl Grey wished to acquire five hundred shares in the International Power Company in 1902, his financial agent, J. Covey Williams, merely instructed a London broker, who telegraphed his contact in New York, as the concern was a United States one and actively traded only there, with the result that the purchase was quickly made. The shares were then to be paid for when they arrived in England with the next mail from the United States.[10] As G. Withers noted in 1907: 'It is just as easy to do business in this fashion [buy and sell] in the stocks quoted on the New York, Boston, Chicago, San Francisco, or any other American exchange, as it is to deal in the stocks quoted on the London list.'[11]

However, improved communications and the creation of an international web of correspondent brokers did more than merely facilitate the purchase and sale of foreign securities on other exchanges. Important as this was in widening the market for securities, the very speed of contact, and the ability to transact business immediately through mutual trust, created a new type of business that could not have existed before. This was international security arbitrage. Defined in 1911 by Poley and Gould, it was 'a traffic consisting of the purchase and sale on one stock exchange, and the simultaneous or approximately simultaneous re-sale or re-purchase on another stock exchange, of the same amount in the same stocks or shares'.[12]

The almost instantaneous communication between exchanges, and the active trading in the same securities in the different markets, created opportunities for members of each to profit from any differences in prices that occurred, by buying in the market where the price was lower and selling where it was higher. This was not just trying to buy in the market where the price was lowest or sell where it was highest, but the making of a living from equalizing supply and demand with little or no interest in the intrinsic worth of the security being bought and sold. As communications continued to improve and working practices between members of different exchanges became better organized, more efficient and more sophisticated, the difference in prices between the same security on different exchanges at which it became profitable to conduct an arbitrage operation fell steadily. Arbitrageurs made their profits from large-scale operations based on momentary and marginal divergence of prices of the level of one-sixteenth or one-eighth of one per cent.[13]

Reflecting historic connections and the chronology of communications developments, the Paris Bourse was the first foreign exchange with which London brokers established an active arbitrage operation. It remained of major importance from then on, interrupted only by the Franco-Prussian War and the Commune in the early 1870s. The issue of the French indemnity loan following the war greatly stimulated transactions between the two centres; and, as that loan was repatriated, attention focused on any securities that were actively traded on both markets, such as Brazilian government stock in 1891 and copper mining company shares in 1908.[14] Active arbitrage between London and other European centres soon followed. The connections with Amsterdam, Brussels and Berlin were the ones of major significance. Trading between London and these centres was largely confined to European government debt at the outset, but that was gradually superseded by other negotiable instruments, such as US railroad securities traded with Amsterdam in 1873, Argentinian government bonds traded with Berlin in 1892 and the shares of traction enterprises from throughout the world traded with Brussels in 1914.[15]

Illustrating the techniques of business as it existed between London and European exchanges is the case of the relationship between the London firm of F. D. Ingall & Co. with its Amsterdam correspondent, Vermeer & Co. According to F. D. Ingall in 1908:

> If Vermeer & Co. sent them an order they did it at the best price obtainable and advised it. Messrs. Vermeer & Co. did a corresponding bargain on their side and advised it: the profit was divided as was the usual practice in Arbitrage business. In the event of failure in London they [Ingall & Co.] bore the loss: if in Amsterdam Vermeer & Co.[16]

This practice had existed since 1876. It indicates a strong degree of partnership and dependency between the two firms, even though they remained separate entities operating on different markets.

Important as was the arbitrage with the Continent, the opening of the Anglo-American telegraph in 1866 created a link of far greater potential, by allowing trading between New York and London. Extensive British purchases of US government debt and the continuance of further purchases, particularly of railroad and later industrial securities, created a much more substantial volume of common securities between the London Stock Exchange and the New York Stock Exchange than between London and any other centre. By November 1873 it was noted by the London Stock Exchange authorities that 'immense transactions in American stocks ... were taking place'.[17] By 1884 a total of £571.0 million in government and railway securities was listed on both exchanges, and this figure had risen to £2,089.9 million in 1914. That amount excluded the growing number of US industrial, mining and urban securities that were to be found on both, such as US Steel and Amalgamated Copper (Table 3.1).

Table 3.1 *London and New York Stock Exchanges: Securities in Common (Paid-Up Capital), 1884 and 1914*

	1884	1914
Railroads, USA	$1,483.8m (£296.8m)	$8,962.1m (£1,792.4m)
Foreign	$79.8m (£15.8m)	$642.1m (£128.4m)
Total	$1,562.6m (£312.6m)	$9,604.2m (£1,920.8m)
Government, USA	$1,292.3m (£258.5m)	$175.6m (£35.1m)
Foreign	— —	$669.5m (£133.9m)
Total	$1,292.3m (£258.5m)	$845.1m (£169m)
Total (Rail. and Gov.)	$2,854.8m (£571.0m)	$10,449.2m (£2,089.9m)

Source: Security statistics from: (1) *Commercial and Financial Chronicle* (New York), 28 February 1914, 24 May 1914, 30 May 1914; (2) *Financial Review* (New York), 1884 and 1914; (3) *Stock Exchange Official Intelligence* (London, 1884 and 1914).

Consequently, close connections developed between members of the London and New York Stock Exchanges for the purpose of conducting arbitrage operations.[18] P. E. Schweder & Co. of London, for instance, conducted an arbitrage operation with

Raymond, Pynchon & Co. of New York, and described the typical method of operation prevailing in 1908:

> The modus operandi of our conducting our Arbitrage business is the same as that of the other Arbitrageurs viz:- that, it is conducted by means of cables direct from the Floor of the Stock Exchange there to the Floor of the Stock Exchange in New York, we keeping a special staff for the decoding of the cables received.[19]

Clearly the business involved considerable commitment, investment and expertise. Another London broker conducting transatlantic arbitrage, Heseltine, Powell & Co., referred to its 'highly trained and specialised clerks' and its 'expensive administrative machinery which has taken many years to perfect'.[20]

Simple as this appeared to be, the creation of such long-distance arbitrage links was not an easy matter, involving as it did the rapid response to cryptic messages upon which rested a vast volume of business at very tight margins. A major difficulty was the achievement of mutual understanding. The economical and speedy use of the telegraph did not permit instructions to be accompanied by extensive details or copious qualification, which might have met all possible circumstances. Frequently one word was all that was permitted. In addition, the physical distance between London and New York, and the time taken by steamship travel (one week each way), did not permit frequent personal consultations through which problems could be resolved. Only by a process of trial and error could effective working relationships develop between the members of the London Stock Exchange and other markets, such as New York.

Even in 1911 when the London firm of Nathan & Rosselli was setting up a new arbitrage operation with E. & C. Randolph of New York, this was preceded by considerable personal discussion and correspondence before a memorandum on the methods of business was drawn up. This memorandum indicates the complexity of arbitrage and the attention to detail it required:

> Any changes in the market are cabled to N.Y. in the morning. Use Com. Cable Co. on very busy days. It is advisable to send duplicate cables by Western Union as they are not overworked.

Nathan and Rosselli code to be used for all orders, executions etc. for their account. Randolph's code to be used for all orders etc. for their account. In addition we use Hartfields Wall Street Code. All orders for account Randolph to be reported net always. All orders are given net.

Any news of importance of newspaper articles are cabled to London early in the morning, also indications, if any. Upon receipt of London prices New York will suggest dealings. Any business done is reported to New York at London prices, and the exchange rate at which we work given. After New York opening Randolph will cable prices promptly giving all important changes, indications, etc. Every cable containing an order, reporting a bargain which has to be undone has to be answered by cable, giving either the execution or quoting the market. All bargains have to be undone the same day, unless agreed upon holding over by both sides. The number of shares bought and sold is checked every evening, as arranged.

Shipments:- Randolph will take shipments we make through the Guaranty Trust for their own account, and will instruct the bank accordingly in London.

The Arbitrage starts on the first August, and Messrs. Randolph will write to us not later than the 1st October from New York on what basis they will agree to do the business for us after this trial. Should the 2 months in question be particularly blank months then a further trial period may be arranged.

Rates of interest on the account to be on as favourable a basis as possible, especially with regard to short. If no exchange of views has taken place you can deal in advance to the extent of about 1,000 shares.

Specialize Penns, Readings, Amals, Annacondas, Chesapeakes, Mops and Utah. All bargains to be cabled at once after execution.[21]

Despite the careful working out of the procedures, and the fact that both firms were experienced arbitrageurs, numerous problems beset the early working of this relationship. As E. & C. Randolph noted on 24 August 1911, for instance:

I do not doubt that with a little patience, we will get our

connection to the point we want it, we have to get accustomed to each others ways of doing things. Since your cable about a week ago I have tried to eliminate as much as possible the speculative feature of the arbitrage, but I must complain about your preaching theories, you do not adhere to yourself.[22]

Difficulties of this kind, and the elaborate nature of the arrangements required, indicate that the individuals and firms involved in inter-exchange security arbitrage were not merely passive pawns in a rearrangement created by changes in communications, securities and markets, but active participants who gradually formulated the techniques and connections necessary to meet the changing circumstances. Their continuous pursuit of new methods and contacts was fundamental to both the actual operation of a world market in securities and its very nature, particularly the role played by London.

A need for understanding was only one of the difficulties that had to be overcome. Differing time zones also created problems. Whereas the difference between London and European centres was of limited significance, and could be easily catered for by slight adjustments of trading hours, that between London and other continents was substantial. New York, for example, was 4 hours 56 minutes behind London; so when the New York Stock Exchange opened at 10 a.m. it was already 3 p.m. in London. This meant that the overlap between the two exchanges' trading was only one hour, since the London Stock Exchange closed at 4 p.m. Because the management of the London Stock Exchange would not agree to a later closing than 4 p.m., those interested in US securities solved the problem by continuing to transact the business after hours, but outside in the courtyards adjacent to the transatlantic telegraph offices. Activity could continue until as late as 8 p.m., by which time the New York Stock Exchange closed.[23]

For more distant centres, time was an even greater problem, as there could be no overlap between the hours at which markets were open. Melbourne, for example, was 9 hours 40 minutes ahead of London, so that dealing on the London Stock Exchange coincided with the hours between 9 p.m. and 2 a.m. there. Nevertheless, arbitrage did take place through either the operation of after- and before-hours markets or the dispatch and receipt of orders to be done when either market opened. The risk was taken that the bargain could be done advantageously in the other market when it opened. If it could not, the original market was resorted to. This involved far greater risk than the simultaneous buying and selling on different exchanges but was resorted to because the potential profits were high.[24] Therefore, though differing market hours created difficulties, methods of business were devised by the arbitrageurs, despite the hindrance of institutions, which either eliminated or reduced the problem.[25] As a result active arbitrage contacts existed between the members of the London Stock Exchange and numerous centres overseas, many of them far distant from Britain. There was an active arbitrage, for example, with Johannesburg in the shares of gold-mining companies, as well as with major centres like Paris, Amsterdam, Berlin and New York and minor centres like Havana, Colombo and Alexandria (Tables 3.2 and 3.3).[26]

Table 3.2 *London Stock Exchange Arbitrage Connections – Centres, 1909*

Centre	No. of firms in London with arbitrage connections	No. of firms in each centre with London connections
Total	262	356
Europe	102	106
Paris	27	27
Berlin	13	13
Hamburg	8	8
Frankfurt	5	5
Amsterdam	16	20
Brussels	16	16
Antwerp	7	7
Vienna	3	3
Geneva	1	1
Zurich	1	1
Rome	2	2
Milan	2	2
Genoa	1	1
North America	60	86
New York	39	61
Boston	3	3
Philadelphia	3	3
Toronto	6	10
Montreal	9	9

Latin America	3	5
Havana	1	3
Buenos Aires	1	1
Valparaiso	1	1
Middle East	8	8
Constantinople	1	1
Cairo	5	5
Alexandria	2	2
Southern Africa	23	27
Johannesburg	10	14
Cape Town	4	4
Durban	2	2
Pietermaritzburg	2	2
Pretoria	1	1
Salisbury	1	1
Bulawayo	2	2
Beira	1	1
Far East	8	11
Singapore	2	4
Kuala Lumpur	2	2
Penang	1	2
Colombo	1	1
Madras	1	1
Shanghai	1	1
Australia and New Zealand	58	113
Melbourne	9	32
Adelaide	11	23
Sydney	6	12
Brisbane	6	8
Perth	3	5
Launceston	2	2
Kalgoorlie	3	6
Charters Towers	3	6
Townsville	2	2
Coolgardie	1	1
Broken Hill	1	1
Auckland	5	6
Wellington	3	6
Dunedin	2	2
Reefton	1	1

Source: London Stock Exchange: Committee for General Purposes, 4 January 1909–8 November 1909.

Arising from the increasingly complex nature of arbitrage, it came to be undertaken by only a small proportion of the membership of the London Stock Exchange.[27] In 1909 only 262 firms registered their arbitrage contacts, for example (Table 3.2). This did not mean that the other members did not possess or retain overseas contacts, for many did. But it meant that the bulk of international transactions was increasingly carried out by those who made it their prime business. Sales and purchases of less actively traded securities, which required time and negotiation before a bargain could be completed, were still the preserve of the general broker and his correspondents abroad. However, arbitrage in active securities, which was the main conduit of contact between different markets, became dominated on the London Stock Exchange by a few relatively large firms. Heseltine, Powell & Co., Raphael & Co. and Higgins & Clarke were largely responsible for the Anglo-American business; George Wilson, F. Healy & Co. and Morton Bros. for Anglo-Australian; Govett & Co. for Cuba; L. Powell & Sons for Penang; Baker, Mason & Co. for Alexandria. Other firms maintained worldwide contacts, such as Vivian Gray & Co., which had connections in fourteen different centres, ranging from Berlin to Bulawayo.[28]

Table 3.3 *London Stock Exchange Arbitrage Connections –*
Regions, 1909

Region	No. of firms in London with arbitrage connections	No. of firms in each region with London connections
Europe	102 (39%)	106 (30%)
North America	60 (23%)	86 (24%)
Latin America	3 (1%)	5 (1%)
Middle East	8 (3%)	8 (2%)
Southern Africa	23 (9%)	27 (8%)
Far East	8 (3%)	11 (3%)
Australia and New Zealand	58 (22%)	113 (32%)

Even for trading between only two centres, such as London and New York, certain firms specialized in particular branches, like individual railroads, mining, or industrial securities. This required specialist contacts in New York, which themselves concentrated upon the appropriate part of the market. The London firm of

Chinnery Brothers claimed in 1911 that 'It was only by going to the right person in New York and being kept posted by that correspondent that they were enabled to run a book on this side and make reasonably close prices.'[29] Consequently, a firm like Chinnery Brothers offered a specialist service by being always ready to trade in a restricted group of securities between the London and New York Stock Exchanges.

As the overall volume of business grew on the London Stock Exchange, so an increasingly specialized class of broker appeared who devoted his time to trading not merely between London and other centres but in specific securities and to specific markets. These brokers could normally buy and sell certain securities at much closer prices, and for any amount or time, than others in the exchange and so attracted most of the trading in the field in which they specialized.[30]

Arbitrage involved not only rapid buying and selling on behalf of foreign contacts but also the continuous quotation of prices in selected stocks in order to maintain business, so it was inevitable that it would undermine the broker/jobber divisions existing on the London Stock Exchange. Brokers were meant to buy and sell on behalf of the investing public, being in the position of passive agents, while jobbers were expected to make a market in securities by being always ready to quote prices and buy or sell as desired. However, brokers such as Heseltine, Powell & Co., with an interest in US securities, began to quote prices in these both inside and outside the exchange so as to stimulate interest and develop an active market, which would make arbitrage easier.[31] Similarly the brokers Morton Bros. were the founders of the market in certain colonial stocks, claiming in 1907 that 'Both non-members and Jobbers came to them to learn the price and they constantly negotiated between non-members either here or by wire in Australia.' They went on to comment: 'The market was practically in their office and there were many other cases in which Brokers were the market rather than the Jobbers.'[32]

At the same time, the ease of communications allowed jobbers to be in constant contact not only with brokers on the floor of the London Stock Exchange but also with brokers on other exchanges, through the telegraph and, later, the telephone. They were thus able to quote bid and sell prices outside the Stock Exchange, and to make a market generally, which is what they did. In fact, such was the competition for business among the jobbers that many offered to share with their foreign contacts any profits to be made in trading between London and overseas financial centres.[33]

The members of the London Stock Exchange were forced to alter their working methods not only because of the opportunities that arbitrage created but also as a result of growing competition for the business from outside. Other individuals and institutions appeared in London dealing in international securities more actively and at closer prices than either brokers or jobbers. The firm of S. Japhet & Co., for example, was established in London in 1896 and specialized in transatlantic and continental arbitrage operations, using German experts and techniques. It was not a member of the Stock Exchange, as it undertook some merchant banking functions, but it dealt extensively on the street after hours with members of the exchange, when trading was not properly covered by the rules and regulations. Japhet himself claimed that his was the leading arbitrage firm before 1914.[34] Much of the activity in rubber plantation shares between London and centres such as Singapore from 1910 was also undertaken by firms outside the Stock Exchange, who eventually set up their own market in Mincing Lane.[35] The boom in South African securities in the mid–1890s also created a number of powerful mining finance houses that held extensive portfolios of stocks and shares in a wide variety of South African companies. In order to dispose of these securities these houses began to sell them directly to brokers and undercut the prices quoted by London jobbers.[36]

While these developments increasingly posed direct threats to the membership of the London Stock Exchange in specific areas, the establishment of branches of continental banks in London posed a more general challenge. Banks such as Crédit Lyonnais, Deutsche Bank, Swiss Bankverein and Oesterreichische Laenderbank all created agencies in London offering to buy and sell securities at terms or prices competitive with those of the Stock Exchange jobbers, reflecting their involvement in the securities market in their own countries.[37] Eight London jobbers complained in 1900 that 'Many large foreign Financial Houses have set up Agencies in London who carry on business in stocks and shares, and who induce Brokers, by the offer of a commission, to transact clients' business with them, which otherwise would have been effected on the Stock Exchange.'[38]

These foreign banks, which were often members of their domestic stock exchanges – a practice not allowed in London – maintained direct telegraph or telephone links between London and their continental offices, along which business could be passed. Such was the case with the Deutsche Bank, which had a direct telephone line between its London and Paris branches for the purpose of dealing in securities between the two centres.[39] Though these foreign financial institutions and others did capture a significant part of the arbitrage business, especially in US corporate bonds and South African gold-mining and Malayan rubber plantation company shares, the bulk of the inter-stock-exchange dealing continued to flow through the members of the London Stock Exchange. In fact, the appearance of such outsiders, especially the continental banks, generated increased business in London from foreign centres, which all could share in. The foreign banks, South African finance houses, outside rubber brokers and arbitrage specialists all conducted considerable buying and selling operations with Stock Exchange brokers and jobbers as an integral part of their operations. Japhets alone, for instance, claimed in 1912 to be paying *c*. £50,000 per annum in commissions to Stock Exchange members.[40] Though competing with the London Stock Exchange, such firms were also complementary to it, through providing considerable business for its membership in general as well as extending and deepening the geographic contacts and the range of transactions engaged in.

Arbitrage and the convenience of investors were not the only advantages stemming from the changes that were taking place in the international securities market after mid-century. Through the existence of active markets in different time zones, such as London, New York and Melbourne, it was possible to operate in an almost continuous securities market. By holding the appropriate securities, financial institutions could simultaneously improve their yields and liquidity, because they could hold interest-paying assets which could be readily sold at almost any time. Neither the opening hours of stock exchanges nor the conventions of the working day could now prevent banks and other financial houses from either employing their funds remuneratively and securely, or realizing their investments so as to minimize the risks arising from a sudden liquidity crisis.[41]

Nevertheless, the opening hours of the London Stock Exchange, and the after-hours operations of its membership, coincided with those of major exchanges in continental Europe and North America. As S. S. Pratt noted in 1903: 'London can trade by cable in American stocks during all the time the New York Exchange is open, as when it closes it is only eight o'clock in London.'[42]

Again, this was not only conducive to arbitrage and investment, but also meant that London could compete with New York for the buying or selling of orders in those securities in which both exchanges had an active market. By offering closer prices, faster deals, or lower commission charges, deals could be attracted to one market rather than another through the communications and business links in existence. The American W. E. Rosenbaum observed in 1910:

> When consideration is taken by the fact that there is always a very large and broad market on the London Stock Exchange for many of the stocks listed on the New York Stock Exchange and at certain times even a much better market for some stocks than here, the great value of the London market to people on this side should be fully appreciated, for by its use there is constantly offered the double or alternative field which is not at the command of those limiting their transactions only to the market on this side.[43]

There existed a growing volume of trading in internationally held securities that could be conducted on any market, but would gravitate to the best and cheapest. Clearly, to an informed contemporary like Rosenbaum, that market was London.

It was not inevitable that the London Stock Exchange would gain rather than lose by this new competitive environment. Through the links to other markets it was now possible for British investors to channel their buying and selling abroad, bypassing the London Stock Exchange entirely. British investors possessed large holdings of such securities as foreign government bonds and US railroad stocks, of which the greater proportion continued to be held abroad. Consequently, the most active markets in these securities might be expected to be abroad, rather than in London, and so the buying and selling would take place there rather than on the London Stock Exchange, once the difficulties of communications and contact had been removed. Withers, in 1907, for example, was of the opinion that

> More than three-quarters of the entire transactions in American bonds and stocks, tho' nominally done in London, are in reality done through the arbitrageurs on the American Exchanges – the London broker comes to a London jobber and the London jobber in turn either cables to America for his supply, or else he disposes in America of the stock he has bought.[44]

This raises the questions of how important in the international market London was and why it was important.

Not all factors were conducive to the London Stock Exchange and its membership playing a major role in the world security market. Each stock exchange had been formed to provide a forum for its members, physically present on or near the trading floor, and its organization and rules reflected such an arrangement. The growing ease of external communications and the proliferation of contacts outside the exchange threatened the accepted modes of conducting business and, eventually, the very existence of a single stock exchange building. Consequently, those who owned and managed the London Stock Exchange resisted any changes that undermined its exclusiveness. However, a policy of outright opposition gradually gave way to one of grudging acceptance as they perceived the extra business and membership that resulted from the improvements that had been won from them. The management was never in the forefront of change, but it could be persuaded by the membership to introduce the new developments as they became available or necessary.[45]

Developments ranged from the use of such new technology as the telegraph, telephone and pneumatic tubes to the expansion of the building and the rearrangement of the trading floor, in order to give the foreign markets more space conveniently sited for communications purposes.[46] Typical of the process of continuing change, and the increasingly positive attitude of the management, was the response to the first international telephone link between London and Paris. The arbitrageurs made immediate use of this facility, which required quick and immediate access to a telephone. As a result, the management moved the Paris telephone so that it was adjacent to the Foreign Telegraph Office, and also arranged that members with private telephones could have calls directly routed to them. In addition, an indicator board was installed in the exchange, which gave members warning when their Paris call was imminent.[47] By the early twentieth century the Stock Exchange authorities were more than willing to co-operate with the membership in providing it with all the facilities it required for the conduct of foreign business. International communications never created the type of hostility that the domestic arrangements did; probably they were never seen as such a threat.[48]

However, many of the members did not share this helpful attitude. Though the international business was of growing importance, it was the main occupation of only a minority of the membership. Consequently, the majority were often unwilling to change their practices to meet the particular needs of this minority.[49] H. S. Carey, of the General Post Office, reported in 1908, after discussing continental telegraph arrangements with influential members of the Stock Exchange:

> the members who do the arbitrage and other business which requires a very rapid delivery of foreign telegrams are few in number and, in his opinion, without influence on the Committee, or with the general body of members. In fact, I gather that they are a small and unpopular set.[50]

This would have mattered little if those with foreign contacts had not had special requirements, especially with regard to opening hours. In the years before the continental telegraph service was fully established, much information and many orders did not arrive until the late afternoon, leading to those interested staying on the floor to conduct business between themselves. Rather than accept this extension of hours, which the majority had no need of but were afraid would apply to them, it was decided to pass a regulation that the exchange had to be cleared at four o'clock. However, for continental business this ceased to be a problem once the telegraph service improved, as the London and European trading hours overlapped.[51]

The first real clash over hours came with the Anglo-American telegraph of 1866, for the London and New York Exchanges overlapped only between 3 and 4 p.m. (GMT). As dealing in US securities grew rapidly it could not be encompassed within this one hour, especially as the New York Stock Exchange continued to trade actively until 8 p.m. (GMT). The consequence was that the buying and selling of US securities had to take place after hours, and therefore outside the Stock Exchange. This had to be sufficiently close so that the telegraph offices were on hand and the membership could easily transfer from the floor of the house to another site without interrupting business. Naturally enough, those involved in the American market desired proper accommodation, especially in the winter months, and repeatedly appealed to the exchange management to make proper provision. After some initial hesitation the management agreed to the request, worried by the possibility that the American dealers would set up a separate exchange. At the same time the unregulated and animated throng in Throgmorton Street and Shorters Court was considered a public nuisance, which gave the Stock Exchange a very poor image. As the managers put it in October 1891:

> The business in American securities forms at the present moment a very considerable factor in Stock Exchange business and the difference of meridian between New York and London leads inevitably to transactions at late hours. A very large number of members are engaged in these transactions and the managers are desirous of making some attempt to provide them with suitable accommodation in a place where they may be sheltered from the inclemencies of an English winter, where sufficient light shall be provided for the due transaction of business in an orderly and proper manner, and where the jurisdiction of the committee shall be free from any doubt or question.[52]

This was all very sensible, but the rest of the membership was unwilling to countenance any extension of hours – no matter the discomfort, nuisance, threat, or importance of the US market. It was considered impossible to extend the hours of one particular market without this inevitably lengthening the period over which the whole Stock Exchange was open for business. Consequently, while a petition in 1891 to provide proper accommodation for the US dealers received the support of 116 members, a counter-proposal opposing any change was signed by 1,070.[53] The problem was that in numerical terms the American dealers were far outnumbered by members who were not directly involved, and it was impossible to persuade the majority to make concessions to the minority.[54] This refusal to grant official recognition and proper accommodation to the American market nevertheless had compensations. Those involved in American securities, whether members of the Stock Exchange or not, could continue to meet and form a market between 4 and 8 p.m. largely unhindered by institutional and other controls over admissions, changes, or strict rules of conduct. A non-member firm such as Japhets could play a prominent role, while generally the market could respond quickly to changing circumstances at home and abroad, and so remain competitive.[55]

While the London Stock Exchange was able to meet the problem of trading hours posed by European, American and later South African and Australian securities by ignoring it, and allowing after-hours markets to coexist with it, the undermining of the jobber/broker functions posed more fundamental difficulties. The jobber/broker division was not simply an artificial creation but reflected a need to separate the buying and selling of securities for commission and the dealing in securities for one's own account. In the former, the broker sought to obtain the best deal possible for his client, while in the latter he looked for the best bargain for himself. This could pose a conflict of interest where both functions were undertaken by the same individual, with sales and purchases for clients being done at prices that benefited the broker as buyer or vendor. Nevertheless, as the changing international circumstances led brokers to become market makers, and jobbers to develop outside contacts, the Stock Exchange authorities tried to ignore the implications for the traditional division of functions.[56]

It was not the potential conflict of interest that provoked a reaction to the change but the growing complaints from jobbers, who saw their livelihood threatened by brokers quoting prices and making markets, and from brokers, who felt that direct contact between jobbers and outsiders meant that a source of commission income bypassed them. Since those with direct foreign interests were always a minority, they did not have the numerical strength to resist the attacks of those who felt threatened by the collapse of the traditional functional organization. However, the committee of the London Stock Exchange tended to take a wider and longer-term viewpoint, and saw that external connections could generate increased business from which all could benefit. Thus it was reluctant to take any action in enforcing the rule forbidding dual capacity.[57] Eventually, though, pressure of opinion against the flagrant abuse and disregard of the dual capacity rule reached such a level that action had to be taken.

Attempts were made to have the rule abolished, which came near success, but the outcome was that the rule prohibiting dual capacity was to be properly enforced from July 1909 onwards. Within that rule, however, so many exceptions were allowed for international business that the established methods continued virtually unchanged. In fact, dual capacity was accepted as necessary for the conduct of arbitrage.[58] Similarly, the introduction of minimum commission charges in 1912 left so many loopholes for arbitrage and foreign business as to make its application ineffective. For example, it was possible to remit up to 75 per cent of the commission charge for recognized foreign agents, or 'remisiers'. Moderate as these regulations were for international business, it was also clear that the committee of the Stock Exchange was declining to enforce them in any effective manner, despite the continuing complaints of other members.[59]

At the same time a substantial proportion of the foreign business continued to be done in the after-hours markets, in which it was almost impossible to enforce any kind of rules, regulations, or discipline, especially as a number of the participants were not even members of the Stock Exchange. The following incident, which took place in January 1903, illustrates the way business was conducted outside the exchange and the impossibility of policing it. According to W. W. Ellis, of Higgins & Clarke:

> someone called out 'B & O'. He – Ellis – not knowing him asked him if he were a Jobber and he reported 'Yes. Laurie'. The bargain was then done. It was dark and he could not see if he was wearing a badge and he took no steps to ascertain if he was authorised . . .
>
> If it had been in the House he would have taken precautions, but in the street it was the usual practice to deal with anybody,

unauthorised Clerk or Principals – the practice was very casual in these matters in the street.[60]

Laurie, of H. W. Laurie & Co., who specialized in American and South African stocks, denied that such a deal ever took place. Under conditions such as these the rule changes introduced from 1909 onwards had little impact on the international market, especially as they contained numerous loopholes and were little enforced for foreign business. Nevertheless, the new regulations did limit the ability of Stock Exchange members to compete for business through being more flexible in terms of commission rates or methods of business. This led at least one firm, Helbert Wagg & Co., to resign from the exchange in 1913.[61]

For almost the entire period from 1850 until the First World War, then, the London Stock Exchange provided only minimal controls over its membership's involvement in international securities, and left it to adjust to the dictates of the market. Much the same philosophy existed for admission, which remained both easy and cheap. Foreigners could become members with little difficulty, with one contemporary in 1851 claiming that 'Jews flock to it from every quarter under heaven'.[62] In quantitative terms, out of the 2,297 new members admitted between 1900 and 1909 a total of 99 were foreign, or 4 per cent. These were mainly Germans, or Jews from the general area of central Europe, and excluded those who had become naturalized or were from the British Empire itself.[63] Though foreigners were, therefore, not numerous among the membership there was no attempt to limit their numbers, and they played a strategic role in enhancing London's importance.

Foreign firms retained strong links with their country of origin and so could direct business to London which would otherwise have bypassed it. Nathan & Rosselli, for example, had a total of 74 clients in continental Europe in 1910, including 67 spread throughout Germany, for whom they bought and sold in London.[64] Similarly, when Japhet established himself in London in 1896 he already possessed a wide range of individual and institutional clients on the Continent which he retained but reorientated away from the German exchanges to London. As Japhet himself reminisced: 'The two branches in Berlin and Frankfurt were the London firm's natural feeders.'[65] These foreign–originated firms preserved their contacts by drawing on their overseas institutional clients for staff, ensuring that they were always dealing with people whom they know and who were familiar with their methods. Nathan & Rosselli's foreign department, for instance, received a total of twenty staff from various German and Swiss firms between February 1903 and July 1914, and sixteen of these returned home.[66] London's willingness to accept immigrants into its financial community, allowing them to become members of the Stock Exchange, not only added enterprise and initiative but also established strong and continuing links with the securities markets of other countries, especially on continental Europe, In contrast, stock exchanges elsewhere were much more restrictive of entry.[67]

Where the London Stock Exchange did have a restriction on entry was the refusal to admit institutions or firms which did more than a broking business. This precluded those foreign banks present in London, and a few merchant banks, which did trade in securities. However, as long as there were no minimum commission rates this lack of membership was easily overcome by brokers agreeing to handle the large volume of business these banks generated either at very low commission rates or for a salary. Essentially, the banks and other institutions were in a position to employ a member of the London Stock Exchange at much the same cost as membership and the payment of their own staff would have been. This meant that London was a very competitive market in terms of charges, which could be varied to suit the nature and volume of business, and so attracted buying and selling from countries where the commission rates were regulated by statute or stock exchange rules.[68]

Eugene Karminski, manager of the Crédit Lyonnais in London, explained the position clearly in 1912, though perhaps with some exaggeration:

> In the case of Stock Exchange business, it is an undeniable fact that the [foreign] Banks have always been the natural channel through which orders have been brought to the London Stock Exchange from abroad, and it has been largely through their intermediary that the London Stock Exchange has developed into an international market for stocks and shares.[69]

He went on to indicate that the new minimum commission rules would interfere with the arrangements these banks had for having their business done on the London Stock Exchange at low cost, and so discourage them from passing as much through London as formerly. This view was echoed by other contemporaries; for the inability of the banks and other financial institutions to become members of the London Stock Exchange made their trading there particularly vulnerable to fixed commission rates. These were introduced from 1912 onwards and did damage the London Stock Exchange's international competitiveness. However, the London Stock Exchange's policies on such matters as admissions, regulation of business, listing of securities and minimum commissions was in general much more liberal and flexible than those of most other stock exchanges, such as New York or Paris, and this attracted business to London.[70]

The same position prevailed with regard to state controls on stock exchanges. While the British government interfered hardly at all, that was not the case abroad. Most seriously, the Bourse Law passed in Germany in 1896, which attempted to outlaw speculation, curbed the normal operations of the German stock exchanges and led to the transfer of business abroad, notably to London. By 1897 seventy agencies had been formed outside Germany which channelled German buying and selling of securities to foreign stock exchanges, and the arrival of such people as Saemy Japhet and Max Karo in London coincided with this restrictive legislation. Whereas in 1893 twelve major German banks, located in Berlin, Hamburg and Frankfurt, received orders from abroad to buy or sell securities amounting to £26 million, and placed orders abroad totalling £2.2 million, by 1902 they received only £3.6 million but sent £11 million. The London Stock Exchange undoubtedly gained a substantial volume of business because of the German legislation.[71] Similarly, the French legislation of 1893 and 1898, which was also designed to curb speculation, drove business to London, as did the controls imposed by the government on the listing of foreign securities on the Paris Bourse.[72] Laws passed in Europe, then, particularly in Germany, France, Austria and Italy, restricted the freedom of continental stock exchanges to operate and diverted dealing elsewhere, with London picking up a significant proportion.[73]

The one area where the British government did interfere was in taxation, specifically through the imposition of stamp duty on stock exchange transfers. As early as 1871 all stock and share certificates had to bear a revenue stamp, though not until 1879 was it realized that this applied to foreign securities. When this duty was raised in 1892 it produced considerable opposition, leading to it being abandoned in 1893, as the government had become convinced that its imposition encouraged foreigners to bypass London. The reimposition of the duty at a level of half a per cent was also considered to have lost London business, with an even greater loss threatened by the proposal to raise the rate to one per cent. Medwin & Lowy, dealers in international securities, warned of the consequences, based on the European experience, in 1909:

> Other countries have introduced heavy stock exchange duties with the result that they have minimised transactions in their larger exchanges and have entirely wiped out some of their smaller ones. However desirable it may be to encourage investors to take up more Home and Colonial Stocks, the importance of foreign dealings must not be lost sight of, and a stamp duty which would hamper foreign business would practically have the effect of reducing the present dominating position of London to that of a small Exchange where chiefly local stocks are dealt in.[74]

Though the government continued to impose a stamp duty, this was in line with most continental European countries and the State of New York, where the rates tended to be higher. At the same time it was not difficult to avoid the duty for foreign securities, since the certificates could be kept on deposit in a foreign bank, while many Stock Exchange deals were never completed and so did not produce transfers requiring a stamp.[75] Consequently, the attitude of the British government to the London Stock Exchange was a largely passive one, in which it was left free to respond to the dictates of the market. This was in marked contrast to the position in certain continental countries where the laws passed considerably circumscribed the stock exchanges, and drove personnel and business out of the country, which greatly benefited London.

With British brokers and jobbers rapidly developing overseas contacts, and foreign firms and financial institutions establishing themselves in London, the members of the London Stock Exchange soon came to possess extensive connections abroad, either directly or indirectly. These connections varied from the arbitrageurs, who turned over a vast business daily through a close working relationship with members of other exchanges, to the remisiers or foreign agents who channelled orders to London for a share of the commission. R. M. Bauer, a remisier for Solomon & Co., described his function in 1911:

> It is the foreign agent's business to inform his London house of everything going on in the country where he is domiciled and to draw its attention to the opportunities for profitable investment. Apart from this he has to show to his friends the advantages which the London Stock Exchange offers to the investor and speculator, and in procuring orders for his house he contributes towards the greatness of the Stock Exchange.[76]

It was through this web of contact, which existed at all levels, that the London Stock Exchange came to be in receipt of a constant stream of information and orders from throughout the world, but especially from Europe, North America, Australia and South Africa (Table 3.3). Orders were bypassing the smaller and less active foreign exchanges and being sent to London for execution, via either the remisiers, the branch networks of foreign banks, or local brokers.[77] At the same time the operations of the arbitrageurs ensured that the prices prevailing on the London Stock Exchange, and the volume and nature of the business that could be done, were equal to those on any other stock exchange, if not in excess of them.[78] The rapidity of communications, the relative freedom from governmental and institutional restrictions and the willingness to absorb and adapt allowed the membership of the London Stock Exchange to place itself at the very centre of the world's securities market. Lionel Cohen, a jobber with extensive European connections, had already recognized the London Stock Exchange's position by 1878, when he reported:

> The advantage of our London market is now very much secured to the continent by the rapidity of communication between the two places, and we continually get the telegrams from the Bourses abroad saying 'will you buy' or 'sell this or that in London', because they cannot find anyone to deal in their own country.[79]

In the years that followed, this role was increased in terms of the volume of business, widened in terms of the regions of the world served, and extended in terms of the securities involved. The London Stock Exchange became the market-making institution for the world in respect of international securities.[80] As *The Statist* divined in 1886: 'Arbitrage, in fact, is simply jobbing "writ large" carried on between two markets instead of in one.'[81] By being always ready to buy and sell any amount at any time at close prices, and by possessing the contacts to offer this service worldwide, the members of the London Stock Exchange attracted business, offering a ready market for the widest range of securities.

In 1910, when the paid-up value of all negotiable securities in the world was placed at £32.6 billion, a total of £10.7 billion, or 32.8 per cent, was found on the London Stock Exchange, which was far greater than that of any other stock exchange.[82] Though many of these securities did not have an active market in London, the figures indicate the importance of the London Stock Exchange for the world securities market. For the Stock Exchange itself, one statistical illustration of the growth and change that took place was the fact that the paid-up value of the foreign securities (payable in London) which it quoted rose from $101 million in 1853 to at least £5,080.8 million in 1913, or by £83 million per annum. In proportional terms, foreign securities rose from 8.3 per cent of all quoted securities to 53.2 per cent (Tables 2.3 and 2.4). Both the international securities market and the London Stock Exchange's participation in it had been transformed between 1850 and 1914. One market now existed, and London was by far its single most important component.

Having gained such a position, the London Stock Exchange possessed a commanding lead over its rivals. With a reputation as a market where the widest range of securities could always be bought and sold at the keenest prices, the Stock Exchange attracted business. This, in turn, produced a greater volume and variety of turnover, which encouraged specialization and expertise, further increasing the attractions of the London market. As long as nothing interfered to diminish the volume of business, to limit the flexibility of the personnel, to increase the costs and charges, or to restrict access either way, then the London Stock Exchange could maintain its competitive edge and preserve its position as the central market for international securities.[83]

One should perhaps ask whether this international orientation was to the detriment of the market for domestic securities provided by the London Stock Exchange and its membership. At the simple level of physical capacity, the Stock Exchange was regularly expanded throughout the nineteenth century, to cater for increased demand. In this expansion, the foreign markets tended to be given the least consideration. Both the American and South African markets overflowed into the adjoining courts and streets at busy times, while the Malayan plantation securities found an alternative home in Mincing Lane, being formalized into an independent market in 1909.[84] There was never any sign of foreign securities driving domestic ones from the floor; rather, the overseas markets had to use what capacity they could, whether inside or outside.

A similar situation existed in employment. Many of the brokers and jobbers in foreign securities came from abroad, as did some of their staff, attracted to London because of the opportunities that existed there. Stock Exchange membership grew substantially, with numbers reaching 5,000 by 1908, of whom around 2,000 were jobbers. These jobbers dealt on their own account and seemed willing to trade in any securities where a profit could be made, and this meant both domestic and foreign.[85] The skills these people had were often dependent upon expertise and contacts acquired abroad, and London gained as a result of their participation in securities trading. This was especially true in arbitrage, which would have been much more limited without personnel from abroad. Loewenstein, for instance, was reputed to be the foremost arbitrageur in London in the Edwardian period, and he had been recruited in Germany in 1901 by Saemy Japhet, himself an immigrant, because of his skill and experience as a currency dealer, a business that was relatively neglected in London.[86]

The externally orientated firms, however, did not confine themselves to international business but lent their abilities to trading in domestic securities, when the need occurred or openings arose. G. H. & A. M. Jay, for example, had been arbitrage traders between London and Amsterdam from the 1870s, but switched increasingly to London–Glasgow arbitrage with the coming of the telephone and the opportunities its introduction created. The techniques and knowledge that had been used to develop a better market in international securities could, and were, used in the improvement of the domestic market for industrial securities.[87] Consequently, it is very unlikely that the international orientation of the London Stock Exchange crowded out domestic securities in terms of space, staff, or commitment. The whole market was expanding and responding to the demands put upon it, with the only restriction occurring in the years before the First World War, when the securities that lost out were those of the rubber companies, not domestic industrial issues.

This was not a matter of the international securities expanding at the expense of the domestic, but of both growing rapidly, and the market growing just as rapidly to accommodate them both. Circumstances in the world, and London's response to them, ensured that the growth of international securities would be that much faster; but this did not mean that the growth of domestic securities was any slower as a result. Such a causal connection was absent. In Germany, for example, where the external orientation of the Berlin and Frankfurt stock exchanges was much less than in Britain, there were also poorer markets for domestic securities.

Notes

1   S. Chapman, *The Rise of Merchant Banking* (London, 1984), pp. 8, 14, 38, 59, 202–4; R. W. and M. E. Hidy, 'Anglo-American Merchant Bankers and the Railroads of the Old Northwest, 1848–1860', *Business History Review*, vol. 34 (1960), p. 154; J. A. Kouwenhoven, *Partners in Banking: A Historical Portrait of a Great Private Bank: Brown Brothers, Harriman & Co., 1818–1968* (New York, 1968); D. Greenberg, *Financiers and Railroads, 1869–1889; A Study of Morton, Bliss & Co.* (Newark, 1980), pp. 25, 31–2; D. C. M. Platt, *Foreign Finance in Continental Europe and the United States, 1815–1870* (London, 1984), p. 59.
2   London Stock Exchange (LSE): Committee for General Purposes, 17 November 1851, 30 March 1857, 3 April 1857, 4 February 1909.
3   LSE: Gen. Purposes, 23 August 1889.
4   Chapman, *Merchant Banking*, pp. 47, 49; Greenberg, *Financiers and Railroads*, pp. 31–3; J. E. Hedges, *Commercial Banking and the Stock Market before 1863* (Baltimore, 1938), p. 71; W. J. Duncan, *Notes on the Rates of Discount in London, 1866–1873* (Edinburgh, 1877), p. 146.
5   E. F. Satterthwaite & Co. to R. Irvin & Co. 15 April 1879, 22 April 1879, 3 June 1879, 17 March 1880, 17 February 1880, 26 February 1881 (R. Irvin & Co., Correspondence, New York Historical Society); cf.

Morton Bliss & Co. to Morton, Rose & Co., 16 March 1884, 28 May 1884, 21 June 1884, 23 December 1884, 21 January 1885, 21 February 1885 (George Bliss, Letter Book, NY Historical Society).

6 Chapman, *Merchant Banking*, pp. 22, 25, 43, 77, 106, 108, 114, 120–2, 125, 172; J. A. Kouwenhoven, *Partners in Banking*, p. 169.

7 LSE: Gen. Purposes, 11 January 1858; Chapman, *Merchant Banking*, pp. 49–50.

8 *Royal Commission on the London Stock Exchange, Minutes of Evidence* (British Parliamentary Papers, 1878, XIX), pp. 113–14; *Financial Times*, 25 January 1908; Chapman, *Merchant Banking*, pp. 59, 67; cf. C. A. Jones, 'Competition and Structural Change in the Buenos Aires Fire Insurance Market: The Local Board of Agents, 1875–1921', in O. M. Westall (ed.), *The Historian and the Business of Insurance* (Manchester 1984), p. 119.

9 E.g. LSE: Gen. Purposes, 6 December 1854, 3 February 1863, 25 October 1870.

10 J. Covey Williams to Earl Grey, 12 June 1902; cf. B. Lenman and K. Donaldson, 'Partners' Incomes, Investment and Diversification in the Scottish Linen Area, 1850–1921', *Business History*, vol. 13 (1971) pp. 11–12; J. H. Treble, 'The Pattern of Investment of the Standard Life Assurance Company, 1875–1914', *Business History*, vol. 22 (1980), p. 184; Hidy and Hidy, 'Anglo-American Merchant Bankers', p. 166.

11 G. Withers, 'English Investors and American Securities', *Financial Review of Reviews* (*FR*), March 1907, p. 34.

12 A. P. Poley and F. H. Gould, *The History, Law and Practice of the Stock Exchange* (London, 1911, 2nd edn), p. 86.

13 W. C. Van Antwerp, *The Stock Exchange from within* (New York, 1913), p. 284.

14 LSE: Gen. Purposes, 24 November 1857, 11 January 1858, 17 October 1870, 21 December 1870, 8 October 1872, 20 April 1875, 9 February 1891, 20 October 1909; Gen. Purposes, Appendixes, 6 January 1879, 20 January 1879.

15 LSE: Gen. Purposes, 17 June 1873, 22 December 1892, 4 February 1895, 19 October 1905, 14 April 1914; Gen. Purposes Subcommittee of Non-Permanent Character, 24 February 1910.

16 LSE: Gen. Purposes, 6 January 1908; cf. 17 June 1873, 2 April 1900, 18 February 1903, 19 October 1908, 14 April 1914.

17 LSE: Gen. Purposes, 20 November 1873; cf. Chapman, *Merchant Banking*, p. 108.

18 LSE: Gen. Purposes, 8 October 1872, 27 October 1873, 25 October 1877, 14 March 1894, 21 March 1894, 27 January 1908, 21 December 1908; Gen. Purposes Subcommittee on Rules and Regulations, 13 April 1910, 19 April 1910.

19 LSE: Gen. Purposes, 3 March 1908.

20 LSE: Gen. Purposes, 2 July 1908.

21 Nathan & Rosselli, Memorandum on Arbitrage, 1911 (Nathan & Rosselli Papers, Guildhall Library).

22 E. & C. Randolph to Nathan & Rosselli, 24 August 1911; cf. 24 April 1911, 7 June 1911, 8 June 1911, 1 August 1911, 15 August 1911, 22 August 1911, 6 September 1911, 28 September 1911.

23 LSE: Gen. Purposes, 23 January 1884, 16 December 1908. For international times see *The Stockbrokers' Telegraphic Code* (London, 1886 and 1899), p. 157.

24 LSE: Gen. Purposes, 7 February 1907, 2 July 1908, 23 July 1908, 21 December 1908.

25 LSE: Gen. Purposes, 3 February 1908, 8 February 1909, 2 October 1911; Gen. Purposes Subcommitee on Commissions, 21 May 1912, 4 June 1912; Gen. Purposes Subcommittee on Rules and Regulations, 13 April 1910; Gen. Purposes Subcommittee on Settlement Dept, 6 November 1889, 2 January 1895; Gen. Purposes Subcommittee on Non-Permanent Character, 23 September 1909.

26 LSE: Gen. Purposes, 6 December 1906.

27 Cf. G. P. & A. W. Butler, Brokers, New York, Letter Book, 25 September 1906, 10 July 1909, 16 November 1909, 15 December 1909, 21–23 July 1910, 4 August 1910, 11 August 1910.

28 LSE: Gen. Purposes, 3 February 1908, 21 December 1908, 18 January 1909, 8 February 1909, 2 October 1911; Gen. Purposes Subcommittee of Non-Permanent Character, 23 September 1909; E. & G. Randolph to Nathan & Rosselli, 24 August 1911.

29 LSE: Gen. Purposes, 20 March 1911; cf. 20 May 1912, 29 May 1912.

30 LSE: Gen. Purposes, 17 June 1873, 5 February 1908, 21 December 1908; Gen. Purposes Subcommittee on Commissions, 20 August 1913.

31 LSE: Gen. Purposes, 25 October 1877; Vivian Gray & Co. to Sec., Gen. Purposes, 12 June 1889; *The Times*, 17 January 1908.

32 LSE: Gen. Purposes, 7 February 1907.

33 LSE: Gen. Purposes, 2 April 1900, 18 February 1903, 22 November 1906, 28 November 1906; *Financial News*, 8 March 1905, 11 April 1906, *Financial Times*, 10 January 1908.

34 S. Japhet, *Recollections from my Business Life* (London, 1931), pp. 23–5, 62, 76–8, 112; L. Dennet, *The Charterhouse Group, 1925–1979: A History* (London, 1979), pp. 73–6; LSE: Gen. Purposes Subcommittee on Commissions, 2 May 1912; NYSE: Committee on Securities, 11 August 1913; Chapman, *Merchant Banking*, p. 50.

35 LSE: Gen. Purposes, 17 December 1902, 7 January 1903, 4 July 1904.

36 LSE: Gen. Purposes, 17 December 1902, 7 January 1903, 4 July 1904, 11 July 1904, 20 November 1906, 19 December 1906.

37 LSE: Gen. Purposes, 19 April 1900, 15 October 1906, 15 November 1906.

38 LSE: Gen. Purposes, 27 June 1900.

39 LSE: Gen. Purposes, 1 February 1909, 14 March 1910.

40 LSE: Gen. Purposes, 7 February 1907; LSE: Gen. Purposes Subcommittee on Commissions, 2 May 1912.
41 W. E. Rosenbaum, *The London Stock Market: Its Features and Usages* (New York, 1910), pp. 4–5.
42 S. S. Pratt, *The Work of Wall Street* (New York, 1903), p. 114; Huebner, *Stock Market*, pp. 87–9.
43 Rosenbaum, *London Stock Market*, p. 4; cf. E. S. Woolf, 'The American Market before 1914', *Stock Exchange Journal*, vol. 8 (1963), pp. 14–15.
44 G. Withers, 'English Investors', p. 34.
45 LSE: Trustees and Managers, 12 April 1859, 3 February 1904, 17 February 1904, 16 March 1904, 7 December 1904, 24 May 1905, 7 July 1907; Gen. Purposes, 24 September 1888.
46 LSE: Trustees and Managers, 11 December 1879, 29 January 1880, 1 March 1899, 15 March 1899, 6 January 1904, 19 February 1908.
47 LSE: Trustees and Managers, 17 February 1909.
48 LSE: Gen. Purposes, 26 October 1908, 6 November 1911.
49 *Financial Times*, 25 January 1908.
50 H. S. Carey to L. T. Horne, 3 December 1908 (GPO Archives).
51 LSE: Gen. Purposes, 17 January 1851; Trustees and Managers, 17 June 1884.
52 LSE: Trustees and Managers, 7 October 1891; cf. 17 June 1884, 10 December 1885, 3 December 1890, 25 September 1891, 14 October 1891, 28 October 1891, 2 December 1908, 10 November 1909, 4 December 1909, 16 November 1910.
53 LSE: Trustees and Managers, 7 October 1891.
54 LSE: Gen. Purposes, 23 January 1884, 20 November 1885, 21 December 1885, 8 November 1886, 22 October 1891.
55 LSE: Gen. Purposes, 16 December 1908; Woolf, 'The American Market', pp. 14–15; Japhet, *Recollections*, pp. 77–8, 92, 96–7, 112.
56 LSE: Gen. Purposes, 25 October 1877, 17 December 1902, 18 February 1903, 11 July 1904, 15 October 1906, 15 November 1906, 20 November 1906, 22 November 1906.
57 LSE: Gen. Purposes, 18 October 1900, 21 May 1903, 10 February 1908.
58 LSE: Gen. Purposes, 23 July 1909; cf. Minutes 1906–9.
59 LSE: Gen. Purposes, 1 June 1912, 30 September 1912, 14 April 1914; Gen. Purposes Subcommittee on Commissions, 20 January 1913.
60 LSE: Gen. Purposes Subcommittee of Non-Permanent Character, 2 February 1903.
61 A. R. Wagg, 'The History of the Firm' (typescript in possession of Schroder Wagg & Co.)
62 *Knight's London Cyclopaedia* (London, 1851), p. 647.
63 LSE: Gen. Purposes, Appendixes, Statement of Foreigners Admitted as Members, 1 January 1900–31 December 1909.
64 Nathan & Rosselli, Note and Address Book, 15 January 1910; cf. LSE: Gen. Purposes Subcommittee on Commissions, 2 May 1912; F. E.

Born, *International Banking in the 19th and 20th Centuries* (Leamington Spa, 1983), p. 163; Chapman, *Merchant Banking*, p. 50.
65 Japhet, *Recollections*, p. 72; cf. pp. 19, 24, 60–62, 76; Dennet, *Charterhouse Group*, pp. 73–4. For the similar case of E. Spiegal & Co. see M. Karo, *City Milestones and Memories: Sixty-Five Years in and around the City of London* (London, 1962), pp. 1–2.
66 Nathan & Rosselli, Staff Memorandum, Foreign Department (no date); cf. Japhet, *Recollections*, p. 76.
67 LSE: Gen. Purposes, 15 October 1906; cf. Chapter 9, below, on London and New York.
68 LSE: Gen. Purposes, 4 October 1909.
69 LSE: Gen. Purposes Subcommittee on Commissions, 16 May 1912.
70 Wagg, 'History of the Firm'; LSE: Gen. Purposes, 25 April 1912.
71 *The Times*, 23 February 1908; H. C. Emery, 'Ten Years' Regulation of the Stock Exchange in Germany', *Yale Review*, May 1908, pp. 823–9; Karo, *City Milestones*, pp. 1–2; Japhet, *Recollections*, pp. 62, 68.
72 M. Myers, *Paris as a Financial Centre*, (London, 1936), p. 137; W. Parker, *The Paris Bourse and French Finance* (New York, 1920), pp. 27, 34.
73 LSE: Gen. Purposes Subcommittee of Non-Permanent Character, 3 June 1909, 13 May 1909; Gen. Purposes, 15 October 1906; Born, *International Banking*, pp. 119, 123, 172.
74 LSE: Gen. Purposes Subcommittee of a Non-Permanent Character, 3 June 1909; cf. Gen. Purposes, 25 January 1871, 15 May 1893, 28 November 1906; Gen. Purposes, Appendixes: F. B. Garnett, Inland Revenue, to F. Levien, 19 March 1879, Memorandum on Stamp Duty, 24 April 1899.
75 LSE: Gen. Purposes, 24 April 1899; Gen. Purposes Subcommittee of Non-Permanent Character, 20 May 1909; Gen. Purposes, Appendixes, Memoranda on Stamp Duty, 13 May 1909, 11 July 1909, 13 July 1909; W. R. Lawson, *American Finance* (London, 1906), p. 13; M. L. Weil, *The ABC and Manual of the Curb Market* (New York, 1908), p. 10.
76 LSE: Gen. Purposes, 15 May 1911; cf. 30 June 1871.
77 LSE: Gen. Purposes Subcommittee on Commissions, 9 May 1912, 16 May 1912.
78 Financial Times, *Investors' Guide* (London, 1913), p. 114.
79 *Royal Commission on the London Stock Exchange, Minutes of Evidence*, p. 114.
80 As an illustration of the emergence of this function see *Knight's Cyclopaedia*, p. 647; *The Economist*, 11 October 1856, 3 July 1880; W. J. Duncan, *Notes, 1866–1873*, p. 19; G. R. Gibson, *The Stock Exchanges of London, Paris and New York: A Comparison* (New York, 1889), p. 64; A. H. Woolf, *The Stock Exchange: Past and Present* (London, 1913), p. 112; Financial Times, *Investors' Guide*, p. 13. For a view of the London Stock Exchange from abroad see G. R. Gibson, *The Vienna*

Bourse (New York, 1892), pp. 30–1; F. W. Field, *Capital Investment in Canada* (Toronto, 1911), pp. 43, 51, 147; E. Vidal, *The History and Methods of the Paris Bourse* (Washington, 1910), p. 232; A. R. Hall, *The Stock Exchange of Melbourne and the Victorian Economy, 1852–1900* (Canberra, 1968), p. 233.

81 *The Statist*, 14 August 1886, pp. 179–80.
82 M. A. Neymarck, *Le Statistique Internationale des Valeurs Mobilières* (La Haye, 1911), pp. 3, 23; *Stock Exchange Official Intelligence* (London, 1911), p. 1709.
83 E. McDermott, *The London Stock Exchange: Its Constitution and Modes of Business* (London, 1877), p. 35; E. T. Powell, *The Mechanism of the City* (London, 1910), pp. 43–5; H. Withers, *The English Banking System* (Washington, 1910), p. 116; Financial Times, *Investors' Guide*, p. 13.
84 LSE: Gen. Purposes Subcommittee of Non-Permanent Character, 23 September 1909.
85 *Financial Times*, 27 January 1908, 24 June 1908.
86 Dennett, *Charterhouse Group*, p. 74. For other examples see LSE: Gen. Purposes, 22 November 1906; Gen. Purposes Subcommittee on Rules and Regulations, 13 April 1910.
87 LSE: Gen. Purposes, 27 January 1910, 17 October 1910.

4 The London Stock Exchange and the Capital Market

The functions of the London Stock Exchange and its membership have traditionally been associated with the capital market and its provision of long-term finance for government and business. During the nineteenth century the British capital market grew in size and sophistication, with the City of London coming to occupy an increasingly central and influential position. As the needs of the economy for capital became larger and more varied, it necessitated an expansion in the number and nature of institutional and individual intermediaries, to replace the informal and intermittent methods of the past. These intermediaries were largely located in London, whence they could offer a national or even international service, utilizing the improved communications available.[1]

One measure of London's growing importance in the capital market is the paid-up capital of the securities quoted on the London Stock Exchange, compared to the value of all UK real assets, whether domestic or foreign. In 1873 quoted securities were equivalent to 43 per cent of real assets, while in 1913 the proportion was 77 per cent. However, this gives a false impression of London's significance, as a large proportion of the overseas securities quoted were not owned in Britain, while much of the domestic securities consisted of government debt, for which no equivalent assets existed. A more realistic comparison is between those securities representing real assets, such as railways, urban utilities, commercial and industrial enterprises, and all domestic real assets. The paid-up value of such securities totalled only £440.8 million in 1873, or a mere 9 per cent of domestic assets, while in 1913, when their value had reached £2,570 million, they still represented only 32 per cent of the total.[2] London's importance was increasing but it was by no means dominant even by the First World War.

Perversely, a few contemporaries saw in this growth of a more organized and centralized market a major distortion of the financial arrangements of the country, with detrimental repercussions for the rate and pattern of economic growth. As Kindleberger later generalized, there existed a 'strong suspicion of the Populist type that the financial center sucked funds to it to pour abroad in search of commissions, at some cost to the capital needs of industry in the provinces, which had to rely primarily on internal funds'.[3] This viewpoint has been echoed, however, by numerous serious investigators since, with the result that there is today an almost unanimous belief that the Victorian/Edwardian capital market failed to direct finance to where it was most needed in the domestic economy because of the malignant influence of London. The most thorough investigation conducted into Britain's economic performance, and covering this period, concluded that the capital market did exhibit a definite bias against domestic investment, and Kennedy has made this bias his central explanation for the slowing down of economic growth, and the lack of industrial innovation, that appears to have taken place at this time.[4] Those like Cairncross, Hall, Anderson and Cottrell, who have looked at the operation of the capital market, also stress the separation that existed between London and provincial finance, and consider it a major source of weakness.[5]

Even those who have examined British society in this period highlight the division between London and the rest of the country in financial operations, and consider it a serious problem. Rubinstein, Weiner, Scott and, recently, Ingham have all arrived at this conclusion, though pursuing different lines of research. Ingham, for example, in the suggestively titled *Capitalism Divided?*, was of the opinion that 'Britain's movement towards modern mass production industry was impeded by the structure of the domestic financial system. This was not simply a matter of the export of capital, but also the absence of any close institutional links between finance and industry.'[6] There is, then, a large and diverse body of opinion that sees in the operation of the capital market between 1850 and 1914 a principal source of Britain's economic problems.

However, much of the criticism of the City and its institutions either is misdirected or displays considerable ignorance about an increasingly complex and integrated mechanism. The capital market involved many individual and specialist components that complemented each other in the functions they performed, rather than undertaking everything themselves. The raising of capital by the sale of securities, for example, was done not via the Stock Exchange but through the personnel and institutions of the new issues market. The Stock Exchange provided a secondary market for people who wished to buy and sell those securities already in circulation. Yet this distinction is largely absent from the debate on the role performed by the London Stock Exchange in the finance of domestic enterprise.[7] Members of the London Stock Exchange were involved in company promotion, for instance, but this did not mean that the institution to which they belonged was party to such activities.[8]

At its simplest level, the capital market was the means by which the owners and users of finance could be brought together. This was not always necessary, for much capital formation took place at the individual level, with the single entrepreneur, partnership, or firm undertaking both the saving and investment on an annual basis. The growth of large-scale corporate enterprise added a new dimension to this process, since the management could decide to retain a proportion of earnings for employment in long-term development. Altogether, undistributed profits were the single most important source of finance in the nineteenth century, providing approximately half the additions to capital in industrial concerns by the First World War.[9] There existed considerable coincidence of supply and demand in capital formation, which reduced the requirement for specialist intermediaries, and this remained the case throughout the period before 1914.

Nevertheless, financing was becoming more complex because of the increasing size and variety of demand and the growing separation of function in a sophisticated economy. Between 1856 and 1913 domestic fixed assets in the United Kingdom rose from £4.22 billion to £12.86 billion, at constant fixed prices, while inventories expanded from £0.6 billion to £1.3 billion. Within the increase of £9.34 billion, there were substantial changes in the nature and location of capital formation. New sectors, like manufacturing and urban services, absorbed ever greater sums, while others, principally agriculture, suffered relative or even absolute decline (Table 4.1). In aggregate terms alone it became important to improve constantly the transfer mechanism that would permit or

101

encourage savings to flow from one sector or region to another in response to demand. Reflecting the change was the fact that financial services of all kinds gave employment to only 0.1 per cent of the labour force in 1856 but to 1.1 per cent in 1913.[10]

Table 4.1   *Distribution of Capital in the British Economy, 1856, 1873 and 1913*

Category	1856 %	1873 %	1913 %
Housing and construction	27.3	25.1	24.1
Transport and communications	18.5	22.6	23.4
Gas, water and electricity	1.7	2.7	4.8
Agriculture, fishing and forestry	19.1	15.4	6.2
Mining and quarrying	1.6	2.2	2.1
Manufacturing	12.9	14.6	18.5
Commerce	12.4	11.2	9.8
Public and professional services	6.5	6.2	11.1

Source: R. C. O. Matthews, C. H. Feinstein and J. C. Odling-Smee, *British Economic Growth, 1956–1973* (Oxford, 1982), pp. 222–3.

The demand for capital was not homogeneous. It varied enormously in the individual amounts required and the security and return offered. 'The nature of investments varies so much and the guarantees offered are so different that to bring them all to the same test is impossible,' declared the *Investor's Monthly Manual* in 1909.[11] It was not to be expected, therefore, that the capital market would cater for each demand in exactly the same way. A small venture in a novel field would make an entirely different appeal than a large enterprise in an established business, and would require a different method of financing.[12] Diversity and specialization in the capital market existed because different means were appropriate for different ends.

Within the British economy the single greatest demand for finance in the nineteenth century came from housing, especially the provision of working-class accommodation in the rapidly expanding towns and cities. Approximately one-quarter of all capital formation took place in housing between 1856 and 1913 (Table 4.1). Though a few individuals were sufficiently wealthy to buy or build homes from their own savings, and others had accommodation provided for them by employers, local authorities, or charitable foundations, the great majority were reliant upon borrowing to finance house purchase or construction. Despite the growth of owner-occupation, most people lived in rented property, and most of that was privately rented. Altogether, around 90 per cent of the population lived in property owned by landlords, who regarded it as an investment, with a return being obtained in the form of the rent paid, minus management and other costs.[13]

Housing made demands upon the capital market at two principal stages. First, there was the finance required for the builder as the property was being constructed. This necessitated the provision of short-term credit to bridge the gap before sale, and was a normal component of any commercial bank lending. Secondly, once the property had been sold, longer-term finance was needed by the purchasers. Houses provided ideal collateral for mortgage loans, as they were fixed, tangible assets of certain use. Consequently, it was easy for owners to contribute only a proportion of the cost, usually up to a third, and borrow the remainder on mortgage. All but 10 per cent of dwellings were under mortgage before 1914.[14]

As an investment, house property required constant management in order to ensure that responsible tenants were found, rents were regularly collected and necessary maintenance was undertaken. This was easiest done if the owners themselves were able to exercise personal supervision. Housing was also an easily divisible investment, with even the collective ownership of one house being possible. Central to the process was the ubiquitous local solicitor who, through his clients, was in touch both with those interested in investing in house property and with those with actual or prospective property for sale, such as a local builder or another client. Consequently, the typical property owner, of whom there were around a million in total by 1913, was a shopkeeper or tradesman who invested a part of his profits in houses for rent in his own town, under the aegis of his solicitor. Even in London the property market remained a local one. Of the three thousand or so house sales handled by the London Auction Mart in 1893, 82 per cent were for London and the suburbs, with the remainder being in the surrounding counties of Essex, Kent, Middlesex and Surrey. Elsewhere, the market was in the hands of the 16,845 solicitors who were in practice in England and Wales in 1910, supplemented by the emerging profession of estate agents, who also operated locally.[15]

Even in the provision of mortgages the local solicitor and his contacts were of central importance. By 1912 banks provided 20 per cent of all mortgage finance, closely followed by insurance companies with 18.5 per cent, while local building and friendly societies collectively lent a further 12.5 per cent. However, non-institutional bodies still provided 49 per cent of mortgages, and this was mainly done through the local solicitor directing the savings of one group of clients towards loans secured by the property owned by another set. The institutional element was important in that it facilitated geographical mobility, and it was providing a growing share of mortgage finance, but local sources locally organized remained dominant.[14]

This did not meant that housing finance was not a part of the national capital or uninfluenced by events elsewhere in the economy. Investors in house property could find alternatives both in their own locality and elsewhere, whether in the form of bank deposits, government stock, or other securities, and this became progressively easier as the market became more integrated. 'Bank rate governs sale of properties – when low an incentive to invest in property, when high people content with bank interest,' wrote Stimson & Sons, a firm of London estate agents, in 1896.[17] In the 1890s, a shortage of suitable investments led to a rise in property prices and a boom in housing construction which lasted until 1904, after which a reaction set in due to an accumulation of unsold and unlet property, uncertainty about future demand, higher interest rates and growing opportunities elsewhere. Another firm of London estate agents, Elsworth & Knighton, tried to encourage sales with a hint of optimism in its circular of December 1907: 'As soon as the money market recovers its normal condition and demand for capital in manufacturing districts slackens, there will probably be an improved demand for first-class property for investment.'[18] Unfortunately for the estate agents, however, interest in housing as an investment did not fully revive until after 1911. Sales at the London Auction Mart, which had risen from £2.4 million per annum in 1891 to a peak of £6.6 million in 1898, and remained at around that level until 1904, had fallen to a low of only £2.3 million by 1910, before a slow recovery started.[19]

This did not mean that the capital market was not functioning properly, by failing to direct finance into housing. Rather, the overbuilding of the 1890s reduced the real returns to be obtained from renting out property and discouraged further new construction until effective demand revived. Housing obtained all the finance it was willing to pay for, through the medium of rents and mortgage interest, largely by informal means. These were sufficiently responsive both to absorb large amounts of additional finance, as in the 1890s, and to redirect funds elsewhere, as after 1904 when the circumstances of supply and demand changed.[20]

All this capital formation in housing took place without the need for the facilities of either the Stock Exchange or its membership. Few domestic property companies were formed before 1914, and even fewer were successful (Table 4.2).[21] It was only through the lending of the quoted banks and insurance companies that the Stock Exchange played an indirect role, and even their activities were subsidiary to that of the local solicitor, aided by the growth of the building–society movement. Exactly the same situation prevailed in the finance of domestic agriculture and the ownership of land, with the only involvement coming via the provision of working capital to farmers by the banks and long-term capital to the owners on mortgage, especially by the insurance companies. What agricultural enterprises there were quoted on the London Stock Exchange all operated abroad (Table 4.2). Consequently, another sector of the economy, which absorbed 19.1 per cent of domestic capital formation in 1856 and 6.2 per cent in 1913 (Table 4.1), functioned largely independently of any connection with the Stock Exchange. The collapse of investment in land was a result not of any inadequacies of the informal capital market but of a natural response to the international competitive forces to which agriculture was increasingly exposed in the late nineteenth century.[22]

The capital requirements of other substantial sectors of the British economy were, initially at least, met in much the same fashion as those of construction and housing or agriculture and land. This included most industrial and commercial activities like manufacturing and retailing, personal services such as law and accountancy and even, in the realm of transport, road haulage and shipping – as well as mining and quarrying generally. Where the funds required were somewhat beyond the means of a single individual it was relatively easy to raise the amounts required among a restricted circle of friends, relatives, business acquaintances and

Table 4.2 *Securities Quoted on the London Stock Exchange (Paid-Up Value), 1853, 1873 and 1913*

Category	1853 %	1873 %	1913 %
Housing and construction	—	—	—
Transport and communications	21.2	32.7	39.7
Gas, water and electricity	0.6	0.9	1.4
Agriculture, fishing and forestry	—	0.1	0.2
Mining and quarrying	0.7	0.4	0.8
Manufacturing			
Commerce	2.1	1.8	7.7
Public and professional services	75.4	64.2	49.9

Source: *Stock Exchange Official Intelligence* (London, 1884), p. CXXIV, (1914) p. 1707.

others.[23] Though capital requirements did grow during the nineteenth century, putting increased pressure on the savings of any single individual or small group, there were few radical transformations. At the same time new openings, with limited initial investment needs, were continually appearing, such as the manufacture of bicycles, motor cars and electrical products, and they continued to be financed in the traditional manner.[24]

Shipping is an ideal example of the operation of the capital market in the provision of this level and type of finance. Shipping involved the purchase of a substantial asset in the shape of a steamship (approximate cost £10,000) and considerable risk in its operation, as it could fail to secure cargoes or be lost at sea. Though large integrated companies were formed, running regular passenger and freight services, and these concerns were quoted on the Stock Exchange, the bulk of British shipping was not of this kind. Most ships were owned by small groups of individuals and collectively managed on their behalf by shipbrokers or agents. Numerous single-ship companies existed, each drawing its capital from the inhabitants of a particular port, supplemented by funds obtained through trade and other links. As a Cardiff newspaper, the *Maritime Review*, accurately observed in 1904:

> The composition vendor; the ship-repairer; ropes, paints and oils purveyors; packing people; ship-chandlering folk; owners of small collieries etc. have a little flutter in steamer shares because

of the promise of supplies held out to them, in which case, they argue, even supposing the boat leaves nothing to the ordinary investor, there will still be a bit for themselves. Beyond the few mentioned, shipping is extremely unpopular in the district.[25]

By such informal means of finance, British shipping retained world leadership before 1914. Thirty-four per cent of the world's ocean-going fleet was British, carrying about one-half of all world trade. Shipping was one of Britain's great successes in the late Victorian and Edwardian eras, despite increasing foreign competition, which was often in receipt of subsidies.[26]

Thus for every activity there existed an interested group who could be called upon to supply the necessary finance, and who were willing to do so because of the direct benefits they saw for themselves or because they had high expectations of the enterprise or its projector. Each made a specific appeal to a specific type of investor.[27] By April 1913 there were in Britain a total of 60,754 separate incorporated enterprises, with an average paid-up capital of only £39,927; numerous other family firms, partnerships and individual operations also existed, and their capital requirements were much smaller.[28] For most of these enterprises, especially those in the process of formation, what was important was access to a capital market that not only possessed the requisite finance but was also knowledgeable concerning the intended business and those carrying it out, so that a sympathetic reception could be obtained.

This element of familiarity was vital, for bankruptcy and fraud were common occurrences in Victorian and Edwardian business, and only an intimate knowledge of the entrepreneur and his intentions could minimize the risks involved. Even so, of the 1,076 companies registered in 1880, 27.5 per cent never got into operation, while of the remainder 57 per cent had ceased to exist after ten years and 70 per cent after twenty.[29] Even the simple matter of timing could determine whether a new venture was to be a success or failure, and only those with a specialist knowledge of market conditions in the particular trade to be entered were in a position to hazard a guess about future prospects.[30] According to the *Investor's Monthly Manual* in 1909: 'Looked at coolly, the flotation of an industrial company is really an extraordinary thing, involving a wonderful exercise of faith on the part of the investor.'[31]

Luckily, it was not the public at large who were expected to take these risks, but those among them who had more information and insight through contact and knowledge. In coal-mining, iron and steel, and cotton-spinning the necessary finance came largely from the locality in which operations were undertaken, and where there was the greatest concentration of informed investors. As early as 1875 it was estimated that one-fifth of the population of Oldham had been drawn upon to finance the expansion of the local spinning mills, and other networks of informed investment were evident elsewhere in the country.[32] Consequently, Kennedy's criticism of a capital market in which investors were largely ignorant of the prospects of the companies they were investing in misses completely the geographical, social and business environment it was located in.[33]

There is also no evidence that this informal market was failing to meet the demands put upon it. Between 1870 and 1914, for example, well over one hundred firms were privately floated in London and the Midlands in the relatively novel fields of cycle and tyre manufacturing. On average, up to £10,000 was raised in such a fashion, though much larger sums could be and were obtained.[34] Matthews, Feinstein and Odling-Smee could find no overall shortage of capital in manufacturing industry in this period, which would suggest that the informal market was too good at directing finance into industry, rather than the reverse.[35]

Nevertheless, despite the continued existence of this informal market, numerous public companies did appear in industry, commerce, mining and services, with the result that they dominated some branches of the economy. The paid-up value of corporate enterprise quoted on the London Stock Exchange, excluding railways and utilities, rose from a mere £42.4 million in 1853 to £1,643.3 million in 1913. Iron, steel and coal companies alone had a paid-up capital of £329.8 million by then, while breweries and distilleries had £103.8 million, and shipping £45.3 million. Even a miscellaneous collection of financial trust, land, mortgage and investment companies had a paid-up capital of £248.7 million, which was not far short of banks, with £294.4 million, and much greater than insurance companies' £66.4 million.[36]

Certain areas of business did experience a substantial rise in their capital requirements because of changes in technology or marketing, which placed them beyond the means of the informal market. However, the instances of this happening were relatively rare, given that it was possible to raise £200,000 or so privately in Edwardian times.[37] Capital requirements continued generally to be modest and within reach of many, in a society which was itself steadily becoming more affluent, in terms of both the number and the size of its individual fortunes. Those in receipt of an annual income of £160 or above – which left considerable scope for saving – rose from 280,000 in 1860 to 1,190,000 in 1913, by which date there were more than 13,000 receiving £5,000 and over. Similarly, Britton came to the conclusion that the number of wealthy people in Scotland doubled between 1876 and 1913, indicating their regional dispersion.[38] Consequently, the provision of the necessary finance for most areas of economic activity continued to remain within the reach of the informal networks.

It was rarely the need to raise capital that led to the adoption of the joint-stock form and the acquisition of a Stock Exchange quotation, but a variety of other requirements. In banking, insurance and other investment concerns, the incentive was to spread risk, stimulate custom and share the cost of management and expertise. Many insurance companies never called up the whole amount of their shares, while others successfully utilized the mutual, or co-operative, form of organization for the conduct of business, as did building societies. Among industrial, commercial, mining and similar enterprises, the convenience of the joint-stock form was often of major significance. By the late nineteenth century succession was becoming a problem in some of the business empires built up in the past, for many had grown so big by continuous reinvestment that it was difficult to find individuals wealthy enough to purchase and run them, if none of the heirs were interested. Under these circumstances an obvious alternative was to convert the enterprise into a joint-stock company, issue shares to its former partners and their heirs and hire competent staff to manage the business. The company then developed a life that could long outlast its founders, while the difficulties of trying to withdraw capital could be avoided if a market was created for the securities issued. Similarly, mergers to limit competition could be more easily achieved by an amalgamation of rival firms into one joint-stock company, with previous owners holding shares in proportion to the size of their businesses, rather than by a cartel arrangement. The growth of joint-stock companies did not indicate an abandonment of informal means of finance because of its inadequacies, but an awareness of the flexibility and convenience that the joint-stock form gave to established business, especially as they grew in size and scale, and as their owners aged.[39]

Those industrial and commercial joint-stock companies that were established in the late nineteenth and early twentieth centuries, and which did obtain a Stock Exchange quotation, were almost entirely the conversion of established businesses, already provided with their capital, rather than new concerns seeking to raise finance. In fact their appearance seems to owe at least as much to demands from the public for suitable investments as to the desire of the captains of industry to release ownership and control to a publicly quoted joint-stock company. It still remained possible and common, though less convenient or profitable, for owners to sell out in return for cash obtained from a mortgage on the firm's assets and a share of the future profits. The conversion of established businesses was concentrated in particular years, such as the late 1890s and 1906–7, when the public was eager to invest because of a scarcity of alternatives. The type of firm converted reflected public interest in particular activities, like brewing or motor vehicles, rather than the financial circumstances of individual industries.[40]

Before 1914, then, few branches of industrial and commercial enterprise needed to use the facilities of the formal capital market to raise the finance they required. The numerous issues that were made were generally well received by the public – though expectations were rarely fulfilled – and were more a response to the public's willingness to invest than a need to raise capital for the finance of a further stage of development.[41] Roughly three-quarters of capital formation in 1856 and two-thirds in 1913 were undertaken either without the intermediation of the Stock Exchange and its membership, or with only a limited need for and use of the services they provided (Table 4.1).

In complete contrast to this position, the informal market was of little use in meeting the financial requirements of government in the nineteenth century. Government needed to raise large sums of money within short periods, in particular to meet the demands of warfare, and this meant tapping the resources of a substantial part of the nation. For this a formal market mechanism was required, which even the local authorities used when they began large-scale borrowing in the 1880s, for it was better suited to their requirements than anything their own locality could provide. Few of the uses to which central government applied the finance it raised resulted in productive assets, with wars being the principal expenditure. Local authorities, however, raised capital for the provision of buildings and services and the improvement of roads, water supply and sewage disposal, while central government did end up providing postal, telegraph and telephone communications. Even so, the regular needs of central and local government for finance were met from the income received by way of taxation and rates, rather than borrowing.[42]

The paid-up value of the National Debt alone rose from £853.6 million in 1853 to only £1,013.0 million in 1913 despite a series of colonial and other wars, such as the Crimean and Boer wars. Even the new development of borrowing by local authorities and other public bodies produced a debt of only £277.1 million quoted on the London Stock Exchange in 1913, compared to £46.6 million in 1883. This increase of £436.5 million in overall government borrowing was relatively modest in comparison to that of British railways, whose quoted paid-up capital rose from £211.4 million in 1853 to £1,217.4 million in 1913, or by £1,006 million.[43] Increasingly it was the finance of infrastructure, especially railways, that depended upon the formal capital market because of the need to commit large amounts of finance from the outset, with no possibility of withdrawing at will. It was not possible to build a railway line in small sections, financing the next stage out of reinvested profits, as was the pattern in most of business. A return came only when a substantial part of the line was in existence and so could generate traffic. In the course of the nineteenth century more components of the infrastructure came to require this type of finance, with the central production and distribution of gas, electricity and water, the creation of urban mass transit systems and the development of telegraph and telephone communications. This branch of the economy's capital requirements rose accordingly from 20.2 per cent of the total in 1853 to 28.2 per cent in 1913 (Table 4.1).

Undertaking the provision of this kind of infrastructure were joint-stock companies possessing Stock Exchange quotations from the outset and raising the necessary finance on the public capital market (Table 4.2). Though some of this was done in the provinces, with railways, tramways, electric undertakings and telephone companies relying on local sources of finance, London increasingly came to dominate, especially after the emergence of large companies operating nationally or regionally.[44] Here, the capital market does appear to have been deficient in supply. Whereas Britain had pioneered the railway and the telegraph, amply supplying them with finance, the provision of electricity and the telephone lagged behind that of major competitors, despite much of the technology being British. However, both these developments were enthusiastically received by the investing public and actively supported by the capital market. The problem was that this initial interest waned in the face of legislative impediments imposed by central and local government, which discouraged the capital market from supplying finance. Municipal authorities, for example, frequently decided to supply electricity themselves, and refused to give companies the opportunity of doing so, while the government, through the Post Office, restricted the business of the telephone companies, eventually taking over their functions itself. There are far more plausible explanations for Britain's tardy progress in electrification and telecommunications in the late nineteenth century than any bias or inadequacies of the capital market.[45]

On the domestic front, therefore, the formal capital market was responsible for only around a quarter, rising to a third, of capital formation taking place in the British economy between 1856 and 1913, and this was largely concentrated in the field of infrastructure (Table 4.1). In this it was of crucial importance, for it was beyond the means of the informal capital market to finance such developments as the railways. However, the most rapid growth of capital was taking place not domestically but in those foreign assets owned by British people. At constant (1938) prices, net overseas assets rose from £0.5 billion in 1856 to £7.3 billion in 1913, or from 9.3 per cent of all assets to 34 per cent, and most of these were acquired through the mechanism of the formal capital market.[46]

Investment did flow abroad through informal means, with the direct purchase of foreign assets, especially with the growing ease of travel. Grohman, writing in 1880 on the topic of US cattle ranches, claimed that he had 'heard of some half-dozen gentlemen in England who are reported to draw 15 and 20 per cent interest from the capital they advanced to their former camp-fireside companions'.[47] It was even possible for particular groups in Britain to channel funds overseas through the existence of links derived from migration and trade.[48] Similarly, there was a slow but gradual move among established British firms to expand their operations abroad, whether to develop new sources of raw materials, like the steel companies with iron ore, or to obtain new markets for their products through establishing manufacturing plants, such as was the case with J. & P. Coats in cotton thread.[49] However, the close knit webs that made the informal capital market so effective within Britain were largely lacking in overseas investment. Foreign assets were alien and unfamiliar to most investors and discouraged the calculated risk-taking that was common at home.[50]

Consequently, business that would be privately financed within Britain would need to use the formal capital market if located abroad. Paish calculated that the stock of direct foreign investment by 1913 was only £300 million out of a total of £4,000 million, or a mere 7.5 per cent. Recently Platt has revised Paish's estimates, to produce a figure for direct investment of £750 million, or 30 per cent of his new £2.5 billion total.[51] This still means that the formal capital market was relatively much more important for overseas investment than it was for the finance of the domestic economy. One illustration of the difference is the fact that the paid-up capital of tropical agricultural companies, producing tea, coffee and rubber, totalled about £25 million by 1913, while there were no equivalent domestic enterprises.[52] Similarly, because of the greater difficulties and risks involved, overseas investment needed to be much more managed than its domestic counterpart. This led to a proliferation of investment, trust and mortgage companies, which had between them funds totalling £195 million by the beginning of 1914, almost all of which was placed abroad.[53]

Within the role played by the formal capital market in overseas investment, that of London was paramount, and this was only to be expected. Simon calculated that between 1865 and 1914 36 per cent of the value of all foreign issues made in London were for governments, with another 10 per cent guaranteed by them, while much of the remainder was for the finance of infrastructure investment, especially railways (Table 4.3). It was in the finance of these very types of investment that London specialized; and without the privileged access to local sources that British railways or utilities possessed, foreign enterprises would naturally try London, as it had the greatest concentration of potential investors as well as the market mechanism to draw in others nationally and internationally.[54] Thus by its very nature foreign investment made far greater calls upon London and the organized capital market than did the needs of the domestic economy.

Table 4.3 *Public Issues of Foreign Securities in London, 1865–1914 (£m)*

Category	1865 –74	1875 –84	1885 –94	1895 –1904	1905 –14	1865 –1914
Government	236.3	216.4	259.3	260.6	504.5	1,477.1
Government-guaranteed	73.7	45.9	111.3	44.9	119.8	395.6
Non-government	179.9	203.6	375.5	433.0	1,017.4	2,209.4
Infrastructure	361.3	334.9	533.1	413.0	1,185.6	2,827.9
Primary	31.1	32.8	66.4	154.6	199.6	484.5
Secondary	4.1	6.7	41.9	26.4	63.3	142.4
Tertiary	93.4	91.5	104.7	144.5	193.2	627.3
Total	489.9	465.9	746.1	738.5	1,641.7	4,082.1

Source: M. Simon, 'Pattern of New British Portfolio Foreign Investment, 1865–1914', in A. R. Hall (ed.), *The Export of Capital from Britain, 1870–1914* (London, 1968), pp. 42–3.

The institutions and individuals of the City were all involved in this capital market to a lesser or greater extent. Government issues, whether home or overseas, were largely in the hands of the merchant banks, with competition slowly developing from the commercial banks and other financial intermediaries, such as investment trusts. Between 1815 and 1904 the two leading merchant banks – Rothschilds and Barings – together handled 205 separate government issues totalling £2,003.6 million, disposing of them through a well-established circle of wealthy individual and institutional contacts, many of whom, in turn, had their own clients.[55] Arthur Grenfell, for instance, through his Canadian Agency, issued 35 loans for £16.4 million between 1906 and 1913, and did so largely through a list of some 20,000 potential investors and intimate City connections (Table 4.4). Few stockbrokers were numbered among the issuers of government stock, but they were one group among the contacts used, because of their links with investors. However, this put members of the Stock Exchange in a very subsidiary role.

Table 4.4 *Principal Issues made to the Public by the Canadian Agency 1906–13*

Category	Number	Amount	Sub-totals
Canadian provinces	2	£919,500 ⎱	£2,193,926
Canadian municipalities	6	£1,274,426 ⎰	
Canadian railways	4	£2,310,600 ⎱	£5,310,600
Chilean railways	3	£3,000,000 ⎰	
Canadian industrials	8	£4,210,000 ⎱	£6,910,000
Canadian land and mortgage	9	£2,700,000 ⎰	
South African mining	2	£833,000 ⎱	£1,973,000
Russian oil	1	£1,140,000 ⎰	
Total	35	£16,387,526	

Source: Arthur Grenfell, Memorandum on the Canadian Agency, 1914.

In the field of corporate enterprise of all kinds, brokers were more active, being numbered among the company promoters of their time. James Capel & Co. indulged in the flotation of a number of railways in the mid-1840s, while Foster & Braithwaite concentrated upon the formation of electric power, traction and engineering companies in the 1880s and 1890s.[56] Again, though, stockbrokers were only one among many groups and individuals who undertook company promotion because of the rewards it offered. Solicitors had long been the principal agents, because of their wide range of clients and the necessary legal work, and they remained important. A few solicitors such as the London firm of Ashurst, Morris & Co. even specialized in company promotion, the latter having been involved with 145 different enterprises in existence by 1895.[57] Newly emerging professions, such as accountants, also dabbled in company promotion, like the London and Manchester firm of Adamson, Collier & Chadwick, which concentrated upon coal and iron companies.[58] A few individual financiers even appeared who made a profession of arranging the conversion of established businesses into joint-stock concerns or the flotation of entirely new companies. Numbered among these were Grant, Hooley and O'Hagan.[59]

Familiarity with government loans also led merchant banks to become involved in corporate finance at an early stage. Barings and Rothschilds handled between them 109 non-government issues, totalling £244.1 million, between 1815 and 1904, and such business became increasingly common over time. Some of the newer merchant banks, like Grenfell and his Canadian Agency, concentrated upon corporate issues, with 87 per cent of the capital he raised being for them between 1906 and 1913 (Table 4.4). One measure of the importance of the various groups involved in corporate finance can be gleaned from those handling US and Canadian railroad issues between 1865 and 1890. In that period a total of £185.4 million was raised, and 65.2 per cent of this came via merchant banks, with another 6.7 per cent from other banks and discount houses. Investment trusts, stockbrokers and others provided the remaining 28.1 per cent; within that, the only significant contribution from members of the Stock Exchange came from L. Cohen & Sons and R. Raphael & Sons, who provided 1.9 per cent and 1.2 per cent of the total respectively.[60]

Stockbrokers were thus responsible for only a relatively small proportion of the vast number of public issues and company promotions that were taking place. Between 1865 and 1894 alone there were 9,100 separate issues made in London for foreign and colonial governments and corporations.[61] In addition, few British companies domiciled outside London bothered with London institutions or professionals when they were making an issue, unless they were particularly large enterprises or local authorities.[62]

The level at which the members of the London Stock Exchange were important in the operation of the capital market was essentially through the contacts they possessed with the investing public, and that public's growing confidence in their advice and judgement. This role was recognized by those handling issues, for they paid brokers a commission on all the subscriptions obtained from their clients. The Imperial Land Company, for instance, paid out a total of £1,200 to 25 London and 66 provincial brokers on the subscriptions received to 18,000 shares. However, this was a very passive role in comparison with the merchant banks and others who were largely responsible for bringing new issues to the attention of the public in the first place, often supported by considerable newspaper advertising and a direct appeal to the investing public. Even in terms of contact and advice, solicitors, bankers and accountants were equally well positioned and at least equally well regarded.[63] Even in the process of encouraging the public to subscribe to new issues, by dealing before allotment, which gave the impression that the offer was in demand and would thus go to an immediate premium, stockbrokers were not the initiators of the buying operations but merely the agents of the promoters. In any case that mechanism was soon devalued by exposure and gradually replaced by underwriting, in which stockbrokers again had only a minor representation.[64]

Consequently, any suggestion that the members of the London Stock Exchange were central to the capital market through their participation in new issues is largely erroneous. They did contribute to both company formation and government borrowing but in a minor and subsidiary way. They normally acted at the behest of others, putting their links with the investing public at the disposal of those who wished to issue securities. The stocks and shares in which the brokers and jobbers dealt were, therefore, largely the creation of others, reflecting the separation that existed between the new-issue market and the secondary market, which only a few brokers bridged.

The function of the London Stock Exchange and its membership was not to participate directly in the provision of capital, but to provide a market for those transferable securities issued as a result. Through the existence of a secondary market it was far easier to persuade investors to purchase new securities than it would otherwise have been. Few investors could spare all or a substantial part of their saving indefinitely, but this was what lending to government and the finance of infrastructure demanded. However, many were willing to invest if there was a strong possibility – or better still, a certainty – that they could easily convert the assets they acquired back into money, or into other assets. The existence of this secondary market thus expanded the pool of savings which could be drawn upon to finance capital formation, especially long-term projects like railway construction. As the ability to buy and sell securities readily on the Stock Exchange grew in the course of the nineteenth century, so did the proportion of total savings that could be tapped to meet the growing capital requirements of an increasingly urban and industrial economy. At the same timè, the existence of this market lowered the cost of finance by expanding supply. Increased marketability was recognized by contemporaries as increasing the price and lowering the yield of any given security.[65] The existence of the London Stock Exchange, and the growing perfection of the securities market it provided, rendered easily accessible sources of finance that would not have normally been available, and allowed them to be directed into sectors of the economy where there was a growing demand for capital, which could not be provided through informal means. In this the securities market made an important contribution to economic development at home and abroad; for it assisted in the rapid creation of an infrastructure that would not have been easily attained otherwise, and this infrastructure was a necessary adjunct to continuing growth and change in both the British economy and numerous economies throughout the world.

Crucial as the Stock Exchange's contribution to the capital market was in an indirect fashion, then, its direct involvement lay with the investing public rather than the needy entrepreneur, company, or government. The flexibility created by the ability to buy and sell issued securities not only made it easier to raise capital but encouraged the public to invest, particularly in easily transferable assets. It allowed the investor to liquidate, augment, or change his holdings at will, choosing what securities to purchase from the whole range of those in existence, rather than those being currently issued. Flexibility and choice, increasingly geared to meet the investor's every requirement, progressively reduced that proportion of the nation's savings that remained idle because of lack of suitable opportunities, as well as directing those savings to where each could obtain its highest possible rate of return, within the confines of perceived risk.[66]

Within Britain both the number of investors in securities and the diversity of their requirements grew rapidly in the second half of the nineteenth century. One estimate suggests that there were only 250,000 investors in 1870, a mere 0.8 per cent of the population or, more realistically, 2.5 per cent of those males over 15. By 1913, in contrast, the number of investors had risen to at least one million, 2.2 per cent of the population or 6.4 per cent of adult males. In 1870 these investors had confined their attention almost wholly to government stock and railway securities; by the early twentieth century they were holding a wide variety of British and foreign

118

securities. The number of investors in domestic joint-stock companies, excluding railways and utilities, rose from around 50,000 in 1860 to half a million in 1910. Similarly, by the eve of the First World War a selection of twenty-two Canadian industrial companies numbered around 7,000 British investors among their shareholders.[67]

Despite the absolute and proportional growth of the investing class, it nevertheless remained a small élite in Victorian and Edwardian society. In 1911–13 an estimated 66–9 per cent of the nation's wealth was held by only one per cent of the population; and it was a group numbering around half a million people that owned most of the securities. The holding of stocks and shares was highly skewed towards the very wealthy, for those with moderate savings tended to place most of them in house property and business premises, or only indirectly in securities through insurance companies, banks and friendly societies.[68]

Although a relatively small number of investors used the facilities of the Stock Exchange, they were by no means a homogeneous grouping with uniform requirements. As the stockbrokers Walker & Watson concluded in 1894:

> If there is a wide variety among investments, there is a corresponding variety, in respect both to their requirements and their tastes, among investors themselves – comprising every shade, from the conservative believer in nothing but the 'Funds', to the speculative investor who is content to face the risk of loss for the sake of a 10 or 20 per cent return or a prospective increase in market value.[69]

Age, class, education, wealth, environment, temperament and numerous other factors combined to differentiate one investor from another, influencing the amount invested, when, for how long and in what.

There were wealthy rentiers with no business or other involvements who could afford to invest for the long term, selecting from among the safest of securities. Lord Overstone, the retired banker, had a total of £1.7 million invested in securities by 1881, of which 93 per cent was in government and railway stocks, while the Earl of Leicester, a wealthy landowner, had £0.4 million in securities in 1891, with 85 per cent in railways and governments. On a smaller scale Peter Brough, a retired Paisley draper, had £120,000 in securities by 1880, and this was all in the issues of four railway companies, mainly in England. However, few individuals were so divorced from other influences as to be able to invest solely on the criteria of risk and return. The Duke of Sutherland had £0.8 million in securities by 1879, and two-thirds of these were in the railways, mines and industrial companies connected with his large English and Scottish estates.[70]

The growing number of wealthy investors emerging from business or professional backgrounds in the late nineteenth century tended to own securities issued by companies whose operations they were familiar with, through either trade connections or proximity. W. E. Allen, a Sheffield steel manufacturer, was largely interested in other industrial undertakings, while Samuel Chick, a London lace warehouseman, invested in a London property company and a Nottingham textile manufacturing concern. Typically, John Cory, a Welsh coal-owner and exporter, concentrated upon local railways and collieries and companies providing bunkering services overseas. Circumstances presented many with investment opportunities of which they had a particular knowledge, and this was readily taken advantage of. Among the professions solicitors were particularly well placed, with some like C. E. Cockram and L. E. Milburn specializing in particular investments – British insurance companies and American breweries respectively – while others spread themselves more widely. Bankers, engineers, surveyors, estate agents and a host of others, including stockbrokers, were similarly placed. Travel also widened investment opportunities. G. P. Doolette and H. K. Rutherford returned from Australia and Ceylon respectively, and became involved in gold mines and plantations as a consequence.

Few investors confined themselves solely to a few familiar investments, but increasingly spread themselves over a diverse range of securities. Sir J. S. Barwick, a Sunderland coal-owner, invested locally in quarrying, shipbuilding, ship-owning, dockworks, banking and insurance, and in oil, gold and nitrates abroad. Much the same picture emerges from the interests of Sir Charles Tennant, a Glasgow chemical manufacturer who invested in eight British companies mainly related to his business, such as

United Alkali and Nobel's Explosives, or to his locality, like the Union Bank of Scotland, Linlithgow Oil and the Steel Company of Scotland. However, he was also a major shareholder in nine overseas concerns – of which only one – Tharsis Sulphur & Copper – was related to his business; the others were largely very risky Indian gold mines.[71]

In a survey of 6,120 joint-stock companies conducted in 1901, a cumulative total of 3,369,000 shareholders was discovered, but allowing for duplication this was estimated to be only 445,000 separate individuals. This implied that each investor was involved in seven or eight different companies, and ignored holdings in railways, governments and foreign-based enterprises. Lowenfeld, writing in 1907, was of the opinion that the average portfolio contained fifteen different investments, and this was based on his experience of advising numerous investors.[72] Of course, some had only one investment, such as C. F. Hitchins, a civil engineer, who concentrated upon the British Vacuum Cleaner Company, while others had innumerable holdings, like R. Ashworth, a Manchester felt manufacturer, who was a shareholder in 370 different companies.[73]

In addition to the individuals who were investors, there were also an increasing number of institutional investors. Traditional institutions, such as the banks and insurance companies, grew in both number and size, while an ever-larger proportion of their assets was committed to securities rather than mortgages, loans, or land. The assets of life insurance companies rose from £108.8 million in 1870 to £530.1 million in 1913, and the proportion of these in securities rose from 24.4 per cent to 50.6 per cent. At the same time specialist investment companies appeared, as well as individuals who managed a portfolio of investments on behalf of numerous clients. The conditions under which these institutions and professionals operated also differed considerably. Banks were always aware that the money they had to invest was placed with them on deposit, and could be withdrawn at immediate or short notice. In contrast, life insurance companies had to aim for long-term capital growth in order to pay out, on death, the sum they had agreed upon. Differing circumstances such as these conditioned the type of investment each was able to purchase, and what proportion of its assets each would compromise.[74]

It was thus of crucial importance for institutions such as these to have constant access to a market where they could either invest in a wide variety of securities the funds placed at their disposal or realize securities they owned to repay depositors or make payments to the bereaved. Without the Stock Exchange these institutions would have had to have kept a much larger proportion of their funds idle to meet every eventuality, which would have reduced the returns they paid to depositors or premium holders, and restricted the supply of finance available for the economy. Even for the individual, the existence of a secondary market was more than a matter of mere convenience. One illustration of this comes from the interaction of age and the investor. In youth, for example, the individual combined his talents with the limited funds at his disposal to develop a business of his own. As he got older, and the prospect of retirement came nearer, it became necessary to obtain a source of income that depended less on his own energy and management for one that yielded a safe, steady return without risk or supervision. In the past land had provided the safe haven required, supplemented by holdings in the National Debt. However, the difficulties of agriculture after 1870 and the relative shrinkage of government borrowing forced a change upon the investor. The result was a switch to a more diversified portfolio of safe securities, such as railway stock and industrial debentures with a proven track record. However, this portfolio might not suit the investor's heirs, who might have their own businesses to establish or require expenditure on setting up homes. Part might therefore be sold off, to be acquired by others who were gradually relinquishing the reins of their business. It was increasingly important for investors to alter their investments through their individual life cycle, and to do this using the widest range of securities on offer, especially those already issued and with a proven reputation. Again, without this flexibility it would have been difficult to diversify wealth and make it more secure, leaving individuals either to hoard idle balances to meet their future needs or to continue channelling their funds into land or government debt.[75]

The individual and institutional investor in stocks and shares needed the services provided by the London Stock Exchange and its membership, and this need grew in the course of the nineteenth century as a growing proportion of wealth was in the form of transferable securities. With the existence of the secondary market, and the continuous improvement in its operation, the inhibitions to investment were progressively reduced, so that the investor was willing to part with a growing proportion of his savings at less interest, while the economy obtained a growing supply of capital at less cost.[76] This was of particular importance in the provision of an infrastructure but slowly pervaded all other areas of the economy, as well as contributing to the development of countries overseas, especially those to which British migrants went.

Was this overseas orientation of the London capital market harmful to the domestic economy? In terms of demand it is difficult to detect any resistance from those issuing securities and promoting companies to domestic enterprise. Even established merchant banks of foreign origin became involved in domestic projects when the opportunities arose. The German bank of E. Spiegel & Co. turned to property development at Frinton-on-Sea when the South African mining boom collapsed with the Boer War. The Central Underground Railway was promoted by a consortium of four different merchant banks, all noted for their overseas connections, and it was successfully completed in 1900 at a cost of £3,725,000. The very fact that London-based joint-stock companies were more prevalent on the London Stock Exchange than London's importance in the economy would warrant indicates that City promoters were responsive to approaches made to them. There were also numerous new entrants to the London capital market in this period, all looking to make a living out of handling promotions and issues.[77]

These new entrants and established firms responded not only to approaches (or lack of them) within Britain, but also to increasingly international opportunities. Issues were made, and flotations organized, in London to attract not only the British investor but also those from continental Europe. The Argentine North-Eastern Railway, for instance, issued a loan for £1.5 million in 1888, and though 62.5 per cent was taken in Britain 18.9 per cent went to France and 18.5 per cent to Germany. This was typical of the circumstances in which the financial institutions and intermediaries of London operated by the late nineteenth century. As a consequence, there was considerable flexibility in the issues handled, the companies floated and the countries involved, with much switching from one to another as circumstances changed.[78] For example, in 1906 Arthur Grenfell, a partner in the merchant bank Chaplin, Milne & Grenfell and founder of the Canadian Agency, switched from South African mines to Canadian industrials, which was a deliberate response to changing opportunities (Table 4.4).[79]

The conclusion is largely inescapable that the reason the London capital market was so involved in foreign rather than domestic investment was because that was from where the demands were made and where the remunerative opportunities lay. British industrial and commercial companies just did not require the services offered by the City in most cases, having more familiar means readily available to them either to raise finance or to convert themselves into joint-stock companies.[80] It is inconceivable that a man like Arthur Grenfell – who between 1906 and 1913 made eight separate issues totalling £4.2 million for Canadian industrial companies like Lake Superior Steel and Canada Cement – would not have turned his attention to British companies if he had been given the opportunity (Table 4.4). It was not a failure of the formal capital market but a failure of demand from the domestic economy that gave the City of London its appearance of bias in favour of foreign investment. If the British government had cared to borrow more to finance expenditure on the improvement of human capital through the better provision of health and education, the institutions and individuals of the City would have responded with alacrity, though for a fee.[81]

Notes

1 For such a development in accountancy see E. Jones, *Accountancy and the British Economy, 1840–1980: The Evolution of Ernst & Whinney*, (London, 1981), pp. 24, 61, 72, 102–8, 267–8.

2 R. C. O. Matthews, C. H. Feinstein, J. C. Odling-Smee, *British Economic Growth, 1856–1973* (Oxford, 1982), pp. 128–9; *Stock Exchange Official Intelligence* (London, 1884), p. CXXIV, (1914), p. 1707.

3 C. P. Kindleberger, 'Financial Institutions and Economic Development: A Comparison of Great Britain and France in the Eighteenth and Nineteenth Centuries', *Explorations in Economic History*, vol. 21 (1984), p. 116.

4 Matthews, Feinstein and Odling-Smee, *British Economic Growth*, p. 356; W. P. Kennedy, 'Foreign Investment, Trade and Growth in the United Kingdom, 1870–1913', *Explorations in Economic History*, vol.

11 (1974), p. 425; W. P. Kennedy, 'Institutional Response to Economic Growth: Capital Markets in Britain to 1914', in L. Hannah (ed.), *Management Strategy and Business Development* (London, 1976), pp. 155–6; W. P. Kennedy, 'Economic Growth and Structural Change in the United Kingdom, 1870–1914', *Journal of Economic History*, vol. 42 (1982), p. 112.

5   A. K. Cairncross, *Home and Foreign Investment, 1870–1913* (Cambridge, 1953), pp. 90, 95–6, 101; A. R. Hall, *The London Capital Market and Australia, 1870–1914* (Canberra, 1963), pp. 26, 67–8, 186–7; B. L. Anderson, 'Law, Finance and Economic Growth in England: Some Long-Term Influences', in B. M. Ratcliffe (ed.), *Great Britain and her World, 1750–1914* (Manchester, 1975), pp. 112, 116; P. L. Cottrell, *Industrial Finance, 1830–1914* (London, 1980), pp. 146–53, 189.

6   G. Ingham, *Capitalism Divided? The City and Industry in British Social Development* (London, 1984), p. 169; cf. pp. 10, 35, 149, 153, 227–8, 241–2; W. D. Rubinstein, 'The Victorian Middle Classes: Wealth, Occupation and Geography', *Economic History Review*, vol. 30 (1977), p. 62; W. D. Rubinstein, 'Wealth, Elites and Class Structures of Modern Britain', *Past and Present*, vol. 76 (1977), p. 116; M. J. Weiner, *English Culture and the Decline of the Industrial Spirit, 1850–1980* (Cambridge, 1981), pp. 129, 166; J. Scott, *The Upper Classes: Property and Privilege in Britain* (London, 1982), pp. 94–5.

7   A. R. Hall, 'A Note on the English Capital Market as a Source of Funds for Home Investment before 1914', *Economica*, vol. 24 (1957); and the subsequent debate with A. K. Cairncross in *Economica*, vol. 25 (1958).

8   R. F. Henderson, *The New Issue Market and the Finance of Industry* (Cambridge, 1951), p. 42; K. W. Paish, 'The London New Issue Market', *Economica*, vol. 18 (1951), p. 2; cf. 'The Functions of the Market', in R. C. Michie, *Money, Mania and Markets: Investment, Company Formation and the Stock Exchange in Nineteenth-Century Scotland* (Edinburgh, 1981).

9   Matthews, Feinstein and Odling-Smee, *British Economic Growth*, p. 347; Cairncross, *Home and Foreign*, p. 98; Hall, *London Capital Market*, p. 25.

10 Matthews, Feinstein and Odling-Smee, *British Economic Growth*, pp. 129, 224.

11 *Investor's Monthly Manual*, February 1909.

12 B. A. Williams, *Investment in Innovation* (London, 1958), p. 31.

13 A. Offer, 'Property and Politics: A Study of Landed and Urban Property in England between the 1880s and the Great War' (D. Phil. thesis, Oxford University 1978), p. 48.

14 *The Land: The Report of the Land Enquiry Committee* (London, 1914), Vol. II (Urban), p. 81; Offer, 'Property and Politics', pp. 79–81.

15 R. A. Ward, *A Treatise on Investments* (London, 1852), pp. 35–8; *The*

Land, pp. 82–4; Offer, 'Property and Politics', pp. 30, 34, 36. Data calculated from *Land and House Property Year Book for 1893* (London, 1894). For a case study of housing and its finance see R. J. Springett, 'The Mechanics of Urban Land Development in Huddersfield' (PhD thesis, Leeds University, 1979), pp. 209, 271, 275, 352.

16 S. B. Saul, 'House Building in England, 1890–1914', *Economic History Review*, vol. 15 (1962–3), p. 133; E. J. Cleary, *The Building Society Movement* (London, 1965), p. 151; Offer, 'Property and Politics', pp. 83–4.

17 *Estates Gazette*, 26 December 1907.

18 *Estates Gazette*, 28 December 1907.

19 *Estates Gazette*, 1896–1910; Offer, 'Property and Politics', pp. 32, 192, 205, 214, 231; Michie, *Money, Mania and Markets*, pp. 133–6.

20 *The Land*, pp. 82–4, 90; Offer, 'Property and Politics', p. 214.

21 P. L. Cottrell, 'Investment Banking in England, 1856–1882: Case Study of the International Financial Society' (PhD thesis, Hull University, 1974), p. 147.

22 F. M. L. Thompson, 'The Land Market in the 19th Century', *Oxford Economic Papers*, vol. 9 (1957), pp. 285–99; S. W. Martins, *A Great Estate at Work: The Holkam Estate and its Inhabitants in the 19th Century* (Cambridge, 1980), pp. 36, 60; T. W. Beastall, *A North Country Estate* (London, 1974), pp. 184–7, 207; R. C. Michie, 'Income, Expenditure and Investment of a Victorian Millionaire: Lord Overstone, 1823–83', *Bulletin of the Institute of Historical Research*, vol. 58 (1985), pp. 61–3, 67–70; D. Deuchar, 'Investments', *Journal of the Federation of Insurance Institutes*, vol. 1 (1898), pp. 309–14.

23 For a selection of examples see D. A. Farnie, *The English Cotton Industry and the World Market, 1815–1896* (Oxford, 1979), pp. 236, 252, 257, 260, 289; A. Birch, *The Economic History of the British Iron and Steel Industry, 1784–1879* (London, 1967), pp. 198–9; R. A. Church (ed.), *The Dynamics of Victorian Business: Problems and Perspectives to the 1870s* (London, 1980), pp. 11, 94, 103, 123.

24 Cf. R. C. Michie, 'The Social Web of Investment in the Nineteenth Century', *Revue Internationale d'Histoire de la Banque*, vol. 18 (1979); R. C. Michie, 'Options, Concessions, Syndicates and the Provision of Venture Capital, 1880–1913', *Business History*, vol. 23 (1981); R. C. Michie, 'The Finance of Innovation in Late Victorian and Edwardian Britain: A Preliminary Investigation', *Journal of European Economic History* (forthcoming).

25 *Maritime Review*, 24 February 1904; cf. P. L. Cottrell, 'The Steamship on the Mersey, 1815–80: Investment and Ownership', and R. Craig, 'William Gray & Co.: A West Hartlepool Shipbuilding Enterprise, 1864–1913', in P. L. Cottrell and D. H. Aldcroft (eds.), *Shipping, Trade and Commerce* (Leicester, 1981), pp. 153–5, 75; W. B. Forwood, *Recollections of a Busy Life* (Liverpool, 1910), p. 72; Michie, *Money, Mania and Markets*, pp. 144–6.

26 F. Crouzet, *The Victorian Economy* (London, 1982), pp. 312–13.
27 E. T. Powell, *The Mechanism of the City* (London, 1910), pp. 29–30.
28 *Stock Exchange Official Intelligence* (London, 1914), p. 1706; A. E. Musson, *The Growth of British Industry* (London, 1978), pp. 245–7; A. Essex-Crosby, 'Joint-Stock Companies in Great Britain, 1890–1930' (M.Com. thesis, London University, 1938), pp. 228–30; J. B. Jefferys, 'Trends in Business Organisation in Great Britain since 1856' (PhD thesis, London University, 1938), p. 130.
29 Jones, *Accountancy*, pp. 47–8, 56, 98, 158; D. H. MacGregor, *Economic Journal*, 'Joint-Stock Companies and the Risk Factor', vol. 39 (1929), pp. 495–6; S. F. Van Oss and F. C. Mathieson, *Stock Exchange Values: A Decade of Finance, 1885–1895* (London, 1895), p. li.
30 Ward, *Treatise on Investments*, p. 87; Jefferys, 'Trends in Business Organisation', pp. 345, 359, 363; H. S. G., *Autobiography of a Manchester Manufacturer* (Manchester, 1887), p. 98.
31 *Investor's Monthly Manual*, July 1909; cf. November 1909, and W. G. Cordingley, *Guide to the Stock Exchange* (London, 1893 and 1901), p. 80.
32 C. M. M'Laren, 'Prospects of Iron and Steel Investments', *Financial Review of Reviews (FR)*, October 1906; A. R. Foster, 'Cotton Spinning Companies as Investments', *FR*, February 1907; M. M. Mason, 'Dangers of Colliery Investments', *FR*, November 1913; H. Lowenfeld, 'Investment Crazes', *FR*, March 1906; *Investor's Monthly Manual*, February 1905; Farnie, *English Cotton Industry*, p. 252; J. Scott and M. Hughes, *The Anatomy of Scottish Capital* (London, 1980), pp. 20, 37, 44, 46; D. C. Coleman, 'Gentlemen and Players', *Economic History Review*, vol. 26 (1973), p. 105.
33 Kennedy, 'Economic Growth and Structural Change', pp. 113–14
34 A. E. Harrison, 'Growth, Entrepreneurship and Capital Formation in the United Kingdom's Cycle and Related Industries, 1870–1914' (PhD thesis, University of York, 1977), pp. 364–8.
35 Matthews, Feinstein and Odling-Smee, *British Economic Growth*, pp. 350, 354, 381–2; L. E. Davis, 'Capital Market and Industrial Concentration: The US and UK: A Comparative Study', *Economic History Review*, vol. 19 (1966), p. 259.
36 *Stock Exchange Official Intelligence* (London, 1914), p. 1707.
37 P. L. Payne, 'Iron and Steel Manufactures', in D. H. Aldcroft (ed.), *Development of British Industry and Foreign Competition* (London, 1968), p. 95; W. Hamish Fraser, *The Coming of the Mass Market, 1850–1914* (London, 1981), p. 85; Harrison, *Growth, Entrepreneurship and Capital Formation*, p. 368; Cottrell, *Industrial Finance*, p. 184; Cottrell, 'Investment Banking', pp. 23, 76–9.
38 W. D. Rubinstein, *Men of Property: The Very Wealthy in Britain since the Industrial Revolution* (London, 1981), p. 48; R. Britton, 'Wealthy Scots, 1876–1913', *Bulletin of the Institute of Historical Research*, vol. 58 (1985), pp. 78–94; Hall, *London Capital Market*, pp. 23–6.

39   G. L. Ayres, 'Fluctuations in New Capital Issues on the London Money Market, 1899 to 1913' (M.Sc. thesis, London University, 1934), pp. 188–9, 202; Musson, *British Industry*, pp. 249–50, 254; Cairncross, *Home and Foreign Investment*, p. 95; Hall, *London Capital Market*, p. 21, Michie, *Money, Mania and Markets*, ch. 12.

40   Cf. A. R. Hall and A. K. Cairncross, 'English Capital Market', *Economica*, vol. 24 (1957), vol. 25 (1958); Harrison, *Growth, Entrepreneurship and Capital Formation*, pp. 354, 358–9, 437; *Investor's Monthly Manual*, March 1906; J. D. Walker & Watson, Stockbrokers, *Investors' and Shareholders' Guide* (Edinburgh, 1894), pp. 53, 267.

41   Hall, *London Capital Market*, pp. 23–6, 82; Walker & Watson, *Investors' and Shareholders' Guide*, pp. 109–10; Van Oss and Mathieson, *Stock Exchange Values*, pp. xxiii, lix.

42   E. V. Morgan and W. A. Thomas, *The Stock Exchange* (London, 1962), chs. 3 and 7; Hall, *London Capital Market*, p. 18; Sir Henry Drummond Wolff, *Rambling Recollections* (London, 1908), Vol. II, p. 61.

43   *Stock Exchange Official Intelligence* (London, 1884), p. CXIV, (1914), p. 1707.

44   J. S. Jeans, *Railway Problems* (London, 1887), p. 23; *Investor's Monthly Manual*, January 1887; cf. Michie, 'Finance of Innovation', pp. 2–4, 13–20.

45   L. Hannah, *Electricity before Nationalisation* (London, 1979), p. 43, I. C. R. Byatt, *The British Electrical Industry, 1875–1914* (Oxford, 1979), p. 7; Hall, *London Capital Market*, p. 22; P. Young, *Power of Speech: A History of Standard Telephones and Cables, 1883–1983* (London, 1983), pp. 7, 19, 23; J. Kieve, *The Electric Telegraph: A Social and Economic History* (Newton Abbot, 1973), pp. 200–6, *Investor's Monthly Manual*, May 1882, July 1882, November 1897; *Daily News*, 18 November 1907. For the development of this argument see Michie, 'Finance of Innovation', pp. 26–9.

46   Matthews, Feinstein and Odling-Smee, *British Economic Growth*, p. 129.

47   W. B. Grohman, 'Cattle Ranches in the Far West', *Fortnightly Review*, vol. 28 (1880), p. 450.

48   Michie, 'Social Web', pp. 170–3; Michie, *Money, Mania and Markets*, pp. 154–9; D. G. Paterson, *British Direct Investment in Canada, 1890–1914* (Toronto, 1976), pp. 41–2.

49   J. M. Stoppard, 'The Origins of British-Based Multinational Manufacturing Enterprises', *Business History Review*, vol. 48 (1974), pp. 316–17, 323–5; P. J. Buckley and B. R. Roberts, *European Direct Investment in the USA before World War I* (London, 1982), p. 49.

50   H. Lowenfeld, *All about Investment* (London, 1909), p. 101.

51   D. C. M. Platt, 'Britain's Stock of Investment Overseas at the End of 1913' (circulated typescript, 1985), pp. 4, 32–3.

52   *Stock Exchange Official Intelligence* (London, 1914), p. 1707; cf. C. C.

Spence, *British Investments and the American Mining Frontier, 1860–1901* (Ithaca, 1958), p. 220.

53 R. C. Michie, 'Crisis and Opportunity: The Formation and Operation of the British Assets Trust, 1897–1914', *Business History*, vol. 25 (1983), pp. 125–6, H. Burton and D. C. Corner, *Investment and Unit Trusts in Britain and America* (London, 1968), pp. 1, 15, 29, 43; L. A. McFarlane, 'British Investment and the Land: Nebraska, 1877–1946', *Business History Review*, vol. 57 (1983), pp. 260–71.

54 E. Rosenbaum and A. J. Sherman, *M. M. Warburg & Co., 1798–1938: Merchant Bankers of Hamburg* (London, 1979), pp. 84–90, 101–2; S. Chapman, *The Rise of Merchant Banking* (London, 1984), p. 158.

55 Chapman, *Merchant Banking*, pp. 16, 160; *Report of the Royal Commission on Loans to Foreign States* (British Parliamentary Papers, 1875, II), pp. xxxvii–xlv; and evidence of Henry White (Barings), 11 March 1875; *Report of the Royal Commission on the London Stock Exchange*, (British Parliamentary Papers, 1878, XIX), p. 168.

56 M. C. Reed, *A History of James Capel & Co.* (London, 1975), pp. 38–9; W J. Reader, *A House in the City* (London, 1979), pp. 98–100.

57 C. A. Jones, 'British Financial Institutions in Argentina, 1860–1914' (PhD thesis, Cambridge University, 1973), p. 302; C. A. Jones, 'Great Capitalists and the Direction of British Overseas Investment in the Late Nineteenth Century: The Case of Argentina', *Business History*, vol. 22 (1980), pp. 166–7; T. C. Barker and M. Robbins, *A History of London Transport* (London, 1963 and 1974), Vol. II, p. 25; Jefferys, 'Trends in Business Organisation', pp. 331–2, 345, 359, 363.

58 Cottrell, 'Investment Banking', pp. 420–4.

59 H. O. O'Hagan, *Leaves from my Life* (London, 1929), Vol. I, pp. 22–3, 29, 149.

60 Chapman, *Merchant Banking*, pp. 16, 25, 96, 158; J. Camplin, *The Rise of the Plutocrats: Wealth and Power in Edwardian England* (London, 1978), pp. 59–60.

61 M. Simon, 'Pattern of New British Portfolio Foreign Investment, 1865–1914', in A. R. Hall (ed.), *The Export of Capital from Britain, 1870–1919* (London, 1968), p. 20.

62 M. Edelstein, 'Rigidity and Bias in the British Capital Market, 1870–1913', in D. McCloskey (ed.), *Essays on a Mature Economy: Britain after 1840* (London, 1971), pp. 87–92; Michie, *Money, Mania and Markets*, pp. 188–90; London Stock Exchange: Committee for General Purposes Subcommittee on Commissions, 9 May 1912.

63 *Financial Times, Investor's Guide* (London, 1913), p. 59; *Royal Commission on London Stock Exchange*, pp. 166, 184, 239–43; Reader, *House in the City*, p. 93.

64 *Royal Commission on London Stock Exchange*, pp. 144, 153–60, 164, 243; Reader, *House in the City*, p. 93.

65 J. M. Stone, 'Financial Panics: Their Implications for the Mix of Domestic and Foreign Investments of Great Britain, 1880–1913',

Journal of Economics, vol. 85 (1971), p. 323; J. H. Murchison, *British Mines Considered as a Means of Investment* (London, 1854), pp. 15–17; F. Gore-Browne and W. Jordan, *A Handy Book on the Formation, Management and Winding-up of Joint-Stock Companies* (London, 1902), pp. 453–4.

66   Cf. Chapter 5, 'The London Stock Exchange and the Money Market', for the further implications of this.

67   Hall, *London Capital Market*, p. 38; Musson, *Growth of British Industry*, p. 253; Jefferys, 'Trends in Business Organisation', p. 435; Matthews, Feinstein and Odling-Smee, *British Economic Growth*, pp. 52, 56; B. R. Mitchell, *Abstract of British Historical Statistics* (Cambridge, 1971), pp. 6–7; *Investor's Monthly Manual*, January 1887; A. G. Webb, *The New Dictionary of Statistics* (London, 1911), p. 78; F. W. Field, 'How Canadian Stocks Are Held', *Monetary Times* (Toronto), January 1915.

68   Scott, *Upper Classes*, pp. 116–17; Hall, *London Capital Market*, p. 42; Cairncross, *Home and Foreign Investment*, p. 85.

69   Walker & Watson, *Investor's and Shareholder's Guide*, p. 262; cf. Michie, 'Social Web of Investment'.

70   R. C. Michie, 'Income, Expenditure and Investment of a Victorian Millionaire: Lord Overstone, 1823–1883', *Bulletin of the Institute of Historical Research*, vol. 58 (1985), pp. 73–4; Martins, *A Great Estate at Work*, pp. 267–9; J. B. Sturrock, *Peter Brough: A Paisley Philanthropist* (Paisley, 1890), p. 211; E. Richards, 'An Anatomy of the Sutherland Fortune: Income, Consumption, Investments and Returns, 1780–1880', *Business History*, vol. 21 (1979), p. 54.

71   These two sections are largely based on two books by H. N. Bassett, published between 1900 and 1912, which list British business men and give brief details of the investments of many, as well as their general financial interests: H. H. Bassett (ed.), *Men of Note in Finance and Commerce* (London, 1900–01); H. H. Bassett (ed.), *Businessmen at Home and Abroad* (London, 1912).

72   *Stock Exchange Gazette*, 30 March 1901; H. Lowenfeld, 'Money Market Article and the Private Investor', *FR*, February 1907.

73   Cf. note 71.

74   Hall, *London Capital Market*, pp. 49, 53, 55; Michie, 'Social Web of Investment', pp. 173–4; Michie, 'Crisis and Opportunity', pp. 125–6, 130.

75   R. J. Morris, 'The Middle Class and the Property Cycle during the Industrial Revolution', in T. C. Smout (ed.), *The Search for Wealth and Stability* (London, 1979); M. B. Rose, 'Diversification of Investment by the Greg Family, 1800–1914', *Business History*, vol. 21 (1979), pp. 91, 93; Sturrock, *Peter Brough*, p. 211, Michie, 'Overstone', pp. 61–2; Rubinstein, *Men of Property*, p. 218; Scott, *Upper Classes*, p. 84.

76   F. W. Paish, *Long-Term and Short-Term Interest Rates in the United Kingdom* (Manchester 1966), p. 53.

77   Chapman, *Merchant Banking*, p. 25; Reader, *House in the City*, pp.

106–8; Camplin, *Plutocrats*, p. 60; Jones, 'Great Capitalists', pp. 155, 166–7; Barker and Robbins, *London Transport*, Vol. I, pp. 38–42, Edelstein, 'Rigidity and Bias', p. 87; A. R. Wagg, 'The History of the Firm, (unpublished, n.d.); M. Karo, *City Milestones and Memories* (London, 1962), pp. 1–4.

78   Chapman, *Merchant Banking*, p. 158, A. H. Woolf, *The Stock Exchange: Past and Present* (London, 1913), p. 112; D. R. Adler, *British Investment in American Railways, 1834–1898* (Charlottesville, 1970), p. 149; J. H. Lenfant, 'British Capital Export, 1900–1913' (PhD thesis, London University, 1949), pp. 14, 63.

79   A. Grenfell to Lord Grey, 28 August 1906, 20 November 1906.

80   C. P. Kindleberger, *A Financial History of Western Europe* (London, 1984) p. 206; Cottrell, 'Investment Banking', p. 837; Chapman, *Merchant Banking*, pp. 43, 77, 98–9, 170.

81   J. G. Williamson, *Did British Capitalism Breed Inequality?* (Boston, 1985), pp. 100–1. For an exhaustive review of the debate on overseas investment see S. Pollard, 'Capital Exports, 1870–1914: Harmful or Beneficial?', *Economic History Review*, vol. 38 (1985).

5 The London Stock Exchange and the Money Market

'The money market of the United Kingdom is an institution of great importance and of some complexity,' wrote Gairdner in 1888; part of this complexity was a growing interaction between the money market and the securities market, though this is largely ignored by the standard accounts of the London Stock Exchange.[1] The Stock Exchange provided a service that was of use not only to those issuing securities but also to those purchasing them, and it was this latter role that led to its involvement with the money market in a variety of ways and at different levels. No understanding of the operation and functions of the Stock Exchange would be complete without an examination of this dimension of its business, for much that has been dismissed by contemporaries as speculation or gambling becomes a legitimate and necessary activity when examined from the standpoint of those in the money market who bought and held securities.[2] However, before investigating this Stock Exchange–money market connection, it is necessary to gain some knowledge of the money market itself, particularly its role and requirements.

Neither money nor the money market lend themselves to ease of definition, tending to be classified by what functions they performed rather than what they were. Money is seen as a medium of exchange or a store of value; and though certain components, such as coins and notes, can be readily identified, others fit much less easily, fulfilling some of the functions of money only at particular times and in specific circumstances. Cheques, bills of exchange, bankers' drafts and credit facilities enter only the area of quasi-money, but it is with these that the London money market was concerned. It did not deal in coins or banknotes but in credit instruments – claims to future payment. It did this without any formal markets, for its

132

trading took place in and between the offices of those involved in the City of London and, later, with offices at a distance through the telegraph and the telephone.[3]

Money was not a homogeneous commodity but varied in the individual amount that was available and required, in the length of time it was available and required and in the location at which it was available and required. It was the function of the institutions and individuals of the money market to match the supply and demand of credit instruments in terms of amount, time and location, and to make a profit for themselves in the process. Money was like any other commodity, to be allocated to the highest bidder in the market-place and to be used as productively as possible.

Within a market economy such as that of nineteenth-century Britain, money was continually being released and absorbed by different sectors and locations in the daily, weekly or monthly cycle of activity. In agriculture, for example, there was a marked seasonal variation determined by the harvest, with economic activity concentrated in the autumn months. The weather affected other areas, such as construction, coal-mining and gas production. As Chiozza Money put it so succinctly in 1912: 'By no process of law can we make it as convenient to build a house in the winter as in the summer, or cause as great a demand for artificial light in the summer as in the winter in northern latitudes.'[4] Artificial creations such as summer holidays and Christmas led to other seasonal trends in the economy, while periodic booms and slumps created fluctuations from year to year.

Consequently, within the economy there was a need to redistribute money from one sector and one location to another as circumstances altered, in order to make maximum use of the available supply. Within the money market the greatest demands were traditionally placed between August and December, as the harvest was gathered, paid for and stored. Christmas and government taxation kept conditions tight until after March, when money became much easier, as stocks were run down and the government spent its revenue. The cycle then resumed again after the summer.[5] Thus over the period 1870–1913 the rate of interest charged for credit was consistently higher in the winter months than in the summer (Table 5.1); by this time the money market was functioning with considerable expertise.

Table 5.1 Seasonal Interest Rates, by Quarters, 1890–1913

	Deposit rate				Bill rate				Call rate				Yield on consols			
	I	II	III	IV	I	II	III	IV	I	II	III	IV	I	II	III	IV
1870–9	2.04	2.08	2.07	2.80	2.93	2.78	2.82	3.51	1.98	2.05	2.03	2.82	3.20	3.18	3.19	3.19
1880–9	2.07	1.52	2.00	2.84	2.61	1.85	2.52	3.03	2.11	1.42	1.83	2.67	2.95	2.93	2.95	2.94
1890–9	1.43	1.28	1.33	2.08	2.00	1.69	1.98	2.88	1.53	1.22	1.22	2.09	2.66	2.65	2.67	2.67
1900–13	2.39	1.81	1.87	2.82	3.33	2.75	2.99	4.02	2.51	2.06	1.92	2.89	2.95	2.93	2.99	3.02
1870–1913	1.98	1.67	1.82	2.64	2.72	2.27	2.58	3.36	2.03	1.69	1.75	2.62	2.94	2.92	2.95	2.96

Source: F. Capie and A. Webber, *A Monetary History of the United Kingdom, 1870–1982* (London, 1985), Vol. I, pp. 495–9.

Generally, there were always substantial balances that were being held idle in order to meet a wide variety of expected needs in the near future. Some of these were reasonably predictable in timing and amount, such as seasonal operations, while others, like a recovery in consumer demand, were much more problematic. What was certain was that the money could not be committed to long-term investment.[6]

Increasingly this money did not remain in the hands of its owners but was placed at the disposal of the financial system, especially the banks. 'The savings of the nation, when not at once invested by their owners, are deposited with bankers all over the country' wrote Duncan in 1867.[7] Between 1871 and 1913 the number of bank branches in Britain rose from 2,746 to 8,190, providing a network that covered the whole country, while net bank deposits rose from £446 million to £1,032 million over the same period.[8] Since the banks paid interest on much of their deposits, as well as having to meet their own expenses, they were placed under an obligation to find remunerative employment for as large a proportion of the funds they controlled as possible.

This was not just a simple matter of lending to one set of customers what another made available, with a margin in interest rates in their favour, though this was a substantial part of a bank's business. The deposits held by banks were mostly subject to immediate or short-notice withdrawal. Net UK bank deposits, for instance, did fall each year between 1876 and 1879, and this possibility was much greater for any individual bank. Each bank had to follow a lending policy that was essentially a compromise between liquidity and return. Cash yielded nothing but had to be available to meet withdrawals, while mortgages paid a high rate of interest but were illiquid. From this position it is clear that banks were required to hold a range of assets that could be progressively called upon to meet any drain on deposits, and were also sufficient to maintain the banks' profitability.[9]

A large proportion of the temporary money gravitated to London, for it was there that the best, or only, opportunities for its remunerative employment existed. Because of its size, wealth and commercial importance, London possessed the most active money market in Britain, and could thus offer the appropriate combination of liquidity and return so as to attract funds to it.[10] Through links between metropolitan and country bankers, funds were channelled from the rest of Britain into the London money market in growing volume during the first half of the nineteenth century. During the second half of the century these links were formalized within the structure of national banking networks. In 1870, for example, there were only eight banking groups, or 2 per cent of all banks, that operated in both London and the provinces, and their 392 branches comprised only 14 per cent of all branches. However, by 1913, though the number of such groups had risen to only fifteen, or 14 per cent of all banks, their 4,716 branches amounted to 58 per cent of the total. In a parallel trend the Scottish banks, which remained outside this national amalgamation movement, all opened offices in London after mid-century specifically to lend out short-term funds.[11] The proportion of British bank deposits controlled by London and London-and-provincial banks rose from 36 per cent in 1871 to 64 per cent in 1913 (Table 5.2), illustrating the growing London orientation of the financial system. Even without the benefits of employment in the money market, there were advantages to banks in keeping a proportion of their cash reserves in London; for if every bank did likewise this simplified the settling of inter-bank credits and debits by concentrating it in one central location.[12]

Table 5.2 *British Bank Deposits (Excluding Bank of England), 1871–1913*

Year	Total (gross) deposits	London	Deposits by location of banks London/ Provincial	Provincial	Scottish	Irish
1871	£446m	27%	9%	44%	15%	6%
1880	£484m	25%	15%	38%	16%	6%
1890	£609m	22%	22%	35%	15%	6%
1900	£825m	16%	37%	28%	13%	6%
1913	£1,032m	5%	59%	17%	12%	7%

Source: F. Capie and A. Webber, *A Monetary History of the United Kingdom, 1870–1982* (London, 1985), Vol. I, pp. 130, 153, 432.

In the money market the principal use to which these short-term funds were put was in the finance of trade. The gap between production and payment, as the buyer awaited customers while the manufacturer had to meet costs, required the extension of commercial credit. This could be done through direct lending on a renewal basis or by the medium of bills of exchange. The use of bills allowed borrowers to tap credit far beyond the confines of their local bank. Bills were promissory notes given by the purchaser to the vendor and often guaranteed by a bank or other acceptor. By selling such a bill at a discount to its face value – representing the rate of return – the vendor obtained immediate payment, the purchaser was given credit and the holder of the bill obtained remunerative employment for temporary savings. These bills normally ran for 30 to 90 days and represented a reasonably liquid asset which matured at a specified time and at a fixed price. For even greater liquidity, banks could also lend to the bill brokers or discount houses that specialized in borrowing short-term – often on a day-to-day basis – using the money to purchase and hold bills, benefiting from the yield differential obtained.[13]

Illustrative of the whole philosophy behind the operations of these money-market intermediaries was the following explanation for one transaction given by the discount house Smith St Aubyn & Co. in 1894, though referring to debentures rather than to bills in this case:

> Sold per Messel £60,000 Debentures due July 1895 at one and a quarter premium. This may appear rash but the grounds on which it has been done are briefly as follows. We hold the stock to pay us two and a half per cent, money is half a per cent, therefore if we run it we can make two per cent running profit. Now two per cent profit on £100 for 9 months is £1.10 and from that must come 8d in the £1 tax – say 1/- thus 2 per cent profit on £100 for 9 months is £1.9. We sell the stock outright for £1.5 down – and we have the chapter of accidents in our favour. The money to be paid on Monday next.[14]

Bill brokers and discount houses functioned in the expectation that as one source of credit dried up another became available, so that they were always able to finance their bill portfolio using cheap day-to-day money – conditioned, of course, by their expectations of possibilities and risks.[15] However, this required a very large money market in which fluctuations in overall supply and demand could be minimized. Only in London were these conditions to be found within Britain. Therefore, London attracted to it funds from increasingly diverse sources and distant areas, with the result that the opportunities it could offer became progressively superior to those in any other centre.

Scottish lenders and borrowers increasingly turned to London. By the early 1880s the Glasgow-based Union Bank of Scotland employed roughly £1.8 million per annum in the London money market by way of loans and bills, or 17 per cent of its total deposits, which averaged £10.5 million per annum at that time. Similarly, in the 1890s the Edinburgh-based British Assets Trust conducted all its short-term borrowing in London, despite the fact that this was with the Commercial Bank of Scotland, also of Edinburgh.[16] As early as 1840 the Royal Bank of Ireland contrasted the inadequacies of the Dublin money market with the advantages of London, and bemoaned the fact that it had to keep a higher proportion of its funds in non-earning assets as a consequence, with a corresponding impact on its profitability.[17]

However, the needs of trade – as reflected in the supply of bills of exchange – did not always absorb the volume of short-term funds that was being placed in the London money market. Economic activity fluctuated throughout the year, and from year to year, so that the supply of and demand for credit were not always in balance. This was true throughout the nineteenth century and forced bankers and the money market to look for alternative means of employing the funds at their disposal.[18] In fact, the need to find substitutes for the domestic bill of exchange grew in the course of the century, because of changes in the nature of banking. With the formation of national banking networks it became increasingly possible for individual banks to equalize the supply of and demand for credit between activities and locations without the need to resort to bills of exchange, because this could all be achieved by means of transfers within the group. By 1910, for instance, the top five banks in the United Kingdom controlled 36 per cent of all deposits, compared to only 20 per cent in 1870, illustrating the potential for offsetting loans and deposits within the same bank, compared to the localized structure of earlier years. The result was that the volume of domestic, or inland, bills of exchange – after rising rapidly to £0.7 billion in 1876–80 from £0.3 billion in 1836–40 – fell back to £0.6 billion by 1911–13.[19]

At the same time other changes in the economy and in banking were leading to an expansion in the volume of temporary credit available. As domestic agriculture and its products declined in importance in Britain, and as improved transport, communications and marketing economized on stocks of commodities and goods, the funds that had been tied up in financing such operations were now released for other employment.[20] Amalgamation and sophistication within the banking system were also reducing the proportion of money that had to be kept completely idle in the form of cash in order to meet sudden or unexpected demands. Experience allowed events to become more predictable, and so reduced the margin that needed to be maintained, while internal and inter-bank clearing arrangements removed the need to transfer large sums of cash, and so made them available for temporary use.[21] Britain's need for finance was still continuing to grow but it was increasingly in the form of long-term capital, as with the railway system, urban facilities and, later, manufacturing enterprise.

This is where the London Stock Exchange became important, for it was a market where securities already in existence could be bought and sold. The Stock Exchange traded in long-term debt, which was either irredeemable, like shares, or redeemable after many years, like government stock and corporate debentures. Therefore, though the actual securities could not be liquidated, as with a bank loan or a bill of exchange, which matured and was paid, the claim to the promised return could be realized by the sale to another at the prevailing price in the market. To the holder of these securities the commitment of funds could consequently be as long or as short as desired, with the risk being accepted that the price might fall in the meantime. The length of time the borrower required the use of the credit no longer conditioned the length of time the lender had to part with cash in order to earn a return, for the right to principal and interest could be sold in the market, and this process could be repeated indefinitely, without any need to redeem the security. An irredeemable security could possess some of the characteristics of a short-term loan, if there was a market where it could be readily bought and sold at close prices.[22]

The creation and efficient operation of a securities market blurred, or even removed, the conventional distinction between short- and long-term capital. What existed was a single market in assets of varying liquidity, with the Stock Exchange providing the bridge between the traditionally separate money and capital markets. When bills of exchange were in short supply, banks, and others with short-term funds to employ, invested in those long-term securities possessing an active market. Because stocks, particularly fixed-interest ones, tended to rise in price from one dividend and date to the next, as the period to wait for payment progressively shortened, it was possible to purchase a security, hold it for a short period and then sell it at an enhanced price, receiving a return on the money used in the form of the difference between the buying and selling price, minus expenses. This did entail a risk that the security would fall in value, creating a loss rather than a profit, but such a possibility could be avoided through a little additional expense. A 'put' option, for example, could be taken out, allowing the security to be sold for a fixed price in the future. These options or privileges were freely available at mid-century and became progressively more sophisticated so as to meet all requirements. Alternatively, securities could be bought for cash and sold for delivery at the end of the fortnightly account, obtaining a small price differential in the purchaser's favour, as the price paid was less than that received, reflecting the difference between cash and credit terms.[23]

The employment of temporary money directly in long-term securities became an increasingly common practice in the nineteenth century, to be found not only among banks but in other organizations and enterprises. The London County Council, for instance, regularly bought and sold securities in order to employ its revenue profitably until it was required for normal expenditure. Generally, it was reported to the Stock Exchange in 1909 that 'the large English Banks, Discount, Insurance and Trust Companies ... continually enter into large transactions in stock exchange securities for short periods at rates calculated to give only a slight profit over the Bill rates for money'.[24]

Nevertheless, many financial institutions with such funds at their disposal did not use them in constantly buying and selling securities. That would have involved the banks in acquiring considerable expertise and a need to monitor events continuously, though their use of such facilities might be only intermittent. Instead, they mainly left the operation to others, such as Stock Exchange brokers and jobbers, who could devote all their attention, time and knowledge to it, with the banks participating through loans to these intermediaries, when they had the money available. By borrowing short-term money, available at low rates of interest, and using it to hold long-term securities yielding a higher rate of return, these intermediaries could obtain a running profit with only limited risk. This was fundamentally the same type of activity as existed with bills of exchange, out of which the practice grew. Such lending on the collateral of transferable securities became very common in the course of the second half of the nineteenth century. By 1898, for example, the Bank of England itself had £1 million lent out to jobbers,[25] while the *Investors' Review* of 1895 was explicit on the course of action followed by banks: 'Bankers' money which can find no employment in trade goes into securities either directly, by the investments of the banks themselves, or indirectly, through loans to customers who buy and pawn stocks while money is cheap.' Similarly, companies accumulating income not required until dividends were paid out increasingly made a practice of lending it out short-term on the security of stocks and shares.[26]

The nature of the securities in which operations of this kind were conducted was very important. It was vital that they were easily bought and sold and that their price fluctuated little, thus minimizing the risk taken. Only securities issued in large amounts, widely held and actively traded, with an unblemished record of regular interest payments, were considered suitable. In particular, the National Debt was regarded as the most appropriate, as it dwarfed all other issues and could be readily bought and sold at close to the market price whatever the amount, and with little expense. For the first three-quarters of the nineteenth century, therefore, trading in consols dominated the activities of money-market operators in securities.[27] As late as 1877 Maddison recommended that 'where money is to be invested which is likely to be wanted again in a short time, the English Funds are the best security'.[28] Most of the buying and selling operations conducted by London brokers and jobbers were thus for a long time in consols, either on behalf of their institutional clients, such as banks, or for themselves on borrowed funds.[29]

Even where the bank was not itself investing directly it looked carefully at the securities being pledged, so as to ensure that they were readily saleable if the borrower defaulted. 'We always think, beyond the borrower, that if the security was thrown on our hands how easily could we realise it and repay ourselves' was the view of the general manager of the London Joint-Stock Bank in 1909.[30] The only way to operate on more volatile securities, using borrowed funds, was to borrow directly from stockbrokers, who in turn borrowed from banks on the strength of the deposit of more acceptable stocks and bonds. Between 1902 and 1913, for instance, the London stockbroker Wm. Russell lent out £267,893 against securities worth £290,455. Of course, higher interest charges were incurred, as well as commission and costs, for the broker expected to profit from the risk he was taking by charging more for the loan to the client than the bank charged him. Shepherds & Chase made between £14,136 and £65,619 per annum from the interest they charged clients in the second half of the century. This was the most speculative element of Stock Exchange business, involving both greater costs and a higher risk that the price might drop sharply. Conversely, the potential gain was greater, as the price could also rise sharply, and that was its attraction.[31]

The National Debt remained the largest single block of securities on the London Stock Exchange before 1914, and the one possessed of the best market.[32] As late as 1906 the *Financial Review of Reviews* was of the opinion that 'It is the exceeding negotiability of consols and the small transfer expenses attendant upon the purchase and sale of this stock which have tended to make it the most usual method in which bankers and financiers temporarily employ their cash balances.'[33] However, despite increases during the Crimean and Boer wars, the size of the National Debt fell in absolute terms between 1815 and 1914, restricting its availability and decreasing its yield in comparison to other securities. At the same time much was absorbed in permanent investments by institutions, such as the Trustee and Post Office savings banks, or to act as reserves, and so the amount in which there was an active market was reduced, creating the need for supplementary but similar securities. These took time to develop.[34] Even in 1858 it could take days to arrange a sale or purchase of railway stock compared to the hours for government stock, limiting their value as a home for temporary funds. Nevertheless, with the expansion and amalgamation among railway companies, the issues of the larger concerns did come to possess active markets, being readily bought and sold with little price variation. The development of joint-stock manufacturing, mining and commercial enterprises, operating nationally, also produced suitable securities, particularly debentures. In contrast, the issues of smaller and more local companies, and most industrial equity, were too volatile to attract the interest of those with only short-term savings available.[35]

The diversification of securities away from British government debt can be seen in the case of the Bank of England, a very conservative financial institution. Its portfolio of securities, exclusive of UK government stocks, rose from £8.7 million in 1892 to £14.6 million in 1911.[36] In a wider context British life insurance companies increased their holdings of securities from £28.2 million in 1871 to £161.4 million in 1906 (Table 5.3), and within this the proportion that was non-government rose from 47.9 per cent to 74.8 per cent.[37] Certain financial intermediaries were also established with the deliberate policy of lending on more volatile securities. The Guarantee Insurance & Investment Company, formed in 1902, borrowed from banks and lent on the security of mining shares through the Stock Exchange firms of James Shepherd & Co. and Sperling & Co.[38] Nevertheless, in spite of the growth of domestic securities supplementing the money-market role performed by consols, it was increasingly overseas securities that became the popular alternatives. Foreign government issues were comparable in size and nature to the British National Debt, offering similar guarantees, scale and activity. Of those government securities quoted on the London Stock Exchange in 1910, the average size of

Table 5.3 *British Life Insurance Companies: Portfolio of Assets, 1871 and 1906*

Type of asset	1871		1906	
	Amount	*Proportion*	*Amount*	*Proportion*
Mortgages	£51.6m	47.0%	£99.2m	25.1%
Loans	£17.3m	15.8%	£64.7m	16.4%
Property	£4.7m	4.3%	£39.2m	9.9%
Securities	£28.2m	25.7%	£161.4m	40.8%
Miscellaneous	£7.9m	7.2%	£31.2m	7.9%
Total	£109.7m	100.0%	£395.7m	100.0%

Source: A. G. Webb, *The New Dictionary of Statistics* (London, 1911), p. 338.

each individual issue (most governments made numerous separate issues) was £6.9 million. This ranged from the £511.1 million in French *rentes*, through the £76.6 million of British 2½ per cent consols or £10.5 million in various runs of Imperial Japanese bonds, to the average size of £1 million for the issues of Canadian federal and provincial authorities.[39] Only a number of North and South American railroads, and later a few very large industrial and mining corporations, especially from the United States, managed to offer the type of foreign security that the money-market operators required and could find in most major government issues.[40]

Not only was the London money market becoming international in the securities utilized for the employment of its temporary funds; the money upon which it operated was also coming increasingly from throughout the world, after the mid-nineteenth century. This was partly the result of the expansion of British financial institutions abroad. Insurance companies, for instance, rapidly extended their coverage to other countries, and were soon in receipt of a substantial foreign income.[41] More important, however, were the banks formed in Britain, with head offices in London, to operate throughout the world, especially in those countries where modern financial systems were required but lacking, as in much of Asia and the countries of recent European settlement, such as Argentina, Australia, Canada and South Africa. Other banks were established for more specific purposes like the organization and finance of the emerging trade between Britain and individual countries, such as the Anglo-Austrian Bank and the Anglo-Russian Bank. Altogether, sixty-three British overseas banks were founded between 1853 and 1913. By the early twentieth century forty-three of these banks were still in existence, controlling a network of 1,156 branches worldwide (Table 5.4). It was only to be expected that these banks would seek to operate in the same fashion as their domestic counterparts and employ their temporary funds in the London money market, which is what they did.[42]

The foreign money that flowed to London was increasingly less due to Britain's own entrepreneurial, imperial or trading efforts, and more the reflection of the opportunities the London money market offered for the employment of otherwise idle savings at remunerative rates of return. The advantages that the British banks had discovered in London were increasingly available to the financial institutions of other countries, with the improved communications and growing economic integration that was taking place in the world in the nineteenth century.[43] There was developing in money, as in securities, an international market in which those centres which could offer employment at the most competitive rates of return for equivalent risk attracted funds to themselves and away from other markets. By 1870 this position was already apparent in western Europe, according to one observer: 'the price of money throughout Europe is now gradually assimilating. The rates of Germany are approximating, by their downward tendency, to those of England and France; and it is not easy to find signs of prospective divergence.'[44] This trend towards integration accelerated in the forty years before the First World War, so that minor fluctuations in interest rates in one major centre produced a rapid response in all the others, with corresponding flows of money to take advantage of higher returns.[45]

Table 5.4   *British Overseas Banks, 1905 and 1910*

Group	No.	Capital	Total	Branches Europe	Asia	Africa	America	America	Australia
Imperial banks (1905)	19	£12.4m	843	—	45	256	46	13	483
International banks (1910)	24	£19.8m	308	10	192	6	—	100	—
Total (1905–10)	43	£32.2m	1,156	10	237	262	46	113	483

Sources: A. S. J. Baster, *The Imperial Banks* (London, 1929), p. 269; A. S. J. Baster, *The International Banks* (London, 1935), p. 245.

London had a number of advantages for foreign money that made it one of the most attractive centres in the world. At the very least there was convenience. Britain was the world's largest trading nation, and London was the centre through which this was financed, and thus the place where payments were continually made and received. Consequently, by keeping money in London – even idle – it was in the best location for settling trade debts. Since Britain monopolized such a large proportion of world trade before 1914, and British trade was so widespread, no other centre could match the facilities offered by London. 'London is the exchange centre of the British Empire and partly of the entire world,' wrote Brooks, an American, in 1906, and this sentiment was echoed by many others.[46]

It was important to have money readily available in London, as this international trade continued to be financed largely through the use of bills of exchange, which were constantly maturing, and so releasing funds, or being created, and so absorbing funds. If, in the interval between one bill being paid off and another financed, it was possible to employ the funds that were temporarily available in short-term loans to the money market, that would represent an additional bonus over the convenience that London already possessed.[47] The scale of such operations can be seen from the suggestion by Bloomfield that international commercial debt totalled $2.9 billion by 1913.[48]

As well as convenience London had other attributes that made it an attractive centre in which to hold funds. The international acceptability of sterling, backed by a rigid adherence to the gold standard, the policy of free movement of goods and capital and a well-organized financial system all gave funds held in London a safety and mobility that no others could match; this made them desirable irrespective of the rate of return.[49] There was thus an additional incentive for the principal financial institutions of the major economies of the world to locate a proportion of their liquid reserves and short-term funds in London, whence they could easily be dispatched wherever required, or used to meet the fluctuating demands of international commercial credit.[50]

From about 1870 onwards, many foreign banks either established branches in London or linked with British banks, in order to have representation in what was the financial centre of the world economy. By 1910 there were twenty-six branches of foreign banks, primarily from continental Europe, in London, while innumerable others had agents acting for them.[51] Through these banking links came a growing volume of foreign short-term funds to the London money market at the very same time that Britain's own overseas investments were expanding. Spalding noted in 1911 that 'we have at our disposal a large quantity of French, German, Swiss, Austrian and American capital', and such a view was increasingly echoed by numerous other contemporaries, who referred to supplies of money coming from even more sources.[52] The Indian and Japanese governments, for instance, maintained large balances in London in order to meet claims on their countries by way of expatriate salaries or interest charges. The Java Bank, of the Dutch East Indies, reoriented its funds to London and away from Amsterdam in the wake of the shift in the sugar trade.[53]

Those holding money in London for convenience and trade would naturally enough seek to employ it remuneratively when it was not otherwise occupied. Simultaneously, the London money market's ability to employ idle balances encouraged such funds, wherever they were accumulating, to seek an outlet in London rather than remain under-utilized at home. There is abundant evidence that foreign banks and other institutions channelled short-term money to London because of a want of domestic demand for that kind of temporary credit. Even Paris and New York – rival financial centres – used the London money market in preference to their own for a proportion of the funds under their control.[54]

It is unfortunately very difficult to estimate the amount of short-term money from abroad placed in the London money market, though it is clear from contemporary comment that it was both large and growing. In 1850 the amount appears to have been either negligible or small. King suggests that of the £116 million employed in the money market at that date, none came from abroad. However, by the early 1870s, according to Duncan, between £30 and £40 million of overseas funds was employed in the London money market, out of a total of about £350 million, or around 8–11 per cent.[55] From 1877 onwards there are available *The Economist*'s statistics of London deposits held by the overseas banks that possessed either a London head office or branch. These grew from £106.9 million in 1877 to £1,855.2 million in 1914, or from 18 per cent to 65 per cent of all British bank deposits (Table 5.5).

Of the assets of British joint-stock banks in 1913, 23.7 per cent were in the form of cash and money at call or short notice, while a further 9.5 per cent consisted of bills discounted or bought (Table 5.6). Of the cash and call money, 51.4 per cent was composed of coins and notes in 1913. From this it appears that the money-market assets held by British banks totalled 21.0 per cent of all their assets in that year.[56] Applying this ratio to deposits, it implies that £209 million was the sum employed by British banks in the London money market in 1913. If the same ratio was applied to the deposits of overseas banks the total would be a further £389.6 million. This

Table 5.5   *Bank Deposits in Britain, 1877–1913/14*

Year	British bank deposits (net UK)	Foreign and colonial bank deposits (in London)	Total
1877	£501.7m (82%)	£106.9m (18%)	£608.6m
1889	£571.7m (70%)	£240.8m (30%)	£812.5m
1899	£781.8m (74%)	£277.0m (36%)	£1,058.8m
1913/14	£995.2m (35%)	£1,855.2m (65%)	£2,850.4m

Source: F. Capie and A. Webber, *A Monetary History of the United Kingdom, 1870–1982* (London, 1985), Vol. I, pp. 130, 254.

gives a grand total of £598.5 million available to the London money market, 65 per cent of which came from abroad. However, many of the foreign banks were represented in London for the purpose of employing funds in the money market, and acted as international conduits for short-term money flowing from their own country to London. Of the assets of these colonial and foreign banks in 1908, 16.6 per cent consisted of cash and money at call, while bills discounted and bought were included with loans and advances. The cash and call component would consist largely of money at short notice, as these banks had little to fear from a run in London, for that was not where their depositors were resident. Similarly, their investments in securities was half the level of those of the British banks, implying that they were concentrating upon lending (Table 5.7). The amount and proportion of foreign money are thus likely to be an under- rather than an overestimate. At the same time, within the general lending to customers, part would be borrowed directly to finance, for example, speculative security purchases by both market professionals and outside amateurs.

Within the money market much of this money was absorbed in international trade credit. World trade almost tripled between 1876–80 and 1911–13; over the same period bills of exchange drawn on London rose from £1.9 billion to £2.8 billion, and these bills provided most of the business for the discount houses and bill brokers.[57] However, a growing proportion of these bills were not being created as a result of merchandise trade but in the form of finance bills, to move money around the world for whatever purpose it was required. According to Withers in 1910: 'Out of bills

Table 5.6   *British Joint-Stock Banks, 1913*

Assets	England and Wales	Scotland	Ireland	Total	Proportion	
Cash and money at call	£235.9m	£34.0m	£17.2m	£287.1m	23.7%	
Bills discounted and bought	£92.4m	£18.1m	£5.1m	£115.6m	9.5%	15.1%
Cover for acceptances	£61.7m	£5.5m	£0.4m	£67.6m	5.6%	
Investments and securities	£121.2m	£38.0m	£23.9m	£183.1m	15.1%	
Loans and advances	£430.7m	£59.7m	£43.3m	£533.7m	44.0%	
Premises	£21.1m	£4.5m	£1.0m	£26.6m	2.2%	
Total	£963.0m	£159.8m	£90.9m	£1,213.7m	100.0%	
Liabilities						
Deposits	£809.0m	£125.9m	£70.6m	£1,005.8m		

Source: League of Nations, *Memorandum on Commercial Banks, 1913–1929* (Geneva, 1931), pp. 280–93.

of exchange, originally drawn against merchandise actually shipped, grew the finance bill drawn sometimes in anticipation of produce or merchandise to be shipped, sometimes against securities, and sometimes against the credit of the parties to it.'[58] Out of the £350 million in prime bills outstanding in 1913, altogether £210 million, or 60 per cent, represented finance bills.[59] Consequently, even among bills a growing proportion were being used to finance Stock Exchange operations, with the securities purchased being used as collateral for the credit that the discounting of the bill provided.

Table 5.7   *Foreign Joint-Stock Banks, 1908*

Assets	Colonial	Foreign	Total	Proportion
Cash and money at call	£86.6m	£71.3m	£157.9m	16.6%
Loans and advances	£224.3m	£495.1m	£719.4m	75.6%
Investments and securities	£30.8m	£44.0m	£74.8m	7.9%
Total	£341.7m	£610.4m	£952.1m	100.0%

Source: National Monetary Commission, *Statistics of Britain, France, Germany and the United States, 1867–1909* (Washington, 1910).

In addition to commercial and finance bills, this foreign money also found its way directly to the London Stock Exchange through loans to brokers and jobbers, where it was of increasing importance. In 1909 the Stock Exchange was itself one among many contemporaries noting that 'A very considerable amount of foreign capital is employed on the London Stock Exchange for carrying over purposes.'[60] What proportion of funds employed on the Stock Exchange was foreign is impossible to say; but if it reflected the estimate for the money market, then two-thirds would be a legitimate suggestion, and this would fit with the increasing international orientation of the London securities market. It is also difficult to put a precise figure on how much borrowed capital was employed via the Stock Exchange. The only direct estimate comes from investigations made by the Stock Exchange for 31 August 1914, which arose out of the crisis created by the beginning of the First World War. At that time the members of the London Stock Exchange owed to the clearing and other banks, and to other institutions, firms and individuals, a total of £67,032,965 with margin, and £13,728,395 without, making a total of £80,761,360. On the same date the members had open in active securities – ones cleared by the settlement department – a further sum of £24,918,800. Therefore, at that time the members of the Stock Exchange were operating on outside, or their own credit, to the extent of £105,680,160.[61] However, this figure is likely to be a serious underestimate, since the threat and eventual outbreak of war would have led to a desire for extreme liquidity by financial institutions, and a closing of open transactions by brokers and jobbers.[62]

The availability and use of temporary funds were of major importance to the London Stock Exchange. Not only did brokers borrow to finance themselves and accommodate clients, but the market makers – the jobbers and dealers – relied heavily on access to credit to finance their operations. As their business depended on being always willing to buy and sell active securities, this could involve holding stocks in expectation of demand or purchasing securities offered, which they were unable to resell immediately.[63] Cordingley's view in both 1893 and 1901 was that 'as the amount of capital required to hold securities in this way must necessarily be very large, the jobber, in most cases, pledges the securities with his bankers'.[64] Clearly, without the availability of abundant credit, business on the London Stock Exchange would be seriously reduced, as so much buying and selling was induced by the narrow margin between the current yield on fixed-interest securities and money–market rates.[65]

Of more importance for the London Stock Exchange's competitive position, however, was the fact that without abundant credit the very operation of the market would be seriously impaired. What made London unique within Britain was the existence of the jobbers and dealers, who ensured that there was an active market in certain securities, and increasingly more numerous and diverse securities as time passed. The convenience of such market makers was aptly summarized by one of them, James Hall Renton, in 1878:

> The advantages of having the dealer is this, that supposing the broker cannot find a purchaser for his stock in the shape of another broker, he can always rely upon finding a purchaser for his stock by going to a dealer, and the result is that you get your money at the time when you wish it; whereas had you to wait till your broker had found another broker who had the supposed investment to make in stock which you wished to sell, you might be out of your money for a very long time.[66]

The market intermediaries were dependent on credit in order to function, but the existence of an active and ready market in securities – or in certain securities – was in turn dependent upon them. The existence of that type of market allowed banks and others to employ temporary funds in long-term investments. It was the presence of the jobbers and dealers that placed the Stock Exchange firmly within the money market, rather than leaving it on the fringes.

This was true internationally as well as domestically. Arbitrage operations required substantial capital, especially where securities had to be carried in order to meet demand, or were being purchased ahead of delivery in expectation of a price rise, as could be the case in options. Arbitrage firms did not themselves possess the level of finance required and relied on a close relationship with banks for the necessary credit, supported by the securities they were holding.[67] The London arbitrage firm of Nathan & Rosselli, for instance, required a credit line of $1.5 million (roughly £0.3 million) for its transatlantic business, while its European clients could run up debts with the firm to the order of £60,000 without margin and £100,000 with 10 per cent margin. This money was largely obtained from the London branches or agent of continental banks such as Banque Française pour le Commerce et l'Industrie, Compania de Massamedes, Banque de Paris et des Pay Bas, and Louis Hirsch, all of Paris. From these Nathan & Rosselli borrowed at between 2¾ and 5½ per cent – charging, when lending to clients, from 7 to 7½ per cent. Similar circumstances existed for S. Japhet & Co., another arbitrage firm.[68]

With the primacy of the London money market over all others, the members of the London Stock Exchange thus had access to unrivalled sources of finance, a fact of vital importance for the business they conducted and the market in securities they created. Not only did London brokers and jobbers never experience the degree of stringency in the money market that was occasionally evident elsewhere, such as in New York, but interest rates were always lower in London than in other centres. As E. & C. Randolph, of New York, reminded their arbitrage partners, Nathan & Rosselli, in 1911: 'You must not forget that it is much easier to finance positions in London than in New York.'[69] This was not just in comparison with New York. Money was both normally cheaper and more abundant in London than in continental centres like Paris and Berlin.[70] So if a purchase was to be made on credit there was an incentive to direct it to London, where it could be financed more readily and cheaply than anywhere else.[71]

The London Stock Exchange's ability to compete with the stock exchanges of other countries, then, was intimately linked to the existence in London of, as Kennedy puts it, 'a short term money market of unrivalled efficiency', since it was this market that provided the credit upon which the Stock Exchange operated, on better terms than any other money market.[72] Conversely, the existence in London of a more active securities market than in other cities provided the continuous and remunerative employment for short-term funds, which helped make the London money market the foremost in the world.[73] The two markets developed together in the course of the nineteenth century, contributing to each other's progress and competitive ability. Without the one it would be difficult to believe that the other could have been either so successful or so dominant as both became.

The close links that existed between the London security and money markets provided far more than a contribution to the advantages that the London Stock Exchange enjoyed over its rivals. At the very least it ensured that Britain's financial resources, and progressively those of the world, were mobilized for productive use by being channelled into long-term investments in the form of negotiable securities. Savings would probably otherwise have lain dormant, as they were required to safeguard the solvency of banks and other financial institutions from abnormal levels of withdrawals.[74] This was all to the benefit of the British economy, for these temporary funds were available at very low rates of interest, having no immediate alternative use, and could be employed in holding better-yielding stocks and bonds. Britain gained access to a cheap source of finance from abroad, some of which was reinvested overseas in investments paying a higher rate of return. It is difficult to be precise on what Britain's net position as an overseas investor was by the First World War, but it is evident that both the level and nature of that investment were conditioned by the international operations of the London money market and its interaction with the Stock Exchange.[75]

Important as the fuller utilization of idle balances was, the contribution made by the interconnection of the London security and money markets did not cease there. In maintaining the equilibrium of monetary flows within the British economy, without the need for the large and continuous transportation of coins and notes, the existence of readily negotiable and widely held securities supplemented the role played by bills of exchange.[76] However, the development of an integrated banking system after 1850 progressively reduced the need for specific acknowledgements of debt that could be exchanged or held until payment. This was not the case internationally, though, for the growth of the world economy and its transfers of goods, capital and people between countries all required some simple mechanism through which international payments could be made.

Five main characteristics were required from money in the international economy: volume, time, location, cost and acceptability. The right amount of money had to be available at the right time and in the right place at the right interest rate and in the right national currency. When transport and communications were poor, and financial sophistication was limited, gold occupied a unique position; for only gold could be readily shipped in any amount to any centre, at little cost compared to its value, and be immediately accepted at a price that varied little between countries. Gold's position was further enhanced by its price being fixed in terms of the national currency in a growing number of countries in the nineteenth century.[77]

However, with the dramatic improvement in world communications, accompanied by the growth in numbers and expertise of financial intermediaries and institutions, a new era was coming into being after the mid-nineteenth century. This has been largely missed by those who have since looked at the period and have seen its international monetary mechanism solely in terms of the gold standard. The changes occurring made it possible to conduct asset arbitrage over space, creating an exchange of currency in the process. The medium of exchange became steadily irrelevant, for what mattered was if it possessed a large and active market in both the centres between which a transfer was required, so that a simultaneous cancelling sale and purchase could be made. Consequently, numerous other assets came to acquire the characteristics, if only momentarily, that had made gold so crucial to the operation of the international monetary system in the past.[78]

Central to this process was the bill of exchange, which had traditionally been used to settle debts between nations without the need continually to ship gold. The essence of the system was captured by Spicer in 1908: 'When a foreign Bill of Exchange is purchased the transaction resolves itself into buying for a sum of money payable in one country the right to a certain amount of currency in another country, either immediately or at a definite date in the future.'[79] Unfortunately, not all trade led to the creation of bills of exchange, while there were also major imbalances in timing and location. For instance, there was a marked seasonal trend in international trade, with primary producing nations exporting at harvest time but importing throughout the year, leading to serious shortages of bills in different directions at different times of the year.[80]

The solution to this was the finance bill (or banker's draft or cheque), through which credit was extended, at a cost, until payment could be made. The finance bill was essentially a device invented to compensate for the lack of trade bills, and to avoid the expense of having to ship gold, which would have only to be shipped back again. These finance bills could be created in a variety of ways, but one of the commonest and most acceptable – since it was backed by realizable assets rather than simple faith in the guarantors – was the one that emanated from stock exchange operations. By selling, for example, the same security in London and simultaneously purchasing it in New York, a claim in pounds was established through an expenditure of dollars. This claim in pounds could then be sold to those wanting to make payment in London. Thus, by using the London Stock Exchange and its worldwide arbitrage links it was an easy matter to transfer money to the country and currency where it was required.[81]

However, within the world economy trade became increasingly multilateral, with no balance being achieved between any two economies, while countries could and did run overall merchandise deficits and surpluses as their economic fortunes fluctuated. For those countries possessing large and active securities markets, situations of imbalance did not produce the severe crises that had occurred in the past. Instead of, for instance, an outflow of gold and currency producing financial stringency leading to a contraction of credit and demand and resulting in a period of bankruptcy and unemployment, assets could be sold so as to provide a period in which readjustment could take place. The most mobile of assets were naturally stock exchange securities and, among these, those that commanded an international market. As early as the 1870s the movement of securities between Britain and other countries had become of major significance in international settlement, and their importance grew progressively, as well as becoming much more sensitive to the slightest of economic influences.[82] Typical is Escher's description of the interaction between the London and New York Stock Exchanges in 1911:

> With the wires continually hot between the two markets and a number of experts on the watch for the chance to make a fraction, quotations here and abroad can hardly get very far apart, at least in the active issues, but occasionally it does happen that the arbitrageur is able to take advantage of a substantial difference. Always without risk, the bid in one market being in hand before the stock is bought in the other.[83]

Through the links between the security and money markets any tightening or easing of credit, whether evidenced by changes in interest rates or not, would bring an immediate response not only in the local stock exchange but in the principal stock exchanges worldwide, with corresponding consequences for their own money markets. Informed contemporaries were well aware of this situation, including the role played by the stock exchange, and acknowledged its importance for the relatively smooth functioning of the world economy that characterized the period from 1870 to 1914. C. A. Conant, for instance, wrote in 1914:

> If there were not a great mass of sound securities which are quoted in international markets, an adverse balance of trade against a country could be settled only by the shipment of goods or gold. When securities are admitted to the equation, however, they afford a variety of means of tiding over deficiencies in money or capital ... It prevents the violent checks to the money market, which would otherwise occur and which would be expressed through the demand for gold for export, the impairment of bank reserves, the calling of loans to replenish reserves, and the sharpness of the discount rate.[84]

A high degree of interdependency thus existed between the London Stock Exchange and the more amorphous money market of the City of London, and this relationship was of major importance far beyond the confines of the Stock Exchange. 'The international character of the London market forms the safety-valve of financial disturbance, and the preservation of that character is of the highest commercial importance,' wrote the jobbers Medwin & Lowy in June 1909; despite self-interest, they were not understating their case.[85] Examined from the angle of the domestic and international money market, the London Stock Exchange can be seen as an institution playing an essential role. In the first instance it allowed the mobilization of otherwise idle savings, and so partially provided itself with capital for investment by creating a new supply rather than by diverting the existing stream. In the second, its ability to employ and release credit, and its arbitrage links with foreign stock exchanges, provided an automatic mechanism which helped mitigate, or even neutralize, international imbalances that in the past resulted in panics and severe economic dislocation. Fluctuations and difficulties continued to occur, but the existence of the operations of the London Stock Exchange ensured that they were milder, and had less serious repercussions, than had been the case in the past.[86] All this necessitated the constant buying and selling of securities, within a process of continuous adjustment to the needs of national and international money markets, and it was this that appeared to contemporaries, even those in the business, as both wasteful and needless. However, without this constant activity the contribution made by the London Stock Exchange and its members to the functioning of the national and international economy would have been much poorer, and the world's economy would not have performed as well as it did before 1914.[87]

Notes

1 C. Gairdner, *The Constitution and Course of the Money Market* (Glasgow, 1888), p. 3; cf. E. V. Morgan and W. A. Thomas, *The Stock Exchange: Its History and Functions* (London, 1962).

2 For contemporary criticism see: *The Bank – The Stock Exchange – The Bankers' Clearing House – The Minister and the Public: An Exposé* (London, 1821); *Exposure of the Stock Exchange and Bubble Companies* (London, 1854); H.M., *On the Analogy between the Stock Exchange and the Turf* (London, 1885).

3 R. W. Clower, 'Introduction', in R. W. Clower (ed.), *Monetary Theory: Selected Readings* (London, 1969), pp. 13–17; M. Friedman and A. J. Schwartz, *Monetary Statistics of the United States* (New York, 1970), pp. 104–37.

4 L. G. Chiozza Money, *Insurance versus Poverty* (London, 1912), p. 301; cf. S. Kuznets, *Seasonal Variations in Industry and Trade* (New York, 1933), p. 197; D. H. Robertson, *A Study of Industrial Fluctuations* (London, 1915), pp. 12–25, 138, 143, 150; J. P. Lewis, *Building Cycles and Britain's Growth* (London, 1965), p. 25.

5 R. H. Palgrave, *Bank Rate and the Money Market* (London, 1903), pp. 107, 135, 139; W. S. Jevons, *Investigations in Currency and Finance* (London, 1884), p. 3, 7–8, 171; E. V. Holden, 'The World's Money Market', *The Statist*, 24 January 1914.

6 M. Friedman and A. J. Schwartz, *Monetary Trends in the United States and the United Kingdom: Their Relation to Income, Prices and Interest Rates, 1867–1975* (Chicago, 1982), p. 262.

7 W. J. Duncan, *Notes on the Rate of Discount in London, 1856–1866* (Edinburgh, 1867), p. 69.

8   F. Capie and A. Webber, *A Monetary History of the United Kingdom, 1870–1982* (London, 1985), Vol. I, pp. 130, 576–7.

9   M. Collins, 'The Business of Banking: English Bank Balance Sheets, 1840–80', *Business History*, vol. 26 (1984) p. 46; Capie and Webber, *Monetary History*, p. 130; E. V. Holden, *The Depreciation of Securities in Relation to Gold* (Liverpool, 1907), p. 3.

10 Duncan, *Notes*, p. 69; Gairdner, *Constitution*, p. 14; A. Ellis, *The Rationale of Market Fluctuations* (London, 1876), p. 43; W. E. Beach, *British International Gold Movements and Banking Policy, 1881–1913* (Cambridge, Mass., 1935), p. 87.

11 Capie and Webber, *Monetary History*, pp. 576–7; N. Tamaki, *The Life Cycle of the Union Bank of Scotland, 1830–1954* (Aberdeen, 1983), has an excellent discussion of the evolving links between Scotland and the London money market, e.g. pp. 13, 53, 84, 106.

12 Gairdner, *Constitution*, p. 14.

13 W. Bagehot, *Lombard Street: A Description of the Money Market* (London, 1873), p. 12; W. T. C. King, *History of the London Discount Market* (London, 1936), pp. 9, 30, 42, 48, 117, 175, 183; C. A. E. Goodhart, *The Business of Banking* (London, 1972), p. 31.

14 Smith St Aubyn & Co., Business Diary, 19 September 1894.

15 King, *Discount Market*, pp. 42, 99, 175, 183; Capie and Webber, *Monetary History*, pp. 310–13.

16 Tamaki, *Life Cycle*, p. 132; R. C. Michie, 'Crisis and Opportunity: The Formation and Operation of the British Assets Trust, 1897–1914', *Business History*, vol. 25 (1983), pp. 132–3.

17 C. Munn, 'The Emergence of Central Banking in Ireland', *Irish Economic and Social History*, vol. 10 (1983), p. 28.

18 *Bankers' Circular*, 24 July 1829; *Investor's Monthly Manual*, 27 February 1886.

19 C. P. Kindleberger, *A Financial History of Western Europe* (London, 1984), pp. 79, 85; F. Capie and R. Rodrik-Bali, 'Concentration in British Banking, 1870–1920', *Business History*, vol. 24 (1982), pp. 285–7; S. Nishimura, *The Decline of Inland Bills of Exchange in the London Money Market, 1855–1913* (Cambridge, 1971), pp. 72, 79; Capie and Webber, *Monetary History*, pp. 280, 310; King, *Discount Market*, pp. 39, 273; M. Levy-Leboyer, 'Central Banking and Foreign Trade: The Anglo-American Cycle in the 1830s', in C. P. Kindleberger and J.-P. Laffarge (eds.), *Financial Crises: Theory, History, and Policy* (Cambridge, 1982), p. 99; Collins, 'Business of Banking', pp. 47, 53–4.

20 S. Chapman, *The Rise of Merchant Banking* (London, 1984), p. 137; *Investors' Review* (1896), pp. 130–1.

21 Capie and Webber, *Monetary History*, pp. 221, 291; Holden, *Depreciation of Securities*, p. 3; J. W. Lubbock, *On the Clearing of the London Bankers* (London, 1860) pp. 2, 10–11; Friedman and Schwartz, *Monetary Trends*, p. 262.

22 F. Machlup, *The Stock Market, Credit and Capital Formation* (London, 1940), p. 23; E. T. Powell, *The Evolution of the Money Market, 1385–1915* (London, 1915), p. 576.
23 E. T. Powell, *The Mechanism of the City* (London, 1910), p. 46; P. L. Simmonds, *Fenn's Compendium of the English and Foreign Funds* (London, 1860, 7th edn), pp. 105–6; J. Reid, *A Manual of Scottish Stocks and British Funds* (Edinburgh, 1841), p. 130; J. F. Wheeler, *The Stock Exchange* (London, 1913), pp. 59, 64; E. C. Maddison, *On the Stock Exchange* (London, 1877), p. 57.
24 London Stock Exchange (LSE): Committee for General Purposes, 4 October 1909; cf. R. Sayers, *The Bank of England, 1891–1914* (Cambridge, 1976), pp. 25, 38–41; Goodhart, *Business of Banking*, p. 131; *Investor's Monthly Manual*, 31 July 1885.
25 A. Crump, *The Theory of Stock Exchange Speculation* (London, 1874), p. 19; Sayers, *Bank of England*, p. 19; National Monetary Commission, *Interviews on the Banking and Currency Systems* (Washington, 1910), pp, 108, 120, 180; Goodhart, *Business of Banking*, p. 18; Bagehot, *Lombard Street*, p. 284; Financial Times, *Investor's Guide* (London, 1913), p. 21; *Investor's Monthly Manual*, 30 July 1881, 30 September 1882, 31 May 1883, 30 September 1896; E. E. Spicer, *An Outline of the Money Market* (London, 1898), p. 99; F. E. Steele, 'On Changes in the Bank Rate of Discount', *Journal of the Institute of Bankers*, vol. 12 (1891) pp. 496–7; W. A. Cole, 'The Relations between Banks and Stock Exchanges', *Journal of the Institute of Bankers*, vol. 20 (1899), p. 409.
26 *Investor's Review* (1895), p. 41; cf. G. L. Ayres, 'Fluctuations in New Capital Issues on the London Money Market, 1899 to 1913' (MSc thesis, London University, 1934), pp. 128, 131.
27 National Monetary Commission, *Interviews*, pp. 44, 120, 134, 180; Sayers, *Bank of England*, p. 15; Crump, *Theory*, p. 19; Powell, *Mechanism*, pp. 38, 43, 45; Investors' Guardian, *Guide to Investments* (London, 1873), p. 7; F. Playfold, *Practical Hints for Investing Money* (London, 1856), p. viii; *Bankers' Circular*, 20 August 1830.
28 Maddison, *On the Stock Exchange*, p. 108.
29 M. C. Reed, *A History of James Capel & Co.* (London, 1975), pp. 31, 43–5; LSE: Gen. Purposes, 16 February 1848, 3 May 1866, 25 January 1871; G. Clare, *A Money Market Primer and Key to the Exchanges* (London, 1900), pp. 147–8.
30 National Monetary Commission, *Interviews*, p. 73.
31 Wm. Russell, Stockbroker, Ledger Value of Securities against Loans, 1901–1913; Financial Times, *Investor's Guide*, p. 22; Morgan and Thomas, *The Stock Exchange*, p. 154; E. Hennessy, *Stockbrokers for 150 Years: A History of Shepherds & Chase* (London, 1978), pp. 4–5; Maddison, *On the Stock Exchange*, p. 93; E. C. McDermott, *The London Stock Exchange: Its Constitution and Modes of Business* (London, 1877), p. 10.
32 Morgan and Thomas, *The Stock Exchange*, pp. 113, 123.

33 *Financial Review of Reviews (FR)*, January 1906, p. 19.
34 National Monetary Commission, *Interviews*, p. 134; R. C. Michie, *Money, Mania and Markets* (Edinburgh, 1981), p. 132.
35 Gresham Omnium, *A Handy Guide to Safe Investments* (London, 1858), p. 95; General Securities Corporation, *The Investor's Handy Book of Active Stocks and Shares* (London, 1912), pp. xi–xiv; J. B. Mackenzie, *The Story of a Stock Exchange Speculator* (London, 1908), p. 9; E. W. Fithian, 'The Beneficial Effect of International Investment on British Trade', *FR*, February 1909, p. 23.
36 Sayers, *Bank of England*, p. 25; cf. Tamaki, *Life Cycle*, p. 104, 137; A. Ellis, *The Rationale of Market Fluctuations* (London, 1876), p. 112.
37 A. G. Webb, *The New Dictionary of Statistics* (London, 1911), p. 338; cf. 'The Progress of Insurance', *The Statist*, 23 May 1903; B. L. Anderson, 'Institutional Investment before the First World War: The Union Marine Insurance Co., 1897–1915', in S. Marriner (ed.), *Business and Businessmen* (Liverpool, 1978), p. 39.
38 Guarantee Insurance & Investment Co., Minutes, 3 January 1902, 21 January 1902, 14 April 1902, 9 April 1903, 29 January 1907, 27 January 1909.
39 See Table 2.2.
40 Gresham Omnium, *Handy Guide*, p. 33; S. F. Van Oss, *American Railroads and British Investors* (London, 1893), pp. 138, 140.
41 F. Crouzet, *The Victorian Economy* (London, 1982), p. 360; Morgan and Thomas, *The Stock Exchange*, p. 122.
42 A. S. J. Baster, *The Imperial Banks* (London, 1929), pp. 140, 144, 216; A. S. J. Baster, *The International Banks* (London, 1935), p. 76, 258; K. E. Born, *International Banking in the 19th and 20th Centuries* (Leamington Spa, 1983), p. 117.
43 D. Williams, 'The Evolution of the Sterling System', in C. R. Whittlesey and J. S. G. Wilson (eds.), *Essays in Money and Banking* (Oxford, 1968), p. 286; A. I. Bloomfield, *Short-Term Capital Movements under the pre-1914 Gold Standard* (Princeton, 1963), pp. 35, 46; D. N. McCloskey and Z. R. Zecher, 'How the Gold Standard Worked, 1880–1913' in D. N. McCloskey (ed.), *Enterprise and Trade in Victorian Britain: Essays in Historical Economics* (London, 1981), pp. 188–9.
44 *The Financier*, 3 March 1870.
45 E. G. Peake, *An Academic Study of Some Money Market and Other Statistics* (London, 1923), pp. 7, 21, 24, 37, 39; McCloskey and Zecher, 'Gold Standard', p. 188; R. Triffin, *Our International Monetary System: Yesterday, Today and Tomorrow* (New York, 1968), p. 12; F. Escher, *Foreign Exchange Explained* (New York, 1917), pp. 17–18.
46 H. K. Brooks, *Foreign Exchange Text Book* (Chicago, 1906), pp. 3, 136–7; cf. A. W. Margraff, *International Exchange* (Chicago, 1903), p. 227.
47 A. C. Cole, 'Notes on the London Money Market', *Journal of the Institute of Bankers*, vol. 25 (1904), p. 134; W. F. Spalding, 'The

Establishment and Growth of Foreign Branch Banks in London',
Journal of the Institute of Bankers, vol. 22 (1911), p. 455; A. G. Ford,
'International Financial Policy and the Gold Standard, 1870–1914',
Warwick Research Papers, vol. 104 (1977), p. 9; P. L. Cottrell,
'Investment Banking in England, 1856–1882: Case Study of the
International Financial Society' (PhD thesis, Hull University, 1974),
pp. 749, 801–2; A. Cairncross and B. Eichengreen, *Sterling in Decline*
(Oxford, 1983), p. 10.

48 Bloomfield, *Short-Term Capital*, p. 34.

49 G. Rozenraad, 'The International Money Market', *Journal of the
Institute of Bankers*, vol. 23 (1902), pp. 197–8, vol. 24 (1903), p. 101,
vol. 25 (1904), p. 266; Kindleberger, *Financial History*, pp. 70, 264.

50 Escher, *Foreign Exchange Explained*, pp. 11, 73, 117; A. G. Ford, *The
Gold Standard, 1880–1914: Britain and Argentina* (Oxford, 1962), pp. 19,
32; P. Einzig, *The History of Foreign Exchange* (London, 1962), pp. 173,
178; A. G. Ford, 'The Trade Cycle in Britain, 1860–1914', in R. Floud
and D. McCloskey (eds.), *The Economic History of Britain since 1700*
(Cambridge, 1981), vol. 2, pp. 43–4; Crouzet, *Victorian Economy*, p. 10.

51 Spalding, 'Foreign Branch Banks', p. 434; W. M. Scammell, *The
London Discount Market* (London, 1968), p. 165; Duncan, *Notes*, p. 146;
Kindleberger, *Financial History*, p. 125; King, *Discount Market*, p. 280;
G. Jones, 'Lombard Street on the Riviera: The British Clearing Banks
and Europe, 1900–1960', *Business History*, vol. 24 (1982), pp. 186–7.

52 Spalding, 'Foreign Branch Banks', p. 448; cf. J. H. Lenfant, 'British
Capital Export, 1900–1913' (PhD thesis, London University, 1949),
pp. 63–4; F. Schuster, 'Foreign Trade and the Money Market', *Monthly
Review*, vol. 14 (1904) p. 7; London Chamber of Commerce: Gold
Reserves Committee, Minutes, 7 May 1908, 28 July 1908, 20 May
1909; *Investors' Review*, 1892, p. 263.

53 Sayers, *Bank of England*, pp. 21, 38–41; P. Geutzberg and J. T. M. Van
Laaner, *Changing Economy in Indonesia: Money and Banking, 1816–1940*
(Amsterdam, 1980), pp. 48, 120; L. S. Pressnell, 'The Sterling System
and Financial Crises before 1914', in Kindleberger and Laffarge (eds.),
Financial Crises, pp. 148, 156.

54 M. G. Myers, *Paris as a Financial Centre* (London, 1936), pp. 157, 170;
A. H. Burgoyne, 'Bank Reserves from a New Point of View', *FR*,
February 1912, p. 21; M. Patron, *The Bank of France in its Relation to
National and International Credit* (Washington, 1910), pp. 75, 107;
Escher, *Foreign Exchange Explained*, p. 13; W. C. Schluter, *The Pre-War
Business Cycle, 1907 to 1914* (New York, 1923), p. 180.

55 King, *Discount Market*, pp. 191, 265; Duncan, *Notes*, p. 19.

56 League of Nations, *Memorandum on Commercial Banks, 1913–1929*
(Geneva, 1931), pp. 294, 297; F. Capie and A. Webber, *Profits and
Profitability in British Banking, 1870–1939*, City University Centre for
Banking and International Finance Discussion Paper No. 18 (1985), p.
21.

57   Levy-Leboyer, 'Central Banking', pp. 99–100; R. S. Sayers, *Gilletts in the London Money Market, 1867–1967* (Oxford, 1968), pp. 53, 61; W. F. Spalding, 'The Billbroker: Some Account of his Operations on the London Money Market', *Journal of the Institute of Bankers*, vol. 33 (1912), p. 478; Smith St Aubyn & Co., Business Diary, 3 January 1899, 9 October 1900, 14 May 1901, 5 January 1909; G. A. Fletcher, *The Discount Houses in London* (London, 1976), p. 25; Scammell, *London Discount Market*, pp. 164–6; King, *Discount Market*, pp. 280–8.

58   H. Withers, *The English Banking System* (Washington, 1910), p. 55.

59   Levy-Leboyer, 'Central Banking', p. 101; Chapman, *Merchant Banking*, p. 106; Bloomfield, *Short-Term Capital*, p. 38; Nishimura, *Decline of Inland Bills*, pp. 72, 79; Fletcher, *Discount Houses*, pp. 16, 29; Scammell, *London Discount Market*, p. 165.

60   LSE: Gen. Purposes Subcommittee of Non-Permanent Character, Memorandum to Chancellor of Exchequer on 'Stamps', 13 May 1909; cf. Withers, *English Banking*, pp. 37–8; Coles, 'Notes', p. 134.

61   LSE: Gen. Purposes Subcommittee of Non-Permanent Character, Memorandum on Loans, 10 September 1914; F. Lavington, *The English Capital Market* (London, 1921), p. 142; Goodhart, *Business of Banking*, pp. 122, 124.

62   W. C. Schluter, *The Pre-War Business Cycle, 1907 to 1914* (New York, 1923), pp. 168–9, 180.

63   E. McDermott, *The London Stock Exchange* (London, 1877) p. 10; *Investor's Monthly Manual*, 31 May 1883, Clare, *Money Market Primer*, pp. 147–8; Morgan and Thomas, *The Stock Exchange*, p. 154; F. E. Steele, 'On Changes in the Bank Rate of Discount', *Journal of the Institute of Bankers*, vol. 12 (1891) pp. 496–7; H. S. Miller, *Scientific Speculation* (London, 1901), p. 38.

64   W. G. Cordingley, *Guide to the Stock Exchange* (London, 1893 and 1901), p. 49.

65   Clare, *Money Market Primer*, p. 149; Steele, 'Changes in Bank Rate', pp. 95–6; J. F. Wheeler, *The Stock Exchange* (London, 1913), pp. 36, 50, 53; *Investor's Monthly Manual*, 30 July 1881, 30 September 1882, 31 July 1885, 30 September 1896, 30 October 1906.

66   *Royal Commission on the London Stock Exchange* (British Parliamentary Papers, 1878, xix), *Report*, p. 8, *Minutes of Evidence*, p. 25, 44, 102; Wheeler, *Stock Exchange*, p. 36.

67   LSE: Gen. Purposes, 3 March 1908, 21 September 1911; *Royal Commission on London Stock Exchange, Minutes*, p. 37.

68   Nathan & Rosselli, 'Special Notes Regarding Foreign Clients, Accounts, Loans, Dividends, etc.' (1911); cf. S. Japhet, *Recollections from my Business Life* (London, 1931), p. 88; L. Dennet, *The Charterhouse Group, 1925–1979: A History*, vol. I (London, 1979), pp. 73–6.

69   E. & C. Randolph to Nathan & Rosselli, 7 June 1911; cf. W. E. Rosenbaem, *The London Stock Market: Its Features and Usage* (New York, 1910), p. 5.

70 Spalding, 'Foreign Branch Banks', *Journal of the Institute of Bankers*, vol. 32 (1911), p. 448; Ford, 'International Financial Policy' p. 48; Kindleberger, *Financial History*, p. 265; Ellis, *Rationale*, p. 21.

71 H. Schmidt, *Foreign Banking Arbitration: Its Theory and Practice* (London, 1875), p. 184.

72 W. P. Kennedy, 'Institutional Response to Economic Growth: Capital Markets in Britain to 1914', in L. Hannah (ed.), *Management Strategy and Business Development* (London, 1976), p. 155.

73 McDermott, *London Stock Exchange*, p. 35.

74 Powell, *Evolution of the Money Market*, p. 574.

75 For a reassessment of Britain's stock of foreign assets in 1913 see D. C. M. Platt, 'Britain's Stock of Investment Overseas at the End of 1913: A Down Valuation' (circulated typescript, 1913).

76 A Scotch Banker, *The Theory of Money*, (Edinburgh, 1868), pp. 137–41.

77 G. Clare, *The ABC of the Foreign Exchange: A Practical Guide* (London, 1895), p. 34; cf. A. J. Schwartz, 'Introduction', in M. D. Bordo and A. J. Schwartz (eds.), *A Retrospective on the Classical Gold Standard, 1821–1931* (Chicago and London, 1984), p. 24.

78 L. E. Davis and J. R. T. Hughes, 'A Dollar-Sterling Exchange, 1803–1895', *Economic History Review*, vol. 13 (1960–1), p. 52; Kindleberger, *Financial History*, p. 250.

79 Spicer, *Outline of the Money Market*, p. 34; cf. G. J. Goschen, *The Theory of Foreign Exchange* (London, 1864), p. 23; Clare, *ABC*, pp. 43, 89.

80 Ellis, *Rationale of Market Fluctuations*, p. 72; Margraff, *International Exchange*, p. 31.

81 Withers, *Money Changing*, pp. 23–4; Clare, *ABC*, pp. 29–32; Brooks, *Foreign Exchange*, p. 120; Margraff, *International Exchange*, pp. 35–6.

82 Withers, *Money Changing*, pp. 11, 75, 122; Clare, *ABC*, p. 107; Brooks, *Foreign Exchange*, pp. 136, 193; Bloomfield, *Short-Term Capital*, pp. 38, 40, 76; P. H. Lindert, *Key Currencies and Gold, 1900–1913* (Princeton, 1969), pp. 16, 17, 29; Ellis, *Rationale*, p. 27; L. H. Jenks, *The Migration of British Capital to 1875* (New York, 1927), p. 279.

83 F. E. Escher, *Elements of Foreign Exchange* (New York, 1911), p. 5.

84 C. A. Conant, *The Functions of the Stock Exchange* (New York, 1914), pp. 14–15; cf. J. W. Angel, *The Theory of International Prices* (Princeton, 1926), p. 527; Clare, *ABC*, pp. 81–2; Margraff, *International Exchange*, p. 20; G. Paish, *The Trade Balance of the United States* (Washington, 1910), p. 165; Escher, *Elements*, pp. 137–40; Withers, *Money Changing*, p. 136; G. R. Gibson, *The Stock Exchanges of London, Paris and New York: A Comparison* (New York, 1889), p. 3; E. E. Gellender, 'The Relations between Banks and the Stock Exchanges', *Journal of the Institute of Banking*, vol. 20 (1899), p. 497; *Investor's Review*, 1897, p. 195; Davis and Hughes, 'Dollar–Sterling Exchange', p. 64; Bloomfield, *Short-Term Capital*, pp. 4, 34; C. P. Kindleberger, *Manias, Panics and Crashes: A History of Financial Crises* (London, 1978), pp. 49, 119.

85 LSE: Gen. Purposes Subcommittee of Non-Permanent Character, Memorandum by Medwin & Lowy, 3 June 1909.

86 G. H. Phillips, *Phillips' Investors' Manual* (London, 1887), p. 127.

87 Goodhart, *Business of Banking*, pp. 218–19; R. C. O. Matthews, C. H. Feinstein and J. C. Odling-Smee, *British Economic Growth, 1856–1973* (Oxford, 1982), pp. 445, 457.

PART TWO

NEW YORK

6 The New York Stock Exchange and the Securities Market I

During the nineteenth century approximately 250 different stock exchanges were formed in the United States, with all major centres of population coming to possess at least one. However, most of these exchanges had a very transitory existence, disappearing with the collapse of a speculative mania or mining boom, or through a change in investment fashion.[1] Only a few of those that were founded both survived and grew, and they were all in the principal cities, such as Philadelphia, New York, Boston, Chicago and San Francisco. Even fewer of these acquired national significance as judged by whether their activities were of interest and importance for people outside their immediate locality, or whether they catered for more than a narrow focus of investment. Among those that did achieve this status, the New York Stock Exchange soon became paramount, and it retained its premier position thenceforth. Such was the apparent influence of the New York Stock Exchange that the president of one bank – Baldwin of the Fourth National Bank of New York – was reported as claiming that 'Next to the Christian religion, the New York Stock Exchange has been the greatest civilizing influence in the world.'[2]

Certainly, the consensus of contemporary opinion was that the New York Stock Exchange was the dominant force in the US securities market, and that it exerted a pervasive influence throughout the nation. Cornwallis, writing in 1879, felt 'That the New York Stock Exchange exerts a mighty influence over the price of the vast volume of securities dealt within its walls, and indirectly, through sympathy, over all the securities in the United States, must be obvious to the most casual observer of the fluctuations recorded in the daily lists.'[3] The various government committees set up to investigate, directly or indirectly, the workings of the securities market in the years before the First World War also arrived at this conclusion. In the report into the *Concentration of Control of Money and Credit*, which was presented in 1913, the New York Stock Exchange was described as 'the market place of the entire country'.[4]

Subsequent historians have accepted this viewpoint with little attempt to confirm or deny its veracity.[5] However, estimates of a more substantial kind are available by which the extent of the New York Stock Exchange's actual importance can be measured, in terms of both the securities quoted and the business done. In 1913 the New York Stock Exchange listed stocks and bonds with a par value of $26.0 billion. For a year earlier – 1912 – it has been estimated that the value of all United States securities issued and still current totalled $58.1 billion. Thus almost half (44.8 per cent) of the securities in circulation in the United States, by value, were to be found on the New York Stock Exchange and could be bought and sold there.[6] Furthermore, the New York Stock Exchange can be contrasted with its nearest competitor at that time, namely, the Boston Stock Exchange (Table 6.1). From this comparison it can been seen that the New York Stock Exchange quoted 4.4 times as many issues as Boston, with a par value 4.1 times greater, and the area of greatest contrast was in bonds, in both number and value.

Table 6.1   *New York and Boston Stock Exchanges, 1913*

	New York	Boston
Stocks		
Issues	565	195
Par value	$13,385.4m.	$4,130.2m.
Bonds		
Issues	1,089	182
Par value	$12,589.6m.	$2,181.7m.
Total		
Issues	1,654	377
Par value	$25,975.0m.	$6,311.9m.

Source: *Regulation of the New York Stock Exchange: Hearings before the Committee on Banking and Currency* (US Senate 63rd Congress, 2nd Session, Washington, 1914) pp. 437–8, 529.

An even better measure of the New York Stock Exchange against its rivals exists, as there is no guarantee that all the securities quoted were actively traded. The major US stock exchanges kept a record of the number of stocks sold each day, and the value of business done in bonds. These are presented in Table 6.2 for the year 1910, covering the three major New York markets and the three largest exchanges in the rest of the United States. Judging from the contribution made by Chicago, which was the third largest outside New York, turnover on the stock exchanges not included (such as San Francisco, Baltimore, St Louis, Pittsburgh and Cleveland) must have been relatively tiny, and their inclusion would not significantly alter the relative dimensions of the aggregate total. However, there was an important over-the-counter market in bonds which cannot even be guessed at.[7] Compensating for the lack of inclusion of these other markets was the fact that the New York Stock Exchange concentrated on high-denomination securities, which would increase the value of the business done there in contrast to other exchanges. Accepting the general accuracy of these estimates, the indication is that two-thirds of all trading in stocks in the United States took place on the New York Stock Exchange, and almost 90 per cent within New York City as a whole. A similar picture was apparent in bonds, where the New York Stock Exchange's dominance was even greater, reaching 90 per cent of the total on its own (Table 6.2). Informed contemporaries were clearly right about New York's importance, without being aware of the order of magnitude.

Important as these figures are in placing the New York Stock Exchange in perspective, they nevertheless reveal little about why it came to dominate security trading and what was the precise role that it played. If each stock exchange served its own particular segment of the market, whether divided by locality or by the nature of securities traded, and did so largely in isolation, then the New York Stock Exchange was merely large without being powerful.

New York was the most populous city in the United States, and the centre of one of the most consistently wealthy regions. It was also the major port, and the principal channel through which international commerce flowed, as well as a substantial part of inter-regional trade, especially with the opening of the Erie Canal in 1825.[8] It was thus only to be expected that New York would

Table 6.2   *US Securities Markets, Sales in 1910*

Market	Stocks Number	Proportion	Bonds Par Value	Proportion
New York Stock Exchange	164,150,061	68.5%	$635.0m	90.6%
Consolidated Stock Exchange	32,238,773	13.4%	—	—
New York Curb Market	18,671,438	7.8%	$10.8m	1.5%
New York: Total	215,060,272	89.7%	$645.8m	92.1%
Boston Stock Exchange	15,503,336	6.5%	$32.7m	4.7%
Philadelphia Stock Exchange	8,341,599	3.5%	$14.6m	2.1%
Chicago Stock Exchange	894,362	0.4%	$7.4m	1.1%
Total	239,799,569	100.1%	$700.5m	100.0%

Sources: NYSE: New York Stock Exchange, Special Committee on Commissions, Memorandum, 1924; Consolidated: Consolidated Stock Exchange, Annual Report, year ending 31 May 1910; Curb: Jones & Baker, *Profits and Dividends on America's Second Largest Stock Market* (New York, 1919); Boston: J. G. Martin, *Stock Fluctuations* (Boston, 1911); Philadelphia: A. W. Barnes (ed.), *History of the Philadelphia Stock Exchange, Banks and Banking Interests* (Philadelphia, 1911); Chicago: F. M. Huston and A. Russell, *Financing an Empire – History of Banking in Illinois* (Chicago, 1926), vol. I.

possess the largest stock exchange, as its catchment area contained the greatest number of affluent investors, who would require facilities for buying and selling securities.[9]

Philadelphia was the financial centre of the United States in the immediate post-Revolution years, with the first public bank being founded there, as well as the first organized securities market. However, even by the 1790s stockbrokers in Philadelphia accepted that New York had become the most active market for many securities; and New York stockbrokers were confident enough by 1836 to claim, in a memorandum to the New York State Assembly, that transactions 'are much more extensive in this city than at Philadelphia', adding that New York was 'the only market where stocks, to any large amount, could be sold, at any one time, for their intrinsic value'.[10] Philadelphia's position was also undermined by the abolition of the first Bank of the United States (1791–1811), and by the same fate befalling its successor (1816–36) – both had been based in that city. Their existence might have allowed Philadelphia to have preserved more of an equilibrium with New York, which was rapidly outpacing it in terms of commercial wealth and business enterprise.[11]

For much of the first half of the nineteenth century the US stock exchanges that existed were little more than local markets, whose level and nature of business reflected the size, wealth and interest of the local population. The New York Stock Exchange, for instance, was largely engaged in providing a market for the issues of New York-based companies or public bodies. In 1820, of the 30 different securities trading there, 28 were local, belonging to 16 insurance companies, 9 banks, and 3 authorities. Only two were non-local, namely federal government bonds and the stock of the Bank of the United States. By 1835 the list of securities had quadrupled, largely through an expansion in the number of banks and insurance companies and the addition of local railroads and utilities. The non-local proportion had grown, especially among the banks and railroads, but still remained a minority, contributing only 35 out of the 124 securities quoted.[12] The consequence was that the stock exchanges in the main eastern cities of New York, Philadelphia, Boston and Baltimore remained on a par, with New York having only a slight if noticeable lead.[13]

This did not mean that these exchanges traded in isolation of each other, for there were always securities held more widely than in single localities. Government and, later, state debt attracted investors generally throughout the eastern seaboard, as did the stock of the first and second Bank of the United States and, subsequently, the railroad lines linking one city to another.[14] In the 1790s the stock of the first Bank of the United States was held extensively in both Philadelphia and New York, and this led to considerable trading between the security markets of each city, whenever any price differential appeared. Two who became heavily involved in such an operation were Standish Lorde in Philadelphia and Peter Anspach in New York, who decided in February 1792 to enter into a joint-account speculation in US Bank shares. 'As soon as the price can be had make the sale and advise me that I may purchase whole shares at the same time when they can be had so as to leave about 10 per cent profit,' wrote Lorde to Anspach on the 25th of that month, and this type of daily communication continued until October 1792, when they abandoned the business, because of the risks involved. The reasonable proximity of New York to Philadelphia and the existence of express mail made regular contact possible between these two markets; but even so, two or three days had to be allowed for the dispatch and receipt of letters, and a profit of at least 10 per cent on the money employed after all expenses had been met was required in order to make the risks worthwhile. This meant that significant price differentials could exist in common securities, such as the $117 in New York and $112 in Philadelphia (or 4.5 per cent) for US Bank shares on 25 February 1792.[15]

Inter-market dealing, during the age of the letter and the horse, was thus a most speculative affair, rather than a regular business, and was abandoned when the risks were considered uncommensurate with the rewards. Though each exchange was aware of what was happening on its neighbour, though there were always commonly held securities whose ownership could move from one city to another, and though adjustments were made to the price fluctuations as a result, it was local conditions that dominated buying and selling. It took a substantial differential to provoke a reaction, with people like Lorde and Anspach always willing to step in for the quick gains when such chances arose. However, much more important was the regular correspondence between brokers and their clients, or between brokers on different exchanges, giving instructions to buy and sell the local securities that each exchange specialized in, with only limited regard for conditions elsewhere. 'It is not infrequent that orders are received by mail in the morning, for the sale of large amounts of stocks, accompanied by the promise to send the certificates or powers of attorney by transfer in the next mail,' claimed the New York brokers in 1836.[16] The field of competition between the New York Stock Exchange and its rivals was limited by the problems of communication that existed along the extensive eastern seaboard, let alone in the vast hinterland, and by the local nature of much of the securities being traded. Even in 1890 a special express train took 1 hour 38 minutes to complete the Philadelphia–New York journey, indicating that continuous contact through transportation was an impossibility.[17]

However, all this was to change with the introduction of the telegraph in the mid-1840s, which provided for almost instantaneous communication between the different exchanges, and removed the barriers of distance that had preserved local markets.[18] Before the telegraph, the next best system was that arranged between New York and Philadelphia in the 1830s, involving a series of relay stations across New Jersey flashing information from one to another by the use of mirrors. Even this took ten minutes each way, and was subject to climatic conditions. Consequently, as soon as the two cities were linked by the telegraph in 1845, this signalling system was abandoned.[19] New York was soon connected with all the major eastern cities by telegraph, and the rapid expansion of the system throughout the country led to a New York–San Francisco link being established in 1866. Between 1848 and 1912 the US telegraph network grew overall from 3,400 miles of wire to 1,814,200, by which time 103.6 million inland messages a year were being sent. Costs fell, too, particularly on the longer-distance routes. Whereas the cost of a ten-word telegram from New York to Philadelphia was already down to 25 cents in 1850, and remained at that level, the cost for the same telegram to Chicago fell from $1.55 to 50 cents (by 73 per cent) between 1850 and 1908, while one to San Francisco cost $7.45 in 1866 but only $1.00 in 1908, representing a fall in price of 87 per cent. At the same time users of the telegraph became adept at reducing their instructions to one-word codes, further lowering costs. Illustrating the transformation that took place was the fact that by 1887 the delay between the dispatch of a telegram and receipt of a reply between New York and Chicago was a mere one and a half minutes.[20]

The next phase in the transformation of inland communications came with the introduction of the telephone in the late 1870s, which provided instantaneous two-way contact. Though New York and Chicago were connected by telephone in 1892, the principal contribution made by the telephone was for shorter-distance conversations. As late as 1905 one Cleveland, Ohio, brokerage firm noted that 'We never use the telephone to New York. We use our private telegraph wires. Telephoning that distance is expensive.' That firm sent any messages going over 100 miles by telegraph rather than use the telephone, because of the charges. In 1902, while a three-minute call from New York to Philadelphia cost only 55 cents, the same to Chicago cost $5.45, and even by 1915 one to San Francisco cost $20.70. Technical problems and atmospheric problems also continued to hamper long-distance telephone calls, making the connection unreliable. Nevertheless, the telephone became the broker's principal means of communication, and its range was progressively extended, being in regular use between

New York and Philadelphia and New York and Boston by the early twentieth century, if not to Chicago or San Francisco.[21]

Through this alteration in the speed and cost of communication, no buying and selling on other exchanges was immune from the influence of New York, and this manifested itself in two principal ways. One was the continuous dissemination of current New York Stock Exchange prices, which would directly affect trading in securities that were shared with New York, and indirectly affect all other securities through sympathetic movement. Even by 1860, of the securities of 118 different government or corporate bodies that the New York Stock Exchange quoted, a total of 60 (51 per cent) were non-local, being the stocks and bonds, for example, of railroad companies operating throughout the union. The Philadelphia & Reading Railroad Company, for instance, was shared with Philadelphia, and the Canton Company, a property concern, with Baltimore.[22] The telegraph allowed the New York prices of these to be transmitted nationwide, so that dealers on all other exchanges traded in awareness of what was happening on the largest and most active market, and adjusted their prices accordingly. This was greatly facilitated by the development of the ticker-tape machine and its introduction on the floor of the New York Stock Exchange in 1867. According to one observer in 1875:

At convenient points about the hall are telegraphic instruments. Operators are constantly on the floor mingling in the crowds, and as often as a sale or bid is made, the operator rushes to his instrument, and telegraphs the name of the stock with the price at which it is sold, or the bid or offer made for it. The wires from all these instruments concentrate in the headquarters of the two stock telegraph companies.[23]

Through these stock-quotation companies this information was then relayed throughout the United States, to anyone who cared to subscribe to the service. By 1874 the Gold & Stock Telegraph Company alone served 116 cities outside of New York, as well as having numerous clients within the city itself.[24] The prices on the ticker-tape normally ran only two or three minutes behind the trading on the floor, though in very active periods it could be as much as ten minutes behind. However, this was a tremendous change compared to the pre-telegraph era, when the delay could be measured in hours or days, and the time and quality of the information received was uncertain. It was no longer important to be in or near Wall Street to know the current state of trading on the New York Stock Exchange, for, as L. W. Hamilton noted in 1875: 'The echoes of the bids and offers that are daily shouted in its halls are heard in every city and town in the Union.' This continuous transmission of prices had an important psychological effect. It both focused the public's attention on the floor of the New York Stock Exchange as the nation's securities market, and forced brokers elsewhere to monitor constantly what was happening in New York, in case they should be caught by any sudden change. [25]

However, the ticker-tape was only one manifestation of the change taking place because of the transformation in communications. The other was the effect that transformation had upon the operations of the members of the New York Stock Exchange, and on their contacts with both clients and members of other exchanges. 'The advent of electric transmission of messages was probably more of a boon to brokerage than to any other business,' was Nourse's assessment in 1910. [26] The same telegraph wires that could transmit information could also carry buying and selling orders, and the brokers immediately utilized them for that purpose. Clients could be attracted from an ever wider area, for, as the New York firm of Haight & Freese pointed out in 1898: 'Business may be conducted as readily by letter, telegram or telephone as by being on the spot.' [27]

Conversely, it was now also unnecessary for the brokerage firm to be itself in physical proximity to the market it used, for a telephone call or a telegram to a broker on the appropriate exchange would suffice. Again, Clapp & Co., another New York firm, was in a position to claim in 1893 that 'We have the machinery and necessary facilities for buying or selling on all American exchanges.' [28] It was estimated in 1871 that the members of the New York Stock Exchange were receiving from 850 to 2,300 domestic cables a day, especially from connections in other major cities such as Philadelphia, Boston, Baltimore, St Louis, Chicago and San Francisco, as well as from smaller neighbouring centres like Hartford, Connecticut, and Providence, Rhode Island. [29]

The new communications had more than a passive impact in

allowing a physical separation to take place between broker and either the client or the exchange; they also transformed inter-market dealing. By maintaining a telephone line from the floor of the New York Stock Exchange to the broker's office, and thence a telegraph or telephone contact with a broker on another exchange, it was possible to be in constant touch with events on two or more markets widely separated in distance. By 1903, 500 out of the New York Stock Exchange's membership of 1,100 had direct telephone lines between their offices and the floor, while others maintained private wires between New York and all principal cities of the United States for the conduct of business, even at a cost of $16,000 per annum for one to Chicago or $60,000 for San Francisco. Hamilton & Bishop, for instance, had private wire connections to Albany, Troy, Syracuse, Rochester and Utica in New York State as well as to Cleveland and Chicago.[30] Such a private wire was not essential for the conduct of inter-market dealing; the New York firm of G. P. & D. W. Butler, for instance, did not possess any but regularly received and dispatched buying and selling orders through the public telephone and telegraph system. In September 1908 Butlers purchased $61,000 Western Maryland First mortgage 4 per cent bonds for seventy-six and a half from Mackibin, Goodrich & Co. of Baltimore, on the basis of a single telephone call.[31] Nevertheless, those firms with private wires had their exclusive use and could keep them open throughout business hours, which gave them a small but crucial time advantage over those firms using the public system. As a result, the inter-market business gradually became concentrated in the hands of those firms that invested heavily in telephonic and telegraphic communications.[32]

A growing number of New York firms went so far as to establish branches in other cities and acquire membership of other exchanges, so that they could offer a comprehensive national service, while brokers from other parts of the United States also set up in New York and bought seats on the New York Stock Exchange. While this was encouraged by the New York Stock Exchange's minimum commission rules – which allowed cheaper rates only for members, wherever they were located – it reflected the growing integration of the domestic securities market, which the exchange itself recognized in 1881: 'The active development of financial enterprise for whose obligations the New York Stock Exchange provides a market and the desire throughout the country to invest in them have induced many members of the Exchange to seek to extend their business field by the establishment of branch houses and connections with firms in other cities.'[33]

By 1901 a total of 136 New York Stock Exchange members had branches outside the City of New York. As early as 1886 firms such as Spencer, Trask & Co. had offices in Albany and Saratoga in New York State, in Providence, Rhode Island, and in Philadelphia; while Hill & Kennedy had a Chicago branch, and Bernheimer & Speyer one in San Francisco. In addition, there were 119 seats of the New York Stock Exchange owned in 1901 by out-of-town members, who in turn maintained further branches of their own. In 1912 J. C. Wilson & Co. of San Francisco had offices in Los Angeles, San Diego and Coronado Beach, California, in Portland, Oregon, in Seattle, Washington, and in Vancouver, British Columbia. Similarly, Walter Fitch & Co. of Chicago had opened local offices in Ottawa and Bloomington, Illinois, as well as more distant branches in Toledo, Ohio and Minneapolis, Minnesota. Overall, some 23 per cent of the New York Stock Exchange's membership in 1901 either possessed branches elsewhere or were themselves part of out-of-town firms. The United States was coming to have an increasingly integrated network of brokerage firms that were either based in New York or oriented in that direction, while the New York Stock Exchange was itself being gradually monopolized by such firms.[34]

This growing external interest in the New York Stock Exchange, and the increasing use to which its trading facilities were put by investors and institutions not resident in the city, was recognized by the institution itself. 'Many blocks of stocks are sold upon the New York market by telegraph from cities situated at distances of all kinds from the Exchange,' was its considered opinion in 1909. The Stock Exchange's own estimate was that 48 per cent of the business transacted there came from outside New York City by that date.[35] Among the brokers outside New York there was also a rising awareness of the advantages that directing a sale or purchase to New York offered over the local market, and this became increasingly common practice.

The firm of P. J. Goodhart & Co., for instance, a member of both the Cincinnati and New York Stock Exchanges, stated in 1913 that 'a broker in Cincinnati receiving an order to buy or sell securities listed on the New York Stock Exchange, knows immediately where to fill that order and to find the best market where the quotations are regulated by the law of supply and demand' – and thus immediately sent such orders to its partner in New York. A similar opinion was expressed in 1903 by Charles Head & Co., a member of both the Boston and New York Stock Exchanges.[36] One estimate of the extent of New York's attraction for out-of-town business comes from a survey undertaken by the Boston Stock Exchange, between 14 March and 14 April 1904, into sales of five stocks quoted on both Stock Exchanges. In that one-month period Boston sales of these stocks totalled only 286,005 shares, just 5.4 per cent of the New York total, while Boston brokers also completed the sale of 330,565 shares through the New York Stock Exchange, or 15.6 per cent more than they did on the Boston Stock Exchange (Table 6.3).

However, the reverse could also be true. The communications links and branch and other networks established could also be used to channel New York business to other exchanges. G. P. & A. W. Butler received an order in 1910 to sell stock in the Atlantic Mining Company but informed their client that 'the principal market for this stock is in Boston . . . we have placed an order there to sell any part of 50 shares at six and a half'.[37] Similarly, New York brokers redirected orders in such stocks as Detroit Edison to Detroit or Consolidation Coal to Baltimore because the market was better there than on the New York Stock Exchange.[38] The transformation of communications, then, did not simply deliver securities trading in the United States into the passive hands of the New York Stock Exchange and its members, for both had to change and compete in order to retain the business they already had and to gain a growing share of what was being created.[39]

It was not sufficient for the number of brokers in New York simply to expand in line with any increase in the volume and variety of business. That would merely have produced a market that was bigger but not better than elsewhere, and one that might have become worse through the lack of personal contact and the complexity of arranging deals involving so many intermediaries. Increasingly, refinements were added to the operations of the New York Stock Exchange whereby it became better than any of its rivals. In particular, among its membership there were those who

Table 6.3 *New York and Boston Stock Exchanges, Comparison, 1904*

(a) Transactions of brokers having seats in both New York and Boston, 14 March–14 April 1904

			Stocks listed on both exchanges			
	Amalgamated Copper	Atchison, Topeka & SF	Union Pacific	Am. Sugar Refining	US Steel	Total
Boston sales	122,603	42,192	48,938	29,916	42,356	286,005
New York sales	853,000	902,000	2,215,600	174,500	1,129,400	5,274,500
Boston sales in New York	63,093	57,854	103,803	27,260	78,555	330,565

(b) Business of the Boston Stock Exchange, 2–14 May 1904

Category	Total amount	Proportion
Local Stocks	137,693	65.7%
Arbitrage Stocks	71,887	34.3%
Total	209,580	

Source: Boston Stock Exchange: Committee on Ways and Means of Increasing the Business of the Exchange, Minutes 14 April 1904, 15 May 1904, 3 June 1904.

began to concentrate upon particular aspects of the securities market, with the result that they became experts, able to offer a service superior to that of any of their competitors. The personnel of the New York Stock Exchange, as in the other eastern cities, consisted initially of brokers buying and selling securities for their clients on commission, and giving advice on the state of the market. Few if any of these operated as full-time stockbrokers, but combined it with a variety of other pursuits. However, as turnover grew these brokers began to devote themselves full time to dealing in stocks and bonds. This was certainly the case with the New York broker James W. Bleecker, who did more in marine insurance than stockbroking in his early years before coming to concentrate on securities. By the 1840s professional stockbrokers had emerged in New York.[40] For many exchanges outside New York this was as far as specialization went, with the whole market consisting of commission brokers conducting a buying and selling business directly for the general public, plus a few deals for themselves because of their expert knowledge and suitable connections. In New York, though, a much more sophisticated pattern evolved. On the one hand, new classes of brokers emerged, who still bought and sold on commission but for different reasons and in particular segments of the market. On the other hand, there developed various groups of brokers who largely ceased to do business for the general public, and concentrated upon dealing in securities for the benefit of themselves or for the firms in which they were partners.[41]

The capacity of the New York Stock Exchange member to conduct business of any kind was also greatly enhanced in this period through the adoption of 'special' partners. By this means it required only one partner of a New York brokerage firm to be a member of the Exchange for all to receive the privileges of membership, especially that of buying and selling at reduced commission rates. Seats on the Stock Exchange were consequently owned more and more by large and often diversified firms, which supported their securities operations with a large staff and substantial capital.[42] Even as early as 1821 the New York brokerage firm of Clarkson & Co. was financed by a loan of $16,000 from John O'Connor, an army officer, but the scale became much greater later in the century. A single broker with a seat on the exchange, such as Eugene Del Mar, still required a loan of $90,000 from his brother Walter in 1891 in order to support his operations; while a larger firm like Field, Lindley & Co. employed in 1882 $650,000 belonging to Cyrus W. Field alone.[43] Illustrative of the scale of operations by the early twentieth century was the firm of Hayden, Stone & Co., which was a member of both the New York and Boston Stock Exchanges. Between 1909 and 1913 this firm bought and sold securities totalling $990 million, or $198 million per annum, of which 72.5 per cent was done in New York and 27.5 per cent in Boston. For this it received in commission income alone a total of $1.66 million gross, or $1.2 million net, but paid out over $2 million in expenses, principally on salaries to staff (56 per cent), communications (11 per cent) and office rent (10 per cent). The firm also engaged in borrowing and lending money, and in selling newly issued securities (Table 6.4).

In addition to the capital possessed by the brokerage firm itself, New York brokers had access to far greater amounts. Through intimate connections with the New York banks large lines of credit could be obtained, with the securities purchased by the firm – on either its own or its clients' account – being used as collateral. Banks would usually lend 80 per cent of the market value against gilt-edged securities, such as first-class railroad or government bonds.[44] Thus Hayden, Stone & Co.'s capital of $3.8 million in 1906 could, if fully utilized, be translated into a potential credit of $10 million, when it was used as a 20 per cent margin with banks for loans against securities.[45] In addition, it was common practice for brokers to extend loans to clients for up to 90 per cent of the market value of the securities involved, on condition that these securities remained in the possession of the firm and could be pledged with a bank at the 20 per cent margin. Indicative of the extent to which this happened is the fact that over 50 per cent of the common stock of US Steel was held in brokers' names at any one time between 1905 and 1913, and the same picture was true for other active securities belonging to large corporations.[46]

In turn, other clients often left money on interest-bearing deposit with brokerage firms when they were not employing it themselves, such as between selling one security and buying another. The result was that the finance available to any individual broker or firm was far greater than that supplied by the partners themselves, which itself expanded enormously in the course of the nineteenth century. New

Table 6.4   *Hayden, Stone & Co., Boston and New York, 1909–13*

(a)   Volume of business, 1909–13

Location	Purchases	Sales	Total	Proportion	Per annum (average)
New York	$349.2m	$368.2m	$717.4m	72.5%	$143.5m
Boston	$135.0m	$137.4m	$272.4m	27.5%	$54.5m
Total	$484.2m	$505.6m	$989.8m	—	—
Average (per annum)	$96.8m	$101.2m	$198.0m	—	—

(b)   Communication expenses, 1909–13

	Telegraph	Telephone	Ticker	Total
Total	$14,335	$18,968	$16,566	$49,869
Proportion	28.7%	38.0%	33.2%	—
Average (per annum)	$2,867	$3,794	$3,313	$9,974

(c)   Commission and interest, 1909–13

	Commission		Interest	
	Total	Annual Average	Total	Annual Average
Received	$1,595,191	$319,038	$7,076,525	$1,415,305
Paid	$351,019	$70,204	$6,205,891	$1,241,178
Net	$1,244,172	$248,834	$870,634	$174,127

(d)   Comparative costs: Boston and New York, 1909–13

	Total		Selected items	
		Salaries	Rent	Communications (incl. post and circulars)
Boston	$965,237	$486,465	$110,803	$114,383
New York	$1,028,952	$632,270	$95,410	$107,220
Total	$1,994,189	$1,118,735	$206,213	$221,603
Proportion of total		56.1%	10.3%	11.1%

Source: Hayden, Stone & Co., Summary Ledger (Harvard Business School, Baker Library).

York brokerage firms regularly extended credit to brokers on other exchanges with whom they had close business connections; Logan & Bryan had a $0.5 million loan outstanding to an interior firm in February 1913, for example.[47] By 1912 altogether 22 per cent of the entire banking reserves of the United States were placed with banks and trust companies located in New York City, and New York banks had a total of $767 million outstanding, secured on Stock Exchange collateral.[48] On the New York Exchange the individual brokers of the early nineteenth century, financed either by themselves or by friends and relatives, had by the early twentieth century been largely replaced by partners in large, well-staffed and well-equipped firms commanding vast capitals, both directly and indirectly.

As the number of securities traded increased, the volume of business grew and the physical size of the floor expanded, brokers were forced to spend more and more of their time touring the market, buying and selling for customers. This led to the appearance of the $2 broker, so called because he charged a commission to fellow members of only one-fiftieth of a per cent. The $2 broker specialized in accepting commissions from other brokers and then roving the market until they were completed. As a consequence, the normal commission broker was released to deal with other business, such as keeping in touch with his clients and generating more buying and selling to be passed through to the floor and the $2 broker. The efforts of the $2 broker thus ensured that sales and purchases could be made rapidly and at the best price, despite the growing scale of operations on the Exchange.[49]

The growing financial requirements of security trading also led to the creation of money brokers. These were brokers who developed intimate connections with the principal New York banks and trust companies, receiving commission on the money they lent. They became important channels through which these institutions lent out money to brokers. A firm such as Griesel & Rogers received money from the City, Chase and Hanover banks; from the Bank of Commerce; and from investment bankers like Kuhn, Loeb & Co., Goldman Sachs & Co. and Speyers, which they then lent out to other brokers. By 1912 these money brokers were handling $40 to $50 million a day on the floor of the Exchange. At the same time most brokers made direct arrangements with specific banks to cover their normal volume of business, using the money broker to meet sudden or exceptional needs.[50] A few other brokers in addition became intermediaries in arranging the lending or borrowing of securities, again receiving commission for their trouble. This was essential under the daily delivery system that operated on the New York Stock Exchange, as it was not always possible to produce in time the securities which had been sold. Not only had purchases to be financed by borrowing from the money brokers, but sales had to be fulfilled through borrowing the appropriate stocks and bonds from other brokers.[51]

A growing number of members of the New York Stock Exchange abandoned the commission business entirely or largely, and went into business on their own account, buying and selling solely for the profit such transactions brought. Such individuals had begun to make their appearances before the Civil War, and by 1865 they were well established, according to Hamon: 'Many who belong to the Stock Board never execute an order, or make a purchase or sale of stock, except on their own account – they are known especially under the name of stockjobbers.'[52]

These stock jobbers, variously known as merchants, traders, or market makers, employed their own and borrowed funds to buy, sell and hold securities in expectation of making a living from the difference between the buying and selling prices that occurred during the course of a day's trading, or over a longer period. Their contribution to the New York Stock Exchange was that, by being willing to buy when other brokers wanted to sell, and to sell when the rest wanted to buy, they created a market where securities could be readily bought and sold in the required amounts at whatever time. Without them any large selling order would produce a dramatic collapse of price, through an inability of the market to absorb that amount of securities, while a large buying order would create a steep price rise through a failure of the market to meet demand. The existence of these market makers meant that the dealing by call in twice-daily sessions, whereby a list of securities was read out and business conducted in rota, was already irrelevant long before it was officially abandoned, as it had been replaced by a continuous market in the active securities.[53]

With the growth of this market in both volume and variety these market makers themselves became more specialized, leading to the appearance of the aptly named 'specialist'. The specialist concentrated upon trading in one or a few securities, and dealt in that throughout the day, quoting buy and sell prices with a small spread to yield a profit, and being always ready to purchase or deliver what was required. However, the specialist did accept orders from other brokers, at a commission of one-fiftieth per cent, to buy or sell securities at a certain price, or within a certain price range, when that became possible. Again, this freed the commission broker from spending the whole day in the market trying to arrange a deal at the price requested by a client.[54] As the *New York Tribune* reported in 1914: 'The specialist was born out of the inability of the average commission house broker to be in a dozen places at once.'[55] The result was that almost every stock listed on the New York Stock Exchange by the First World War was covered by at least one specialist, who made a market in it or was willing to accept commission orders. Many less active securities shared the same one, while the most heavily traded commanded the attention of numerous specialists. US Steel, for instance, had eleven specialists devoted to making a market in it, while a railroad such as the Reading involved nine, and the Union Pacific and Erie had seven apiece. The more a security was bought and sold, the greater the number of specialists who traded in it, and thus the easier it was to transact business at the most competitive prices, with a tiny spread between bid and sell.[56]

Complementing the specialist, who remained stationary at his post all day, was the floor trader, who also operated on his own account but continually moved throughout the market. The floor trader concentrated upon a range of similar securities, with which he became familiar and whose prices he monitored continually. Sales and purchases were made depending on the evaluation of future trends in the market as a whole or due to discrepancies that appeared in individual price trends. However, these floor traders were always willing to switch attention to any part of the market that became particularly active. The actions of the floor traders ensured that the prices of any security, or group of securities, did not get out of line with the others traded on the Exchange, for they would tend to sell a stock whose price appeared to be rising too rapidly or to buy one whose price was falling too quickly. They added both stability and flexibility to the market and ensured that all prices moved broadly in line.[57]

One of the last specialists to develop was the odd-lot broker. On the New York Stock Exchange the conventional minimum dealing unit was for 100 shares, and few brokerage firms would deal for less than this, or for amounts that were not simple multiples. Small deals did not repay the time spent, while strange amounts involved considerable administrative inconvenience. As a result amounts of under 100 units or odd numbers traded at a slight discount or premium to the current market price, depending on the nature of demand. Hence, there appeared brokers who specialized in either buying these odd lots, combining them to form normal units and then selling them at the market price, or buying standard lots and splitting them to make the amounts required.[58] The actions of the odd-lot broker, in combination with the other specialists and floor traders, ensured that the New York Stock Exchange could offer a market that would meet the needs of any broker's client to buy and sell whenever he wanted and in the amounts he desired, without the broker having to spend time and effort on negotiating a special deal, which would involve both delay and expense.

Finally, there also developed a class of brokers called arbitrageurs who specialized in trading between the New York Stock Exchange and other exchanges. Many of the securities quoted in New York were not unique to itself but were common to most securities markets, especially the larger and more active issues. In 1904, for instance, New York shared with Boston the market in the Atchison, Topeka & Santa Fe and Union Pacific railroads, the Amalgamated Copper and American Sugar Refining companies, as well as US Steel (see Table 6.3). Some of these, plus others, were also shared with other markets not only within the United States but also abroad. The *Commercial and Financial Chronicle* noted in 1890: 'Many new issues are listed almost simultaneously in New York and London', and added that the same was increasingly true for New York and Amsterdam, Berlin and Frankfurt.[59] Wherever the identical securities were being traded, there were opportunities for arbitrageurs to profit from buying in one market and selling in another when price differences arose.

Even before the telegraph, arbitrage of a kind took place, as witness Lorde and Anspach in the 1790s, but it grew enormously once an almost instantaneous means of communication was provided, while the number of mutually quoted securities also rose, especially during and after the Civil War.[60] This led New York brokerage firms to establish trading relationships with members of other exchanges for the buying and selling of shared securities. Groesbeck & Scholey of New York, for example, had an arrangement with De Haven & Townsend of Philadelphia in 1880 to trade in the stock of the Northern Pacific and Reading railroads between the two markets. This involved the two firms operating in joint account, whereby all costs and profits were shared and no commission was charged for any purchases or sales made.[61] However, these arrangements between separate brokers in different markets were gradually replaced by operations within those brokerage firms which purchased membership on the appropriate exchange, invested heavily in private wires and telephone lines and employed expert staff. By 1894 there were twenty-six members of the New York Stock Exchange that were also members of the Boston Stock Exchange, and it was through these jointly represented firms, like Charles Head & Co. and Barnes & Cunningham, that the arbitrage business was almost entirely conducted between those two cities.[62]

Such was the degree of competition existing between those firms engaged in domestic arbitrage, especially between New York and Boston and Philadelphia, that every effort was made to provide the fastest possible inter-market communications. The *New York Tribune* observed in 1892 that 'In order to benefit by the difference in markets the transactions have to be done quickly, and to facilitate the operation the brokers use a system of signalling with the fingers from the floor of the exchange to men stationed at telephones. Some houses have as many as five special men to attend to this business alone.'[63] Through these means, and the general improvement in communications and expertise, the differential in prices between the principal East Coast exchanges, in the securities that they traded in common, was reduced. The difference between New York and Philadelphia in Reading railroad stock in 1870 averaged a mere 0.19 per cent, while by 1904 it took a gap of less than one-eighth per cent (0.125 per cent) to provoke an immediate rush of compensating buying and selling orders from the arbitrageurs, which restored price equality. Thus 1870 registered a 24-fold improvement over the 4.5 per cent of the 1790s, while 1904 showed a 36-fold gain.[64]

A similar development occurred internationally with the completion of the first transatlantic cable in 1866. The London Stock

Exchange already quoted certain US securities that were traded on the New York Stock Exchange, such as US government bonds, and these were augmented by numerous other US securities, which were also increasingly found generally in western Europe. This led to arbitrage connections being established between members of the New York Stock Exchange and their counterparts in London, initially, and later Amsterdam, Berlin, Frankfurt and Paris. Though a few New York brokerage firms did open offices abroad, they were denied membership of European stock exchanges, and so arbitrage operations continued to take place on the basis of joint-account trading between separate firms. Nevertheless, it reached a very high degree of sophistication that was sufficient to reduce the difference in the prices of active securities between New York and London, for instance, to the level of only one-eighth or even one-sixteenth per cent by the early twentieth century.[65]

Eames described the procedure for international arbitrage in 1894:

> In the foreign arbitrage operations, the member gives the New York quotation to his clerk outside the rail, who writes the cable message, passes it to the telegraph office within the Exchange, from which it starts for London or other European Stock Exchange. An answer from London is expected in four minutes, within which time . . . the Atlantic Ocean has been twice traversed, a distance of over six thousand miles.[66]

This involved both considerable skill and confidence in the correspondent on the other exchange, and so the New York firms that engaged in international arbitrage often either drew their staff or partners from abroad or had the foreign broker or his clerk to work with them for a short time. N. E. Holden from London, for instance, spent some time on the floor with Knauth, Macleod & Kuhne, while C. F. Woerishoffer, who arbitraged between New York and Frankfurt, had migrated from Germany.[67] Another firm, Raymond Pynchon & Co., even paid Sir Arthur Elliot in London a salary of $10,000 per annum, because 'the details of their foreign business . . . have grown so complex that they find it necessary to have an experienced man, familiar with both the foreign and domestic markets'.[68]

The consequence of this domestic and international arbitrage was that an integrated securities market was created which covered both

North America and western Europe, with the New York Stock Exchange as its principal American component, maintaining constant contact with exchanges as distant as Chicago, San Francisco, Montreal and Toronto. Price divergences in the numerous commonly held securities were quickly rectified, and through that a great degree of uniformity and stability was possible. On the very eve of the partial collapse of the system with the outbreak of the First World War, the *New York Tribune* concluded:

> Arbitrage operations among the great security markets of the world tend to annihilate space and time. They come as close to establishing the same price for the same thing at the same time in all important markets as anything humanly devised could hope to do. In that way they tend to reduce fluctuations in prices and place investors all over the world on an equal footing.[69]

At the same time as the arbitrageurs made New York essential to the maintenance of a North American and transatlantic securities market, the continuing specialization among all the membership of the New York Stock Exchange resulted in that institution being able to provide a more continuous and active market than any other within the United States. In terms of the volume of securities to be bought or sold, the speed at which it could be done, the narrowest spread between buy and sell prices, and the ease of arranging finance, no other stock exchange in the Americas could challenge the New York Stock Exchange, and so it attracted business from throughout the nation, channelled through the broker networks and contacts, and the telegraph and telephone lines.[70]

Notes

1 M. V. Sears, 'Gold and the Local Stock Exchanges of the 1860s', *Explorations in Entrepreneurial History*, vol. 6 (1968–9), p. 198.
2 Quoted in T. W. Lawson, *High Cost Living* (Dreamworld, Mass., 1913), p. 85.
3 K. Cornwallis, *The Gold Room, and the New York Stock Exchange and Clearing House* (New York, 1879), p. 37. For a similar opinion written in 1908 see H. Clews, 'Some Notes on the American Position', *Financial Review of Reviews*, May 1908.

4 *Report of the Committee Appointed to Investigate the Concentration of Control of Money and Credit* (US Congressional House Committee, 28 February 1913), p. 115.

5 Cf. J. E. Hedges, *Commercial Banking and the Stock Market before 1863* (Baltimore, 1938), p. 38; R. N. Owens and C. O. Hardy, *Interest Rates and Stock Speculation: A Study of the Influence of the Money Market on the Stock Market* (New York, 1965), p. 53.

6 H. S. Martin, *The New York Stock Exchange* (New York, 1919), p. 182; US Department of Commerce, *Historical Statistics of the United States* (Washington, 1975), Series F 377–421.

7 J. H. Hollander, *Bank Loans and Stock Exchange Speculation* (Washington, 1911), p. 23; cf. *Manual of Statistics* (New York, 1901).

8 US Department of Commerce, *Historical Statistics*, Series F 287–96; H. Porter, 'One Hundred Years of New York Commerce', in C. M. Depew (ed.), *One Hundred Years of American Commerce, 1795–1895* (New York, 1895), pp. 55–62.

9 J. E. Meeker, *The Work of the Stock Exchange* (New York, 1930), ch. III.

10 Memorial and Remonstrance of the Board of Stock and Exchange Brokers of the City of New York to the State of New York Assembly, 23 March 1836, Standish Lorde, Philadelphia, to Peter Anspach, New York, 19, 21, 22 March 1792.

11 H. E. Kroos and M. R. Blyn, *A History of Financial Intermediaries* (London, 1971), pp. 19–22, 33; J. P. Townsend, 'Wall Street', in Depew, *American Commerce*, pp. 67–75.

12 D. K. Van Veghten, Prices of Stocks and Rates of Exchange, 27 October 1820–18 April 1821; G. A. Rollins, Call Quotation Book, 17 September 1835–26 March 1836; R. Sobel, *The Big Board* (New York, 1965), pp. 22–4, 44.

13 R. B. Duboff, 'The Telegraph and the Structure of Markets in the United States, 1845–1890', *Research in Economic History*, vol. 8 (1982), p. 261; cf. C. W. Barren *et al.*, *The Boston Stock Exchange, 1839–1893* (Boston, 1893), no pagination.

14 V. S. Pratt, *The Work of Wall Street* (New York, 1903), p. 50; J. G. Martin, *A Century of Finance: History of the Boston Stock and Money Markets, 1798–1898* (Boston, 1898), p. 29.

15 Standish Lorde to Peter Anspach, 25 February 1792; cf. 12 February 1792–2 October 1792.

16 Memorial and Remonstrance, p. 7.

17 *New York Tribune*, 13 February 1890.

18 Cf. C. P. Kindleberger, *The Formation of Financial Centers: A Study in Comparative Economic History* (Princeton, 1974), p. 11.

19 A. W. Barnes, *History of the Philadelphia Stock Exchange, Banks and Banking Interest* (Philadelphia, 1911), p. 9; Newcomen Society, *The Story of the Philadelphia Stock Exchange* (Philadelphia, 1976), p. 11.

20 US Department of Commerce, *Historical Statistics*, Series R71–4 1271–4; Duboff, 'Telegraph and Structure of Markets', pp. 253–7;

Hedges, *Commercial Banking*, pp. 39, 112; Pratt, *Work of Wall Street*, p. 15; *Railroad Review*, 24 December 1887.

21 US Department of Commerce, *Historical Statistics*, Series R 13–16; F. S. Dickson, *Telephone Investments and Others* (Cleveland, 1905), pp. 40–1; Duboff, 'Telegraph and Structure of Markets', p. 268; J. E. Hudson, 'The Telephone', in Depew, *American Commerce*, p. 134. G. P. & A. W. Butler, New York, to William Stanley, Charleston, South Carolina, 6 December 1909; *New York Tribune*, 20 September 1892.

22 Sales on the New York Stock and Exchange Board, 1860. W. A. Armstrong, *Stocks and Stock-Jobbing in Wall Street* (New York, 1848), pp. 29, 32; H. Hamon, *New York Stock Exchange Manual* (New York, 1865), pp. 240, 307.

23 Tunbridge & Co., *Secrets of Success in Wall Street* (New York, 1875), pp. 9–10.

24 Gold & Stock Telegraph Co., Statement to New York Stock Exchange, 2 March 1874; cf. F. L. Eames, *The New York Stock Exchange* (New York, 1894), p. 90; Reply by the New York Stock Exchange to the Governor's Committee on Speculation in Securities and Commodities, 15 February 1909.

25 L. W. Hamilton & Co., *Stock Speculation* (New York, 1875), p. 3; cf. John Hickling & Co., *Men and Idioms of Wall Street* (New York, 1875), p. 4; E. C. Stedman, (ed.), *The New York Stock Exchange* (New York, 1905), pp. 434, 437, 441; S. S. Huebner, *The Stock Market* (New York, 1922), p. 180.

26 E. G. Nourse, *Brokerage* (New York, 1910), p. 24.

27 Haight & Freese, *Guide to Investors* (New York, 1898), pp. 48, 52; cf. C. W. Morgan & Co., *How to Speculate Successfully in Wall Street* (New York, 1900), p. 59.

28 Clapp & Co., *Weekly Market Letters for 1893* (New York, 1984), 3 March 1893; cf. Hickling & Co., *Men and Idioms*, p. 4.

29 J. K. Medbery, *Old Times in Wall Street* (New York, 1871, repr. 1891), pp. 39, 195–6; cf. Eames, *New York Stock Exchange*, p. 90.

30 Stedman, *New York Stock Exchange*, p. 11; Pratt, *Work of Wall Street*, pp. 102, 142; *Report of Committee . . . Concentration of Control*, p. 33; Lawson, *High Cost Living*, p. 82; B. E. Schultz, *Stock Exchange Procedure* (New York, 1936), p. 12; *New York Stock Exchange* (New York, 1886), p. 77.

31 Cf. Correspondence of G. P. and A. W. Butler, 11 July 1906, 3 January 1907, 15 February 1907, 16 March 1907, 19 March 1907, 10 September 1908.

32 New York Stock Exchange (NYSE): Committee on Commissions, Minutes, 14 March 1904.

33 NYSE: Committee on Commissions, Minutes, 20 June 1881.

34 Pratt, *Work of Wall Street*, p. 93, NYSE: Committee on Clearing House, Minutes, 28 July 1903; *New York Stock Exchange* (1886) pp. 63, 69, 115.

35 Reply by NYSE to Committee on Speculation, p. 26.
36 US Senate, *Regulation of the Stock Exchange: Hearings before the Committee on Banking and Currency* (Washington, 1914), pp. 453, 529; NYSE: Special Investigation Committee, Continuous Quotations, Transcripts, 27 January 1903; cf. US Congress, *Investigation of Financial and Monetary Conditions* '(Money Trust Investigation'; Washington, 1912), pp. 827, 835.
37 Butler to M. Goebel, 13 December 1910.
38 NYSE: Committee on Commissions, Minutes, 9 July 1909, 4 January 1911.
39 Duboff, 'Telegraph and Structure of Markets', p. 262.
40 Cf. Correspondence of J. W. Bleecker, New York City, 1804–1863; Sobel, *Big Board*, p. 31, 62, 73; Stedman, *New York Stock Exchange*, pp. 445–6.
41 Stedman, *New York Stock Exchange*, pp. 448–50; *Harper's Monthly Magazine* 71, November 1885.
42 Cf. the activities of the following firms: Haight & Freese, *Guide to Investors*; N. W. Harris & Co., *Municipal Bonds* (New York, 1897); Fisk & Hatch, *Memoranda Concerning Government Bonds* (New York, 1882).
43 Clarkson & Co. to John M. O'Connor, 11 October 1821, 27 May 1822; Walter Del Mar & Co., Article of Agreement, 3 April 1891; Field Lindley & Co. to C. W. Field, 1 February 1882.
44 Hamon, *New York Stock Exchange Manual*, p. 17; Hamilton & Co., *Stock Speculation*, p. 8; Cornwallis, *The Gold Room*, p. 35; Pratt, *Work of Wall Street*, p. 93.
45 Hayden, Stone & Co., Private Ledger, 1899–1906.
46 US Congress, Money Trust Investigation, p. 798; Pratt, *Work of Wall Street*, pp. 181, 185.
47 NYSE: Committee on Commissions, Minutes, 11 February 1913; Haight & Freese, *Guide to Investors*, p. 6; Harris & Co., *Municipal Bonds*, p. 33, Fisk & Hatch, *Memoranda*, p. 288.
48 W. M. Blaisdell, *Financing Security Trading* (Philadelphia, 1935), pp. 27, 45; US Congress, Money Trust Investigation, pp. 55, 955–6.
49 H. J. Howland, 'Gambling Joint or Market Place? An Inquiry into the Workings of the New York Stock Exchange', *The Outlook*, 28 June 1913, p. 427; Pratt, *Work of Wall Street*, p. 94; Huebner, *The Stock Market*, pp. 148–53; Schultz, *Stock Exchange Procedure*, p. 55.
50 US Congress, Money Trust Investigation, pp. 743–8, 753–4; Huebner, *The Stock Market*, pp. 148–53; Howland, 'Gambling Joint', p. 431.
51 Stedman, *New York Stock Exchange*, pp. 448–50.
52 Hamon, *New York Stock Exchange Manual*, p. 107, cf. pp. 106, 109.
53 J. H. Failing, *A Treatise on Stock-Dealing and the Gold Conspiracy* (Fort Plain, 1870), p. 4; Medbery, *Old Times in Wall Street*, p. 39; Hamilton & Co., *Stock Speculation*, p. 27; Eames, *The New York Stock Exchange*, p. 50.
54 Pratt, *Work of Wall Street*, p. 94; Howland, 'Gambling Joint', p. 427;

Huebner, *The Stock Market*, pp. 143–8; Schultz, *Stock Exchange Procedure*, p. 58; W. C. Van Antwerp, *The Stock Exchange from within* (New York, 1913), pp. 279–80; Reply by NYSE to Committee on Speculation, pp. 35–6.

55 *New York Tribune*, 6 July 1914.

56 NYSE: Special Committee on Ways and Means Subcommittee on Odd Lots, 19 July 1921; *New York Tribune*, 6 July 1914.

57 Pratt, *Work of Wall Street*, p. 94; Huebner, *The Stock Market*, pp. 143–8, Schultz, *Stock Exchange Procedure*, p. 64; US Congress, Money Trust Investigation, Brief of Counsel on Behalf of the New York Stock Exchange, p. 530; *New York Herald*, 4 May 1902; NYSE: Committee on Commissions, 25 November 1900.

58 S. A. Nelson (ed.), *The ABC of Wall Street* (New York, 1900), p. 18; Howland, 'Gambling Joint', p. 438; Huebner, *The Stock Market*, pp. 143–8; *Regulation of the Stock Exchange, Hearings*, p. 140.

59 *Commercial and Financial Chronicle*, 5 July 1890, cf. chapters on the London Stock Exchange and the international securities market.

60 Van Antwerp, *Stock Exchange*, p. 283, Huebner, *The Stock Market*, pp. 87, 143–8; US Congress, Money Trust Investigation, NYSE, p. 530.

61 NYSE: Committee on Commissions, 30 December 1880, 5 January 1881, 11 January 1881.

62 NYSE: Committee on Arrangements, 14 March 1904; NYSE: Committee on Commissions, 23 April 1894; Barren *et al.*, *Boston Stock Exchange*; NYSE: Special Investigation Committee, Continuous Quotations, 21, 22, 27 January 1903.

63 *New York Tribune*, 20 September 1892; cf. Eames, *New York Stock Exchange*, p. 90.

64 NYSE: Sales of Stock, 1870; Gelpin & Co., Record of Prices and Sales on the Philadelphia Stock Exchange, 1904; NYSE: Committee on Arrangements, Appendix, 14 June 1904.

65 S. F. Streit, *Report on European Stock Exchanges* (New York, 1914), p. 9; Pratt, *Work of Wall Street*, p. 114; Van Antwerp, *Stock Exchange*, pp. 283–4; Huebner, *The Stock Market*, pp. 88–97; A. Cragg, *Understanding the Stock Market* (New York, 1929), pp. 210–13.

66 Eames, *New York Stock Exchange*, p. 90.

67 NYSE: Common Arrangements, 14 December 1903, 14 February 1905, 20 November 1905, 27 November 1905, 18 December 1905, 26 December 1905; *New York Tribune*, 11 May 1886.

68 NYSE: Committee on Commissions, 29 December 1910.

69 *New York Tribune*, 15 June 1914.

70 Huebner, *The Stock Market*, pp. 20–30; Howland, 'Gambling Joint', p. 436; Reply by NYSE to Committee on Speculation, pp. 35–6.

7 The New York Stock Exchange and the Securities Market II

Most of the changes that took place in the New York Stock Exchange, or with which it was associated, assisted it in becoming the premier securities market of the United States. Its willingness to incorporate all the new advances in communications technology from their first appearance aided its national coverage, while the freedom it allowed its membership to specialize in function, spread in location and increase in capital helped to improve the quality and availability of the service it provided. This was not the case in all instances, though, for a number of the rules under which the Stock Exchange forced its membership to operate restricted or discouraged the members from actively competing for all business. Measures taken to enforce certain of these rules also undermined the position of the Stock Exchange in the securities market, both at home and abroad. Rival exchanges were always ready to exploit any restrictions that New York might impose, while there was no law that forced brokers to become members of a stock exchange in order to trade. The success of the New York Stock Exchange rested upon the self-interest of its members and the benefits they obtained from joining, not upon any monopoly conferred upon it by legislation at city, state, or federal level.

The most obvious restriction that the New York Stock Exchange imposed was the limitation on membership. After the merger with the 'Open Board', in 1869, the number admitted was set at 1,060; and this was increased only once, by 40 in 1879, before the First World War. At the same time the volume of business expanded considerably (Table 7.1). Between 1879 and 1909 the amount of common stock sold rose from 73 million to 212 million, while its

Table 7.1   New York Stock Exchange, Sales, 1879–1913

Year	Stocks (million)	Bonds (million)
1879	73	571
1880	96	644
1881	117	486
1882	117	294
1883	98	314
1884	96	527
1885	93	682
1886	104	649
1887	86	374
1888	63	353
1889	62	398
1890	59	379
1891	72	392
1892	87	503
1893	78	301
1894	33	355
1895	52	503
1896	42	386
1897	63	542
1898	86	872
1899	121	752
1900	139	579
1901	265	995
1902	187	893
1903	158	686
1904	187	1,033
1905	261	1,026
1906	282	677
1907	195	530
1908	195	1,081
1909	212	1,314
1910	164	635
1911	127	890
1912	131	675
1913	83	502

Sources: E. C. Stedman (ed.), The New York Stock Exchange (New York, 1905), pp. 473–4; P. Wyckoff, Wall Street and the Stock Markets: A Chronology, 1644–1971 (Philadelphia, 1972), p. 155; US Department of Commerce, Historical Statistics of the United States (Washington, 1975), Series X 531–53.

estimated value increased from $4.16 billion to $19.1 billion, or a threefold rise in number and fivefold in value. Reflecting the fact that membership was restricted, and did not meet demand, was the fact that the cost of purchasing a place rose between $14,000 and $26,000 in 1880 to between $65,000 and $94,000 in 1910, or approximately fourfold.[1]

The consequence was that there were many brokers who could not gain admission to the New York Stock Exchange because of either cost or the lack of availability of seats to purchase. They became a sizeable group in New York and competed for business with the members. Simultaneously, those brokers who were admitted to membership could not cope with all the available trade, despite the growing size and sophistication of the brokerage firms. 'They have as much business as they can attend to now, and the present brokers have so much else to do that they could not attend to orders in mining stocks' was the conclusion of one member in 1879, and a similar view was expressed in 1906.[2] The only solution would have been to liberalize entry, but that would have reduced the benefits enjoyed by the existing membership, and so was strongly resisted. Thus, by limiting numbers the New York Stock Exchange both reduced its own ability to transact all the available business and created a group of non-members who would undertake anything left undone.

Arising from the control on membership was the Stock Exchange's increasing unwillingness to grant a quotation to all the securities for which application was made. Even before the Civil War the Exchange was beginning to concentrate upon the larger and more active issues, as it was these that produced the maximum amount of turnover with the smallest commitment of time. The occasional transaction in the stock of a local gas or insurance company involved considerable trouble for a small commission, while the regular buying and selling of the securities issued by the government or an inter-state railroad produced a large volume of business and a correspondingly large aggregate commission. Thus the Stock Exchange progressively dropped the securities of individual small local concerns and refused the quotation of others, in order to concentrate upon the large issues.[3] This tendency was accelerated during the Civil War when trading in the federal debt, which rose from $65 million in 1860 to $2.8 billion in 1866, dominated all activity on the Exchange.[4]

The New York Stock Exchange emerged from the Civil War as a specialist market in individually large issues of securities, as represented by the borrowings of government, and this was a position it maintained thenceforth. Trading in insurance company shares was abandoned, despite its earlier importance, while mining securities were similarly neglected, though earlier attempts had been made to stimulate activity in the stocks of the larger coal-and copper-mining enterprises.[5] As dealing in federal and state debt declined through redemption, the stocks and bonds of the largest railroads took their place, and they were continually supplemented by the securities of the leading concerns in the fields of urban transit and manufacturing. By the four-year period 1880–3 the proportion of federal debt in the turnover in bonds had already fallen to 8 per cent, compared to the 92 per cent provided by state and railroad bonds. In 1910–13 all forms of government debt comprised only 7 per cent of turnover, while the corporate sector provided the rest. Within the corporate sector railroads slowly gave way to the securities issued by companies operating in increasingly more diverse areas of the economy, but this came mainly after 1900. As late as 1897, 69 per cent of the turnover in stocks was provided by railroads, but this had fallen to under half (48 per cent) by 1912.[6]

Illustrating the large individual size of the securities quoted by the New York Stock Exchange was the fact that in 1913 the average par value of the 1,089 different issues of bonds was $11.6 million, while for the 565 stocks it was $23.7 million. Many of these stocks and bonds in turn belonged to the same corporations. The 215 stocks listed in 1893 had been issued by only 155 companies, for instance. These securities were also actively traded, with 4,635 transactions per bond issue (assuming a par value of $100) and 162,131 per stock issue in 1913, and that year was a poor one for Stock Exchange business. In 1901, for example, the figures were 11,632 for bonds and 699,037 for stocks. Within these some were far more actively bought and sold than others. The stocks issued by the ten most traded companies provided 62.3 per cent of total turnover in 1893 compared to the 0.003 per cent accounted for by the ten least traded, though both comprised 6.5 per cent of the companies quoted.[7] The Stock Exchange specialized in providing a market for a limited number of stocks and bonds belonging to an ever smaller number of organizations and, within that, concentrated upon trading in a tiny minority of these.

The New York Stock Exchange did not discriminate solely on size and potential turnover; for there was also a strong prejudice against volatile securities or those of unproven companies, because of the risks involved. Sudden price changes could cause large losses, resulting in the collapse of individual brokerage firms and undermining the stability of the market, while the failure or difficulties of quoted companies would reflect badly on the others, lowering their status and discouraging investment. For these reasons the Stock Exchange was extremely careful to vet the stocks and bonds it admitted to quotation, seeking for reasons to refuse rather than accept. The securities most affected by this policy were those of mining companies, which tended by the very nature of their business to have an erratic and often brief life. Oil was similarly regarded, as were industrial and commercial concerns until they had proved themselves both individually and as a sector. The Stock Exchange was not a market for either small, new, or risky ventures but one for large, established and secure corporations or the issues of governments, at all levels but with unblemished records.[8]

Too often the members of the New York Stock Exchange assumed that trading in non-listed securities was only a temporary phenomenon and would soon collapse, as did happen from time to time. The volume of business on their own Exchange did fluctuate considerably from year to year (Table 7.1). Eventually, though, it was recognized that outside trading in certain securities, especially those of mining and manufacturing concerns, had become of major importance. The solution found was to form in 1885 an unlisted department where such securities could be traded without giving them the recognition of an official quotation. This unlisted market lasted from 1885 until 1910, when it was abandoned because there was no longer any rational justification for the division that existed. Even on the unlisted market all securities had to pass the same stringent examination concerning size of capital, number of shareholders and proven track record, while business was also dominated by the stocks of a tiny number of companies. In 1895, for instance, 435 industrial stocks were covered by the unlisted department and they generated sales of 13.6 million, but of this 94 per cent was in the securities of only three companies, namely, American Sugar Refining, National Lead and US Leather. Despite the intentions the unlisted department did not provide a substitute market for those securities denied a quotation, since the Exchange did not have the membership to handle it. Thus the principal unlisted stocks were included in the main list, and the rest were dispensed with. By then the Stock Exchange had recognized that it could not provide a general market.[9]

In order to facilitate the transaction of such a volume of business using a finite number of members the New York Stock Exchange not only restricted the securities quoted but also imposed a high minimum on the number of units in which it would deal. The normal lot was 100 stocks or bonds, or an approximate value of $10,000, which was high for most investors. This altered with the appearance of the odd-lot broker in the 1890s, but the members were never keen to undertake small sales or purchases or ones that were not simple multiples of 100. Again, the Stock Exchange concentrated upon serving the needs of the substantial investor, such as an institution, and this also had repercussions for the nature of the US securities market.[10]

Apart from the control of membership, the other restriction the New York Stock Exchange imposed that had a major consequence for the securities market was the rule that required all members to charge a minimum commission of one-eighth per cent on every transaction they handled for non-members. At a minor level, as this commission was based on a $100 par value and not the market or nominal price, it placed low-denomination or under-par securities at a serious disadvantage in terms of the costs involved in buying and selling. The outcome was that low-value securities tended not to be traded. In 1912, for example, of the 131 million shares sold, less than 19 per cent were priced at under $50, while 43 per cent were over $100. As it was mainly industrial and mining companies that used small-denomination securities to attract investors, it was they that the minimum commission rules discouraged from being traded on the Stock Exchange.[11]

More generally, however, a fixed minimum commission of one-eighth encouraged non-members to under-cut, in order to attract business away from the New York Stock Exchange. Rival brokers in New York normally charged one-sixteenth per cent, and this was the rate adopted by the Philadelphia Stock Exchange. Through the telegraph and telephone links it was relatively easy to divert orders from one market to another, and Philadelphia's lower charges helped it to attract trading in US Steel in 1904, for example. This switch was not particularly difficult for the integrated brokerage firms which had members on more than one stock exchange, such as the twenty-four New York firms with seats on the Philadelphia Stock Exchange in 1913. The only official exception the New York Exchange allowed to the commission rule was trading by members for their partners, wherever they were located, and this could go as low as one-fiftieth per cent on the floor or one-thirty-second outside.[12] Again, for the New York Stock Exchange, the result was a concentration upon business for the large security dealers who could afford to purchase seats or were partners in member firms.

In its attempts to preserve this minimum commission the New York Stock Exchange undertook measures that further altered the structure of the US securities market and, eventually, the international securities market. The introduction of the ticker-tape in 1867 and the telephone in 1878 gave non-members access to current prices; so they could deal at Exchange prices without purchasing a seat, and could charge whatever commission they chose. During the 1880s the members of the New York Stock Exchange increasingly believed that they were losing business, through customers getting their sales and purchases transacted by other brokers at less cost but at current prices. Certainly there does appear to have been a decline of sales at that time (Table 7.1). Attempts were made to restrict the availability of exchange prices by denying outside brokers access to the ticker, but this proved impossible to enforce. The ticker was too valuable and too widespread by then to withdraw it from general use, while there were always members of the Exchange who would pass on prices in expectation of the business it would bring them, and they possessed direct communications links to the floor. The most the New York Stock Exchange could do was to ban dual membership of stock exchanges within New York and to prohibit ticker and telephone links between members and non-members. However, that latter embargo was quashed by state legislation in 1913, and the former was evaded through unofficial alliances.[13]

The problem created by the minimum commission rule was not confined to New York itself but extended throughout the United States as communications created a national market. However, ticker, telegraph and telephone contact with the stock exchanges of other cities could not be severed without seriously injuring the work being done by the members of the New York Stock Exchange, which brought considerable business to that institution from throughout the country. Three principal means were used to tackle the difficulty. Joint-account arbitrage was banned, as this directly broke the minimum commission rule. Brokers conducting arbitrage did not charge each other commission and shared the costs incurred, dividing any profits or losses resulting. In the 1880s the New York Stock Exchange insisted that the one-eighth per cent commission was charged on every sale or purchase made for non-members. It also banned the practice of dealing on differences in prices between exchanges – which, of course, was the object of arbitrage. Neither of these measures was effective, because the existence of integrated brokerage firms, represented in New York and elsewhere, internalized these changes and practices and rendered the embargoes ineffective.[14]

The final solution was the prohibition on the sending of continuous quotations, upon which arbitrage depended. After a number of attempts this was implemented in an effective form in January 1898. Rapid as the ticker service was, it was too slow to take immediate account of every variation in a rapidly changing market, and so reliance upon it alone increased the risks of arbitrage. By stopping the sending of continuous quotations between New York and other exchanges, it was assumed that the completion of deals on other markets, where the commission rates were lower, would cease, as their prices would no longer reflect the current position on the floor of the New York Stock Exchange. This it appears to have done, even though certain brokerage firms still continued to conduct an active domestic arbitrage, though less obtrusively than in the past. Charles Head & Co., E. & C. Randolph and De Haven & Townsend, for example, conducted active arbitrage between New York and Boston in 1902–3 in the stocks of Amalgamated Copper and American Sugar.[15] The effect on the US securities market was to confine most of the arbitrage between New York and other exchanges to those brokerage firms that purchased dual memberships, and to divert some of this arbitrage away from the New York Stock Exchange itself to other exchanges or brokers.

These restrictions on domestic arbitrage were not applied by the Stock Exchange to its international counterparts, since it saw no threat to its minimum commission rule from the exchanges of foreign countries. In contrast, New York welcomed international arbitrage as stimulating business and encouraged it by providing for its special needs. The arbitrageurs involved were given a special position with easy access to the transatlantic telegraph (the arbitrage rail), and spaces there were increased from sixteen in 1903 to forty-two by 1910 in response to demand. The time taken to communicate between the floor and the telegraph offices was also reduced to a minimum; arbitrage put a premium on time, and firms were willing to pay $1,500 for the best places on the arbitrage rail.[16] International arbitrage also relied on joint-account trading, but in its case this violation of the rules was ignored. However, it slowly became apparent that deals could be completed more cheaply in London than in New York, and that domestic business was being lost overseas. By 1910 this drain was considered sufficiently large to warrant action, and so it was decided in April 1911 to ban joint-account arbitrage for international business. This was far more serious for international arbitrage than it was for domestic, because New York brokerage firms were not members of foreign stock exchanges and thus could not obtain the reduced commission rates.[17]

Joint-account trading was not the only means by which international arbitrage was conducted but it was by far the cheapest and most convenient. This was acknowledged by the New York Stock Exchange itself in June 1914: 'joint account arbitrage is the most scientific method, economically speaking, of trading between international markets, in that it increases freedom of operation between parties each in close touch with the local market, enlarging the volume of business. It adds broadness and stability to both markets.'[18] The result of such a ban was therefore to reduce the efficiency and increase the costs and difficulties of international arbitrage, even though it was evaded, with seventeen out of the twenty-eight New York arbitrage firms still doing joint-account business in 1914. As early as February 1912 just under half the membership of the New York Stock Exchange (528) asked for the ban to be repealed, as it was damaging business in general. This request was refused but was renewed in February 1914, when it had the support of 746 members, over two-thirds of the membership. However, the First World War intervened; the matter was allowed to lapse, with only minor modifications, but sales fell dramatically on the Stock Exchange after 1911 (Table 7.1).[19]

In its attempt to maintain the minimum commission rule, the New York Stock Exchange created barriers between itself and the other components of the securities market, at home and abroad, from the 1880s onwards. The overall results were probably minor, but their effect was to reduce slightly the broadness, stability and uniformity of the market enjoyed by US securities, with repercussions for the demand they enjoyed, especially from 1898 onwards domestically and 1911 onwards internationally.[20]

At the same time the actions of the Stock Exchange influenced the shape and operation of the securities market, for it both attracted business through its specialization and repelled it through its various restrictions. The New York Exchange dominated the securities market in the United States, judged by volume, but it did not attempt to provide a service for all securities and all investors – concentrating, rather, upon particular securities for particular investors. Even if it had, there would still have been considerable scope for other institutions and individuals. Despite the integration of the securities market there remained a need for facilities which New York was not equipped to provide. Geographically, for example, there were numerous securities owned in a particular area and requiring nothing more than a local market. This relationship of the New York Stock Exchange to the rest of the securities market can be examined both with regard to its position within New York – the financial centre of North America – and its role both domestically and internationally.

Within its own city the New York Stock Exchange was seldom unique. Both outside brokers dealing in the street and rival stock exchanges existed before and after the Civil War, though the merger with the Open Board in 1869 temporarily reduced their numbers and importance.[21] Despite the potential problems that this situation created, the New York Stock Exchange existed in relative harmony with its competitors from 1869 until the mid-1880s. As long as the outside brokers and their exchanges dealt in securities which the New York Stock Exchange ignored there was an acceptance of a rough division of function, which led to co-operation rather than rivalry. Members of the New York Stock Exchange were themselves involved in the establishment of some of these additional exchanges and became members, especially those involved with mining and petroleum. Eventually, all these other exchanges formed to deal in specific securities amalgamated in 1885 to form the Consolidated Stock and Petroleum Exchange with an initial 2,403 members, of whom three to four hundred were also members of the New York Stock Exchange.[22]

It is from this date that real rivalry began. The Consolidated was unwilling to confine its activities to those securities which the New York Stock Exchange neglected. The creation of such a substantial exchange, and the prospect that trading in mines and petroleum would collapse as it had in the past, encouraged the Consolidated to compete with its long-established rival. It therefore began to quote railroad stocks and bonds. With commission rates set at half the New York level (one-sixteenth per cent) and a minimum trade of only ten units, the members of the Consolidated could offer clients an attractive service. The ease and low cost of membership and the facilities of an account system and clearing organization also made membership attractive to brokers. In consequence, turnover expanded rapidly and was based largely upon trading in the railroad, and later industrial, stock that the New York Stock Exchange quoted (Table 7.2).[23] As the Consolidated Stock Exchange itself noted in 1886, this growth was 'accomplished against the most strenuous opposition of our neighbor, the New York Stock Exchange, which has applied to us a principle of "boycotting", more violent than the most extreme of the trade unionists'.[24] This spirit of animosity continued right up to the First World War.

Ineffective as many of the barriers imposed were, their existence nevertheless undermined the operations of the Consolidated Stock Exchange and reduced its attractiveness to brokers and their clients, leading to a decline of business in the 1890s. Attempts were made to revive the mining and petroleum market and to diversify into grain, but none proved successful (Table 7.2). Renewed growth came after 1898 when the New York Stock Exchange's restriction on continuous quotations led to some switching of domestic arbitrage to the Consolidated, which had direct communications links with the principal regional exchanges, as well as maintaining access to current New York Stock Exchange prices. By 1909/10, for example, the Consolidated claimed to be trading in US Steel at a level that was a quarter or a third of that of the New York Stock Exchange. However, the New York Stock Exchange responded by discouraging the members of the exchanges outside New York from dealing with the

Consolidated, and by preventing easy access to its own prices. This resulted in a collapse of arbitrage business, leaving the Consolidated with little more than the buying and selling of securities in fractional lots or small amounts, and the odd-lot broker on the New York Stock Exchange increasingly competed for that. Membership on the Consolidated thus declined to 671 in 1913, many of whom were inactive, while a growing number of Consolidated brokers purchased seats on the New York Stock Exchange, to which they transferred

Table 7.2   *Consolidated Stock Exchange, Turnover, 1885–1912/13*

Year	Railroads and industrials		Mining stocks (million)
	Stocks (million)	Bonds (million)	
1885/6	17.9	58.7	3.2
1886/7	51.4	60.4	8.6
1887/8	50.6	35.5	7.7
1888/9	61.7	48.2	5.4
1889/90	72.6	29.2	4.3
1890/1	75.8	22.1	3.2
1891/2	80.7	40.9	1.8
1892/3	66.1	29.3	1.0
1893/4	52.7	27.7	0.3
1894/5	53.8	18.8	0.4
1895/6	57.6	16.0	1.0
1896/7	56.0	8.6	0.8
1897/8	69.2	16.3	1.1
1898/9	72.4	27.3	1.1
1899/1900	81.1	?	?
1900/1	103.6	4.9	1.5
1901/2	91.4	4.4	1.5
1902/3	106.8	2.7	2.1
1903/4	125.6	4.2	1.7
1904/5	145.4	2.1	1.7
1905/6	133.1	—	2.4
1906/7	131.4	—	2.5
1907/8	127.0	—	3.2
1908/9	141.8	—	2.7
1909/10	59.8	—	2.3
1910/11	42.2	—	1.9
1911/12	39.4	—	1.8
1912/13	24.8	—	1.8

Sources: Consolidated Stock Exchange, Annual Reports, 1885/6–1912/13; S. A. Nelson, *The Consolidated Stock Exchange of New York* (New York, 1907), p. 3.

their business, whether it was in odd lots or domestic arbitrage.[25]

Faced with the hostility of not only the New York Stock Exchange but also the established stock exchanges in the other major US cities, the Consolidated Stock Exchange attempted to set up a rival exchange network for the conduct of domestic arbitrage.

> We must expand our business by offering to the public the very best facilities for legitimate execution of orders. This can be accomplished by establishing closer relations with exchanges now organized in cities throughout the country, or by establishing branch exchanges in the larger cities, the head exchange at New York to be the hub of the wheel . . .

was the tenor of the 1913 Annual Report, and this is what the Consolidated tried to do in the years to come.[26] The other reason that the Consolidated was on the defensive and losing business was the revival of the street market, being conducted by brokers belonging to no exchange. These outside brokers confined themselves to securities which the New York Stock Exchange did not quote, and so avoided the animosity of that institution.[27] Stedman, for example, a member of the New York Stock Exchange, recognized the need for an alternative market when he wrote in 1905:

> The flood of new securities which has come upon the market within the past few years, by the consolidation of mercantile and manufacturing establishments, has caused the Stock Exchange to be more careful as to what is admitted to its list, with the result that the market for the overflow has gone back to the street, and makes what is now known as the market on the 'curb'.[28]

These circumstances led to the rapid growth of the street market from 1899 onwards. By 1908 between 150 and 300 brokers were actively involved at any one time, and a rudimentary organization already existed. These curb (kerb) brokers were willing to deal in any securities for which an active market existed or was in prospect, and were continually dropping those that produced little business and including others. In 1908, for instance, the Curb Market quoted 174 different mining companies, but only 70 (40 per cent) had an active market.[29] Over the four-year period 1911–14 total turnover on the Curb averaged an estimated $0.5 billion per annum, of which 57 per cent was in mining securities and a further 22 per cent in oil stocks, with the remaining 21 per cent being in the issues of industrial and other companies.[30] Clearly the Curb was a speculative market for either mining and oil securities or those issued by the newer industrial and related concerns.

The Curb existed in uneasy harmony with the New York Stock Exchange, never officially recognized but extensively utilized by its membership to fill orders for clients from throughout the country. Some New York Stock Exchange brokerage firms even set up branches to operate on the Curb. An estimated 85 per cent of the Curb's total business was on behalf of members of the New York Stock Exchange, with whom constant contact was maintained through the use of messenger boys, signalling from upper-floor office windows, and conveniently sited telephones at ground-floor window level.[31] The Curb was slowly integrated into the securities market and given a specific role to play, in a way the Consolidated was never allowed to do. Weil, a broker on the Curb, was of the opinion in 1908 that 'The curb market serves as a preliminary market for practically all stocks and bonds that are eventually listed on the New York Stock Exchange.'[32] The New York Stock Exchange was not so candid but came close to admitting this in 1909: 'The curb market represents, first, securities that cannot be listed; second, securities in the process of evolution from reorganization certificates to a more solid status; and third, securities of corporations which have been unwilling to submit their figures and statistics to the proper committees of the Stock Exchange.'[33]

The brokers of the Curb undertook to provide a market in the riskier securities, for whatever reason that was, and when these securities passed out of that category they were either dropped, if inactive, or given a quotation on the New York Stock Exchange, if they represented large and established enterprises. When a security that had been traded on the Curb was quoted by the Stock Exchange, the Curb brokers ceased to deal and looked for a replacement, and so did not compete with that institution. Essentially, the Curb complemented the Stock Exchange by providing a trial market where the performance of a security could be judged before a full quotation was granted. This had a considerable double benefit. Quotation on the Stock Exchange conferred the status of being safe on any security that passed the stringent tests imposed, while the existence of the Curb meant that an active market existed for those securities upon which such a status could not yet be conferred.[34]

For those securities that were little traded in New York, the telephone allowed the creation of a widespread and effective broker-to-broker or over-the-counter (OTC) market, which was far superior to the old system of brokers visiting each other's offices. Centred in New York but operating nationwide, this system provided a means whereby, for example, the smaller issues of cities or utilities could be relatively easily bought and sold at prices that had general currency. This made these securities much more attractive than they would otherwise have been, and they were extensively held by institutions as a consequence.[35]

In New York alone, then, the New York Stock Exchange coexisted or competed with three other components of the securities market. The over-the-counter market met the needs of inactive securities, the Curb was the market where securities could serve an apprenticeship before some progressed to the Stock Exchange, while the Consolidated catered for the requirements of the small investor. Only between the Consolidated and the New York Stock Exchange was there a kind of warfare, as there was no functional division through the securities traded. The result was that in New York the New York Stock Exchange developed as a specialist component of the securities market, shedding certain of its roles to others, with which it slowly developed a working relationship, but not without some difficulties that undermined the unity of the market. Even within New York it would be mistaken to regard the Stock Exchange as completely dominant, for it monopolized only the large deals in large active issues.

The New York Stock Exchange was also one of many existing within the United States. Those stock exchanges formed in the first half of the nineteenth century, like Philadelphia, Boston, Baltimore and New Orleans, continued to play a role after improved communications permitted the creation of an integrated national securities market. The role they continued to play was that of providing a market for local securities; but, for some, the nature of these local securities changed substantially. There was not only the development of new forms of corporate enterprise, as economies expanded and changed, such as in the fields of power supply, urban transit and manufacturing industry, but also a considerable widening in what was accomplished by local finance.[36] Eastern investors, in particular, invested heavily in undertakings in other parts of the United States, and often did so on a local basis. 'Boston, while being a railroad centre of her own, has been profligate in the millions upon millions furnished for the development of these enterprises in all sections of the country,' wrote Martin in 1898.[37] A railroad such as the Atchison, Topeka & Santa Fe, which operated in the south-west of the United States, was largely organized and financed from Boston, and its success led to Boston investors becoming substantial shareholders in the Mexican Central Railway, which was a natural extension of its network.

Numerous other companies located in other parts of North America also had their head offices in Boston, such as the Dominion Coal Company of Nova Scotia and the American Bell Telephone Company, while the copper-mining industry of Michigan and Montana was largely controlled from that city.[38] The consequence for Boston, according to one contemporary writing in 1893, was that there 'many of the leading railroad stocks, bonds, and other securities of the country find their marketable value and established quotations'.[39] Since ownership was concentrated in a particular locality, New England, it was only to be expected that the best market would lie in the local exchange, which was Boston. The same situation also prevailed for Philadelphia.[40]

However, exchanges like Boston and Philadelphia had difficulty holding on to the market in large national or regional concerns as their shareholders became geographically diversified. The New York Stock Exchange began to quote them, and trading gradually moved there, as that was where the most active market came to be, with transactions being carried out for customers located throughout the United States and abroad. In the 1890s, for example, the market in Atchison, Topeka & Santa Fe switched from Boston to New York, so that by 1904 the volume of trading in it on the New York Stock Exchange was twenty-one times greater than on the Boston Stock Exchange. This was repeated time and again, but the Boston Stock Exchange was powerless to stop it, with even its own members coming to deal on the basis of New York prices, and channel orders to New York – both the Stock Exchange and the Curb.[41]

The established East Coast stock exchanges, apart from New York, were slowly transformed into what they had begun as, and that was markets in the locally held securities of locally operating companies. However, this was not entirely the case, for they did preserve some specialities. Boston retained until the First World War the market in the stocks of copper-mining companies and attracted business in these from throughout North America and western Europe, including New York itself.[42] Charles Head, a member of both the New York and Boston Stock Exchanges, reported in 1903: 'There is not very much done there [Boston] excepting in the local securities which are not listed here . . . we do a pretty large business in Boston which does not come to this city [New York] at all – where the customers are Boston men, and the business is done there. We do a large business in these Boston stocks – in all the copper stocks.'[43] By 1904 two-thirds of the turnover on the Boston Stock Exchange was in local stocks, particularly New England railroads, utilities and manufacturing enterprises, while one-third was in national concerns like Amalgamated Copper and Union Pacific Railroad, for which it took its lead from New York.[44] However, not all local companies could get their securities quoted on their local exchange, for those that offered little prospect of business were either refused quotation or subsequently deleted from the list, a practice the Boston Stock Exchange adopted in 1899. Dealing in securities such as these was done either on the kerb market, if one existed, or through the telephone on the over-the-counter market.[45]

The relationship between the New York Stock Exchange and its established East Coast rivals was thus similar to that existing between itself and the Curb. They came to act as proving-grounds for securities which, if they gained a national prominence and established reputation, gradually moved to New York. However, these exchanges continued to compete with New York in certain national securities that were local favourites, as well as being important markets for the stocks and bonds issued by corporations operating in the region and attracting largely local investors.

Local securities locally held were also the main force behind the establishment of stock exchanges in other parts of the United States, but only under particular circumstances in most cases. In San Francisco, for example, brokers handled the few transactions there were in local water, insurance and shipping companies, as well as the railways, without the need to establish an exchange. The integrated brokerage firms and wire connections allowed local brokers to channel orders to New York, or other centres, where the best market existed, without having to try to find local buyers and sellers. Early attempts to set up a stock exchange in Chicago foundered on the fact that it was easier to trade in government bonds and later railroad stock through New York than locally even though there was a pool of local investors and the railroads concerned operated out of Chicago.[46]

It took an exceptional burst of activity to create the need for a stock exchange after the Civil War, and that was mainly related to mineral and oil discoveries. The sudden unearthing of minerals and oil created an explosion of interest in the ventures involved, which led in turn to the creation of numerous stock exchanges to cope with the vast turnover in the securities they issued, with which investors hoped to make their fortunes. These exchanges were usually sited either in convenient centres for the mineral fields – such as Virginia City for the Comstock lode and Pittsburgh for the Pennsylvania oil wells – or in populous cities with numerous investors, like San Francisco and Chicago. Most of these exchanges disappeared long before the minerals, but a few did progress to become established securities markets.[47] The Pittsburgh Stock Exchange found a substitute in local gas and transit stocks in the mid-1880s, as trading in oil declined, so that by 1903 its main business was to provide a market in the securities of Allegheny Valley Railroad, Citizens Traction, American Window Glass, Westinghouse Air Brake, Pittsburgh Brewing and others of a like kind. In contrast, the San Francisco Stock Exchange managed to find a succession of mining securities in which to trade, being able to tap an extensive and diverse mineral area, so that it remained a mining exchange throughout the period from its foundation in 1862 to the First World War.[48]

In Chicago the early mining exchange had ceased to exist before a new stock exchange was formed, and that did not become established until 1887, when it abandoned any attempt to compete with New York in railroad stocks and concentrated upon local securities, such as those issued by Chicago Telephone, Drovers' National Bank and, especially, the Chicago Gas Light & Coke Company, capitalized at $25 million. Other large local enterprises

211

followed through amalgamations in urban transit, brewing, meat packing and match manufacture, and their securities were frequently locally issued and locally held, providing a demand for a local exchange.[49] As Lester, the author of a manual on Chicago securities, observed in 1888: 'the Chicago Stock Exchange must, as it does now, depend upon those stocks and securities which are controlled in Chicago';[50] and this was certainly the case by the early twentieth century. Overall, sales of stock on the Chicago Stock Exchange rose from a mere 150,000 in 1889 to 1.2 million in 1893, then to a peak of 3.5 million in 1899, before settling down at the 1.5 million level for the years before 1914. This was almost entirely in the securities of companies that operated in and around Chicago, with only a small proportion being in such national concerns as American Telephone & Telegraph.[51]

There thus existed in the United States a considerable number of other stock exchanges outside New York that largely served the interests of local investors in local securities. In Detroit it was the stocks of automobile and related manufacturers that dominated. A few of these, like San Francisco in mines, were specialist exchanges of national importance, while others were of major regional significance and competed with New York in particular securities, like the position occupied by Boston, Philadelphia and, eventually, Chicago. However, in terms of active trading in large issues they could rarely match the service that the New York Stock Exchange provided, and so sent their investors' orders in those securities to New York rather than keeping them on their own market. These local exchanges were continually losing securities to New York, as companies grew in size and expanded far beyond their local or regional confines; but at the same time they gained business in the local or specialist stocks that they quoted from throughout the country, including New York, as they were the best market in them.[52]

The same picture was also emerging internationally. American securities were held throughout western Europe and were actively traded on the London, Amsterdam, Berlin and other exchanges, in response to the need of local investors, though New York's minimum commission rates did encourage American business to spill overseas. As most American securities continued to be held in the United States, and it was the larger issues that were commonly held overseas, the New York Stock Exchange was their principal market, and the European stock exchanges took their lead from it. However, these European stock exchanges did retain a substantial market in US securities, even after the transatlantic cable of 1866 and the improvement to communications. This was because of the considerable holdings in western Europe, especially Britain, aided by the five-hour time differential that separated them from New York, as well as the competitive power they possessed in being large, active and sophisticated markets in their own right. The New York Stock Exchange was thus forced to share its trading in many of the larger US security issues, which it dominated domestically, with overseas exchanges, particularly London. In turn, it did gain business from Canada in the largest of Canadian issues, like Canadian Pacific for which it was the principal North American market.[53]

From this examination of the New York Stock Exchange's relationship with the rest of the securities market at home and abroad, it is evident that it became an increasingly specialist institution of national and international importance. It dominated the buying and selling of the securities that it quoted, and these belonged to the largest corporations in the country and attracted considerable foreign interest. As a result of this concentration, however, and its self-imposed restriction on expansion through an increase of membership, there was a need for other exchanges both at a local level and within New York to cater for the business that the members of the New York Stock Exchange neglected. Here problems appeared, for the Stock Exchange refused to recognize that all these fulfilled a necessary function and imposed barriers between itself and them in order to protect its position, especially with regard to its minimum commission charges. This interfered with the working of the domestic securities market in a serious way from 1898 onwards and the international securities market from 1911.

Nevertheless the fundamentals of this securities market were fairly well defined. A moderately traded security would find its place on the over-the-counter market, while a reasonably active security would be traded on either its local exchange or the Curb in New York. Heavily traded securities would have their market on the New York Stock Exchange, where the largest would be shared with the principal exchanges on the other side of the Atlantic, especially London. It was quite possible for the stocks and bonds belonging to any corporation to move between these levels of the securities market, both up and down, and the transition from OTC through local exchanges and Curb to a quotation on the New York Stock Exchange was one followed by a number of securities. The New York Stock Exchange did dominate but, on deeper examination, only in a particular way, and it required the other institutions and individuals to make the securities market function as a whole.

Notes

1 National Monetary Commission, *Statistics of the United States, 1867–1909* (Washington, 1910), p. 9; P. Wyckoff, *Wall Street and the Stock Markets: A Chronology, 1644–1971* (Philadelphia, 1972), pp. 150–1; E. C. Stedman (ed.), *The New York Stock Exchange* (New York, 1905), pp. 473–4.

2 New York Stock Exchange (NYSE): Special Committee on Mining Department, 20 November 1879; Special Investigation of the Curb Market, 29 March 1906.

3 W. Armstrong, *Stocks and Stock-Jobbing in Wall Street* (New York, 1848), pp. 29, 32; H. Hamon, *New York Stock Exchange Manual* (New York, 1865), p. 307; New York Stock and Exchange Board: Miscellaneous Committee, 5 October 1847.

4 US Department of Commerce, *Historical Statistics*, Series Y 493–504; W. C. Mitchell, *Gold, Price and Wages under the Greenback Standard* (Berkeley, 1908), p. 1–2; R. Sobel, *The Big Board* (New York, 1965), p. 70.

5 NYSE: Committee on NY Petroleum and Mining Board, 16 April 1866; Committee on Stock List, 9 November 1874, 9 July 1884, 6 October 1884; J. K. Medbery, *Old Times in Wall Street: A Study for Today* (New York, 1871), p. 17.

6 *History of the New York Stock Exchange* (New York, 1887), pp. 17–19; Stedman, *New York Stock Exchange*, pp. 473–4; B.E. Schultz, *Stock Exchange Procedure* (New York, 1936), p. 14; US Department of Commerce, *Historical Statistics*, Series X 531–53.

7 US Senate, *Regulation of the New York Stock Exchange: Hearings before the Committee on Banking and Currency* (Washington, 1914), pp. 437–8; Clapp & Co., *Weekly Market Letters for 1893* (New York, 1894); F. L. Eames, *The New York Stock Exchange* (New York, 1894), p. 94; Wyckoff, *Wall Street*, p. 155; R. H. Owens and C. O. Hardy, *Interest Rates and Stock Speculation* (New York, 1925), p. 18.

8 NY Stock and Exchange Board, Minutes, 28 March 1864; NYSE: Special Committee on Mining Department, 20 November 1879; Special Joint Committee on Copper Stocks, 18 May 1903; Special Joint Committee on the Curb Market, 14 and 17 May 1909; Committee on Mining Securities, 7 March 1879, 20 April 1880, 28 April 1880, 13 December 1881; Special Committee on Mining Exchanges, 21 December 1880; Van Antwerp to C. T. Rice, 13 November 1913; Medbery, *Old Times*, pp. 274, 278–9.

9 NYSE: Committee on Arrangements, 10 June 1881; Committee on Unlisted Securities, 3 September 1897, 17 November 1897, 22 March 1906, 10 January 1907; Governing Committee, 11 May 1886, 13 April 1887, 12 November 1902, 27 May 1903, 16 March 1910; Special Committee on Unlisted Department, Minority Report, 22 January 1906; Special Investigation of the Curb Market, 29 March 1906, 24 April 1906; *New York Tribune*, 28 March 1886; *New York Evening Post*, 3 May 1913; S. S. Pratt, *The Work of Wall Street* (New York, 1903), pp. 86, 153.

10 NYSE: Special Committee on NY Mining and National Petroleum Exchange, 16 January 1885; C. W. Morgan & Co., *How to Speculate Successfully in Wall Street* (New York, 1900), p. 61; S. A. Nelson (ed.), *The ABC of Wall Street* (New York, 1900), p. 18.

11 NYSE: Special Committee on Commissions, 1924; Governing Committee, 11 May 1886, 13 April 1887, 12 November 1902, 27 May 1903, 16 March 1910, 30 March 1910; Special Joint Committee on Copper Stocks, 18 May 1903.

12 NYSE: Committee on Commissions, 8 June 1883, 14 May 1889, 5 January 1904, 12 May 1904; Governing Committee, 12 November 1902; Special Committee of Inquiry into Stock Commission Business, 2 August 1887; Special Investigation of the Curb Market, 29 March 1906; *New York Times*, 23 January 1885, 15 February 1885; Van Antwerp to G. A. Neeley, 30 June 1913.

13 NYSE: Special Committee on New York Mining and National Petroleum Exchange, 16 January 1885; Special Committee on Bucket Shops, Digest, 25 June 1913, p. 45; Committee on Arrangements, 2 November 1878, 25 March 1884, 11 December 1884, 9 February 1885, 1 June 1885, 3 March 1886, 10 May 1886, 10 February 1887, 21 February 1887, 9 January 1893; US Congress, Money Trust Investigation, pp. 387, 818; US Senate, *Regulation of the Stock Exchange*, p. 78; *History of the New York Stock Exchange*, p. 99.

14 NYSE: Committee on Arrangements, 9 May 1904; Special Joint Committee on Copper Stocks, 18 May 1903; Special Investigation Committee, Continuous Quotations, 27 January 1903; Law Committee, 28 June 1905; Eames, *New York Stock Exchange*, p. 90.

15 NYSE: Committee on Arrangements, Appendices, 14 June 1901; Committee on Arrangements, 1 July 1895, 16 August 1897, 29 October 1900, 10 March 1902, 18 February 1903, 26 October 1903, 14 June 1904;

Committee on Commissions, 22 November 1881, 21 February 1894, 5 January 1904, 12 May 1904; Special Investigation Committee, Continuous Quotations, 21 January 1903, 22 January 1903, 27 January 1903; Reply by NYSE to the Governor's Committee on Speculation in Securities and Commodities, p. 27; *New York Times*, 14 February 1886, S. S. Huebner, *The Stock Market* (New York, 1922), p. 85; Pratt, *Work of Wall Street*, p. 115; Stedman, *New York Stock Exchange*, p. 441.

16 NYSE: Committee on Commissions, 1 June 1882, 29 December 1910; Committee on Securities, 24 December 1880, 19 March 1881; Building Committee, 6 January 1903, 27 January 1903, 25 February 1903, 7 April 1903; Committee on Arrangements, 14 June 1904, 3 October 1904, 10 October 1904, 25 September 1905, 23 October 1905, 26 February 1906, 1 February 1909, 7 June 1909, 6 July 1909, 10 October 1910; New York Stock and Exchange Board, 6 January 1869.

17 NYSE: Committee on Arrangements, 14 December 1910, 14 July 1911, 29 February 1912, 9 April 1912, 30 October 1912, 15 November 1912; Special Committee on Foreign Business, Report, 23 February 1911, 8 March 1911.

18 NYSE: Special Committee on Foreign Business, Digest 1934–5, cf. 24 June 1914 and 20 April 1911.

19 NYSE: Special Committee on Foreign Business, Digest 1934–5, cf. 24 June 1914; Committee on Commissions, 29 February 1912, 9 April 1912, 30 October 1912; Governing Committee, 25 February 1914; *Brooklyn Daily Eagle*, 1 March 1914; S. F. Streit, *Report on European Stock Exchanges* (New York, 1914), p. 9.

20 Pratt, *Work of Wall Street*, pp. 114–15; W. C. Van Antwerp, *The Stock Exchange from within* (New York, 1913), p. 283; Huebner, *Stock Market*, pp. 86–97; A. Cragg, *Understanding the Stock Market* (New York, 1929), pp. 210–13.

21 New York Stock and Exchange Board, Minutes, 27 April 1869, 11 May 1869; Armstrong, *Stocks and Stock-Jobbing*, p. 18; Eames, *New York Stock Exchange*, p. 50; Sobel, *Big Board*, pp. 51, 60; Medbury, *Old Times*, p. 131; H. G. S. Noble, *The New York Stock Exchange in the Crisis of 1914* (New York, 1915), p. 18.

22 New York Stock and Exchange Board: Committee on NY Petroleum and Mining Board, 16 April 1866; NYSE: Special Committee on Bucket Shops, Digest, 25 June 1913, p. 83; Engineering and Mining Journal, *The New York Mining Stock Market for 1879* (New York, 1880), pp. 3–4; *The World*, 4 December 1883; *New York Times*, 18 July 1884; Medbury, *Old Times*, pp. 278–9, 282; Stedman, *New York Stock Exchange*, pp. 457–8; *History of New York Stock Exchange*, pp. 97–100; *New York Curb Exchange* (New York, 1937), p. 8.

23 S. A. Nelson, *The Consolidated Stock Exchange of New York* (New York, 1907), pp. 3–5, 25, 33, 39–40, 48; L. C. Van Riper, *Ins and Outs of Wall Street* (New York, 1898), pp. 25–6; Consolidated Stock Exchange (CSE), Annual Reports, 1885/6–1912/13.

24 CSE, Annual Report, 1886, p. 32
25 Nelson, *Consolidated Stock Exchange*, pp. 7, 23, 40, 45, 75; Nelson, *ABC of Wall Street*, p. 73; Reply by NYSE to Committee on Speculation, p. 428; Money Trust Investigation, pp. 756–7, 768–9; NYSE: Special Committee on Bucket Shops, Digest, 25 June 1913; CSE, Annual Reports, 1890/1–1912/13; Morgan & Co., *How to Speculate*, p. 57.
26 CSE, Annual Report, 31 May 1913, pp. 19–20; cf. Annual Report, 31 May 1921, p. 19.
27 NYSE: Special Investigation of the Curb Market, 29 March 1906, 24 April 1906; Committee on Unlisted Securities, 22 March 1906, 10 January 1907.
28 Stedman, *New York Stock Exchange*, pp. 457–8.
29 Nelson, *ABC of Wall Street*, p. 68; G. E. Vigouroune, 'Mines on the New York Curb', in T. Gibson, *Special Market Letters for 1908* (New York, 1909), p. 117; E. G. Nourse, *Brokerage* (New York, 1910), p. 88; Pratt, *Work of Wall Street*, pp. 153–5; Huebner, *The Stock Market*, p. 8.
30 Jones & Baker, *The History of the New York Curb* (New York, 1916), p. 11. Value of turnover in stocks was estimated using $25 as the average price of each share being traded, while all turnover in bonds was attributed to industrial and miscellaneous.
31 NYSE: Special Investigation Committee, Continuous Quotations, 16 December 1910; Money Trust Investigation, pp. 472, 827; Nelson, *ABC of Wall Street*, pp. 68–9, 73; New York State, *Report of Committee on Speculation*, pp. 431–3; Huebner, *Stock Market*, pp. 8–9; *New York Curb Exchange* (New York, 1937), p. 14; R. Sobel, *The Curbstone Brokers: The Origins of the American Stock Exchange* (New York, 1970), p. 85.
32 M. L. Weil, *The ABC and Manual of the Curb Market* (New York, 1908), p. 8.
33 Reply by NYSE to Committee on Speculation, p. 44.
34 NYSE: Special Investigation of the Curb Market, 4 April 1906; Money Trust Investigation, pp. 478, 1297–300; Jones & Baker, *Profits and Dividends of America's Second Largest Stock Market* (New York, 1919), p. 15; Jones & Baker, *History of the New York Curb*, pp. 10–11; Weil, *ABC and Manual*, pp. 7, 20–1; Nelson, *ABC of Wall Street*, pp. 68, 73.
35 Money Trust Investigation, p. 405; Nelson, *ABC of Wall Street*, pp. 22, 69; Medbery, *Old Times*, pp. 114–15; Huebner, *The Stock Market*, p. 7; S. A. Nelson, *The Bond Buyers' Dictionary* (New York, 1907), pp. 81, 126–7; Fisk & Hatch, *Memoranda Concerning Government Bonds* (New York, 1882), p. 23; N. W. Harris & Co., *Municipal Bonds* (New York, 1897), pp. 19–20; Haight & Freese, *Guide to Investors* (New York, 1898), pp. 6, 69; N. W. Halsey & Co., *The Most Satisfactory Bonds* (New York, 1912), p. 15; L. Chamberlain, *The Work of the Bond House* (New York, 1912), p. 57.
36 Henry Ewing, List of Sales on the Philadelphia Stock Exchange, 14

May 1844–24 August 1844; Newcomen Society, *The Story of the Philadelphia Stock Exchange* (Philadelphia, 1976), p. 11; C. W. Barron *et al.*, *The Boston Stock Exchange* (Boston, 1893), no pagination; J. G. Martin, *A Century of Finance: A History of the Boston Stock and Money Markets, 1798–1898* (Boston, 1898) p. iv; *The Boston Stock Exchange* (Boston, 1930), pp. 7–8; M. V. Sears, 'Gold and the Local Stock Exchanges of the 1860s', *Explorations in Entrepreneurial History*, vol. 6 (1968–9), pp. 221–2.

37 Martin, *Century of Finance*, p. 144.

38 Barron *et al.*, *Boston Stock Exchange*, p. 21; Medbury, *Old Times*, pp. 278–9.

39 Barron *et al.*, *Boston Stock Exchange*.

40 A. W. Barnes (ed.), *History of the Philadelphia Stock Exchange, Banks and Banking Interests* (Philadelphia, 1911), p. 11; Richard Irvin & Co., NY, to E. F. Satterthwaite & Co., London, 20 May 1879.

41 Boston Stock Exchange (BSE): Governing Committee, 7 October 1891, 20 November 1895, 11 April 1898, 20 March 1914; Arbitration Committee, 30 August 1892; Secretary's Notices, 7 March 1905; Committees on Ways and Means of Increasing the Business of the Exchange, 14 April 1904; Barron, *et al.*, *Boston Stock Exchange*.

42 NYSE: Special Joint Committee on Copper Stocks, 18 May 1903; Nelson, *ABC of Wall Street*, p. 73, *New York Stock Exchange* (1886), pp. 99, 110.

43 NYSE: Special Investigation Committee, Continuous Quotations, 27 January 1903.

44 BSE: Ways and Means, 14 April 1904; *Boston Stock Exchange*, p. 21; US Senate, *Regulation of the Stock Exchange*, pp. 437–8, 447, 450.

45 BSE: Stock List Committee, 11 July 1899, 19 July 1899, 27 July 1899, 31 July 1899; J. G. Martin, *Stock Fluctuations* (Boston, 1903 and 1907); Barnes, *Philadelphia Stock Exchange*, p. 13.

46 J. L. King, *History of the San Francisco Stock and Exchange Board* (San Francisco, 1910), p. 3; I. A. Fleming, *The Chicago Stock Exchange: An Historical Sketch* (Chicago, 1894), no pagination; W. Rice, *The Chicago Stock Exchange: A History* (Chicago, 1923), p. 8; F. M. Lester, *Chicago Securities: A Manual for Bankers, Brokers and Investors* (Chicago, 1888), pp. 69, 71–2.

47 Sears, 'Gold and Local Stock Exchanges', pp. 198–9; J. B. Barbour, 'Sketch of the Pittsburgh Oil Exchanges', *Western Pennsylvania Historical Magazine*, vol. 11 (1918), p. 127; King, *San Francisco*, pp. 14–15; Fleming, *Chicago Stock Exchange*; Rice, *Chicago Stock Exchange*, pp. 12–13.

48 *The Pittsburgh Stock Exchange, 1894–1929* (Pittsburgh, 1929), pp. 3–5; Barbour, 'Pittsburgh Oil Exchanges'; Pittsburgh Stock Exchange, *Stocks and Bonds* (Pittsburgh, 1903); King, *San Francisco*, pp. 22–7, 49, 78, 295.

49 Chicago Stock Exchange: Governing Committee, 21 June 1887, 17

August 1887, 17 January 1891, 17 October 1893, 4 November 1895; Fleming, *Chicago Stock Exchange*; Rice, *Chicago Stock Exchange*, pp. 26–8; F. M. Huston and A. Russell, *Financing an Empire: History of Banking in Illinois* (Chicago, 1926), vol. I, p. 524; D. M. Dailey, Investment Banking in Chicago (Urbana, 1931) pp. 8–15.

50 Lester, *Chicago Securities*, p. 74; cf. NYSE: Committee on Admissions, 29 January 1902.

51 Clapp & Co., *Weekly Market Letters for 1893* (New York, 1894), p. 320; Huston and Russell, *Financing an Empire*, p. 534; compare Chicago Stock Exchange Official Quotations, 30 December 1882 and 3 January 1910.

52 *Manual of Statistics* (New York, 1901); NYSE: Special Committee on Multiple Exchange Trading, 1939–40; US Senate, *Regulation of the Stock Exchange*, p. 529; Pratt, *Work of Wall Street*, p. 93; cf. *Detroit Stock Exchange, 1907–1931* (Detroit, 1931), pp. 10–12.

53 NYSE: Special Committee on Foreign Business, Digest 1934–5; Committee on Commissions, 15 November 1912; Nourse, *Brokerage*, p. 109; George Bliss to Levi Parsons Morton, 16 May 1884.

8 The New York Stock Exchange and the US Economy

Within the rapidly expanding US economy of the nineteenth century the financial sector was of steadily growing importance. Between 1869 and 1910–13, when national income more than quadrupled, that share attributable to finance, insurance and real estate rose from 11.5 per cent to 12.7 per cent. In terms of manpower the increase was more dramatic; those engaged in these activities grew from 0.4 per cent of the labour force in 1869 to 1.6 per cent in 1909, and that was a period in which the size of the total labour force almost tripled.[1] Generally, financial institutions and intermediaries were coming to play a central role in all facets of the economy, expanding far beyond their origins in the major northeastern cities and an early concentration upon servicing only trade and government. Their ability simultaneously to increase the supply of finance and reduce its cost became an important dynamic element in an economy short of capital.[2]

Over this period the financial sector experienced considerable change, with a growing level of sophistication being accompanied by an increasing number and variety of the institutions and individuals involved, and the specialist tasks that they performed. The commercial banks, fire-insurance companies and general brokers that predominated at the beginning of the century not only expanded in number and size but were supplemented by developments such as investment banking, industrial insurance and savings and loan organizations.[3]

Within the financial sector those intermediaries and institutions concerned with the issue, distribution and resale of securities were of increasing significance, as the obtaining of finance by the issue of transferable stocks and bonds became steadily more common. By 1900, when the total assets of the United States reached an estimated

$156.8 billion, the intangible proportion was already 43.6 per cent, as opposed to physical property's 56.4 per cent. Within total assets securities comprised 14.2 per cent of the total, but 32.6 per cent of all intangible assets, which included bank deposits, loans, mortgages and insurance as well. The share of assets in the form of securities was a rapidly rising one; for even by 1912, when total assets reached $306.2 billion, securities now provided 19 per cent, or 41.1 per cent of all intangible assets.[4]

Nevertheless, though tangible assets were of diminishing importance, and securities were quickly becoming the single most popular alternative, this did not mean that they achieved universal use, let alone dominate financing arrangements. Even by the First World War large sections of the US economy were little reliant on the issue of securities in order to obtain the capital they required, either directly or indirectly. In agriculture, for example, self-finance supplemented by trade credit and borrowing on mortgage remained normal practice. By 1910 the value of all farm property totalled $41 billion, while farm debt was only $3.2 billion, or equivalent to a mere 8 per cent of the total. The family-owned farm still typified farming, despite the size of the agricultural sector.[5] A similar situation emerges with the finance of urban residential property, though its aggregate capital requirements were also vast. Between 1896 and 1916 the value of housing, excluding that on farms, rose from $11.3 billion to $31.6 billion, while the mortgage debt outstanding fell from an equivalent of 24 per cent of the total to 21 per cent, indicating a growing equity interest among the numerous individual owners. Financial institutions were becoming central to the provision of mortgage finance, with their share rising from 50 per cent to 63 per cent between 1896 and 1916, but virtually all of this was derived from banks, savings and loan, and insurance.[6]

Even in business direct or informal methods of financing remained commonplace rather than the formation of public corporations and the issue of securities. The total number of businesses in the United States, for instance, rose from 204,000 in 1857 to 1,708,000 in 1916, by which time there were 341,300 corporations, or less than one-fifth of the total. Much of business remained the preserve of the owner-operator, family, or partnership, with finance being obtained from a very close circle rather than a general appeal to the investing public.[7] However, developments were taking place that put considerable pressure on such traditional means of finance and rendered them incapable of providing the amounts required within the time span available, forcing the adoption of different methods.

The capital employed in the railroad network increased from $0.3 billion in 1950 to $9–10 billion in 1890 and to $21.1 billion in 1916. Such were the requirements of the railroad system that no single entrepreneur or small group could provide even the minimum amount required to commence a viable operation, while it was not possible to stagger the requirement over a long period, so that the accumulation of self-generated finance would suffice. The capital utilized by the average railroad company, for example, rose from $8.7 million in 1890 to $17.0 million in 1916. Railroads were increasingly joined by other enterprises with similar financing requirements, such as street and electric railways, electric light and power companies, and telegraph and telephone corporations.[8] A tendency towards increasing capital requirements was also evident in sectors of the economy that had previously been financed by traditional means. In manufacturing the average capital employed in each factory rose from $42,309 in 1899 to $77,436 in 1914. Though the average capital requirements in manufacturing remained low throughout, and well within the scope of traditional methods of finance, this varied enormously from one branch to another. The clothing industry was labour- rather than capital-intensive, while the reverse was true with steel production and petroleum refining. Consequently, manufacturing offered opportunities for all types of financial arrangement, ranging from the most informal to the most sophisticated. Similar variety also existed in such other branches of business as distribution and mining.[9]

Inevitably, new means of raising capital had to be devised if such facilities as improved transport, communications and urban services were to be provided, or if the increasing scale of operation in many areas of the economy was to be facilitated. The system generally adopted was the establishment of large corporate enterprises financed through the issue of transferable stocks and bonds to members of the public, who held them for the yield they promised. Among railroads and utilities by 1913 the $493.9 million in stocks issued by the Pennsylvania Railroad were held by 86,804 people, or an average of $5,690 per person, while the 53,737 shareholders in American Telephone & Telegraph provided it with a capital of $344.5 million, or $6,411 from each. Within manufacturing the largest corporation was US Steel, which by 1913 had issued $508.3 million in common stock to 44,398 shareholders and $360.3 million in preferred stock to 77,420 people, or an average of $11,449 and $4,654, respectively, to each. General Motors was tiny in comparison, with a capital stock of only $31.5 million held by 2,907 investors, or $10,836 each, in 1913. One of distribution's giant enterprises was Sears, Roebuck & Company, but its capital was a mere $48.0 million in 1913, provided by 2,853 people, or $16,824 from each. Standard Oil of New Jersey, part of the dismembered Standard Oil Trust, had a capital stock of $98.3 million in 1913, and this was owned by 6,201 investors, at an average of $15,852 each.[10]

Altogether, by 1913 the 76 leading railroads possessed a capital stock of $5.5 billion held by 0.5 million shareholders averaging $11,000 each, while the capital stock of the 252 principal industrial enterprises totalled $6.8 billion and came from 0.9 million investors at an average of $7,556 from each.[11] By then the major undertakings in such areas of the economy as transportation, communications, urban utilities, banking, insurance, mining, manufacturing and distribution were financed by way of publicly held stocks and bonds. There nevertheless remained numerous enterprises in these and other activities which did not rely on the issue of securities to meet their capital requirements.[12]

The productive needs of the US economy were not the only source of demand for capital that created changes in the way it was mobilized. The waging of the Civil War, for example, led to a vast expansion in the government's need for finance, which was partly met by the issue of bonds. In 1860 the public debt of the federal government alone stood at $64.8 million, while by 1866 it had reached $2.8 billion, or $75 per person. After the war, as the federal government successfully reduced its debt burden, reaching $1.2 billion or $12 per person in 1913, the state and other authorities steadily increased theirs, in response to a growing need for improved community services and infrastructure. By 1913 total public indebtedness was $5.6 billion, of which only 21 per cent was federal, with the rest consisting of the borrowing of numerous state, city and other bodies. However, even with this great increase in non-federal issues, the burden of public debt, at $58 per person in

223

1913, remained significantly less than it had been at the end of the Civil War. This represented a substantial amount of savings that could be utilized for other purposes in the economy, especially if borrowers could issue the same type of security, with similar guarantees, that investors had been willing to accept from government.[13]

The potential supply of finance was certainly in existence. National savings were growing rapidly in the second half of the nineteenth century, more than quadrupling in the short period from 1897 to 1913, when they rose from $0.79 billion to $3 69 billion per annum. Rising incomes and profits among a rapidly expanding population generated this increase in savings, which remained largely at the disposal of individuals and unincorporated businesses. These people wanted to place their savings less in the direct ownership of physical assets and more with financial institutions or in financial instruments, because of the greater convenience involved at all stages of the process.[14] Those who could tap this desire could gain easy access to a major source of finance, at costs approaching the low rates at which government could borrow, and so gain a considerable advantage over their competitors.

The railroads were not the first branch of enterprise to make use of this possibility, being preceded by canals, urban utilities, banking and insurance. However, they were in the position to make the greatest use of it, as they both required large amounts of capital within short periods and could offer a steady return backed by physical assets and regional or route monopoly of an essential service. The large railroad corporation with a network spanning thousands of miles, drawing traffic from a huge and diverse area which could generate a regular income, was very attractive to investors, since it offered the same kind of security as a government could with its tax-gathering capacity. The Atchison, Topeka & Santa Fe railroad, for instance, controlled a total mileage of 6,481 by 1896 and dominated a large area of the south-west. Altogether, by 1906 the top seventeen railroads possessed a capital of $9 billion, or 62 per cent of the total railroad capital, illustrating the size of the corporate enterprises involved. It was only when the momentum of railroad construction slackened in the late nineteenth century that other sectors of the economy were given the opportunity to tap this source in a major way. and only then when railroads were temporarily embarrassed by scandals, defaults and low yields. The merger mania and public flotation of manu-facturing enterprises, for example, was not a movement of inevitable progression, as it sometimes appears in retrospect, but one condi-tioned by the willingness of investors to purchase the securities being issued as a result.

Of the 4,191 industrial mergers that took place between 1895 and 1916, involving a capital of $9.8 billion, 63 per cent by number and 65 per cent by value took place in the five year period 1898–1902, which comprised only 23 per cent of the period. Most of these mergers were no more than the conversion of established companies into larger groupings, involving little fundamental change or any need to obtain finance for major new developments. It was a revolution in organization stemming from the value placed on the emerging corporation by the investing public, as opposed to the individual vendors, rather than from an immediate or essential need to reorganize in order to obtain economies of scale from new developments in technology or marketing. That trend was there but hardly critical in the period 1898–1902 when most change took place. The limitation of competition, for instance, which prompted some combinations, could equally well have been achieved without formal mergers and public issues. Conditions within various industries and activities may very well have determined which sectors saw the emergence of giant enterprises, but it was the availability of funds and the desire of the investor for a particular type of investment that underlay their appearance both as a group and at that time.[15]

The need for and importance of formal financial intermediation in the United States, then, were growing in the course of the nineteenth century, and securities were becoming of major significance. At the same time the nature of this financial inter-mediation, and the implications of its existence, were not condi-tioned solely by the demand for capital in the different branches of the economy at different times, but also by the interests of those supplying capital, which could influence not only the timing of developments but also their character. It is with that in mind that the role performed in the economy by the New York Stock Exchange and its membership should be examined, for they served both those wishing to issue stocks and bonds and those desirous of purchasing them.

There were three distinct components involved in the process of raising capital through the medium of transferable securities, namely, their issuing, marketing and trading. Of primary importance was the role of issuing stocks or bonds in order to obtain the finance required. In the *ante bellum* period this process was largely dominated by unspecialized middlemen, particularly lawyers, merchants and bankers. However, as the needs of the users of capital became larger and more complex, a group of professionals specializing in the business began to appear. Even before the Civil War the railroads' requirement of large sums in short periods from many people over a wide area was leading to the development of specialist firms, and this was greatly accelerated by the federal government's bond financing operations. As a consequence, in the *post bellum* era there emerged a distinct and coherent group controlling all large-scale issues of stocks and bonds, and these were the investment bankers.[16]

Between 1907 and 1912, for example, four such firms – J. P. Morgan, Lee Higginson, Kidder Peabody and Kuhn Loeb – together handled issues estimated at $2.8 billion, or $645 million per annum. This was equivalent to almost 40 per cent of all the personal new investment in securities during that period.[17] In addition, other banking institutions were also major issuers, such as National City Bank, First National Bank and the Central Trust Company, while other investment banking firms also existed or were constantly making their appearance. These smaller firms tended to concentrate on particular areas neglected by the major issuers, such as Goldman Sachs's involvement with the securities of automobile manufacturers and retail chains, or the commitment of firms outside the North-east to the stocks and bonds of local enterprises and authorities. The Chicago investment bankers, for instance, made only twelve issues, totalling $7.8 million, in 1900, but seventy-nine for $58.9 million in 1912, and virtually all related to the Midwest. These were small issues, for the larger ones, such as those on behalf of the railroads, continued to be handled by eastern firms.[18]

The process of issuing itself became more demanding and complicated, moving far beyond the stage of a simple commission business. Increasingly the investment bank was required, at the very least, to underwrite the issue, while it soon became normal practice to purchase the issue outright and then resell it to investors. By this means the body or enterprise for whom the issue was being made obtained the finance it required at a price fixed in advance, leaving the investment banker to accept any risk of the securities not being taken up by the public. Of course, the investment banker was paid for this by receiving the securities at a discount to face value, with the profit to be made in the difference between the purchase and resale price.

Illustrative of both the procedure and the expectation of one of the bankers involved is the following comment by Henry Seligman in 1910, on a proposed issue of $15 million in short-term bonds for General Motors, which his firm was handling along with Kuhn Loeb, Lee Higginson and the Central Trust:

> I consider it an excellent piece of business and the terms most liberal, which we were only able to get on account of the company having gone ahead too rapidly and found itself short of working capital owing to the enormous growth of the business. I believe we will have very little difficulty in placing the notes, as they show earnings of practically ten times the fixed charges.[19]

By 1910 this had become standard practice, but it was already commonplace in the 1870s.[20]

This placed an obligation on the investment bankers to mobilize huge sums in order to purchase on favourable terms the securities which corporations or authorities wished to issue. As a result syndicates of investment bankers, financial institutions and wealthy individuals were formed which were capable of financing the largest imaginable issue using their own and borrowed funds. The firm of J. P. Morgan, for instance, was reputed in 1910 to be able to raise around $3 billion for the purchase of any securities it agreed to take, and did raise $200 million for the issue of US Steel made in 1901. On a more typical level, Kuhn Loeb paid $10 million in 1908 for an issue of 4 per cent convertible and redeemable bonds by Western Union and then had them 'distributed among at least several hundred holders both in this country and in Europe', according to the New York Stock Exchange. Insurance companies increasingly participated in syndicate purchases, and so obtained securities directly rather than via the market, as had been the case in the past.[21] From the position of being the commissioned agent, in the United

States the issuer of the securities became the arranger of the finance, receiving in return stocks and bonds which could then be sold to institutional or individual investors, or carried by the firm itself using both its own funds and those borrowed from banks. That latter practice had also become commonplace by the late nineteenth century.[22]

Though the members of these syndicates did agree to purchase securities for their own portfolios, most expected to resell them at a profit to their clients, who might in turn be financial intermediaries with their own clients to whom the stocks or bonds could be sold. By this process securities were distributed to the investing public, of whom there were some two million members by 1912, with an average holding of $25,700 each.[23] In order to tap this numerous, widespread and diverse number, the investment bankers took to extensive advertising and the employment of salesmen, as well as steadily accumulating a client base that could be circulated with all offers. Specialist retailers of securities also appeared, such as Harvey Fisk & Sons and N. W. Harris, which built up extensive sales networks capable of absorbing vast amounts of stocks and bonds. One Wall Street firm had some 22,000 clients by 1907 and handled sales of bonds totalling $100 million per annum. Altogether, in bonds alone about $1.5 billion per annum was being distributed each year by 1912, with one-third being taken by financial institutions like insurance companies, trust companies and banks, and the remainder by the private investor.[24]

These middlemen increasingly dominated the marketing of securities in the United States, but there remained many smaller issues which were neither underwritten, purchased outright, nor distributed through specialist networks. For example, there were 7,045 banking companies in the country by 1910, and the general opinion was that their shareholders were 'generally made up largely of people who either live in the immediate vicinity or have had opportunities of personal acquaintance with the management'.[25] Under circumstances like these there was no need to employ the sophisticated apparatus of investment bankers in order to obtain the finance required, because that could be achieved through informal and local networks. Nevertheless, for the larger issues the specialist financial intermediaries had become essential if the required amount was to be raised at the price and time required.[26]

Within this system of issuing and distributing securities the New York Stock Exchange did play a direct role in that many of its members were active participants. A number of the principal investment banks, for example, had purchased seats. However, membership of the Stock Exchange often came long after the investment bank had created an established business, while others never became members. Even those that were members maintained a clear division between the issuing or distribution of securities and trading activity on the floor of the Exchange, frequently passing on orders from their clients to other members because it was outside their main activities. Membership was important not because of its direct value to issuing and distribution but because it brought with it the privilege of obtaining discount commission rates, which was denied to non-members. The investment banks needed to buy and sell issued securities, both to employ their own funds and on behalf of clients or syndicate members, and so any reduction on the fixed minimum commission rates was of value to them. Nevertheless, very few new securities were disposed of by sale on the Exchange, as only small lots of the most actively traded issues could be absorbed in that way.[27]

Other than this the only other direct involvement of New York Stock Exchange members with the issue and distribution of stocks and bonds was the commission they were paid for any purchases made by their clients. Many brokers possessed extensive contacts among investors; and through them this network could be tapped to sell new securities. However, the existence of specialist retailers of securities in the United States greatly reduced the importance of broker contacts in persuading investors to purchase.[28] Consequently, the Stock Exchange played a very limited role in the means by which government bodies and corporate enterprise obtained the finance they required. That was largely the preserve of institutions, individuals, or firms which were either not members or to which membership was not an essential part of the mechanism. Thus the concept of raising finance through an issue on the New York Stock Exchange bears little or no relationship to the course of actual events. The Stock Exchange's contribution to the capital market was not a direct one but took place indirectly.

In order to encourage investors to purchase securities not only had they to be attractive in their own right but a market was required where they could be subsequently bought and sold. Few investors could afford to commit their savings indefinitely, or for long periods, but this is what those issuing the securities, like the government and railroads, required. Thus the right to transfer was all important but it had to be supported by an assured market if it was to be meaningful. Investment bankers realized this difficulty and took trouble to ensure that the resale facility did exist, even if it involved them making a market in and between their own offices. More generally, it was this market that the various stock exchanges provided, and the better it was the readier investors were to purchase and hold securities rather than any other type of asset, whether tangible or intangible.[29] The importance of this was clearly recognized, as in this comment of 1875 by one New York brokerage firm:

> The Stock Exchange, with its enormous daily transactions, affords to institutions and private investors a regular market for buying and selling securities. It gives at all times to their bonds and stocks a definite price, at which they can be turned into money at a moment's notice; every day's newspaper tells them the exact cash value of their securities, and they are as sure of it as if they held the amount in money.[30]

The existence of this facility made an enormous difference to the willingness of investors to buy and hold not only securities in preference to other investments but also one security rather than another, for it was those with the most active market that were the most desirable.[31]

However, in the provision of this secondary market the role of the New York Stock Exchange was lessened by the fact that it was not the only means through which issued stocks and bonds could be bought and sold. By 1913, for example, the Stock Exchange's quotation of securities totalled $26 billion – not all of which were actively traded – and this was equivalent to around 45 per cent of all securities in existence in the United States by that date. In fact, the Stock Exchange's importance in the securities market was on the wane. At the turn of the century approximately 60 per cent of all US securities had been quoted there. The picture is clear if one examines railroad securities.[32] In 1884 the Stock Exchange listed

$4.4 billion in US railroad stocks and bonds, which was 83 per cent of the total known to the investing public. By 1914 the exchange's listings had risen to $18.7 billion, but this was only 70 per cent of all those in general circulation.[33] Altogether, by the eve of the First World War the New York Stock Exchange quoted only 511 different stocks and 1,096 bonds, confining itself to the issues made by the principal railroad and industrial corporations and the government. The unlisted department had been abandoned in 1910, while certain securities, such as the Standard Oil stocks, had never been given a market.[34]

The New York Stock Exchange nevertheless had an importance in the secondary market far greater than the impression conveyed by a concentration on the proportion of securities quoted or the restricted economic sectors served. The Stock Exchange increasingly concentrated on the largest issues, neglecting or refusing all others. In railroad securities, for instance, the average size of each single issue it quoted was $7.3 million in 1884 but $21.4 million in 1914. In contrast, the average size of those not quoted was only $0.7 million in 1884 and $2.6 million in 1914. A similar situation prevailed among industrial and commercial securities; the average size of those listed in 1914 was $24.7 million compared to $7.5 million for those not granted that privilege. Thus it was the Stock Exchange that provided the market for securities with a national, or even international, appeal wherever they operated or whatever they did. Also, within the securities it quoted, there was a concentration upon bonds rather than stocks. In 1913, while the Stock Exchange provided a market for only 35 per cent of the nation's stocks, it listed 63 per cent of its bonds.[35] This reflected the New York Stock Exchange's central role as the principal link between the United States capital and money markets, as opposed to any other security trading organization or system.

Part of the turnover of the New York Stock Exchange did consist of the regular sale and purchase of securities for investment purposes, as holders constantly exchanged stocks and bonds amongst themselves to reflect changing individual circumstances. It was this flexibility that made securities so attractive an investment as opposed to other assets.[36] However, this type of business was in a minority on the Stock Exchange, being much more characteristic of the other markets. Municipal bonds, for example, of which there were $1.1 billion in existence by 1890, were largely purchased for investment purposes, and they were mainly traded via a telephone market conducted by the investment bankers on behalf of their clients, especially banks, insurance companies and trustees, who wished to purchase as they received funds which had to be invested, or who were required to make sales as payments became due.[37] In contrast, the investigation into the concentration of control of money and credit, which reported in 1913, concluded that

> It has appeared that sales of stocks on the New York Stock Exchange average $15,500,000,000 annually; that but a small part of these transactions is of an investment character; that whilst another part represents wholesome speculation, a far greater part represents speculation indistinguishable in effect from wagering and more hurtful than lotteries or gambling at the race track or the roulette table because practised on a vastly wider scale and withdrawing from productive industry vastly more capital; that as an adjunct of such speculation quotations of securities are manipulated without regard to real values and false appearances of demand or supply are created, and this not only without hindrance from, but with the approval of the authorities of the exchange, provided only the transactions are not purely fictitious.

The report's final condemnation was one probably echoed throughout the country, since many even in Wall Street could not see the value of their own business: 'the facilities of the New York Stock Exchange are employed largely for transactions producing moral and economic waste and corruption'.[38]

Any examination of turnover certainly produces ample verification for such a viewpoint. In 1893, for instance, the stock issued by only twenty-one corporations, or 14 per cent of those listed, produced 84 per cent of total stock sales, while those of sixty corporations, or 39 per cent of the total, generated a mere 0.2 per cent of turnover. The normal picture was of business on the Stock Exchange being dominated by extensive trading in a few selected securities, which far outran the value of their issues capital.[39] For the single year 1901 turnover in the common stock of the Union Pacific Railroad was twenty-two times greater than the amount quoted, and a similar situation existed in the stock of a few other railroad and industrial enterprises. The case of the Reading Railroad provides one measure of the extent to which buying and selling did not represent genuine investment interest. Between January 1906 and November 1912 the 1.4 million shares of this company generated 216.6 million sales, or approximately 30.9 million shares sold per annum, but only a total of 18.6 million ever had ownership transferred on the books of the company. Therefore, the common stock was turned over an average of twenty-two times a year, but only 8.6 per cent of this reached the stage of payment and delivery, leaving 91.4 per cent as purely speculative.[40] It was this that the general public saw, with the result that the New York Stock Exchange was sometimes regarded as not only contributing little to the economy but actually diverting investment to valueless ends.

However, the existence of an active and continuous market in a small number of large security issues was of major importance within an economy in which institutional control of the money supply was becoming paramount. In 1870 the money stock totalled $2.21 billion, of which 58 per cent consisted of bank deposits – as opposed to cash, currency and gold. By 1916 the money supply had risen to $30.0 billion, with 79 per cent being bank deposits, and this was the component that was being most actively used, as the popularity of payment by cheque grew rapidly. In Wall Street, for instance, all transactions were paid for by cheques, with cash never to be seen. There thus existed a vast supply of short-term funds in the hands of financial institutions which could not be invested long-term because they could be either immediately or quickly withdrawn, as in the case of a bank and its deposits, or required for another purpose, as with an insurance company. Even if only 10 per cent of bank deposits were kept as a liquid reserve this produced a sum of $0.1 billion in 1870 and $2.4 billion in 1916, which could not be locked into long-term investment. At the same time these institutions were under pressure to employ such funds remuneratively either to cover the interest they were paying to the depositors or to meet their own running costs. Thus, if some means could be devised to match this supply of short-term money with the demand for long-term capital, the economy would gain access to a vast new source of finance.[41] The New York Stock Exchange was intimately involved with this process; it offered an increasingly sophisticated service to those who either wanted a profitable and suitable home for their savings or required to gain access to the appropriate finance at the lowest cost.

The existence of the New York Stock Exchange and the market it provided allowed investors to buy securities for the shortest of periods, with the expectation that they could be easily and quickly resold if required. Securities issues for purposes of long-term finance could thus be held by a continuous succession of investors using funds only temporarily released from other purposes. The motive was profit, as the value of bonds in particular appreciated as they gained entitlement to interest, and so an enhanced price between purchase and sale could be obtained. Otherwise, a bond could be bought immediately before, and sold immediately after, the interest became due for a profit that consisted of the income received minus the decline in price. An active market offered innumerable opportunities for small but quick gains, and so financial institutions, especially, constantly employed idle balances in the buying and selling of stocks and bonds. High-grade listed bonds, in particular, were always readily saleable and possessed a price that deviated little from a predictable pattern.[42] As a consequence it was noted as early as 1871 that

> During the summer months, when money rules low, many savings banks, insurance companies and similar institutions purchase these bonds for the very purpose of realizing this distinct and fixed interest, thus creating an active demand for these securities at that season, as well as furnishing a good supply of the same when they dispose of them in the fall.[43]

United States insurance companies increasingly employed the premiums they received in securities both for the income and capital growth they generated and as a short-term home for funds either awaiting long-term investment or required to meet sudden payments. As a result, while the total assets of life insurance companies alone rose from $2.69 million in 1870 to $3,876 million in 1910, the proportion in securities grew from 17.8 per cent to 46.2 per cent, of which over 90 per cent was in bonds. A similar situation also developed with state and national banks. Even large industrial corporations that were constantly receiving and making payments employed a proportion of their capital in readily marketable securities rather than keeping it all in idle cash.[44]

However, the direct investment of temporary funds in securities by financial institutions and others was only one part of the process. There was also an enormous expansion of lending based on stocks and bonds as collateral, and, as Woodlock observed in 1908: 'The existence of a market for securities is the first requisite for any system of lending on securities.'[45] The longer money was borrowed for, the higher the rate of interest charged, with lending on a day-to-day basis on the floor of the New York Stock Exchange yielding the lowest return. Thus, by borrowing on a daily basis but lending longer-term, a profit of the differential between the two interest rates could be made. In 1910 a broker borrowing on call could make a running profit ranging from 3.32 per cent per annum (if the proceeds were invested in preference stocks) to 1.51 per cent, if railroad bonds were chosen.[46] This was before any expenses had been met.

Generally, the greater the liquidity of the investment chosen the smaller the risk, and this was reflected in the margin between the market value of the security and the amount lent, which could vary from 10 to 50 per cent, and in the interest charged on the loan. If interest rates rose or money became tight, the securities could be sold and the arrangement terminated; the easier the sale, the less risk there was attached to the process. To safeguard their position the banks and other lending institutions consequently tried to restrict their loans to collateral that altered little in price and could be readily sold, if necessary; while, to increase their profits, brokers were always trying to use borrowed funds to invest in slightly less liquid but more remunerative securities. As John Hickling put it in 1875: 'When an abundance of money is in circulation it is more easily obtained at low rates; so you buy stocks because it is easy to carry them. On the other hand, if money is scarce the rates become higher; you therefore sell to avoid the expense of carrying.'[47] This practice produced occasional crises, as banks overlent and brokers overborrowed, during periods of easy money. For, when circumstances changed, producing sharp if often temporary contractions in credit, the overall amount available for lending on securities was reduced, forcing sales at declining prices. This caught out those banks and brokers that had made the least provision for such an eventuality. H. Kennedy & Co., a New York brokerage firm, failed in April 1877 carrying 30,000 railroad shares financed as to 5 per cent by its own capital and the rest borrowed. Similarly, Mayer & Co. failed in February 1908 carrying 27,000 shares of the Delaware & Hudson Railroad and 35,000 shares of International Pump. The suspension in November 1890 of the brokerage firm Decker, Howell & Co. led in turn to the suspension of the Bank of North America; the firm left debts of about $10 million, and $0.9 million came from that one bank, which then could not cover its obligations to other banks, and faced a run because of its known substantial involvement with that particular brokerage firm.[48] Failure was rare, however, with only an average 0.54 per cent of all New York Stock Exchange members becoming bankrupt in any one year between 1900 and 1913, which was a lower proportion than in banking or in commerce.[49]

By 1912 between $40 and $50 million a day was being lent out on behalf of banks, trust companies and others on the floor of the New York Stock Exchange itself. Certain brokers, like Griesel & Rogers, specialized in the operation, maintaining extensive contacts with both lending institutions and borrowing brokers. However, this was only one part of the process, for most brokers had private arrangements with one or more banks, borrowing on both time and call, and using the money broker to meet sudden additional needs. In addition, there were numerous other private and institutional investors who borrowed using marketable securities as collateral. It was estimated that between 1868 and 1913 from one-third to one-half of all loans by national banks were in the form of call loans being used to purchase stocks and bonds, and this ratio was fairly typical of commercial banking as a whole. Thirty-one New York financial institutions alone had $789.8 million outstanding in 1912, secured by stock collateral, and this had risen from $641.5 million by twenty-nine institutions in 1908.[50]

No other centre could match New York's importance in the nation's money market. Even before the Civil War balances were accumulating in New York because of the need to have funds available there to make payments in both internal and international commerce. These funds were increasingly employed in making call loans to brokers, both for their own use and for their clients. As a result more funds were attracted to New York, as interest was paid there on money that remained unemployable elsewhere in the country.[51] The banking and currency legislation of the mid-1860s further enhanced the importance of New York by compelling banks to keep a proportion of their reserve funds there, but New York had little need for such assistance – its dominance was already established. In the period after the Civil War an integrated and national money market appeared, reflected in a significant narrowing of inter-regional interest-rate differentials, though variations still remained by the First World War.[52]

Within this money market New York was of paramount importance. In 1909, for instance, though that city contained less than one per cent of all the nation's banks, these 159 banks controlled 15 per cent of all bank capital, 21 per cent of all bank assets and 23 per cent of all deposits, while they also undertook 18 per cent of all lending and maintained 35 per cent of liquid reserves. A similar degree of domination existed with other financial intermediaries like life insurance and trust companies, savings institutions and investment banking. In terms of activity in the money market, however, the dominance of New York was even greater; for approximately 60 per cent of all inter-bank clearings took place there, with the New York volume rising from $7.2 billion in 1860 to $147.2 billion in 1916, despite attempts to economize on use, such as the introduction of clearing on the New York Stock Exchange itself in 1892.[53] As the United States progressed towards the creation of a single money market, New York emerged as the dominant centre, providing a clearing mechanism for all monetary transactions through the extensive links maintained by New York banks with their counterparts elsewhere. One New York bank, the Hanover Bank, had 4,074 correspondents nationwide by 1912, while some thirty New York financial institutions lent out on average approximately $130 million per annum on behalf of out-of-town banks between 1908 and 1912.[54]

The result was that a substantial proportion of securities were held using finance borrowed short-term from lenders in the money market with the expectation that as one loan was withdrawn another was made available. In addition there existed a small but significant amount of floating debt, consisting of the securities of the most actively traded securities, which acted almost as a form of currency among the market participants. In the period 1881–4 an estimated 39 per cent of the shares of Western Union, for example, were in the hands of the brokers, while by the twentieth century attention had switched to such securities as those issued by US Steel, where

57 per cent of the common stock was held by brokers between 1909 and 1913. As a security was gradually withdrawn from the market by investors, trading became less active and attention switched to another issue of stocks or bonds. It was not the intrinsic value of the security that mattered, only that it was very actively traded, for this meant that it could always be readily bought and sold. Thus it was both a liquid reserve and a remunerative investment whose possession provided a cushion before more remunerative but less liquid securities had to be sold in any contraction of loans. The nearer a stock or bond approached the level of universal acceptability that notes or coins had, the more it was valued as a medium of exchange rather than as an interest-bearing asset. This was the position that an active market imparted to certain securities within the confines of the financial intermediaries that were involved.[55]

The criticism that the New York Stock Exchange absorbed funds that could be more productively employed elsewhere can therefore be seen as an unjust one, since the Stock Exchange's very existence both allowed the mobilization of savings that would have remained unused and allowed other savings to be channelled into activities where finance was in short supply. Obviously the system by which this was achieved was abused, but that did not mean that the Stock Exchange did not itself perform a necessary and valuable function. However, the necessity for daily delivery and the limited clearing arrangements made, particularly before 1892, did mean that the Stock Exchange's performance of its role was rendered less smooth than it need have been, and absorbed more savings than required. Daily delivery tied up a great deal of bank credit because it required the outside financing of sales and purchases rather than having them carried on the basis of trust between members. At the same time the close and extensive connections between brokerage firms and banks could lead to the transmission of failure on the Stock Exchange to banking collapses and a general crisis in confidence in financial circles, with consequences for both the credit provision for business and long-term investment. Consequently, the way the Stock Exchange organized its system of trading created strains within the money market that contributed to the frequent and sometimes severe cyclical behaviour of the US economy at this time. While it would not have been possible to avoid these altogether, the adoption of a system where more dealing was conducted on trust might have reduced both the frequency and severity of credit contractions by putting less pressure on the money supply at times of difficulty.[56]

The contributions of the New York Stock Exchange to the US economy can now be clearly seen to lie in its involvement with both the capital and money markets and its dual serving of lenders and borrowers. Of primary importance was the way it expanded the supply of capital for long-term investment by allowing governments and corporations to tap the much larger pool of short-term funds. The success of this can be seen both in the growing popularity of security finance as opposed to any other and, more specifically, in the use of bonds rather than stocks. Between 1910 and 1916 a total of $1.7 billion in securities was issued in the United States; 72 per cent of this was in bonds and only 28 per cent in stocks. Earlier, judging from the capital structure of railroads, stocks had been of at least equal importance.[57] Without a securities market, and particularly the New York Stock Exchange, it is most unlikely that this level of funding could have been provided, with major consequences for the whole pattern and pace of US economic development, especially the creation of such capital-intensive projects as the railroads.

However, the benefits that the New York Stock Exchange provided did not end with its role in expanding the supply of finance, for it also contributed to capital mobility. On a domestic level it was in the settled regions of the North-east that the ownership of stocks and bonds was concentrated, but much of the investment they represented took place elsewhere, especially in the case of the railroad network. Conversely, investors in these areas, especially financial institutions, had need of openings for short-term funds as the prosperity of their own regions grew, and so directed them to New York. The outcome of this was that the West and South obtained from outside an enhanced supply of relatively cheap capital to undertake the necessary infrastructure investment, and part of this was financed by the employment in security loans in New York of the funds they themselves were directing there.[58]

Internationally, a similar position existed with respect to Canada. Canadian banks and insurance companies employed a substantial proportion of their liquid funds on the New York money market in either loans on securities or purchases of US stocks and bonds.

The Bank of Montreal, for example, had placed some $50 million in New York by 1913. Canada did not possess a money or securities market which could absorb their loans, purchases and sales without the severe fluctuations which the financial institutions wished to avoid. Conversely, US investors purchased extensively such Canadian securities as the stock of the Canadian Pacific Railroad as well as numerous smaller issues. There was a constant flow of short-term funds from Canada to New York, because that was where they could be fully employed, and a return flow of long-term capital from the north-eastern United States, via New York, to Canada in response to favourable opportunities there.[59]

In the case of western Europe, the relationship was one where investors there both purchased large amounts of US stocks and bonds and lent heavily on the New York money market. By 1914 the United States owed foreign investors, mainly European, a total of $7.2 billion, of which 75 per cent was in securities and 7 per cent short-term borrowings. In the *post bellum* era European investors purchased the issues of US railroads in particular, especially the bonds, creating a common transatlantic market in many of these securities, in which there was a continuous ebb and flow between the principal financial centres. By 1913, for instance, twenty-three foreign banking houses were carrying more than $100 million of US Steel common stock, and this could be readily switched from one country to another depending upon demand.[60]

Not only did the existence of the New York Stock Exchange expand the available supply of funds for investment, then, but it also facilitated its movement from one region and sector to another both within the United States and internationally. Savings were not homogeneous but possessed infinite variety, as did the potential uses to which they could be put. What the Stock Exchange did was to ensure that as few barriers as possible existed to the mobilization and matching of lenders and borrowers. A myriad of financial currents appeared in the United States, many of which appear to have involved wasteful duplication, such as the movement of funds to and from New York from the West and abroad. However, if they had not existed, would the same volume of supply of finance have been available or the same willingness to lend and invest?

This can be seen most clearly in the seasonal nature of turnover on the New York Stock Exchange. Over the years 1897–1913 business was 7 per cent above the monthly average for stocks, and 13 per cent above for bonds, in the months from October to April, while for both it was 10 per cent under in the period May to September. In bonds November, December and January were the most active months, while July, August and September were the slackest. This reflected the Stock Exchange's response to the harvest cycle. Agriculture made its greatest demands for money when the crops were being harvested, marketed and sold, with the finance being gradually released as stocks were run down, before the sum was required again the following autumn. Investment in securities provided a counter-balance to this seasonal demand, through the connection between the Stock Exchange and the money market, as well as allowing funds to be obtained internationally to assist in the huge financing operations that United States agriculture required. The financial requirements of the harvest could therefore be diffused not only throughout the United States but also abroad through the mechanism provided by the Stock Exchange for switching ownership of securities at will and absorbing or releasing short-term funds.[61]

Though the seasonal cycle was predictable, a similar position existed with the periodic crises that from time to time affected the functioning of the world economy and disrupted relationships between countries. During the Baring crisis of 1890, for example, British investors found themselves locked into Argentinian investments which could be sold only at very low prices if at all. However, these investors were able to realize cash in order to meet their commitments by selling US railroad bonds, which were absorbed by US investors who had not been involved in Argentinian investments. As the *New York Times* put it on 8 November 1890:

London, caught loaded with unmarketable rattletraps from the furthermost ends of the earth, has been forced into a great financial liquidation; and the result has long been felt here – for finding the readiest market for their American stocks, the Europeans have sold back to us the greater portion of the United States railway stock investments.[62]

The ability to share the consequences of any financial disaster through the links between different securities markets did not result in the disappearance of crises but did mean that their consequences were neither so severe nor so long lasting as they might have been. Security movements provided a necessary equilibrium both between economies and through links with the money market.[63]

When the relationship between the New York Stock Exchange and the capital and money markets is investigated, the institution's central role in the economy thus becomes clear. Not only did it contribute significantly to the mobilization of the finance but it was one of the major instruments of the fine tuning that maintained equilibrium in an economy which had neither a central bank nor an interventionist government. Though crises did occur, and organizational changes within the Exchange might have moderated these, the role it performed was an essential one. Only through a failure to recognize the strength of this link between the Stock Exchange and the money market, both at home and abroad, can most of its activities be dismissed as wasteful speculation rather than being seen as part of the process whereby the supply and demand for credit, within an increasingly complex national and international economy, were equalized with a fair degree of success. Few contemporaries recognized the importance of this role, let alone the brokers on the floor who sought to do nothing more than turn a profit on every deal, but it existed nevertheless.

Notes

1 US Department of Commerce, *Historical Statistics of the United States* (Washington, 1975), Series F 250–61.

2 S. Kuznets, *Capital in the American Economy: Its Formation and Financing* (Princeton, 1961), pp. 112, 136; L. E. Davis, 'The Investment Market, 1870–1914: The Evolution of a National Market', *Journal of Economic History*, vol. 35 (1965), pp. 335, 391.

3 H. E. Kroos and M. R. Blyn, *A History of Financial Intermediaries* (New York, 1971), p. 19; J. A. James, *Money and Capital Markets in Postbellum America* (Princeton, 1978), p. 36; M. Friedman and A. J. Schwartz, *Monetary Trends in the United States and the United Kingdom: Their Relation to Income, Prices and Interest Rates, 1867–1975* (Chicago, 1982), p. 3; Davis, 'Investment Market', p. 385.

4 US Department of Commerce, *Historical Statistics*, Series F 377–421; S. S. Huebner, 'Scope and Functions of the Stock Market', in S. S. Huebner (ed.), *Stocks and the Stock Market* (Philadelphia, 1910), p. 2.

5   US Department of Commerce, *Historical Statistics*, Series F 250–61, K 1–16, 361–75, V 41–53.

6   US Department of Commerce, *Historical Statistics*, Series N 196–99, 262–77.

7   H. C. Livesay and G. Porter, 'The Financial Role of Merchants in the Development of US Manufacturing 1815–60', *Explorations in Economic History*, vol. 9 (1971), p. 67; N. R. Lamoreaux, *The Great Merger Movement in American Business, 1895–1904* (Cambridge, 1985), p. 56; US Department of Commerce, *Historical Statistics*, Series P 1–12, V 20–30, 41–53.

8   US Department of Commerce, *Historical Statistics*, Series Q 283–312, 346–55, 356–66, Series V 271–84.

9   US Department of Commerce, *Historical Statistics*, Series P 1–12, 123–76, 197–204, Series T 220–4, Series V 41–53.

10 A. D. Chandler, *The Visible Hand: The Managerial Revolution in American Business* (Cambridge, Mass., 1977), pp. 168–9, 376; D. O. Whitten, *The Emergence of Giant Enterprise, 1860–1914: American Commercial Enterprise and Extractive Industries* (Westport, 1983), pp. 61, 130, 169, 176; *Wall Street Journal*, 26 November 1913; *New York American*, 9 January 1914; J. E. Meeker, *The Work of the Stock Exchange* (New York, 1930), p. 587; A. D. Chandler, 'The Beginning of "Big Business" in American Industry', in R. L. Andreano (ed.), *New Views on American Economic Development* (Cambridge, Mass., 1965), p. 279.

11 *Wall Street Journal*, 26 November 1913; *New York American*, 9 January 1914.

12 *New York American*, 9 January 1914; Huebner, 'Scope and Functions', p. 2.

13 US Department of Commerce, *Historical Statistics*, Series Y 493–504, 522–32, Series X 393–409.

14 US Department of Commerce, *Historical Statistics*, Series F 337–52, 540–1, 638–67.

15 US Department of Commerce, *Historical Statistics*, Series Q 356–66, Series V 38–40; Whitten, *Giant Enterprise*, pp. 114, 123, 169, 176; New York Stock Exchange (NYSE): Committee on Stock List, Listing Statements, e.g. Southern Pacific Company, 1 May 1889; Edison General Electric Co., 29 January 1890; National Starch Manufacturing Co., 6 June 1890; Distilling & Cattle Feeding Co., 18 June 1890; American Tobacco Co., 16 June 1890; US Rubber, 1 December 1892; Atchison, Topeka & Santa Fe, 7 April 1896; US Steel, 6 March 1901, 1 April 1901; R. Sylla, 'Federal Policy, Banking Market Structure and Capital Mobilization in the United States, 1863–1913', in R. Cameron (ed.), *Banking and Economic Development: Some Lessons of History* (New York, 1972), p. 256; N. R. Lamoreaux, *The Great Merger Movement in American Business, 1895–1904* (Cambridge, 1985), pp. 87, 111–13, 117, 189–90; Chandler, 'Beginning of "Big Business"', p. 291; T. R. Navin and M. V. Sears, 'The Rise of a Market for Industrial

Securities, 1887–1902', *Business History Review*, vol. 29 (1955), pp. 117, 133; Chandler, *The Visible Hand*, p. 169.

16　V. P. Carosso, *Investment Banking in America: A History* (Cambridge, Mass., 1970), pp. 13, 51, 85; D. C. North, 'Life Insurance and Investment Banking at the Time of the Armstrong Investigation of 1905–6', *Journal of Economic History*, vol. 14 (1954), p. 214.

17　Calculated from US Congress, *Report of the Committee Appointed to Investigate the Concentration of Control of Money and Credit* (28 February 1913), pp. 57, 75–8, 130; US Congress, *Investigation of Financial and Monetary Conditions in the United States* (Money Trust Investigation; Washington, 1912), pp. 1341; North, 'Life Insurance', pp. 213–14; US Department of Commerce, *Historical Statistics*, F 638–67.

18　D. M. Dailey, *Investment Banking in Chicago* (Urbana, 1931), pp. 10–11, 15; North, 'Life Insurance', pp. 213–4; Carosso, *Investment Banking*, pp. 32, 51, 85, 101–2.

19　Henry Seligman to Isaac Seligman, 20 September 1910.

20　Morton Bliss & Co., Letter Books: G. Bliss to L. P. Morton, 30 January 1892, 2 February 1892, 7 March 1892; cf. 24 June 1876, 11 January 1882, 20 January 1882, 23 July 1884, 24 February 1888; D. Greenberg, *Financiers and Railroads, 1869–1889: A Study of Morton, Bliss and Company* (Newark, 1980), pp. 139, 166–7, 193.

21　NYSE: Committee on Stock List, 20 January 1908, 21 March 1901; cf. Greenberg, *Financiers and Railroads*, pp. 43–4, 139, 166–7; North, 'Life Insurance', pp. 211–12, 215; E. G. Nourse, *Brokerage* (New York, 1910), pp. 105, 109; J. E. Hedges, *Commercial Banking and the Stock Market before 1863* (Baltimore, 1938), pp. 43–4; US Congress, Money Trust Investigation, pp. 1660–3.

22　W. Foley, 'Organisation and Management of a Bond House', in W. H. Hull (ed.), *Bonds as Investment Securities* (Philadelphia, 1907), pp. 64, 67, 70.

23　Kroos and Blyn, *Financial Intermediaries*, p. 129; W. C. Van Antwerp, *The Stock Exchange from within* (New York, 1913), p. 15; US Department of Commerce, *Historical Statistics*, F 377–421, U 26–40.

24　S. A. Nelson, *The Bond Buyers' Dictionary* (New York, 1907), pp. 170, 173; L. Chamberlain, *The Work of the Bond House* (New York, 1912), pp. 9, 122; Carosso, *Investment Banking*, p. 102.

25　L. A. Norton, 'Stocks of Financial Institutions', in S. S. Huebner (ed.), *Stocks and the Stock Market* (Philadelphia, 1910), pp. 199–200; US Congress, *Report on Concentration of Control of Money and Credit*, p. 130.

26　S. S. Huebner, *The Stock Market* (New York, 1922), p. 330.

27　Carosso, *Investment Banking*, p. 19; Greenberg, *Financiers and Railroads*, p. 193; Nourse, *Brokerage*, p. 109; Meeker, *Work of the Stock Exchange*, p. 88; N. W. Harris & Co., *Municipal Bonds* (New York, 1897), pp. 33–45; Nelson, *Bond Buyers' Dictionary*, p. 170; Chamberlain, *Bond House*, pp. 11–12.

28　T. R. Navin and M. V. Sears, 'The Rise of a Market for Industrial

Securities, 1887–1902', *Business History Review*, vol. 29 (1955), p. 122; G. P. & A. W. Butler to E. B. Dane, 22 October 1906, and to W. C. Osborn, 2 December 1908; G. Bliss to L. P. Morton, 26 June 1876.

29 Meeker, *Work of the Stock Exchange*, p. 90; Chamberlain, *Bond House*, p. 57; Carosso, *Investment Banking*, p. 16; US Congress, Money Trust Investigation, p. 405; N. W. Halsey & Co., *The Most Satisfactory Bonds* (New York, 1912), p. 15; Fisk & Hatch, *Memoranda Concerning Government Bonds* (New York, 1882), p. 23.

30 L. W. Hamilton & Co., *Stock Speculation* (New York, 1875), p. 3.

31 Nourse, *Brokerage*, p. 110; J. K. Medbery, *Old Times in Wall Street* (New York, 1871), p. 3; Chamberlain, *Bond House*, pp. 42–3; F. W. Mundy, 'Railroad Bonds as Investment Security', in W. H. Hull (ed.), *Bonds as Investment Securities* (Philadelphia, 1907), p. 123; L. Spitzer, 'Industrial Bonds as an Investment', in Hull, *Bonds*, pp. 183, 191; F. A. Cleveland, 'Bonds in their Relation to Corporation Finance', in Hull, *Bonds*, pp. 227–8; Huebner, *Stock Market*, p. 20.

32 US Department of Commerce, *Historical Statistics*, Series F 377–421; W. C. Van Antwerp to A. Brisbane, 19 November 1913; Pratt, *Work of Wall Street*, p. 82.

33 Calculated from the *Financial Review* (New York), 1884 and 1914.

34 P. Wyckoff, *Wall Street and the Stock Markets: A Chronology, 1644–1971* (Philadelphia, 1972), pp. 32, 155; Meeker, *Work of the Stock Exchange*, p. 260; Carosso, *Investment Banking*, p. 78; Jones & Baker, *The History of the New York Curb* (New York, 1916), pp. 10–11.

35 *Financial Review*, 1884 and 1914; Van Antwerp to Brisbane, 19 November 1913; US Department of Commerce, *Historical Statistics*, Series F 377–421.

36 Navin and Sears, 'Rise of a Market', p. 106.

37 N. W. Harris & Co., *Municipal Bonds* (New York, 1897), pp. 28–9.

38 US Congress, *Report on Concentration of Control of Money and Credit*, p. 116; cf. Pratt, *Work of Wall Street*, p. viii; R. Sobel, *The Big Board: A History of the New York Stock Market* (New York, 1965), p. 94.

39 Calculated from Clapp & Co., *Weekly Market Letters for 1893* (New York, 1894), p. 155; cf. F. L. Eames, *The New York Stock Exchange* (New York, 1894), p. 94.

40 US Congress, Money Trust Investigation, pp. 690, 695, 1120, 1132; Pratt, *Work of Wall Street*, p. 45; B. E. Schultz, *Stock Exchange Procedure* (New York, 1936), pp. 14, 18.

41 US Department of Commerce, *Historical Statistics*, Series X 410–19; cf. M. Friedman and A. J. Schwartz, *A Monetary History of the United States and the United Kingdom, 1867–1975* (Chicago, 1982), pp. 151, 262; James, *Money and Capital Markets*, p. 34; M. G. Myers, *The New York Money Market: Origins and Development* (New York, 1931), p. 238.

42 Nelson, *Bond Buyer's Dictionary*, p. 34; Nourse, *Brokerage*, p. 108; A. Cragg, *Understanding the Stock Market* (New York, 1929), p. 198; W. C. Cornwell, 'Bonds as Additional Banking Reserve', in Hull, *Bonds*,

pp. 101, 114; F. A. Cleveland, 'Relation to Corporation Finance', pp. 227–8; Huebner, *Stock Market*, p. 23–30; James, *Money and Capital Markets*, pp. 47–8.

43 NYSE: Petition from the Dealers in US Bonds, 18 December 1871; cf. G. Bliss to L. P. Morton, 29 February 1888.

44 US Department of Commerce, *Historical Statistics*, Series V 285–305, Series X 588–609, 821–32, 908–17; James, *Money and Capital Markets*, p. 50.

45 T. F. Woodlock, *The Stock Exchange and the Money Market* (New York, 1908), p. 23.

46 US Department of Commerce, *Historical Statistics*, Series X 444–55, 474–86.

47 John Hicking & Co., *Men and Idioms of Wall Street* (New York, 1875), p. 18; cf. Cragg, *Understanding the Stock Market*, pp. 130, 192, 197; James, *Money and Capital Markets*, pp. 66, 102; H. Hamon, *New York Stock Exchange Manual* (New York, 1865), pp. 133–5; Nourse, *Brokerage*, p. 213; Pratt, *Work of Wall Street*, pp. 88, 192, 198; J. H. Hollander, *Bank Loans and Stock Exchange Speculation* (Washington, 1911), p. 4; A. A. Osborne, *Speculation on the New York Stock Exchange, September 1904–March 1907* (New York, 1913), pp. 15, 108.

48 NYSE: Committee on Insolvencies, 12 April 1877, 7 October 1885, 25 August 1888, 17 February 1908; W. M. Grosvenor, *American Securities* (New York, 1885), pp. 23–4, 42–3; *New York Tribune*, 7 May 1884, 15 May 1884, 12 November 1890; Friedman and Schwartz, *Monetary History*, p. 123; Pratt, *Work of Wall Street*, pp. 116, 185, 188, 200; NYSE: General Records, Circular *c.* 1873 (Beating for 'Account').

49 Meeker, *Work of the Stock Exchange*, p. 603.

50 US Congress, Money Trust Investigation, pp. 743–4, 753–4, 955–6, 1193; US Senate, *Regulation of the Stock Exchange: Hearings before the Committee on Banking and Currency* (Washington, 1914), pp. 551–2; Kroos and Blyn, *Financial Intermediaries*, p. 135; James, *Money and Capital Markets*, p. 66; W. M. Blaisdell, *Financing Security Trading* (Philadelphia, 1935), p. 165; Reply by the New York Stock Exchange to the Governor's Committee on Speculation in Securities and Commodities, 15 February 1909, p. 33.

51 J. E. Hedges, *Commercial Banking and the Stock Market before 1863* (Baltimore, 1938), pp. 65–75; W. Armstrong, *Stocks and Stock-Jobbing in Wall Street* (New York, 1848), pp. 10, 35; Medbery, *Old Times in Wall Street*, p. 67; Myers, *New York Money Market*, p. 103.

52 R. Sylla, 'The United States, 1863–1913', in R. Cameron (ed.), *Banking and Economic Development* (New York, 1972), p. 249; M. G. Myers, *A Financial History of the United States* (New York, 1970), p. 121; K. E. Born, *International Banking in the 19th and 20th Centuries* (Leamington Spa, 1983), pp. 93, 179; James, *Money and Capital Markets*, pp. 37, 39, 90–5. For the debate on the development of an integrated

money market see the following: L. Davis, 'The Investment Market, 1870 to 1914: The Evolution of a National Market', *Journal of Economic History*, vol. 25 (1965); R. Sylla, 'Federal Policy, Banking Market Structure and Capital Mobilization in the United States, 1863–1913', *Journal of Economic History*, vol. 29 (1969); G. Smiley, 'Interest Rate Movement in the United States, 1888–1913', *Journal of Economic History*, vol. 35 (1975); J. A. James, 'The Development of the National Money Market, 1893–1911', *Journal of Economic History*, vol. 36 (1976); M. E. Sushka and W. B. Barrett, 'Banking Structure and the National Capital Market, 1869–1914', *Journal of Economic History*, vol. 44 (1984).

53 C. A. E. Goodhart, *The New York Money Market and the Finance of Trade, 1900–1913* (Cambridge, Mass., 1969), pp. 11, 17; US Department of Commerce, *Historical Statistics*, Series X 792–5; Carosso, *Investment Banking*, pp. 105, 117, 151–3.

54 US Congress, Money Trust Investigation, pp. 960–1, 1193; Cornwell, 'Additional Banking Reserve', p. 100.

55 N. Green to Cyrus W. Field, 20 January 1885; Meeker, *Work of the Stock Exchange*, pp. 584–5; K. Cornwallis, *The Gold Room, and the New York Stock Exchange and Clearing House* (New York, 1879), p. 21; Cragg, *Understanding the Stock Market*, pp. 197–8; H. S. Martin, *The New York Stock Exchange* (New York, 1919), p. 170.

56 Blaisdell, *Financing Security Trading*, pp. 3, 33, 151, 165; J. P. Ryan, 'Call Money Rates and Stock Prices', in T. Gibson, *Special Market Letters for 1908* (New York, 1909), p. 96; NYSE: Special Committee of Inquiry into the Stock Commission Business, Report, 2 August 1887; NYSE, Circular, 12 May 1885; Nourse, *Brokerage*, pp. 210, 213; W. C. Schluter, *The Pre-War Business Cycle, 1907–1914* (New York, 1923), pp. 179–80.

57 US Department of Commerce, *Historical Statistics*, Series Q 340–55, 356–86, Series X 510–15.

58 L. E. Davis, 'Capital Mobility and American Growth', in R. W. Fogel and S. L. Engerman (eds.), *Reinterpretation of American Economic History* (New York, 1971), p. 229; James, *Money and Capital Markets*, pp. 55, 102; Smiley, 'Interest Rate Movement', p. 619; Sushka and Barrett, 'Banking Structure', p. 47; Nelson, *Bond Buyers' Dictionary*, pp. 63, 75, 133.

59 R. T. Naylor, 'Foreign and Domestic Investment in Canada: Institutions and Policy, 1867–1914' (PhD thesis, Cambridge University, 1979), pp. 144–5, 263, 267, 277, 286; Myers, *New York Money Market*, p. 112; Goodhart, *New York Money Market*, p. 180.

60 US Department of Commerce, *Historical Statistics*, Series U 26–40; J. G. Williamson, *American Growth and the Balance of Payments, 1820–1913* (Chapel Hill, 1964), pp. 125–6, 136, 259; C. F. Speare, 'Selling American Bonds in Europe', in Hull, *Bonds*, p. 91; Nourse, *Brokerage*, p. 109; *New York American*, 9 January 1914.

61 James, *Money and Capital Markets*, pp. 125, 142; A. Selwyn-Brown,

'Economic Crises and Stock Security Values', in Huebner, *Stocks and the Stock Market*, p. 162; E. W. Kemmerer, *Seasonal Variations in the Relative Demand for Money and Capital in the United States* (Washington, 1910), pp. 28–9, 173, 210, 217–18; R. N. Owens and C. O. Hardy, *Interest Rates and Stock Speculation: A Study of the Influence of the Money Market on the Stock Market* (New York, 1925), pp. 2–6, 18, 23–4, 26; Goodhart, *New York Money Market*, pp. 4–5, 19, 38, 40, 74–5, 79, 83–4, 122–3. Calculations from NYSE, Circular on Monthly Sales, April 1914.

62 *New York Times*, 8 and 16 November 1890; *New York Tribune*, 8, 11, 19 November 1890.

63 Schluter, *Pre-War Business Cycle*, p. 102; F. Escher, *Foreign Exchange Explained* (New York, 1917), pp. 17–18; A. W. Margraff, *International Exchange* (Chicago, 1903), p. 20; H. K. Brooks, *Foreign Exchange Text Book* (Chicago, 1906), pp. 3, 120; G. Paish, *The Trade Balance of the United States* (Washington, 1910), pp. 165, 175; C. A. Conant, *The Functions of the Stock Exchange* (New York, 1914), pp. 14–15; C. A. Conant, *Wall Street and the Country* (New York, 1904), pp. 13, 107; H. G. S. Noble, *The New York Stock Exchange in the Crisis of 1914* (New York, 1915), p. 6; R. Estcourt, 'The Stock Exchange as a Regulator of Currency', *The Annalist* (New York), vol. 14 (1919), pp. 136–8; US Senate, *Regulation of the Stock Exchange*, p. 189, 553; C. A. Conant, 'The Balance of Trade', in Gibson, *Market Letters*, p. 58; C. F. Speare, 'Europe's Interest in American Securities', in Gibson, *Market Letters*, p. 106.

Conclusion   The London and New York Stock Exchanges: an Institutional Comparison

Rather than present a short account of each exchange's institutional structure, this chapter will be comparative from the outset. Selected practices and developments will be chosen for examination, with the aim of showing to what extent real differences existed between the London and New York Stock Exchanges and the consequences this had not only for the Exchanges themselves but also for the securities market and the respective national economies. The first area of investigation is the control exercised over each exchange by its membership, the size and nature of that membership and the ease and cost of entry. This leads to an examination of the restrictions imposed on the activities of the members, with regard to how they organized their business, the additional occupations they were allowed to pursue and, especially, their freedom to charge whatever commission rate they desired. The next area to be analysed is the method of trading adopted in each Exchange, and its success in meeting the demands from a growing volume and variety of turnover. From this, the investigation turns to the policy of each exchange towards providing a market for new securities in different fields, by way of giving them an official quotation.

With this comparative evidence from selected areas of importance, it should be possible not only to highlight the main similarities and differences between the London and New York Stock Exchanges, but also to make some assessment of how well each functioned, within its own particular environment, and to what extent each contributed to, impeded, or altered the creation of a national and international securities market. Both were primarily trade associations representing the collective interests of their membership, facilitating business between members by providing a convenient forum for operating and a common set of rules and regulations to govern it. To do this satisfactorily each required a building in which business could be transacted in an orderly manner and away from the disruptive influence of bystanders. Both institutions rented premises for such purposes at first, but both felt the need to construct, or have constructed, a custom-built central exchange, suited to their particular requirements. The way each did this created a major division between them, which was to have repercussions for the future. When the London Stock Exchange decided to build its own exchange in 1801 it did so by issuing shares which could be purchased by anyone. Consequently, there was a divorce between those who used the building for the conduct of their business – the members – and those who controlled the building and saw it as a business – the owners. In 1878, for example, there were 2,009 members of the London Stock Exchange but only 508 shareholders, a number of whom were non-members. It was only in 1876 that all new members were required to purchase at least one share as a condition of entry, with the members and owners gradually becoming an identical body. This process was not complete by the First World War.[1] In contrast, when the New York Stock Exchange decided to construct its own building, which was not until 1863, the finance was raised from among the membership, by way of high entry and membership fees, and by loans based on the security of the real estate acquired. Thus, there could be no conflict between members and owners in New York, as they were the same group of people.[2]

This difference between the Exchanges was reflected in the way each was run. In London there were two committees which controlled all affairs, namely, the Committee of Trustees and Managers, representing the interests of the owners, and the Committee for General Purposes, which reflected the views of the members. All other committees were subcommittees of these. Power thus rested with the two central committees; where their interests overlapped, there could be considerable friction, with no higher authority available to resolve matters. In contrast, on the New York Stock Exchange there was one Governing Committee, which acted as final arbiter, but most of its power was devolved to other permanent committees which had responsibility for particular areas, such as admissions or commissions.[3] As a result of this difference in control between London and New York, their response to particular developments and problems was different. The contrast is clearest with regard to the new communications technology and the admission of new members.

By means of the ticker-tape machine and, later, the telephone, it became possible to relay information immediately from the floor of the exchange to interested parties outside. This was of great benefit not only in keeping members constantly informed, when they were not in the exchange, but also in widening the market beyond the confines of those present on the floor at any one time. In New York there was an immediate recognition that improved communications could aid the business of members, and so both the ticker-tape (1867) and the telephone (1878) were introduced as soon as they were available.[4] Though the membership of the London Stock Exchange was equally aware of the benefits, the introduction of the new devices was long delayed and its optimum operation was hampered. The owners of the London Stock Exchange were worried that the new technology would give outsiders access to current prices and to the trading floor without having to pay membership fees. This would reduce the value of the institution they controlled, and the income they derived from it, by way of the subscriptions members paid. It was not until 1872 that the opposition of the owners was overcome and the ticker-tape was introduced, while the telephone did not make an appearance until 1882–3. Gradually, however, as more of a common identity between owners and members was created after 1876, the opposition to the new technology declined, and there was little sign of any real resistance after 1890.[5]

A legacy nevertheless remained on the London Stock Exchange of a reluctance to accept and fully utilize the new technology. Both the ticker and telephone services available on the London Stock Exchange were inferior to that possessed by the New York Stock Exchange. By 1907, for example, the London Stock Exchange, with a floor space of 25,600 square feet and 5,400 members, had only one ticker-tape operator and four reporters collecting prices, while the New York Stock Exchange, with 1,100 members and a floor space of 10,500 square feet, employed four operators and twenty-two reporters. As a result the New York prices were current and

251

authoritative and gained a wide currency, while the London prices were considered of limited value and had a limited audience.[6] One importance consequence of the division of control on the London Stock Exchange, as opposed to New York, then, was London's relative failure to adopt and fully exploit the new communications technology at an early stage. If this had continued it could have seriously impaired London's position as the central securities market in Britain. It did not, however, so the delay and limitation were only a minor inconvenience, and relatively unimportant by the First World War.

Of greater and more lasting consequence was the differing attitude towards membership that stemmed from the nature of control in each institution. Those who owned the London Stock Exchange derived their income from the entry and subscription fees paid by the members and they had to be careful that these did not discourage membership or encourage the creation of a rival exchange with lower fees. Consequently, the owners actively wished to expand membership, and did so by keeping the fees they charged at moderate levels. In 1904, for instance, it was estimated that it cost only £1,200 (then about $6,000) for someone to become a member of the London Stock Exchange, even after purchasing the requisite number of shares, while a stockbroker's clerk could gain entry for a mere £440 (about $2,200). The Committee for General Purposes did exercise some control over admission but, until the few years before the First World War, rarely refused any well-qualified candidate. Between 1900 and 1909, 2,297 new members were admitted, or 230 a year, and the general feeling was that it was easy, as well as inexpensive, to gain entry. Only in the years prior to 1914 was any real attempt to vet and restrict applications made. This resulted from overcrowding in the Exchange and from the growing power of the members as they also became owners. Generally, however, as a result of this liberal policy, membership of the London Stock Exchange rose from 864 in 1850 to 5,567 in 1905, before falling back to 4,855 in 1914.[7]

On the New York Stock Exchange a very different approach to membership was adopted. Vested with absolute control of their own institution, the members recognized the special advantages it brought them in security trading, and so were loath to admit others to the privileges that they enjoyed. By 1862 it cost a new member

$3,000 (then about £600) to gain admission, and this was raised to $10,000 in 1866 (about £2,000). Later, through the ownership of their own building, each member of the New York Stock Exchange came to share in a valuable property. To allow retiring members to realize their part of this investment it was decided in 1868 to make memberships saleable; and in order to restrict entry the total number of members was set at 1,060. The only increase in numbers before 1914 came in 1879 when forty new seats were created and sold, in order to finance improvements to the exchange building. The only way a new member could gain admission to the New York Stock Exchange was therefore not only to pay the substantial entry and membership fees, but also to buy the membership or seat of an existing member. These seats varied in price, reflecting the prosperity of the market; whereas in 1870 it cost between $4,000 and $4,500 (£800 to £900) to buy a seat, in 1910 it cost from $64,000 to $94,000 (£13,000 to £18,800), which indicated their security value. Thus, while membership of the New York Stock Exchange rose from 112 in 1848 to around 400 in 1865, between 1868 and 1879 the increase was only 40, and none at all thereafter.[8]

These contrasting attitudes to membership had major consequences for each exchange and the role it occupied in the securities market. The London Stock Exchange's largely 'open-door' policy meant that most who wished to practise as stockbrokers in London, and agreed to abide by the rules and regulations, could and did become members of that Exchange. Throughout the period there were outside brokers who occasionally transacted a substantial business. During the railway mania of the mid-1840s, for example, a portion of the business in railway shares was conducted by non-members. In most cases, though, these outside brokers either were absorbed into the London Stock Exchange, because of the ease and convenience of membership, or merely ceased to do business. In a few cases the trading outside the London Stock Exchange grew to such a level that a rival exchange was established, such as with mining securities at times between 1855 and 1870. However, these other exchanges did not survive more than a few years and failed to establish a permanent place for themselves in the securities market. The one exception was the Mincing Lane market founded in 1909 to provide for dealings in the shares of plantation companies, particularly those involved in rubber growing. It was probably no coincidence that the appearance of this exchange coincided with the growing restriction on membership by the London Stock Exchange.[9] The street markets that were created in London, such as those in Shorter's Court and Throgmorton Street, were not alternatives to the London Stock Exchange. They were after-hours markets catering for either a continuing pressure of business or time differentials, with exchanges in other countries still being open when London was officially closed.[10] With only minor exceptions, then, the London Stock Exchange provided the sole market for securities in London, and it did this by being willing to expand its membership in line with demand until the few years before the First World War. This meant that London possessed one integrated securities exchange without barriers and with a common set of rules, which provided a market that was open to all.

With the New York Stock Exchange reluctant to expand numbers before 1868, and very restrictive afterwards, there was no way that it could cope easily with an increased demand for membership. During the Civil War, for example, there was a great increase in security trading due to the growth of government debt and the general state of uncertainty, but the New York Stock Exchange admitted few new members. The result was the growth of numerous established brokers operating outside the exchange, and the eventual creation of rival bodies. It was not until 1869, when the New York Stock Exchange merged with its main rival, the Open Board, that a unified market was again established. However, because of the policy of limitation it was not long before there was again an active outside market, leading to the formation of other stock exchanges. The most serious challenge came in 1885 when a number of rival exchanges merged to form the Consolidated Stock Exchange, with 2,403 members. From then until the First World War there was considerable rivalry between these exchanges, with the New York Stock Exchange forbidding its members to belong to both institutions, and attempting to stop all telegraphic and telephonic communication between the two floors. In order to avoid incurring the direct opposition of the New York Stock Exchange, many other brokers remained unorganized, unhoused and unregulated, conducting their business in groups on the street, where they formed the Curb Market.[11]

The securities market in New York was therefore divided into three distinct components, each with substantial adherents. In addition to the New York Stock Exchange's 1,100 members, by 1913 the Consolidated had 1,225 and the Curb had at least 200. Both the Curb and the Consolidated Stock Exchange enjoyed a substantial turnover, by dealing either in securities for which the New York Stock Exchange did not provide a market, or in small numbers of securities, often of low individual value, which New York Stock Exchange brokers were not interested in handling. In 1908, for example, the number of shares of common stock traded on the three New York markets was estimated at 424 million, and only 46.5 per cent of that was done on the New York Stock Exchange, compared to 32.4 per cent at the Consolidated and 21.2 per cent on the Curb. Of course, the value of business would be much greater on the New York Stock Exchange, because of the higher individual worth of the common stock it traded and its substantial turnover in bonds. This was estimated at $1.1 billion in 1908 compared to $66 million on the Curb and none at the Consolidated. There was nothing intrinsically disadvantageous with this specialization in the securities market, if common rules of operation and intimate interconnection existed. The problem was, however, that the New York Stock Exchange refused to recognize the existence of the rival exchanges and so prevented the creation of an integrated and organized market composed of these separate components. Artificial barriers were placed between itself and the Consolidated, preventing that exchange from gaining ready access to the current prices on the main market, and so forcing it to deal at wider prices. No restrictions were placed on communication with members of the Curb Market, and an estimated 85 per cent of the business of Curb brokers was derived from members of the New York Stock Exchange. However, fear of such restrictions prevented that market from implementing rules and regulations to govern its conduct, which would have rendered its business more acceptable to the investing public.[12] Thus, whereas the London Stock Exchange encompassed almost the whole market for securities in London, the New York Stock Exchange covered only a part of the New York market, and helped to prevent the remainder operating as efficiently and effectively as possible.

These contrasting attitudes to membership also had significant consequences for those who became members of the London and New York Stock Exchanges. Since the owners of the London Stock

Exchange relied on membership fees for their income, the rules insisted that all the partners of a firm were members. With entry being relatively easy and cheap, there was therefore little incentive for the creation of large firms, which could maximize on the privilege of membership by conducting an extensive business. In addition, in order to deny access to the market to rivals in security trading, such as bankers and lawyers, a member was prohibited from conducting any other business. However, with every partner having to be a member, this ruling meant that no one who was active in any other branch of the economy could take an equity stake in a stockbroking firm, and so denied the profession easy access to capital. The outcome was that the average member of the London Stock Exchange, whether an individual or a firm, traded on a very small capital and relied largely on credit. Certain highly capitalized firms were denied entry to the Stock Exchange because of the interests of either the firm or its partners. Such a firm was the merchant bank S. Japhet & Co., which was one of the major London–New York arbitrage operators and required a capital of £0.4 million (about $2 million) in 1910 to do this successfuly.[13] Nevertheless, there does not appear to have been any shortage of capital among the members of the London Stock Exchange at this time, with the partners of the larger broking or jobbing firms providing what was required.[14] In addition, for most of the time the number of members, rather than the size of member firms, could expand to meet demand.

Circumstances in New York led to the opposite pattern occurring. Even before the sale of seats an individual had to be fairly wealthy to gain access to the New York Stock Exchange. With the rising costs of seats after 1869 it became imperative to make as much use of the membership as possible in order to justify the expense involved. At the same time, though the rules of the New York Stock Exchange prohibited institutions or corporations from membership of both the Exchange and member firms, they did not require every partner in a firm to become a member or restrict the additional occupations followed. Thus, New York broking firms obtained substantial funds from 'special' partners, who provided capital in expectation of a good return but took no part in the business of the firm. As early as 1884 the average capital possessed by ten New York Stock Exchange firms was $240,000 (£48,000), while by 1913 it was felt that a moderate sized firm needed a minimum capital of $0.5 million (£0.1 million). The firm of Hayden, Stone & Co., for instance, employed a capital of $3.8 million (£760,000) by March 1906, and between 1909 and 1914 the sales and purchases it handled on the New York Stock Exchange averaged $143 million (£28.6 million) per annum.[15] The restrictions on membership imposed by the New York Stock Exchange, in conjunction with the freedom in obtaining outside capital, thus stimulated the creation of large, highly capitalized broking firms. Consequently, the growing contrast between the large New York firms and the small London firms, or individual members, was the product of the institutional framework within which each operated, rather than of any overriding need to grow large or to stay small.

Differences between the markets, and those who operated in them, were further encouraged by the attitudes of each exchange towards a common and enforced set of commission rates. Though the London Stock Exchange did issue guidelines on the commissions it expected brokers to charge, these were not mandatory until 1912. Brokers competed with each other in offering favourable rates in order to attract customers, especially those with a large volume of business to transact. As one broker admitted to the commission into the London Stock Exchange in 1878: 'I do business for less than scale where the transactions are numerous, and are both ways, and go on through the whole year; but as a rule, for general transactions, we adhere to one particular scale, and I believe that other brokers likewise do so.'[16] Customers with a limited business were charged according to the official scale, while others could negotiate a special rate reflecting the volume of turnover they could expect to generate. For example, S. Japhet & Co. paid out about £50,000 ($250,000) per annum in commission by 1912 and received favourable rates in return. Some brokers even bought and sold free of commission, by agreeing a price with the customer, then trying to better it in the market, and so keep the difference. Others traded on joint account with outside brokers or clients, by which the costs and profits or losses resulting from buying and selling operations were shared, but no commissions were charged. This was very common in national and international arbitrage operations, where a sale or purchase in one exchange was matched by a purchase or sale in another, in order to profit from differential prices.[17] As a result of this flexibility on

257

commissions the members of the London Stock Exchange could offer large customers – such as banks, finance houses and outside brokers – either very attractive terms or a share in the profits, so that business was attracted to the exchange and other means of trading or alternative markets were little resorted to. Some brokers, for example, operated almost solely for one or a few major customers, being paid a fee by them for the business they transacted rather than a commission on turnover. Thus the embargo on additional occupations, which prevented banks and other financial institutions becoming members, was of little practical importance when large customers could get their business transacted at minimal cost through a relationship with one or more members.[18] However, this flexible and mutually beneficial system was undermined by the introduction of minimum commission rates in 1912. This was a move long desired by many members, in order to reduce competition between themselves and was finally inaugurated as a means of preventing non-members gaining favourable access to the facilities of the Exchange. Exceptions to these mandatory minimum commission scales were allowed in the case of foreign business, where the rates could be reduced by up to 75 per cent, but for domestic customers it meant an increase in charges and resulted in a decline in business.[19]

In complete contrast to London, one of the main motives behind the formation of the New York Stock Exchange was to enforce a common set of charges and to restrict competition; this remained of fundamental importance to the Exchange before the First World War. For example, the Governing Committee pronounced in April 1894 that 'The commission law is the fundamental principle of the Exchange, and on its strict observance hangs the financial welfare of all the members and the life of the Institution itself.'[20] Those who were discovered evading the minimum commission rules could expect to be harshly dealt with, such as F. M. Lockwood & Co., who were expelled from the Exchange in 1881 for not charging the full rate.[21] In the 1860s it was possible to reduce by half the minimum commission rate of one-quarter per cent of par value to such importance customers as bankers and outside brokers. However, when one-eighth per cent became the minimum rate no further reductions were allowed. In 1875, for instance, twenty brokers petitioned the Exchange to be allowed to 'make special contracts with their customers to do business at not less than one-sixteenth per cent where the magnitude or activity of the account shall make such agreement desirable to the broker'.[22] However, permission was refused, and the Exchange proved inflexible on this matter, with every purchase and sale for a non-member having to bear a one-eighth per cent commission charge. This included business for members of other stock exchanges.

The one-eighth per cent commission charged by members of the New York Stock Exchange was considered high by contemporaries, and it encouraged many interested parties to deal with outside brokers or members of other exchanges, where the rates were lower. At the same time the rate, being charged on par value, was particularly onerous on shares with a low real value, such as many mining and later industrial securities, and so discouraged trading in these on the New York Stock Exchange.[23] However, there was one loophole in the New York Stock Exchange's commission law which was exploited to the full in order to have business done at much reduced rates. Members buying and selling for each other were charged at the commission rate of only one-thirty-second per cent, or a quarter the minimum rate, and the rate could go to as low as one-fiftieth per cent for deals on the floor between brokers. This privilege extended to all partners in a member firm. Thus, as only institutions and corporations were denied either membership or partnership with a member, this meant that all individuals, firms and other unincorporated bodies that had much security trading to conduct could do so at advantageous terms by buying a seat or joining a member firm. To gain access to these low rates of commission that membership bestowed, individuals and other unincorporated bodies either bought seats or combined with existing members. The result was the creation of ever larger stockbroking firms conducting a diversified business in which the common theme was the profitable employment of their own or other people's capital, whether in loans, commodities, or securities. Henry Clews & Co., for instance, had an estimated turnover of $1 billion (£200 million) per annum in 1887 from a combination of banking, commodity and stockbroking, and employed a staff of one hundred to undertake it all. Similarly, by 1913 twenty-three members of the New York Stock Exchange were also members of the New York Produce Exchange, and a further thirty-one were members of the New York Cotton Exchange.[24]

In addition, unlike the London Stock Exchange, the rules of the New York Stock Exchange allowed members to join other stock exchanges, though this was rescinded for New York City when the Consolidated Stock Exchange was formed. A member of the New York Stock Exchange could therefore do business for a member of another stock exchange at the reduced rate of commission, provided that both were members of the same firm. C. C. Adsit, a Chicago broker, bought a seat on the New York exchange in 1902 in order to profit from the reduced commission that a member was entitled to. This encouraged the formation of integrated stockbroking firms represented on all the major US markets, such as Boston, Philadelphia, Chicago and San Francisco, as well as New York. By 1912, 106 out-of-town stockbroking firms from twenty-two different cities were members of the New York Stock Exchange, including 31 from Philadelphia, 20 from Boston and 16 from Chicago. The converse was also true, with New York broking firms having a total of 258 out-of-town offices, including 31 in Boston, 24 in Chicago, 20 in Philadelphia, 8 in Baltimore, 6 in New Orleans and 4 in San Francisco. Van Antwerp estimated that in 1913 altogether 33 members of the New York Stock Exchange were also members of the Chicago Stock Exchange, while 24 were members in Philadelphia and 17 in Boston.[25] These firms, represented on more than one market, conducted most of the business that passed between exchanges. It was estimated in 1913 that 48 per cent of the transactions on the New York Stock Exchange originated from outside the city.[26]

Despite this dispensation the New York Stock Exchange found difficulty in defending its high minimum commission rate, especially from the Consolidated Stock Exchange, whose members charged one-sixteenth per cent. With the ticker, and later the telephone, it was possible for non-members to deal at the current market prices but to charge less for the service. In consequence, the New York Stock Exchange had to take progressively more serious measures to prevent competitors gaining access to current prices, without depriving its own members of such a valuable facility. The mere removal of tickers from the Consolidated Stock Exchange and the offices of outside brokers was not sufficient. Through telephone communication with accommodating members of the New York

Stock Exchange, and the continuous quotation of security prices, outside brokers could still gain access to current prices. Even when New York Stock Exchange members were forbidden to have telephonic links with members of the Consolidated Stock Exchange, the practice continued through third parties, such as members of other exchanges, who had legitimate access to New York prices through either tickers or direct telephone lines.[27] At the same time, exchanges distant from New York were seen increasingly as competitors, as rapid communication meant that a security could be bought or sold not only where it was cheaper or dearer but also where the commission charged was less. The very method used to conduct this inter-stock-exchange business was itself eventually deemed to transgress the minimum commission rules. With each broker charging the other commission for buying or selling, the result was that no commission need actually be paid, and so the result was joint-account trading in which costs and profits or losses were divided but no commission was received.[28] The New York Stock Exchange eventually banned joint-account arbitrage within the United States in 1881, repealed the prohibition in 1883 and reinstituted it in 1894, when it remained until the First World War, being further reinforced in 1904. In addition, the dealing in differences between domestic exchanges, or arbitrage, was prohibited in 1896, while the sending out of continuous quotations of security prices was outlawed in 1898. The problem with these embargoes was that they were all very difficult to enforce, because much of the dealing took place within the same firm, being done by members on different exchanges, while telephonic contact was constantly maintained so as to implement genuine buying and selling orders, rather than arbitrage operations or continuous quotation.[29] Nevertheless, though evasion took place on a serious scale, the result of these new regulations was to restrict the amount of business being transacted between the New York Stock Exchange and other domestic exchanges, and to widen price differentials.[30] Finally, when it was realized in 1911 that the London Stock Exchange was becoming a major competitor to the New York Stock Exchange in US securities, joint-account trading between New York and London was prohibited, which forced brokers to charge one-eighth per cent on every transaction. This increased the costs of the operation and discouraged some trading, and so it became more difficult to maintain an active market in certain securities, to match bargains, or to keep prices in line.[31]

The rules of each exchange regarding commissions, then, had important repercussions for both the securities market and its personnel. The freedom that existed in London before 1912 allowed rates to be adjusted to suit all types of customer, and so encouraged the use of the London Stock Exchange by all who wished to buy and sell securities. When this flexibility was largely ended in 1912, it was not accompanied by compensating liberalizations, such as the freedom to undertake other business, obtain capital from outsiders, or become a member of other exchanges. The result was that those with a large volume of business to conduct, such as bankers and brokers on other British exchanges, were denied access to the London Stock Exchange at low rates of commission, and so London became a less attractive market for them to deal in, with an effect on the general level of business. In New York the minimum commission rate and the inflexible way it was applied to non-members did drive business to other exchanges. However, the very favourable rates given to members, and the few restrictions on who could become a member, meant that those with a major interest in security trading could reduce their commission costs by purchasing seats or becoming partners in member firms. The result was the creation of large firms that operated nationally and undertook a variety of other financial activities, apart from stockbroking, such as banking and commodity dealing. By this means the restrictions imposed by the commission rates were reduced. Nevertheless, in order to maintain these minimum charges the New York Stock Exchange was forced to restrict the way members could conduct their business; and, though evasion existed, this was detrimental to the creation of a national securities market from the mid-1890s and to the international market from 1911.

When the London Stock Exchange achieved a formal existence with its own building in 1801, there had long been an active and extensive market, and this merely moved indoors. In this market there had already developed means by which a large volume of business, in a variety of securities, could be expeditiously conducted. Essentially, custom and habit divided the market into clusters of members, each trading in a specific group of securities such as British government funds, foreign government bonds or, later, domestic railway stocks. As new issues appeared they either were accommodated in the most appropriate group or came to form a distinct component in the market, as both US stocks and bonds and industrial and miscellaneous shares did. Thus, with little supervision, the trading floor divided itself into separate areas in each of which specific types of like securities were traded; as interest in these changed, so did the space they occupied. In practice, they comprised markets within markets. [32]

In contrast, when the New York Stock Exchange was founded in 1817, business in securities in New York was still very much a part-time activity for a few people and involved a limited turnover in a small number of securities, few of which generated much activity. This type of business was most easily handled by the call system, in which a short list of securities was read out once or twice a day, and trading was conducted in each in turn. However, as turnover increased it became impossible to confine it to these regular sessions, and brokers took to trading directly with each other throughout the day. As a result, long before calls in stocks were abandoned in 1885 and bonds in 1902, they had ceased to be important components of the market mechanism. Even by 1865 the Stock Exchange had set aside a room where direct dealing took place, with securities being grouped into specific locations. [33] With the aim of improving the organization of this market, the New York Stock Exchange introduced the trading post in 1892. By this system each issue was allocated a specific location at one of the posts which were evenly distributed about the room. However, this was not done so as to group like securities together and create mini-markets, but to distribute business throughout the floor and avoid congestion at any one place. In 1913, for example, at post No. 8 was to be found trading in thirty-nine diverse corporations, including the Missouri, Kansas & Pacific Railroad, the Bethlehem Steel Company, Quicksilver Mining and the Assets Realization Company. The consequence of the trading-post system was that any broker with an interest in a certain type of security had to tour the whole market constantly in order to try to keep in touch. In addition, there was a reluctance to keep adding more securities to the posts, because not only had the location of each new one to be memorized, but it also further complicated the buying and selling taking place at each post. By May 1913, for example, there were 555 different stocks being traded at sixteen posts.[34] The London Stock Exchange, by contrast, provided from an early stage a framework requiring little supervision by which the floor naturally divided itself into distinct markets, and changed over time to accommodate fluctuations in business and new securities. In the same period the New York Stock Exchange abandoned its call system only with great reluctance and then reorganized the floor, not to reflect the needs of the market, but for simple convenience. The outcome was that the trading-post system adopted in New York was not suited to trading in a large number and variety of separate issues,. while that of London was. In 1900, for example, the London Stock Exchange quoted 3,631 different issues of securities in a wide variety of fields, while the New York Stock Exchange quoted only 1,157, most of which were railroads.[35]

A much more serious difference between the two Exchanges than the physical organization of the market was the system of trading adopted in each. In the eighteenth century a time period between sale or purchase and delivery or payment was essential, in order to cope with problems of communication and transportation. By the early nineteenth century this had become a rule on the London Stock Exchange whereby, unless otherwise specified, all deals were done for the next settlement date, when all deliveries and payment had to be made. These settlement times occurred every nineteen or twenty days throughout the year and were known in advance. Business could be done, and was done, for 'cash', but this meant a special arrangement; trading 'for the account' was the normal practice.[36]

The delay between deal and delivery was also found to have other valuable advantages, which encouraged the retention of the system long after improvements in communication had removed its original function. Much of the trading on the London Stock Exchange was of a technical or speculative nature, with operators either buying what they could not pay for or selling what they did not possess, in the expectation of reversing the deal at a profit. This could be done within the account with no need either to pay or to make a delivery. The existence of a settlement date, however, forced either such operations to be concluded by a matching sale or purchase, or the security to be delivered and payment received, or a financial penalty to be exacted if this was not done. As a result of this constant buying and selling, an active and continuous market for securities was created, encouraging the holding of stocks, as they could readily be exchanged for cash. In addition, it was frequently the actions of the speculators, buying for a rise or selling for a fall and then trying to close their deals before settlement day, that helped to smooth fluctuations in the market and thus maintain prices within a reasonably narrow band. Again, this encouraged investors to purchase securities, since they had some confidence that the value was unlikely to collapse within a short period, apart from in exceptional cases.[37] The fortnightly settlement was essentially a compromise between the convenience of constant buying and selling operations of variable duration, and the need to restrain speculative excesses by limiting the period and forcing operators either to pay up, to make delivery, or to come to some other arrangement. Without the settlement it would be difficult to check the creditworthiness of both buyers and sellers; but without the intervening period their ability to establish an active market without violent oscillations would be considerably hampered.

In contrast to London, delivery and payment on the following day was the normal pattern or regular way of trading on the New York Stock Exchange. It was possible to extend the duration of the deal, but this involved paying interest to the broker holding the stock. This system of trading was perfectly adequate for the local investment market that existed in New York in the early nineteenth century, but it posed problems when turnover increased and trading became more speculative. As a result time contracts became common, but these could be costly, with a deposit of 20 per cent of the securities' value and a 7 per cent rate of interest being demanded. Attempts were made repeatedly to introduce a London-style settlement system, in order to ease the problems of the market, but these all foundered. In fact, time contracts themselves, while not being outlawed, were increasingly regarded with ill favour on the Stock Exchange, and ceased to be of importance after 1857. Public opinion in the United States was much more vehemently against gambling than in Britain, and there was always the threat that both existing time contracts and the introduction of any system of delayed settlements would provoke anti-gaming legislation. The New York Stock Exchange and its members took this threat seriously and were reluctant to abandon daily settlement, in case it would provoke state or federal retaliation. At the same time, the early years of the Stock Exchange had created a general air of mistrust among members, so that a day's grace was all many members would extend for either payment or delivery. In particular, the crisis of 1857 had led to the collapse of many stockbroking firms because of speculative excesses, and they left behind a mass of debt and broken promises, by way of time contracts, which brought down many other reputable brokers.[38] This lack of trust lingered long into the second half of the nineteenth century. Consequently, while London had about 24 settlements a year, New York had about 250. This meant that buying and selling operations in New York were constantly interrupted by the need to deliver actual securities or finance real payments, which disrupted the even functioning of the market by discouraging technical and speculative buying and selling operations. In New York the compromise achieved between caution and convenience was too much in favour of the former, and this put the market under considerable strain from time to time, as it attempted to meet the needs of active and continuous security trading.

In the New York system two major difficulties existed: the delivery of securities, and the payment for them. During the day brokers would frequently sell what they did not possess, in the expectation that they would be able to purchase it later at a favourable price. These operations were essential in the creation of a ready market. If the broker found he could not purchase at a suitable price or at all, he 'borrowed' the stock from either another broker or an outside institution, contracting to replace it when asked for. He had to bear the cost of financing the holding of this stock for the actual owner, in return for gaining temporary control over it. This system worked adequately as long as there were holders willing to lend the required stocks. However, it lent itself to cornering operations, where a group would secretly buy up a major holding of a stock and then, one day, place numerous buying orders. The brokers who contracted to sell would find that they could neither purchase nor borrow, as the stock was closely held, and so the price would be driven up, making huge profits for the cornering syndicate. This happened periodically on the New York Stock Exchange and not only disrupted the market when it was in progress but discouraged brokers from selling what they did not own, thus reducing the ready market for securities. In a fortnightly settlement system there was time to bring in vendors from a wider circle. This made cornering difficult, though not impossible, under the London system.[39]

Though corners proved a periodic nuisance, of far greater importance was the need in New York to have access to substantial funds, in order to pay for the securities being held until an advantageous moment for resale occurred. In London much of this took place within the account period and so incurred no finance charges. If it was required to hold the securities for a longer period of time, it was relatively easy to obtain credit from banks, renewable every settlement day. So it was only twice a month that the need for cash, to finance purchases, made itself felt on the London money market. However, call money, or money available only on a daily basis, was also employable on the London Stock Exchange, as securities could be bought for immediate delivery and paid for in cash. There were considerable operations of this kind in British government stock, for instance. On 31 August 1914 the members of the London Stock Exchange owed altogether £80.8 million (about $39 million), mainly to financial institutions, on account of their holdings of securities.[40] Thus, in London with the fortnightly system there was not only much less incessant pressure on the money market, from the need to finance short-term security purchases, but also such a variety of periods for which money was lent, ranging from call loans to fortnightly credit or longer, that any pressure in the market would only gradually be felt as loans were slowly called in, beginning with the day-to-day money. Period settlements, time and variety ensured that in London there was reasonable harmony between the security market and the money market, with each helping the other by either providing remunerative outlets for short-term funds or assisting in the financing of security trading.[41]

The daily settlement system in existence on the New York Stock Exchange did not achieve satisfactory results. Historians such as Myers and Hedges have suggested that it was the very appearance of a call-loan market that led the New York Stock Exchange to persevere with daily settlements, by making money easily and cheaply available to finance the holding of securities. However, an even better short-term money market existed in London at an even earlier date, and it did not encourage any move towards more frequent settlements.[42] In fact, it was those people most involved with the New York money market who kept pressing the New York Stock Exchange to abandon daily settlements. The central problem was that the New York system, by forcing all bargains to be concluded by 2.15 p.m. the following day, did not allow sufficient time for technical and speculative buying operations to be undone before payment had to be made. As a consequence, much of the trading which took place in London within the account period, and never made any demands on the money market, made constant demands in New York. In 1913, for instance, the ratio of security loans to commercial bank deposits was 37.7 per cent in New York compared to only 13.3 per cent in London. The need to finance every transaction lasting longer than a day, therefore, monopolized a substantial proportion of the liquid funds available in New York, which was the principal reserve in the United States, while the London system was much more economical, normally requiring financing only for those securities held for longer than a fortnight.[43]

In addition, the daily settlement system tended to exaggerate crises. Rather than a daily delivery ensuring that no broker would have time to create a vast web of obligations, so that his collapse would bring down innumerable others, the short time before payment was due meant that it was difficult for either bankers or brokers to take avoiding measures. Any tightening of the money available on the call-loan market had an immediate and all-embracing impact, as almost all borrowings were for day-to-day money. This pushed up interest rates rapidly and forced large-scale liquidations of securities by brokers, who could no longer finance their holdings. If stocks could not be liquidated, because everyone was similarly affected, or prices dropped to the extent that loans were no longer covered, the brokers would be unable to repay the banks. If such debts were large enough, this could force the banks to suspend operations, and so spread the crisis to more brokers as well as throughout the financial system. Crises of this kind occurred fairly frequently on the New York Stock Exchange, when brokers who had over-extended themselves and banks that had overcommitted themselves failed, with repercussions for the whole economy. For example, in 1890, when the firm of Decker, Howell & Co. failed, the Bank of North America had to suspend operations because it was owed $0.9 million.[44]

The pressure of the daily settlement system on the money market was even greater before 1892, because the New York Stock Exchange refused to adopt a clearing system. With clearing, brokers' cheques, paying each other for stocks, were passed through a central office. There each broker was debited or credited with the amount he paid out, or was paid, so that only a cheque for the balance need be paid out or received, with all other cheques being cancelled. It was estimated in 1901 that the banks saved at least $50 million a year by the partial clearing system introduced by the New York Stock Exchange in 1892. However, it was not until the New York banks indicated that they would refuse to handle brokers' cheques that the Exchange introduced even this partial clearing system, as it was felt that its existence would reveal too much about each broker's business and encourage the anti-gaming lobby.[45]

Consequently, though the New York Stock Exchange provided a large, essential and remunerative home for the short-term funds lodged in New York banks, the daily settlement system adhered to, despite opposition, meant that they absorbed a much greater proportion of these funds than they need have done, particularly before the introduction of a clearing system in 1892. At the same time, the importance of brokers' loans to banks, and the extreme sensitivity of this lending to the slightest fluctuations in monetary conditions – because of the prevalence of call-money loans – often aggravated temporary restrictions in credit so that minor or major crises resulted. In fact, it was only by being able to call on foreign money markets, especially London, that these crises were so readily modified and surmounted before 1914.[46] As one New York broker put it so clearly during the crisis of 1887: 'We gain nothing by the hourly denunciation of those who avail themselves of the opportunity to corner stocks, or to tie up money. Probably we would do likewise if we had the power. They are not to blame half as much as is the system which makes it possible and invites them to it.'[47] The introduction of partial clearing in 1892 did help matters, but the basic problems remained and changes to the system proved difficult. New York brokers began increasingly to utilize the London Stock Exchange for their operations, because of the convenience of dealing 'for the account' in that Exchange.[48]

One area in which there did appear to be a clear distinction between the London and New York Stock Exchanges was in the division of members into jobbers and brokers in London and the lack of any such distinction in New York. The jobber or dealer made a market in securities by being always ready to quote prices and buy and sell accordingly, while the broker transacted business on commission on behalf of clients. Both categories had long existed in London, but it was not until 1847 that each was forbidden to undertake the activities of the other. This ruling was designed to ensure fair and accurate pricing, by forcing the broker to deal through a jobber, rather than quote his own price to the client.[49] Direct trading between brokers remained common, particularly in the less active securities, where there was not sufficient business to justify jobbers making a market. Nevertheless, as long as the floor of the Stock Exchange encompassed the whole market the demarcation between jobber and broker could be largely preserved. However, when it became easier to communicate between the Stock Exchange and outside, especially with the telephone, the distinction began to collapse. Jobbers established direct and close contacts with brokers on other stock exchanges, both at home and abroad, for whom they also acted as dealers. Brokers with provincial or overseas contacts started to quote prices in order to compete with the jobbers in this trade, while others established links with financial institutions, on whose behalf they tried to make markets in specific securities. The result was that the simple distinction between brokers and jobbers gradually disappeared, with at least seven different types of operator being observed by April 1903.[50]

On the New York Stock Exchange the reverse process took place. As the volume and variety of business grew, brokers began to specialize in specific tasks. As early as 1865 a class of brokers had appeared who traded on their own account and were referred to as stock jobbers. These grew in number and sophistication, with some specializing in making a market in a particular stock or stocks at a single trading post, while others roamed the market dealing in a particular group of securities. Consequently, by the early twentieth century seven categories of operators were also observed in the New York Stock Exchange. To try to ensure that the broker's client received the market price under the New York system, the broker was obliged to declare his bids and offers openly in the ring or pool where the stock was dealt. Hence the 'open outcry' in New York as opposed to the quiet negotiation of London.[51] Thus, apart from the noise created, there was little difference in the specialization of the membership of each Exchange, or at least this was the case until 1909. In that year the London Stock Exchange implemented a new rule which reinforced the clear division between broker and jobber, which had long fallen into abeyance. It was increasingly felt by many members that the direct contacts with provincial brokers established by some jobbers siphoned business away from the London Stock Exchange to other centres. With the aim of breaking these links the jobber/broker distinction was revived. The introduction of minimum commission rates in 1912 was part of the same attack, as it was felt that jobbers continued to maintain such contacts by passing the business through a few accommodating brokers for minimal commission. As a consequence, the flexibility of the London Stock Exchange's membership to respond to the individual needs of its clients was circumscribed by the re-creation of the jobber/broker distinction, and the Exchange lost business as a result, especially from the provinces.[52]

In the matter of the securities they quoted there was a growing divergence between the London and New York Stock Exchanges during the nineteenth century. This was not just the fact that London increasingly provided a market for securities from throughout the world, while New York traded almost exclusively in US stocks and bonds.[53] With the rapid growth and immense opportunities existing within the United States, it was only to be expected that the New York Stock Exchange would confine itself to the domestic front. However, even within the type of security quoted on each, ignoring the geographic dimension, important differences appeared. During the first half of the nineteenth century neither exchange exercised much supervision over the securities quoted, since they were quite happy to list anything that generated business. This consisted mainly of government securities and local banks, insurance companies, utilities and, later, railways.[54] Then, as the number of securities seeking a quotation rose in the second half of the nineteenth century, each Exchange became much more selective. The London Stock Exchange discriminated almost solely by size, with the minimum capital being set at around £100,000 (about $0.5 million) by the early twentieth century. Nevertheless, the London Stock Exchange continued to offer a listing to smaller concerns, especially those with a head office in London. The result was that it was relatively easy

271

to obtain a quotation on the London Stock Exchange. Also, an official listing was not essential for a security to be dealt in on the floor of the Exchange. As a consequence, the paid-up value of the securities quoted rose from £2.3 billion (about $11.5 billion) in 1873 to £8.8 billion ($44 billion) in 1903 and £11.3 billion ($56.5 billion) in 1913. Of course, only a small number of these were actively traded, but the members of the London Stock Exchange were ready to buy and sell most of them.[55] In addition, the expansion of membership, and the organization of the market, ensured that the Exchange could cope with the increased number and value of securities. With the exception of rubber plantation companies' shares from 1909, therefore, the London Stock Exchange offered a home to almost all securities that required a market and could expect to generate business.

Like the London Stock Exchange, New York also faced problems in accommodating the increasing number of securities, but these were much more serious because of that Exchange's limitation on membership and the organization of its market. The value of securities it quoted nevertheless rose from about $3 billion (£0.6 billion) in 1868 to $13.8 billion (£2.8 billion) in 1902.[56] This was about one-third of the London level and reflected a deliberate policy of exclusion rather than any lack of applications for listings. Increasingly more strict conditions were imposed on companies seeking a quotation for their securities, with each issue having to be of large dimension, while at least one year's earnings had to be shown. Even the quality of the stock certificate was closely scrutinized, and could be a cause for rejection if it was not of a high standard. W. C. Van Antwerp summed up the position in 1913: 'the Stock Exchange repeatedly refuses application to list securities, and our requirements in this respect are daily growing more severe'.[57] As a result, whereas by 1914 the average size of each issue from an industrial or commercial company quoted on the New York Stock Exchange was $24.7 million (£4.9 million), the average size of the capital possessed by an industrial or commercial company quoted on the London Stock Exchange was only £1.03 million ($5.1 million). In order to obtain a quotation on the New York Stock Exchange, then, a company had to be at least five times bigger than its London counterpart.[58] The same was true for government securities, with the issues of many city and state authorities being

272

considered too small to warrant a quotation. These excluded securities which were traded either on the Consolidated or the Curb market, or on the 'over-the-counter' market which was maintained by brokers dealing directly with each other by telephone.[59] However, it was not just size that led to exclusion, for the New York Stock Exchange became very discriminating about the type of security it permitted to be quoted. Mining and petroleum companies were refused a quotation for a long time, as the uncertain nature of their business was felt to make trading in their securities a hazardous occupation. A similar view prevailed with industrial and commercial companies in their formative years. Only once such companies had not only established themselves but also gained a market for their securities elsewhere did the New York Stock Exchange grant them access to its floor.[60]

This attitude had major repercussions. By ignoring a wide range of securities because of their size or nature, the New York Stock Exchange encouraged the fragmentation of the securities market. Though this did not deny these securities an active market, such as on the Curb or 'over-the-counter', it did deny them official recognition by way of a quotation. This was of major importance, for without a quotation securities were much less suitable for collateral purposes, and a large proportion of securities were held on borrowed funds. In addition, quoted securities were also regarded as temporary homes for funds which could be quickly called away, forcing rapid realization. Under these circumstances, immediate marketability at a well-publicized price was of prime importance, and this was what a quotation gave. Without a quotation a security was deprived of access to an important part of those funds either seeking an investment in securities or willing to finance security purchases.[61] As the *Report into the Control of Money and Credit* concluded in 1913: 'Manifestly, a security privileged to be bought and sold on such an exchange obtains a wider market and a more definite current value than one which is not.'[62] The consequence was that in New York, much more than in London, there was a premium on obtaining a quotation on the Stock Exchange. Because only heavily capitalized, established corporations could obtain a listing for their securities on the New York Stock Exchange, while much smaller concerns could gain access to the London exchange, there was a far greater incentive given to the creation of large corporations in the United States than in Britain. In both the United States and the United Kingdom there was a movement towards a growing scale of enterprise in business, stemming from changes in the processes of production and distribution. However, these changes were insufficient to account for the size of firms that were created, especially as many mergers involved nothing more than a loose grouping of independent units, without any benefit from economies of scale. Clearly there had to be other forces at work, and while the preferential access of certain individuals to finance was not of crucial significance, the ability to gain a wider market for securities, through a quotation, was considered of major importance. A quotation enhanced the value of a company and allowed it to gain additional and cheaper sources of capital, which in turn allowed it to absorb other, lesser known enterprises by swapping its more valuable quoted securities for their less valuable unquoted stock. In Britain, where many more enterprises had their securities quoted on the London Stock Exchange, the differential to be obtained through amalgamation, by swapping one type of security for another, was much less than in the United States. The merger movement in Britain was therefore neither so widespread nor on the same scale as in the United States, because the financial inducements were much less. In 1905, for example, the average capitalization of the fifty largest British companies was only £4.4 million ($21.3 million), while the equivalent figure in the United States was $79.5 million (£16.4 million).[63]

What, then, can be concluded concerning the differences and similarities between the two Stock Exchanges, and what were the consequences of these? Certainly, before 1909 or 1912 the London Stock Exchange was a fairly liberal institution, which admitted most people who applied for membership and quoted the securities of most companies and governments that requested it. At the same time, though it maintained restrictions on the extra-curricular activities of its members, the way they conducted business within the exchange was left fairly uncontrolled, which allowed the Exchange to cope with an expansion of both membership and the variety and volume of securities. The result was that the London Stock Exchange provided an integrated but fairly open market for securities, which existed in harmony with both the money market and the capital-raising activities of private and public enterprise.

One of its few restrictions involved the introduction and use of modern communications technology, and this declined in significance over time. The other restriction involved its members' access to capital, and their undertaking of additional business, which kept the average member firm small and specialized, even though certain trends encouraged diversification and a larger capital. However, with the new regulations of 1909 and 1912, which reimposed the broker/jobber division and introduced mandatory minimum commissions, added to the gradual restriction on membership, the strengths of the London Stock Exchange were undermined. This was without any compensations by way of liberalization of the size or operations of member firms. In the five years before the First World War the London Stock Exchange's role as an efficient and competitive market, attracting business both nationally and internationally, was slowly eroded.

As a result of the New York Stock Exchange's restrictive policy on membership and quotation, its high and inflexible minimum commission rates and its methods of trading, the securities market in New York was fragmented into a number of distinct components, each dealing in the business the Exchange ignored. By persistently interfering in the relations between itself and these other markets, the New York Exchange reduced the efficient operation of the securities market as a whole. However, adjustments made through the growth of large, diversified broking firms, operating nationally, and the evasion or circumvention of certain of the rules, allowed this market to operate fairly successfully. For example, an intimate working relationship was established between members of the New York Stock Exchange and the Curb Market. Nevertheless, the Stock Exchange's commitment to the daily settlement of trading, and its growing restriction of quotation to large, established corporations, did have profound influences upon the US economy. The former was a destabilizing influence on the financial system, tending to exaggerate crises, while the latter encouraged the creation of ever larger business units operating, first, in railroads and, later, throughout manufacturing industry.

Consequently, by the First World War the London Stock Exchange was entering a new phase of development in which it was much less a passive element in the securities market and more a positive influence, but the results of this had hardly begun to make themselves felt on the British economy. In contrast, the rules and regulations of the New York Stock Exchange, and their enforcement, had ensured that that institution had long been an important and positive influence within the US economy, and adjustments had been made, both within the Exchange and outside, in order to accommodate the particular stance it took. In essence, the London Stock Exchange was, before 1909, much closer to a 'free' market in securities than the New York Stock Exchange; and the performance of the respective markets and the changes engendered in each country were very much a reflection of that difference.

Notes

1 *Royal Commission on the London Stock Exchange* (British Parliamentary Papers, 1875, XIX), *Report*, pp. 5–6, *Minutes*, pp. 4, 16–17; E. V. Morgan and W. A. Thomas, *The Stock Exchange: Its History and Functions* (London, 1962), pp. 70, 74, 143; H. Keyser, *The Law Relating to Transactions on the Stock Exchange* (London, 1850), pp. 20–1.
2 J. E. Meeker, *The Work of the Stock Exchange* (New York, 1930), pp. 64–9.
3 Morgan and Thomas, *The Stock Exchange*, ch. 9; Meeker, *Work of the Stock Exchange*, ch. 16.
4 New York Stock Exchange (NYSE): Stock and Exchange Board, 15 November 1867; Committee of Arrangements, 2 November 1878, 23 December 1881, 9 November 1885, 9 May 1887, 11 July 1895, 12 May 1902; NYSE: N. Green, Gold & Stock Telegraph Co., to Chairman, NYSE, 26 December 1884; NYSE: Memorandum on Foreign Ticker Services, 3 May 1897; Special Committee on Odd Lots, Report, 6 June 1907; E. C. Stedman (ed.), *The New York Stock Exchange* (New York, 1905), pp. 440–1; B. E. Schultz, *Stock Exchange Procedure* (New York, 1936), p. 12.
5 London Stock Exchange (LSE): Trustees and Managers, 7 October 1868, 5 February 1873, 5 November 1879, 29 January 1880, 11 July 1888, 7 November 1888, 2 January 1889, 14 October 1891, 3 June 1903; General Purposes, 1 October 1872, 10 April 1907; Gen. Purposes Subcommittee on Exchange Telegraph Co., 16 April 1886–30 December 1908.
6 NYSE: Memorandum on Foreign Ticker Services, 31 March 1897; LSE: W. King, Managing Director, Exchange Telegraph Co., London, to Secretary, Gen. Purposes, 10 April 1907; Gen. Purposes Subcommittee on Exchange Telegraph Co., 30 December 1908; US Senate, *Regulation of the Stock Exchange: Hearings before the Committee on Banking and Currency* (Washington, 1914), p. 109; *Financial News*

(London), 16 June 1906; W. C. Van Antwerp, *The Stock Exchange from within* (New York, 1913), p. 341.

7 *Royal Commission on London Stock Exchange, Report*, p. 6, Minutes, pp. 10–13, 166; LSE: Trustees and Managers, 14 October 1891; Statement of Foreigners Admitted as Members, 1 January 1900–31 December 1909; F. Chiswell, *Keys to the Rules of the Stock Exchange* (London, 1902), p. 28; J. E. Day, *Stockbroker's Office Organisation, Management and Accounts* (London, 1911), p. 3; Morgan and Thomas, *The Stock Exchange*, pp. 140–4, 157–8, 160.

8 NYSE: Committee on Membership Rights, 17 October 1868; W. Armstrong, *Stocks and Stock-Jobbing in Wall Street* (New York, 1848); H. Hamon, *New York Stock Exchange Manual* (New York, 1965), p. 112; *History of the New York Stock Exchange* (New York, 1887), pp. 1, 5; Schultz, *Stock Exchange Procedure*, p. 13; P. Wyckoff, *Wall Street and the Stock Markets: A Chronology 1644–1971* (Philadelphia, 1972), pp. 150–1; R. Sobel, *The Big Board: A History of the New York Stock Market* (New York, 1965), pp. 86–8.

9 *Royal Commission on London Stock Exchange, Minutes*, p. 27; LSE: Gen. Purposes Subcommittee on Exchange Telegraph Co., 13 August 1894, 13 September 1894; Gen. Purposes Subcommittee on Mincing Lane, 23 September 1909; *A New Survey of London* (London, 1853), Vol. I, p. 378; Universal Stock Exchange, *Stock Exchange Investments* (London, 1897), intro. and pp. 168, 173; R. Burt, 'The London Mining Exchange, 1850–1900', *Business History*, vol. 14 (1972), pp. 126–42; Morgan and Thomas, *The Stock Exchange*, pp. 141, 227.

10 C. Duguid, *The Stock Exchange* (London, 1913), p. 120; *Financial Times, Investor's Guide* (London, 1913), p. 67; Chiswell, *Rules of the Stock Exchange*, p. 71.

11 J. K. Medbery, *Old Times in Wall Street: A Study for Today* (New York, 1886), pp. 10, 131; *The New York Stock Exchange* (New York, 1886), pp. 21, 28; *History of the New York Stock Exchange*, pp. 97–9; S. A. Nelson, *The Consolidated Stock Exchange of New York* (New York, 1909), pp. 45, 23, 25; Consolidated Stock Exchange, Annual Report (1886), p. 68, 73–4, Annual Report (1913), p. 19; W. E. Samson, *The Mysteries of Wall Street* (New York, 1884), p. 66; S. A. Nelson (ed.), *The ABC of Wall Street* (New York, 1900), pp. 69, 73; Jones & Baker, *The History of the New York Curb* (New York, 1916), p. 8; R. Sobel, *The Curbstone Brokers: The Origins of the American Stock Exchange* (New York, 1970), p. 105; S. S. Huebner (ed.), *Stocks and the Stock Market* (Philadelphia, 1910), p. 2; US Senate *Regulation of the Stock Exchange*, p. 78; NYSE: Committee on Arrangements, 31 March 1886.

12 US Congress, *Investigation of Financial and Monetary Conditions in the United States* (Washington, 1912), pp. 1297, 2194; NYSE: Special Investigation of the Curb Market, 29 March 1908; Special Committee on Mining Department, 20 November 1879; Special Committee on the NY Mining Exchange, 16 January 1885; National Monetary Com-

mission, *Statistics for the United States, 1867–1909* (Washington, 1910), p. 9; Consolidated Stock Exchange, Annual Reports, 31 May 1903, 31 May 1908, 31 May 1909; L. C. Van Riper, *Ins and Outs of Wall Street* (New York, 1898), pp. 25–6; E. G. Nourse, *Brokerage* (New York, 1910), p. 88; Van Antwerp, *The Stock Exchange*, p. 428, 431; Wyckoff, *Wall Street*, p. 155; Nelson, *ABC of Wall Street*, p. 18; S. S. Huebner, *The Stock Market* (New York, 1922), pp. 8–9.

13 *Royal Commission on the London Stock Exchange, Minutes*, pp. 11, 13–14, 139; E. McDermott, *The London Stock Exchange* (London, 1877), p. 10; L. Dennett, *The Charterhouse Group, 1925–1979: A History* (London, 1979), pp. 65–73; S. Japhet, *Recollections from my Business Life* (London, 1931), pp. 62, 102–3; LSE: Gen. Purposes Subcommittee on Commissions, 2 May 1912; Chiswell, *Rules of the Stock Exchange*, pp. 28–31, 34; Morgan and Thomas, *The Stock Exchange*, pp. 154, 157–8.

14 LSE: Gen. Purposes, 2 July 1908, 23 July 1908; Financial Times, *Investor's Guide*, p. 59.

15 NYSE: Committee on Commissions, 7 October 1903; Committee on Admissions, 17 December 1902; Committee on Insolvencies, 12 April 1877; K. Cornwallis, *The Gold Room, and the New York Stock Exchange and Clearing House* (New York, 1879), p. 35; S. S. Pratt, *The Work of Wall Street* (New York, 1903), p. 161; Hamon, *Stock Exchange Manual*, p. 112; *New York Times*, 12 November 1885; *The World*, 16 May 1884; T. W. Lawson, *High Cost Living* (Dreamworld, Mass., 1913), pp. 82–3; Hayden, Stone & Co., Summary Ledger 1909–14, Private Ledger, 1 March 1906 (Hayden, Stone & Co. Papers, Harvard Business School).

16 *Royal Commission on the London Stock Exchange, Minutes*, p. 29.

17 *Royal Commission on the London Stock Exchange, Report*, p. 23, *Minutes*, pp. 29, 42–3, 223; LSE: Gen. Purposes, 23 April 1903, 28 November 1906, 2 July 1908; Chiswell, *Rules of the Stock Exchange*, p. 34; Morgan and Thomas, *The Stock Exchange*, pp. 153–4.

18 LSE: Gen. Purposes, 27 June 1900, 11 July 1904, 15 October 1905; Duguid, *Stock Exchange*, p. 34; Day, *Stockbroker's Office Organisation*, p. 80.

19 LSE: Gen. Purposes Subcommittee on Commissions, 8 May 1912, 16 May 1912, 4 July 1912, 30 September 1912, 24 January 1913; Gen. Purposes, 13 January 1912, 15 January 1912, 25 April 1912, 30 April 1912, 1 June 1912, 21 September 1912, 30 September 1912, 20 January 1913, 24 January 1913.

20 NYSE: Governing Committee, 13 April 1894; cf. Constitution of the New York Stock and Exchange Board, 21 February 1820, Article 10.

21 NYSE: Committee on the Constitution, 16 June 1886; Special Committee on Wire Connections, 11 January 1900, *New York Tribune*, 1 May 1881.

22 NYSE: Memorandum on Commissions, 1875; cf. New York Stock and Exchange Board, 30 November 1861, 13 December 1861; Com-

mittee on Commissions, 2 June 1875, 5 January 1881, 12 May 1904, 25 April 1911; *New York Times*, 15 February 1885.

23 NYSE: Committee on Commissions, 14 May 1889, 29 March 1910; Governing Committee, 23 October 1878, 22 May 1889, 12 November 1902, 30 March 1910; Special Investigation of the Curb Market, 4 April 1906; Special Committee on Bucket Shops, Digest, 25 June 1913, p. 83.

24 *Railroad Review*, 24 December 1887; NYSE: Van Antwerp to G. A. Neeley, 30 June 1913; Committee on Commissions, 8 January 1883; Pratt, *Work of Wall Street*, p. 93; LSE: Gen. Purposes, 13 February 1907; G. R. Gibson, *The Stock Exchanges of London, Paris and New York: A Comparison* (New York, 1889), p. 34.

25 NYSE: Committee on Commissions, 16 May 1881, 20 June 1881, 14 July 1911, 12 November 1913; Committee on Admissions, 29 January 1902; Special Committee on Wire Privileges, 11 January 1900; NYSE: Van Antwerp to G. A. Neeley, 30 June 1913; Boston Stock Exchange, Constitution (1905), Article 29; Armstrong, *Stocks and Stock-Jobbing*, p. 36; *New York Stock Exchange* (New York, 1886), pp. 63, 115; NYSE: Committee on the Constitution, 4 December 1911; *Royal Commission on the London Stock Exchange, Minutes*, p. 139.

26 C. W. Barron *et al.*, *The Boston Stock Exchange, 1834–1893* (Boston, 1893), no pagination; Van Antwerp, *The Stock Exchange*, p. 428; US Congress, Money Trust Investigation, Minutes, p. 827.

27 F. L. Eames, *The New York Stock Exchange* (New York, 1894), p. 90; Stedman *The New York Stock Exchange*, p. 11; NYSE: Committee on Arrangements, 10 May 1886; Committee on Commissions, 21 February 1894; Nelson, *Consolidated Stock Exchange*, p. 75.

28 NYSE: Governing Committee, 13 April 1894; Huebner, *Stocks and the Stock Market*, p. 7.

29 Reply by the New York Stock Exchange to the Governor's Committee on Speculation in Securities and Commodities, 1909 (Horace White Papers, New York Historical Society), p. 27; NYSE: Governing Committee, 12 January 1881, 27 June 1883, 13 April 1894, 23 April 1894, 31 May 1894, 23 December 1897, 26 January 1898; Committee on Arrangements, 1 July 1895, 11 January 1897, 29 October 1900, 18 February 1903, 9 May 1904, 14 June 1904; Committee on Commissions, 5 January 1904; Matter of Domestic Arbitrage and Quotations, 14 June 1904; Pratt, *Work of Wall Street*, p. 115; Stedman, *New York Stock Exchange*, p. 505; Huebner, *The Stock Market*, pp. 85, 213.

30 NYSE: Committee on Commissions, 29 February 1912; Special Committee on Wire Connections, transcripts, 11 January 1900; Special Investigation Committee on Continuous Quotation, transcripts, 21 January 1903–5 February 1903; Special Committee on Copper Stocks, 18 May 1903; cf. Boston Stock Exchange (BSE): Governing Committee, 10 April 1894, 21 February 1898, 11 April 1898, 20 March 1914; BSE: Committee on Ways and Means of Increasing Business, 18 July

1904; W. C. Cornwell, 'Bonds as Additional Banking Reserve', in W. H. Hull (ed.), *Bonds as Investment Securities* (Philadelphia, 1907), p. 118.

31 NYSE: Special Committee of Inquiry into the Stock Commission Business, Report, 21 August 1887; Committee on Commissions, 14 August 1907, 14 December 1910, 29 February 1912, 9 April 1912, 30 October 1912; Governing Committee, 23 February 1911, 20 April 1911, 25 February 1914; Special Committee on Foreign Business, Digest 1934–5; *New York Commercial*, 26 February 1914; *Brooklyn Daily Eagle*, 1 March 1914; Pratt, *Work of Wall Street*, p. 114; Huebner, *The Stock Market*, p. 85; W. E. Rosenbaum, *The London Stock Exchange: Its Features and Usages* (New York, 1910), pp. 3–7; BSE: Committee on Ways and Means, 18 July 1904; BSE: Governing Committee, 20 March 1914.

32 LSE: Joint Committee of Trustees and Managers and General Purposes Subcommittee to Confer on the Arrangements of the Markets, 22 August 1884; *Royal Commission on the London Stock Exchange, Minutes*, p. 15; R. E. Melsheimer and S. Gardner, *The Law and Customs of the Stock Exchange* (London, 1884, 2nd edn), p. 6; W. G. Cordingley, *Dictionary of Stock Exchange Terms* (London, 1901), p. 5; W. G. Cordingley, *Guide to the Stock Exchange* (London, 1893 and 1901), p. 12; Day, *Stockbroker's Office Organisation*, pp. 78–9.

33 Hamon, *New York Stock Exchange Manual*, pp. 112, 118; Medbery, *Old Times in Wall Street*, pp. 20, 39; Sobel, *Big Board*, pp. 22–5; Wyckoff, *Wall Street*, pp. 22, 24; Eames, *New York Stock Exchange*, pp. 50, 69; L. W. Hamilton & Co., *Stock Speculation* (New York, 1875), p. 27; J. H. Failing, *A Treatise on Stock-Dealing and the Gold Conspiracy* (Fort Plain, 1879), p. 4.

34 H. J. Howland, 'Gambling Joint or Market Place? An Inquiry into the Workings of the New York Stock Exchange', *The Outlook*, 28 June 1913, p. 420; NYSE: W. C. Van Antwerp to H. J. Howland, 23 May 1913; Wyckoff, *Wall Street*, p. 35; Pratt, *Work of Wall Street*, p. 100; H. S. Martin, *The New York Stock Exchange* (New York, 1919), p. 68.

35 Meeker, *Work of the Stock Exchange*, p. 547; London Stock Exchange Official List, 31 December 1900.

36 S. R. Cope, 'The Stock Exchange Revisited: A New Look at the Market in Securities in London in the Eighteenth Century', *Economica*, vol. 45 (1978), pp. 8, 15; J. F. Wheeler, *The Stock Exchange* (London, 1913), p. 41; Duguid, *The Stock Exchange*, p. 56; Day, *Stockbroker's Office Organisation*, p. 41; *Royal Commission on the London Stock Exchange, Report*, p. 20, *Minutes*, pp. 21, 45; Messholmer and Gardner, *Law and Customs* (1905, 4th edn), p. 15.

37 For the benefits of an active market, and how it was created, see Howland, 'Inquiry', pp. 436–7; Huebner, *The Stock Market*, pp. 23–30; A. Cragg, *Understanding the Stock Market* (New York, 1929), p. 196.

38 Memorial and Remonstrance of the Board of Stock and Exchange Brokers of the City of New York to the State of New York, 23 March

1836, pp. 2, 4–6, 11; US Congress, *Money Trust Investigation, Report*, p. 116; J. E. Hedges, *Commercial Banking and the Stock Market before 1863* (Baltimore, 1938), pp. 97–8; M. G. Myers, *The New York Money Market* (New York, 1931), vol. I, pp. 132–3, 305, 424; Stedman, *New York Stock Exchange*, pp. 423, 446, 499; Pratt, *Work of Wall Street*, pp. 103–5; Schultz, *Stock Exchange Procedure*, p. 8; Hamon, *New York Stock Exchange Manual*, pp. 12, 112, 116, 118.

39 Reply by the New York Stock Exchange to the Governor's Committee on Speculation, p. 35; NYSE: Circular, Dealing for the Account, 1873; Circular, To the Members of the NYSE, 18 July 1887; *The World*, 21 October 1883 (corner in Northern Pacific); *New York Tribune*, 4 March 1884; Huebner, *The Stock Market*, pp. 168–9.

40 C. A. E. Goodhart, *The Business of Banking, 1891–1914* (London, 1972), pp. 18, 122–7; E. Withers, *The English Banking System* (Washington, 1910), pp. 37–8; E. E. Spicer, *An Outline of the Money Market* (London, 1908), p. 19; A. C. Cole, 'Notes on the London Money Market', *Journal of the Institute of Bankers*, vol. 25 (1904), pp. 134–5; F. E. Steele, 'On Changes in the Bank Rate of Discount', *Journal of the Institute of Bankers*, vol. 12 (1891), pp. 496–7; W. A. Cole, 'The Relations between Banks and the Stock Exchanges', *Journal of the Institute of Bankers*, vol. 20 (1899), p. 409; A. Crump, *The Theory of Stock Speculation* (London, 1874), p. 19; F. Lavington, *The English Capital Market* (London, 1921), p. 142; Chiswell, *Key to the Rules*, p. 11; Cordingley, *Guide to the Stock Exchange*, p. 479; E. C. Maddison, *On the Stock Exchange* (London, 1877), pp. 93–4; *Royal Commission on the London Stock Exchange, Minutes*, pp. 37–40; LSE: Gen. Purposes Subcommittee of Non-Permanent Character, 10 September 1914.

41 Goodhart, *Business of Banking*, p. 218; W. M. Blaisdell, *Financing Security Trading* (Philadelphia, 1935), pp. 33, 48, 84, 151–2; J. H. Hollander, *Bank Loans and Stock Exchange Speculation* (Washington, 1911), pp. 4, 24.

42 Myers, *New York Money Market*, pp. 131–3; Hedges, *Commercial Banking*, pp. 75, 97–8; *Bankers' Circular* (London), 15 February 1828, 19 October 1832; L. E. Davis, 'The Capital Markets and Industrial Concentration: The US and UK – a Comparative Study', *Economic History Review*, vol. 19 (1966), p. 260.

43 Blaisdell, *Financing Security Trading*, pp. 33, 84, 152, 156–8, 165; J. P. Ryan, 'Call Money Rates and Stock Prices', in T. Gibson, *Special Market Letters for 1908* (New York, 1909), p. 96; A. A. Osborne, *Speculation on the New York Stock Exchange, September 1904–March 1907* (New York 1913), p. 108; Nourse, *Brokerage*, pp. 209–10, 214–15, 223; Huebner, *The Stock Market*, pp. 221–30, 292–5, 313; H. S. Martin, *The New York Stock Exchange* (New York, 1919), p. 188.

44 T. F. Woodlock, *The Stock Exchange and the Money Market* (New York, 1908), pp. 28–9; Pratt, *Work of Wall Street*, pp. 183–5, 452; Huebner, *The Stock Market*, pp. 227–30, 292–5; *New York Tribune*, 28 October

1879, 7 May 1884, 15 May 1884, 12 November 1890, 19 November 1890; Ryan, 'Call Money Rates', p. 96; C. A. E. Goodhart, *The New York Money Market and the Finance of Trade, 1900–1913* (Cambridge, Mass., 1969), p. 17; Cragg, *Understanding the Stock Market*, p. 160.

45 NYSE: Governing Committee, 1 September 1887, 23 November 1887; Circular, Dealing for the Account, 1873; Special Committee of Inquiry into the Stock Commission Business, Report, 1 August 1887; Report on Foreign Stock Exchange Clearing Practice, 27 May 1914; Special Committee on Stock Clearances, Circular, 1873; H. Meigs, Chairman, NY Bankers' Clearing House, to Chairman, NYSE, 5 November 1879, 26 September 1882; R. L. Edwards, President, Bank of the State of New York, to President, NYSE, 12 January 1892; Committee on Clearing House, Report, July 1892; Pratt, *Work of Wall Street*, pp. 116, 120; Cragg, *Understanding the Stock Market*, p. 136; Huebner, *The Stock Market*, pp. 221–3; Blaisdell, *Financing Security Trading*, pp. 16, 84, 150–2, 158; Eames, *New York Stock Exchange*, p. 69.

46 W. M. Grosvenor, *American Securities: The Causes Influencing Investment and Speculation and the Fluctuations in Values, 1872–1885* (New York, 1885), pp. 23–4; H. G. S. Noble, *The New York Stock Exchange in the Crisis of 1914* (New York, 1915), p. 14; Goodhart, *New York Money Market*, p. 17; Nourse, *Brokerage*, pp. 209–10; Blaisdell, *Financing Security Trading*, pp. 156–8; Huebner, *Stock Market*, p. 17; Huebner, *The Stock Market*, pp. 292–5; Stedman, *New York Stock Exchange*, pp. 423, 499; N. N. Owens and C. O. Hardy, *Interest Rates and Stock Speculation* (New York, 1925), pp. 5–6; US Senate, *Regulation of the Stock Exchange: Hearings before the Committee on Banking and Currency* (Washington, 1914), Brief of Counsel on Behalf of the New York Stock Exchanges, pp. 529, 551, 553; S. F. Streit, *Report on European Stock Exchanges* (1914), pp. 8, 16–17.

47 NYSE: Circular, To the Members of the New York Stock Exchange from a Fellow Member, 18 July 1887.

48 Rosenbaum, *London Stock Exchange*, pp. 5–7; E. & C. Randolph, New York, to Nathan & Rosselli, London, 7 June 1911 (Nathan & Rosselli Papers, Guildhall Library).

49 *Royal Commission on the London Stock Exchange, Report*, p. 9; F. Playford, *Practical Hints for Investing Money – with an Explanation of the Mode of Transacting Business on the Stock Exchange* (London, 1856), pp. 10–11; W. E. Hooper (ed.), *The Stock Exchange in the Year 1900* (London, 1900), p. 198; Cope, 'Stock Exchange Revisited', p. 7; Chiswell, *Keys to the Rules*, p. 37; Wheeler, *Stock Exchange*, p. 36; Withers, *English Banking System*, p. 116; Morgan and Thomas, *The Stock Exchange* p. 145; Cordingley, *Guide to the Stock Exchange*, p. 12; Cordingley, *Dictionary of the Stock Exchange*, p. 31.

50 *Royal Commission on the London Stock Exchange, Minutes*, pp. 29, 126, 130, 206; Day, *Stockbroker's Office Organisation*, pp. 44, 218, 219; Gibson, *Stock Exchanges*, pp. 34–6; Maddison, *On the Stock Exchange*,

pp. 7–8; Duguid, *The Stock Exchange*, p. 34; C. Duguid, *The Story of the Stock Exchange* (London, 1901), p. 350; *Financial News* (London), 8 March 1905; *Investors' Review* (London), 15 February 1908; *The Times*, 21 February 1908; LSE: Gen. Purposes, 27 June 1900, 17 December 1902, 23 April 1903, 18 December 1903, 11 July 1904, 15 October 1906, 27 November 1906; E. T. Powell, *The Mechanism of the City* (London, 1910), pp. 43–5.

51 NYSE: Committee on Arrangements, 5 November 1877, 17 March 1884, 22 June 1891; Answers from the Committee of NYSE to Supplemental Questions, 1909 (Horace White Papers, New York Historical Society), pp. 3, 35–6; Hamon, *New York Stock Exchange Manual*, p. 107; Howland 'Gambling Joint', pp. 427–40; Pratt, *Work of Wall Street*, p. 94; Van Antwerp, *The Stock Exchange*, pp. 279–80; Huebner, *The Stock Market*, p. 143; Schultz, *Stock Exchange Procedure*, pp. 55, 58, 64; US Congress, Money Trust Investigation, pp. 743–5; *New York Tribune*, 6 July 1914; *New York Herald*, 4 May 1902; NYSE: W. C. Van Antwerp to Editor, *Saturday Evening Post*, Philadelphia, 13 June 1913; NYSE: Committee on Commissions, 25 November 1900; Martin, *New York Stock Exchanges*, pp. 143–53.

52 W. A. Thomas, *The Provincial Stock Exchanges* (London, 1973), pp. 90–1, 202; LSE: Gen. Purposes, 13 January 1908, 10 February 1908, 17 February 1908, 2 July 1908, 23 July 1908, 11 June 1909, 1 March 1910, 13 January 1912, 1 June 1912, 2 September 1912, 30 September 1912, 8 July 1914; Chiswell, *Key to the Rules*, p. 37.

53 W. J. Greenwood, *Foreign Stock Exchange Practice and Company Laws* (London, 1911), p. 204; A. K. Cairncross, *Home and Foreign Investment, 1870–1913* (Cambridge, 1953), pp. 90, 95; T. Skinner, *The Stock Exchange Year Book and Diary* (London, 1874), p. iii; Morgan and Thomas, *The Stock Exchange*, p. 97; Gibson, *Stock Exchanges*, pp. 92–3; Van Antwerp, *The Stock Exchange*, p. 345–58; Pratt, *Work of Wall Street*, p. 35.

54 C. Fenn, *A Compendium of the English and Foreign Funds* (London, 1837 and 1840); Sobel, *Big Board*, p. 22; Hedges, *Commercial Banking*, p. 35; NYSE: D. K. Van Veghten, Prices of Stocks and Rates of Exchange, 27 October 1820–19 April 1821; NYSE: G. A. Rollins, Call Quotation Book, 17 September 1835–26 March 1836.

55 *Royal Commission on the London Stock Exchange, Minutes*, pp. 29, 59, 66, 77, 79, 150, 369; *The Economist*, 30 May 1885; LSE: Gen. Purposes Subcommittee of Non-Permanent Character, 25 April 1898, 27 April 1899, 25 April 1900, 22 April 1901; Chiswell, *Key to the Rules*, pp. 136–9; Morgan and Thomas, *The Stock Exchange*, pp. 282–3; General Securities Corporation, *Investors' Handy Book of Active Stocks and Shares* (London, 1912), p. ix; M. Edelstein, 'Rigidity and Bias in the British Capital Market, 1870–1913', in D. M. McCloskey (ed.), *Essays on a Mature Economy: Britain after 1840* (London, 1971), p. 87; Melsheimer and Gardner, *Law and Customs*, p. 9.

56 Pratt, *Work of Wall Street*, pp. 51, 82; Schultz, *Stock Exchange Procedure*, p. 14.
57 NYSE: W. C. Van Antwerp to E. F. Abbott, Citizens Bank, Kansas, 7 July 1913; cf. Myers, *New York and the Money Market*, pp. 42–4; Wyckoff, *Wall Street*, pp. 431–2, *New York Evening Post*, 3 May 1913, Greenwood, *Foreign Stock Exchange Practice*, p. 198.
58 Calculation based on the *Commercial and Financial Chronicle* (New York), 28 February 1914, and *Stock Exchange Official Intelligence* (London, 1914). (As with London only a small number of issues were very actively traded, cf. Eames, *New York Stock Exchange*, p. 94.)
59 Nelson, *ABC of Wall Street*, pp. 22, 69; Fisk & Hatch, *Memoranda Concerning Government Bonds* (New York, 1882), p. 23; N. W. Harris & Co., *Municipal Bonds* (New York, 1897), p. 20; S. A. Nelson, *The Bond Buyers' Dictionary* (New York, 1907), p. 81; N. W. Halsey & Co., *The Most Satisfactory Bonds* (New York, 1912), p. 15.
60 T. R. Navin and M. V. Sears, 'The Rise of a Market for Industrial Securities', *Business History Review*, vol. 29 (1955), p. 136; M. V. Sears, 'Gold and the Local Stock Exchanges of the 1860s', *Explorations in Entrepreneurial History*, vol. 6 (1968–9), pp. 200–1; Davis, 'Capital Markets', p. 262; Huebner, *Stock Market*, p. 195; Huebner, *The Stock Market*, p. 7; US Senate, *Regulation of the Stock Exchange*, p. 120; NYSE: Committee on Unlisted Securities, 17 November 1897, 22 September 1908; Committee on Mining Securities, 28 April 1880; Committee on Stock List, 7 March 1872, 9 July 1884; Committee on Arrangements, 10 June 1881; Governing Committee, 25 January 1882, 8 March 1882, 1 November 1882, 11 May 1886, 13 April 1887, 12 November 1902; Special Committee on Unlisted Department, Minority Report, 22 January 1896; Special Committee on Wire Connections, transcripts, 18 January 1900; Greenwood, *Foreign Stock Exchange Practice*, pp. 200, 207; Nelson, *ABC of Wall Street*, p. 73; Stedman, *New York Stock Exchange*, pp. 457–8.
61 J. Hicking & Co., *Men and Idioms of Wall Street* (New York, 1875), p. 17; Reply by the NYSE to the Governor's Committee on Speculation, pp. 32–3; NYSE: Governing Committee, 16 March 1910; Pratt, *Work of Wall Street*, pp. 88, 92; Cragg, *Understanding the Stock Market*, p. 197; Duguid, *Stock Exchange*, p. 110; Powell, *Mechanism of the City*, p. 38.
62 US Congress, Money Trust Investigation, p. 33.
63 P. L. Payne, 'The Emergence of the Large-Scale Company in Great Britain, 1870–1914', *Economic History Review*, vol. 20 (1967), pp. 519, 523, 527, 533–4, 537–40; A. D. Chandler, *The Visible Hand: The Managerial Revolution in American Business* (Cambridge, Mass., 1977), pp. 332–3, 338, 373–4, 376; H. E. Kroos and M. R. Blyn, *A History of Financial Intermediaries* (New York, 1971), p. 129; Davis, 'Capital Markets', pp. 262, 271–2; Myers, *New York and the Money Market* , p. 281; Navin and Sears, 'Rise of a Market', pp. 136–7.

Bibliography and Sources

Primary Material

(The extensive records of the London and New York Stock Exchanges themselves provided most of the original matter consulted.)

Guildhall Library (London)

(1) London Stock Exchange Records, 1848–1914.
(2) Nathan & Rosselli: Correspondence, 1890–1922.
(3) Wm Russell: Ledger, 1902–13.
(5) Smith St Aubyn & Sons: Business Diary, 1891–1914.
(6) Guarantee Insurance & Investment Company: Minutes, 1901–11.

General Post Office (London)

Telecommunications Memoranda (Post 30 and Post 83).

Scottish Stock Exchange (Glasgow)

Glasgow Stock Exchange Records, 1844–1914.

New York Stock Exchange (New York)

New York Stock Exchange Records, 1842–1914.

New York Historical Society (New York)

(1) Peter Anspach: Correspondence, 1789–95.
(2) James W. Bleeker: Correspondence, 1804–63.
(3) John M. O'Conner: Correspondence, 1821–5.
(4) George W. Dow: Correspondence, 1851–71.
(5) Richard Irvin & Co.: Correspondence, 1873–1902.
(6) Horace White: Correspondence, 1856–1910.
(7) George Bliss: Correspondence, 1876–95.
(8) G. P. & A. W. Butler: Correspondence, 1905–11.

New York Public Library (New York)

(1)   Cyrus W. Field: Papers, 1870–85.
(2)   Walter Del Mar: Papers, 1891–8.
(3)   Consolidated Stock and Petroleum Exchange: Annual Reports, 1886–1921.

Baker Library (Harvard Business School, Cambridge, Mass.)

(1)   Andrew Clow & Co.: Correspondence, 1790–9.
(2)   James A. Hamilton: Correspondence, 1835–41.
(3)   Henry Seligman: Correspondence, 1884–1914.
(4)   Hayden, Stone & Co.: Ledgers, 1893–1914.

Boston Stock Exchange (Boston)

Boston Stock Exchange Records, 1855–1914.
Boston Stock Exchange Records, 1930.

Midwest Stock Exchange (Chicago)

Chicago Stock Exchange Records, 1882–1914.

Historical Society of Pennsylvania (Philadelphia)

(1)   V. & J. F. Gilpin: Sales Records, 1834–71.
(2)   Henry Ewing: Sales Records, 1844.

Contemporary Works

Armstrong, W. A., *Stocks and Stock-Jobbing in Wall Street* (New York, 1848).
Bagehot, W., *Lombard Street: A Description of the Money Market* (London, 1873).
The Bank – the Stock Exchange – the Bankers' Clearing House – the Minister and the Public: An Expose (London, 1821).
Barnes, A. W., *History of the Philadelphia Stock Exchange, Banks and Banking Interest* (Philadelphia, 1911).
Barron, C. W., et al., *The Boston Stock Exchange, 1839–1893* (Boston, 1893).
Bassett, H. H. (ed.), *Men of Note in Finance and Commerce* (London, 1900–1).
Bassett, H. H. (ed.), *Businessmen at Home and Abroad* (London, 1912).
Belding, Keith & Co., *United States Bonds and Securities* (London, 1867).
Brooks, H. K., *Foreign Exchange Text Book* (Chicago, 1906).
The Calumnious Aspersions Contained in the Report of the Subcommittee of the Stock Exchange Exposed and Refuted (London, 1814).
Chaloz, E. and de Saugy, E., *Vade-Mecum des Bourses de Bâle, Zurich, Genève, 1907/8 and 1913* (Zurich, 1907 and 1913).
Chamberlain, L., *The Work of the Bond House* (New York, 1912).

Bibliography and Sources

Chiswell, F., *Key to the Rules of the Stock Exchange* (London, 1901).
China Stock and Share Handbook (Shanghai, 1914).
Chiozza Money, L. G., *Insurance versus Poverty* (London, 1910).
Chiozza Money, L. G., *Riches and Poverty* (London, 1910).
Clapp & Co., *Weekly Market Letters for 1893* (New York, 1894).
Clare, G., *The ABC of the Foreign Exchange: A Practical Guide* (London, 1895).
Clare, G., *A Money Market Primer and Key to the Exchanges* (London, 1900).
Conant, C. A., *Wall Street and the Country: A Study of Recent Financial Tendencies* (New York, 1904).
Conant, C. A., *The Functions of the Stock Exchange* (New York, 1914).
Cordingley, W. G., *Guide to the Stock Exchange* (London, 1893 and 1901).
Cornwallis, K., *The Gold Room, and the New York Stock Exchange and Clearing House* (New York, 1879).
Crump, A., *The Theory of Stock Exchange Speculation* (London, 1874).
Day, J. E., *Stockbrokers' Office Organisation, Management and Accounts* (London, 1911).
Depew, C. M. (ed.), *One Hundred Years of American Commerce* (New York, 1895).
Deuchar, D., 'Investments', *Journal of the Federation of Insurance Institutes*, vol. 1 (1898).
Dickson, F. S., *Telephone Investments and Others* (Cleveland, 1905).
Duguid, C., *The Story of the Stock Exchange* (London, 1901).
Duguid, C., *The Stock Exchange* (London, 1913).
Duncan, W. J., *Notes on the Rates of Discount in London, 1856–1866 and 1866–1873* (Edinburgh, 1867 and 1877).
Eames, F. L., *The New York Stock Exchange* (New York, 1894).
Ellis, A., *The Rationale of Market Fluctuations* (London, 1876).
Escher, F., *Elements of Foreign Exchange* (New York, 1911).
Escher, F., *Foreign Exchange Explained* (New York, 1917).
Exposure of the Stock Exchange and Bubble Companies (London, 1854).
Failing, J. H., *A Treatise on Stock Dealing and the Gold Conspiracy* (Fort Plain, 1870).
Fawcett, W. L., *Gold and Debt: An American Handbook of Finance* (Chicago, 1877).
Fenn, C., *A Compendium of the English and Foreign Funds* (London, 1837 and 1840).
Field, F. W., *Capital Investment in Canada* (Toronto, 1911).
Field, F. W., 'How Canadian Stocks Are Held', *Monetary Times* (Toronto), January 1915.
Financial Times, *Investor's Guide* (London, 1913).
Fisk & Hatch, *Memoranda Concerning Government Bonds* (New York, 1882).
Fleming, I. D., *The Chicago Stock Exchange: An Historical Sketch* (Chicago, 1894).
Forwood, W. B., *Recollections of a Busy Life* (Liverpool, 1910).

Gairdner, C., *The Constitution and Course of the Money Market* (Glasgow, 1888).

General Securities Corporation, *The Investors' Handy Book of Active Stocks and Shares* (London, 1912).

Gibson, G. R., *The Stock Exchanges of London, Paris and New York: A Comparison* (New York, 1889).

Gibson, G. R., *The Vienna Bourse* (New York, 1892).

Gibson, G. R., *The Berlin Bourse* (New York, 1908).

Gibson, T., *Special Market Letters for 1908* (New York, 1909).

Gore-Brown, F., and Jordan, W., *A Handy Book on the Formation, Management and Winding-up of Joint-Stock Companies* (London, 1902).

Goschen, G. J., *The Theory of Foreign Exchange* (London, 1864).

Greenwood, W. J., *Foreign Stock Exchange Practice and Company Law* (London, 1911).

Gresham Omnium, *A Handy Guide to Safe Investments* (London, 1858).

Grohman, W. B., 'Cattle Ranches in the Far West', *Fortnightly Review*, vol. 28 (1880).

Grosvenor, W. M., *American Securities* (New York, 1885).

H.M., *On the Analogy between the Stock Exchange and the Turf* (London, 1885).

H.S.G., *Autobiography of a Manchester Manufacturer* (Manchester, 1887).

Haight & Freese, *Guide to Investors* (New York, 1898).

N. W. Halsey & Co., *Municipal Bonds* (New York, 1875).

N. W. Halsey & Co., *The Most Satisfactory Bonds* (New York, 1912).

Hamilton, H., *An Inquiry Concerning the Rise and Progress, the Redemption and Present State of Management of the National Debt* (Edinburgh, 1818).

L. W. Hamilton & Co., *Stock Speculation* (New York, 1875).

Hamon, H., *New York Stock Exchange Manual* (New York, 1865).

N. W. Harris & Co., *Municipal Bonds* (New York, 1897).

Haupt, O., *The London Arbitrageur, or the English Money Market in Connexion with Foreign Bourses* (London, 1870).

Hemming, H. G., *Hemming's History of the New York Stock Exchange* (New York, 1905).

J. Hickling & Co., *Men and Idioms of Wall Street* (New York, 1875).

Hirst, F. W., *The Credit of Nations* (Washington, 1910).

History of the New York Stock Exchange (New York, 1887).

Hobson, J. A., *The Economic Interpretation of Investment* (London, 1911).

Holden, E. V., *The Depreciation of Securities in Relation to Gold* (Liverpool, 1907).

Hollander, J. H., *Bank Loans and Stock Exchange Speculation* (Washington, 1911).

Hooper, W. E. (ed.), *The Stock Exchange in the Year 1900* (London, 1900).

Howland, H. J., 'Gambling Joint or Market Place? An Inquiry into the Workings of the New York Stock Exchange', *The Outlook*, 28 June 1913.

Huebner, S. S. (ed.), *Stocks and the Stock Market* (Philadelphia, 1910).
Hull, W. H. (ed.), *Bonds as Investment Securities* (Philadelphia, 1907).
Ingall, G. D., and Withers, G., *The Stock Exchange* (London, 1904).
Investors' Guardian, *Guide to Investments* (London, 1873).
Japhet, S., *Recollections from my Business Life* (London, 1931).
Jeans, J. S., *Railway Problems* (London, 1887).
Jevons, W. S., *Investigations in Currency and Finance* (London, 1884).
Karo, M., *City Milestones and Memories: Sixty-Five Years in and around the City of London* (London, 1962).
Kemmerer, E. W., *Seasonal Variations in the Relative Demand for Money and Capital in the United States* (Washington, 1910).
Keyser, H., *The Law Relating to Transactions on the Stock Exchange Board* (San Francisco, 1910).
King, J. L. *History of the San Francisco Stock and Exchange Board* (San Francisco, 1910).
Knight's London Cyclopaedia (London, 1851).
Land and House Property Year Book for 1893 (London, 1894).
The Land: The Report of the Land Enquiry Committee (London, 1914).
Lawson, T. W., *High Cost Living* (Dreamworld, Mass., 1913).
Lawson, W. R., *The Scottish Investors' Manual* (Edinburgh, 1884).
Lawson, W. R., *American Finance* (London, 1906).
Le Maistre, G. H., *The Investors' India Year Book* (Calcutta, 1911).
Lester, F. M., *Chicago Securities: A Manual for Bankers, Brokers and Investors* (Chicago, 1888).
Liesse, A., *Evolution of Credit and Banks in France* (Washington, 1909).
Lowe, J., *Present State of England in Regard to Agriculture, Trade and Finance* (London, 1823).
Lowenfeld, H., *All about Investment* (London, 1909).
Lubbock, J. W., *On the Clearing of the London Bankers* (London, 1860).
Mackenzie, J. B., *The Story of a Stock Exchange Speculator* (London, 1908).
Maddison, E. C., *On the Stock Exchange* (London, 1877).
Manual of Statistics (New York, 1901).
Margraff, A. W., *International Exchange* (Chicago, 1906).
Martin, J. G., *A Century of Finance: History of the Boston Stock and Money Markets, 1798–1898* (Boston, 1898).
Martin, J. G., *Stock Fluctuations* (Boston, 1903, 1907, 1911).
McDermott, E., *The London Stock Exchange: Its Constitution and Modes of Business* (London, 1877).
Medbery, J. K., *Old Times in Wall Street: A Study for Today* (New York, 1871).
Melsheimer, R. E., and Gardner, S., *The Law and Customs of the Stock Exchange* (London, 1884, 1891, 1905).
Miller, H. S., *Scientific Speculation* (London, 1901).
C. W. Morgan & Co., *How to Speculate Successfully in Wall Street* (New York, 1900).

Murchison, J. H., *British Mines Considered as a Means of Investment* (London, 1854).
Nash, R. L., *A Short Inquiry into the Profitable Nature of our Investments* (London, 1881).
National Monetary Commission, *Interviews on the Banking and Currency Systems* (Washington, 1910).
National Monetary Commission, *Statistics of Britain, France, Germany and the United States, 1867–1909* (Washington, 1910).
Nelson, S. A. (ed.), *The ABC of Wall Street* (New York, 1900).
Nelson, S. A., *The Bond Buyers' Dictionary* (New York, 1907).
Nelson, S. A., *The Consolidated Stock Exchange of New York* (New York, 1907).
A New Survey of London (London, 1853).
Neymarck, A., *French Savings and their Influence upon the Bank of France and upon French Banks* (Washington, 1910).
Neymarck, A., *Le Statistique Internationale des Valeurs Mobilières* (La Haye, 1911).
Noble, H. G. S., *The New York Stock Exchange in the Crisis of 1914* (New York, 1915).
Nomura Shoten, *Handbook of Japanese Securities* (Osaka, 1910).
Nourse, E. G., *Brokerage* (New York, 1910).
O'Hagan, H. O., *Leaves from my Life* (London, 1929).
Osborne, A. D., *Speculation on the New York Stock Exchange, 1904–1907* (New York, 1913).
Paish, G., *The Trade Balance of the United States* (Washington, 1910).
Palgrave, R. H. I., *Bank Rate and the Money Market* (London, 1903).
Patron, M., *The Bank of France in its Relation to National and International Credit* (Washington, 1910).
Phillips, G. H., *Phillips' Investors' Manual* (London, 1887).
Pinto, E., *'Ye Outside Fools': Glimpses inside the Stock Exchange* (London, 1877).
Pittsburgh Stock Exchange, *Stocks and Bonds* (Pittsburgh, 1903).
Playfold, F., *Practical Hints for Investing Money* (London, 1856).
Poley, A. D., and Gould, F. H., *The History, Law and Practice of the Stock Exchange* (London, 1911).
Porter, G. R., and Hirst, F. W., *The Progress of the Nation* (London, 1912).
Powell, E. T., *The Mechanism of the City* (London, 1910).
Pratt, S. S., *The Work of Wall Street* (New York, 1903).
Reid, J., *A Manual of the Scottish Stocks and British Funds* (Edinburgh, 1841).
Robinson, K., *The Mining Market* (London, 1907).
Rosenbaum, W. E., *The London Stock Market: Its Features and Usages* (New York, 1910).
Samson, W. E. *The Mysteries of Wall Street* (New York, 1884).
Schmidt, H., *Foreign Banking Arbitration: Its Theory and Practice* (London, 1875).

Bibliography and Sources

Schuster, F., 'Foreign Trade and the Money Market', *Monthly Review*, vol. 14 (1904).

A Scotch Banker, *The Theory of Money* (Edinburgh, 1868).

Simmonds, P. L., *The Stock Exchange Year-Book* (London, 1874).

Simmonds, P. L., *Fenn's Compendium of the English and Foreign Funds* (London, 1860).

Skinner, T., *The Stock Exchange Year Book and Diary* (London, 1874).

Spicer, E. E., *An Outline of the Money Market* (London, 1898).

Stedman, E. C. (ed.), *The New York Stock Exchange* (New York, 1905).

Stockbrokers' Telegraphic Code (London, 1886 and 1899).

Stock Exchange Investments: Their History, Practice and Results (London, 1897).

Streit, S. F., *Report on European Stock Exchanges* (New York, 1914).

Taeuber, R., *Die Borsen der Welt* (Berlin, 1911).

Tunbridge & Co., *Secrets of Success in Wall Street* (New York, 1875).

Universal Stock Exchange, *Stock Exchange Investments* (London, 1897).

Van Antwerp, W. C., *The Stock Exchange from within* (New York, 1913).

Van Oss, S. F., *American Railroads and British Investors* (London, 1893).

Van Oss, S. F., and Mathieson, F. C., *Stock Exchange Values: A Decade of Finance, 1885–1895* (London, 1895).

Van Riper, L. C., *Ins and Outs of Wall Street* (New York, 1898).

Vidal, E., *The History and Methods of the Paris Bourse* (Washington, 1910).

Walker & Watson, *Investors' and Shareholders' Guide* (Edinburgh, 1894).

Ward, R. A., *A Treatise on Investments* (London, 1852).

Watkins, G. P., *The Growth of Large Fortunes* (New York, 1907).

Webb, A. G., *The New Dictionary of Statistics* (London, 1911).

Weil, M. L., *The ABC and Manual of the Curb Market* (New York, 1908).

Wheeler, J. F., *The Stock Exchange* (London, 1913).

Wildshut, H., *General Methods in Vogue with Dealings on the Amsterdam Stock Exchange* (Amsterdam, 1912).

Withers, H., *The English Banking System* (Washington, 1910).

Wolff, H. D., *Rambling Recollections* (London, 1908).

Woodlock, T. F., *The Stock Exchange and the Money Market* (New York, 1908).

Woolf, A. H., *The Stock Exchange: Past and Present* (London, 1913).

Serial Publications

Bankers' Circular (London), 1820s–30s.

Bullionist (London), 1866.

Corporation of Foreign Bondholders: Annual Reports (London), 1874–1914.

Financial Review (New York; Supplement of *Financial and Commercial Chronicle*), 1884, 1914.

Financial Review of Reviews (London), 1904–14.

Investor's Monthly Manual (London), 1880–1914.

Investors' Review (London), 1890–3.
Journal of the Institute of Bankers (London), 1889–1914.
Manual of Statistics (New York), 1884, 1901.
Russian Journal of Financial Statistics (St Petersburg), 1900.
The Statist (London), 1890–1914 (selected).
Stock Exchange Gazette (London), 1901.
Stock Exchange Official Intelligence (originally *Burdett's Official Intelligence*; London), 1884–1914.

Government Reports

British Parliamentary Papers: *Report from the Select Committee on Joint Stock Banks* (BPP, 1837, XIV).
British Parliamentary Papers: *Royal Commission on Loans to Foreign States, Report* (BPP, 1874, II).
British Parliamentary Papers: *Royal Commission on the London Stock Exchange, Report and Minutes of Evidence* (BPP 1878, XIX).
New York State: *Report of Governor Hughes Committee on Speculation in Securities and Commodities* (7 June 1909).
US Congress: *Investigation of Financial and Monetary Conditions in the United States under House Resolutions Nos. 429 and 405 before the Subcommittee of the Committee on Banking and Currency* ('Money Trust Investigation'; Washington, 1912).
US Congress: *Report of the Committee Appointed to Investigate the Concentration of Control of Money and Credit* (28 February 1913).
US Senate: *Regulation of the Stock Exchange: Hearings before the Committee on Banking and Currency* (Washington, 1914).

Secondary Works

Adler, D. R., *British Investments in American Railways, 1834–1898* (Charlottesville, 1970).
Aldcroft, D. H. (ed.), *The Development of British Industry and Foreign Competition* (London, 1968).
Anderson, B. L., 'Law, Finance and Economic Growth in England: Some Long-Term Influences', in B. M. Ratcliffe (ed.), *Great Britain and her World, 1750–1914* (Manchester, 1975).
Anderson, B. L., 'Institutional Investment before the First World War: The Union Marine Insurance Company, 1897–1915', in S. Marriner (ed.), *Business and Businessmen* (Liverpool, 1978).
Angel, J. W., *The Theory of International Prices: History, Criticism and Restatement* (Cambridge, 1926).
Barbour, J. B., 'Sketch of the Pittsburgh Oil Exchanges', *Western Pennsylvania Historical Magazine*, vol. 11 (1918).

Barker, T. C., and Robbins, M., *A History of London Transport* (London, 1963 and 1974).

Barty-King, H., *Girdle round the Earth: The Story of Cable and Wireless and its Predecessors* (London, 1979).

Baster, A. S. J., *The Imperial Banks* (London, 1929).

Baster, A. S. J., *The International Banks* (London, 1935).

Beach, W. E., *British International Gold Movements and Banking Policy, 1881–1913* (Cambridge, Mass., 1935).

Beastall, T. W., *A North Country Estate* (London, 1974).

Birch, A., *The Economic History of the British Iron and Steel Industry, 1784–1879* (London, 1967).

Blaisdell, W. M., *Financing Security Trading* (Philadelphia, 1935).

Bloomfield, A. I., *Short-Term Capital Movements under the pre-1914 Gold Standard* (Princeton, 1963).

Bordo, M. D., and Schwartz, A. J. (eds.), *A Retrospective on the Classical Gold Standard, 1821–1931* (Chicago and London, 1984).

Born, K. E., *International Banking in the 19th and 20th Centuries* (Leamington Spa, 1983).

Britton, R., 'Wealthy Scots, 1876–1931', *Bulletin of the Institute of Historical Research*, vol. 58 (1985).

Buckley, R. J., and Roberts, B. R., *European Direct Investment in the USA before World War I* (London, 1982).

Burt, R., 'The London Mining Exchange, 1850–1900', *Business History*, vol. 14 (1972).

Burton, H., and Corner, D. C., *Investment and Unit Trusts in Britain and America* (London, 1968).

Butt, J., and Ward, J. T., 'The Promotion of the Caledonian Railway Company', *Transport History*, vol. 3 (1970).

Byatt, I. C. R., *The British Electrical Industry 1875–1914* (Oxford, 1979).

Cairncross, A. K., *Home and Foreign Investment, 1870–1913* (Cambridge, 1953).

Cairncross, A. K., and Eichengreen, B., *Sterling in Decline* (Oxford, 1983).

Cameron, R., *France and the Economic Development of Europe, 1800–1914* (Princeton, 1961).

Cameron, R. (ed.), *Banking in the Early Stages of Industrialization* (New York, 1967).

Cameron, R. (ed.), *Banking and Economic Development* (New York, 1972).

Camplin, J., *The Rise of the Plutocrats: Wealth and Power in Edwardian England* (London, 1978).

Capie, F., and Rodrik-Bali, R., 'Concentration in British Banking, 1870–1920', *Business History*, vol. 24 (1982).

Capie, F., and Webber, A., *A Monetary History of the United Kingdom, 1870–1982* (London, 1985).

Capie, F., and Webber, A., *Profits and Profitability in British Banking, 1870–1939*, City University Centre for Banking and International Finance Discussion Paper No. 18 (1985), p. 21.

Carosso, V. P., *Investment Banking in America: A History* (Cambridge, Mass., 1970).

Chandler, A. D., 'The Beginning of "Big Business"', in Andreano, R. (ed.), *New Views on American Economic Development* (Cambridge, Mass., 1965).

Chandler, A. D., *The Visible Hand: The Managerial Revolution in American Business* (Cambridge, Mass., 1977).

Chapman, S., *The Rise of Merchant Banking* (London, 1984).

Checkland, S., *The Mines of Tharsis* (London, 1967).

Church, R. A. (ed.), *The Dynamics of Victorian Business: Problems and Perspectives to the 1870s* (London, 1980).

Cleary, E. J., *The Building Society Movement* (London, 1965).

Clower, R. W. (ed.), *Monetary Theory: Selected Readings* (London, 1969).

Coleman, D. C., 'Gentlemen and Players', *Economic History Review*, vol. 26 (1973).

Collins, M., 'The Business of Banking: English Bank Balance Sheets, 1840–80', *Business History*, vol. 26 (1984).

Cope, S. R., 'The Stock Exchange Revisited: A New Look at the Market in Securities in London in the Eighteenth Century', *Economica*, vol. 45 (1978).

Cope, S. R., 'Bird, Savage & Bird of London, Merchants and Bankers, 1782–1803', *Guildhall Studies in London History*, vol. 4 (1981).

Cottrell, P. L., *Industrial Finance, 1830–1914* (London, 1980).

Cottrell, P. L., 'The Steamship on the Mersey, 1815–80: Investment and Ownership', in P. L. Cottrell and D. H. Aldcroft (eds.), *Shipping, Trade and Commerce* (Leicester, 1981).

Cottrell, P. L., and Aldcroft, D. H. (eds.), *Shipping, Trade and Commerce* (Leicester, 1981).

Cowan, R. M. W., *The Newspaper in Scotland* (Glasgow, 1946).

Cragg, A., *Understanding the Stock Market* (New York, 1929).

Craig, R., 'William Gray & Co.: A West Hartlepool Shipping Enterprise', in P. L. Cottrell and D. H. Aldcroft (eds.), *Shipping, Trade and Commerce* (Leicester, 1981).

Crouzet, F., *The Victorian Economy* (London, 1982).

Dailey, D. M., *Investment Banking in Chicago* (Urbana, 1931).

Davies, A. E., *Investments Abroad* (Chicago, 1927).

Davis, L. E., 'The Investment Market, 1870–1914: The Evolution of a National Market', *Journal of Economic History*, vol. 35 (1965).

Davis, L. E., 'Capital Markets and Industrial Concentration: The US and UK: A Comparative Study', *Economic History Review*, vol. 19 (1966).

Davis, L. E., 'Capital Mobility and American Growth', in R. W. Fogel and S. L. Engerman (eds.), *Reinterpretation of American Economic History* (New York, 1971).

Davis, L. E., and Hughes, J. R. T., 'A Dollar–Sterling Exchange, 1803–1895', *Economic History Review*, vol. 13 (1960–1).

Dennet, L., *The Charterhouse Group, 1925–1979: A History* (London, 1979).

Detroit Stock Exchange, 1907–1931 (Detroit, 1931).

Dickson, P. G. M., *The Financial Revolution in England: A Study in the Development of Public Credit* (London, 1967).

Duboff, R. B., 'The Telegraph and the Structure of Markets in the United States, 1845–1890', *Research in Economic History*, vol. 8 (1982).

Dunning, J. H., *Studies in International Investment* (London, 1970).

Eagly, R. V., and Smith, G. V. K., 'Domestic and International Integration of the London Money Market, 1731–1789', *Journal of Economic History*, vol. 36 (1976).

Edelstein, M., 'Rigidity and Bias in the British Capital Market, 1870–1913', in D. McCloskey (ed.), *Essays on a Mature Economy: Britain after 1840* (London, 1971).

Edelstein, M., *Overseas Investment in the Age of High Imperialism: The United Kingdom, 1850–1914* (London, 1982).

Einzig, P., *The History of Foreign Exchange* (London, 1962).

Escher, F., *Foreign Exchange Explained* (New York, 1917).

Estcourt, R., 'The Stock Exchange as a Regulator of Currency', *The Annalist* (New York), vol. 14 (1919).

Farnie, D. A., *The English Cotton Industry and the World Market, 1815–1896* (Oxford, 1979).

Fletcher, G. A., *The Discount Houses in London* (London, 1976)

Flink, S., *The German Reichsbank and Economic Growth* (1930, repr. New York, 1969).

Fogel, R. W., and Engerman, S. L. (eds.), *Reinterpretation of American Economic History* (New York, 1971).

Ford, A. G., *The Gold Standard, 1880–1914: Britain and Argentina* (Oxford, 1962).

Ford, A. G., 'International Financial Policy and the Gold Standard, 1870–1914', *Warwick Research Papers*, vol. 104 (1977).

Ford, A. G., 'The Trade Cycle in Britain, 1860–1914', in R. Floud and D. McCloskey (eds.) *The Economic History of Britain since 1700* (Cambridge, 1981).

Fraser, W. H., *The Coming of the Mass Market, 1850–1914*, (London, 1981).

Freedeman, C. E., *Joint-Stock Enterprise in France, 1807–1867* (Chapel Hill, 1979).

Friedman, M., and Schwartz, A. J., *Monetary Statistics of the United States* (New York, 1970).

Friedman, M., and Schwartz, A. J., *Monetary Trends in the United States and the United Kingdom: Their Relation to Income, Prices and Interest Rates, 1867–1975* (Chicago, 1982).

Gang, K. L., *Stock Exchanges in India* (Calcutta, 1950).

Goldsmith, R. W., *The Financial Development of Japan, 1868–1977* (New Haven, 1983).

Goodhart, C. A. E., *The New York Money Market and the Finance of Trade, 1900–1913* (Cambridge, Mass., 1969).

Goodhart, C. A. E., *The Business of Banking* (London, 1972).

Greenberg, D., *Financiers and Railroads, 1869–1889: A Study of Morton, Bliss & Co.* (Newark, 1980).

Hall, A. R., 'A Note on the English Capital Market as a Source of Funds for Home Investment before 1914', *Economica*, vol. 24 (1957), vol. 25 (1958).

Hall, A. R., *The London Capital Market and Australia, 1870–1914* (Canberra, 1963).

Hall, A. R., *The Stock Exchange of Melbourne and the Victorian Economy, 1852–1900* (Canberra, 1968).

Hall, A. R., and Cairncross, A. K., 'English Capital Market', *Economica*, vol. 24 (1957), vol. 25 (1958).

Hannah, L., 'Mergers in British Manufacturing Industry, 1880–1918', *Oxford Economic Papers*, vol. 26 (1974).

Hannah, L., *Electricity before Nationalisation* (London, 1979).

Hedges, J. E., *Commercial Banking and the Stock Market before 1863* (Baltimore, 1938).

Henderson, R. F., *The New Issue Market and the Finance of Industry* (Cambridge, 1951).

Hennessy, E., *Stockbrokers for 150 years: A History of Shepherds & Chase* (London, 1978).

Hidy, R. W., and Hidy, M. E., 'Anglo-American Merchant Bankers and the Railroads of the Old Northwest 1848–1860', *Business History Review*, vol. 34 (1960).

Huebner, S. S., *The Stock Market* (New York, 1922).

Huston, F. M., and Russell, G. A., *Financing an Empire: History of Banking in Illinois* (Chicago, 1926).

Ingham, G., *Capitalism Divided? The City and Industry in British Social Development* (London, 1984).

Iversen, C., *Aspects of the Theory of International Capital Movements* (Copenhagen, 1936).

James, J. A., 'The Development of the National Money Market, 1893–1911', *Journal of Economic History*, vol. 36 (1976).

James, J. A., *Money and Capital Markets in Postbellum America* (Princeton, 1978).

Jefferys, J. B., *Business Organisation in Great Britain, 1856–1911* (New York, 1977).

Jenks, L. H., *The Migration of British Capital to 1875* (New York, 1927).

Jones & Baker, *The History of the New York Curb* (New York, 1916).

Jones & Baker, *Profits and Dividends on America's Second Largest Stock Market* (New York, 1919).

Jones, C. A., 'Great Capitalists and the Direction of British Overseas Investment in the Late Nineteenth Century: The Case of Argentina', *Business History*, vol. 22 (1980).

Jones, C. A., 'Competition and Structural Change in the Buenos Aires Fire Insurance Market: The Local Board of Agents, 1875–1921', in O. M. Westall (ed.), *The Historian and the Business of Insurance* (Manchester, 1984).

Jones, E., *Accountancy and the British Economy, 1840–1980: The Evolution of Ernst & Whinney* (London, 1981).

Jones, G., 'Lombard Street on the Riviera: The British Clearing Banks and Europe, 1900–1960', *Business History*, vol. 24 (1982).

Kennedy, W. P., 'Foreign Investment, Trade and Growth in the United Kingdom, 1870–1913', *Explorations in Economic History*, vol. 11 (1974).

Kennedy, W. P., 'Institutional Response to Economic Growth: Capital Markets in Britain to 1914', in L. Hannah (ed.), *Management Strategy and Business Development* (London, 1976).

Kennedy, W. P., 'Economic Growth and Structural Change in the United Kingdom, 1870–1914', *Journal of Economic History*, vol. 42 (1982).

Kieve, J. L., *The Electric Telegraph: A Social and Economic History* (Newton Abbot, 1973).

Killick, J. R., and Thomas, W. A., 'The Provincial Stock Exchanges, 1830–1870', *Economic History Review*, vol. 23 (1970).

Kindleberger, C. P., *The Formation of Financial Centers: A Study in Comparative Economic History* (Princeton, 1974).

Kindleberger, C. P., *Manias, Panics and Crashes: A History of Financial Crises* (London, 1978).

Kindleberger, C. P., 'Financial Institutions and Economic Development: A Comparison of Great Britain and France in the Eighteenth and Nineteenth Centuries', *Explorations in Economic History*, vol. 21 (1984).

Kindleberger, C. P., and Laffarge, J.-P. (eds.), *Financial Crises: Theory, History and Policy* (Cambridge, 1982).

King, W. T. C., *History of the London Discount Market* (London, 1936).

Kouwenhoven, J. A., *Partners in Banking: An Historical Portrait of a Great Private Bank: Brown Brothers, Harriman & Co., 1818–1968* (New York, 1968).

Kroos, H. E., and Blyn, M. R., *A History of Financial Intermediaries* (London, 1971).

Kubicek, R. V., *Economic Imperialism in Theory and Practice: The Case of South African Gold Mining Finance 1886–1914* (Durham, NC, 1979).

Kuznets, S., *Seasonal Variations in Industry and Trade* (New York, 1933).

Kuznets, S., *Capital in the American Economy: Its Formation and Financing* (Princeton, 1961).

Lamoreaux, N. R., *The Great Merger Movement in American Business, 1895–1904* (Cambridge, 1985).

Lavington, F., *The English Capital Market* (London, 1921).

League of Nations, *Memorandum on Commercial Banks, 1913–1929* (Geneva, 1931).

Lee, J. P., 'The Provision of Capital for Early Irish Railways', *Irish Historical Studies*, vol. 16 (1968–9).

Lenman, B., and Donaldson, K., 'Partners' Incomes, Investment and Diversification in the Scottish Linen Area, 1850–1921', *Business History*, vol. 13 (1971).

Levy-Leboyer, M., 'Central Banking and Foreign Trade: The Anglo-

American Cycle in the 1830s', in C. P. Kindleberger and J.-P. Laffarge (eds.), *Financial Crises*, op. cit. (1982).

Lewis, J. P., *Building Cycles and Britain's Growth* (London, 1965).

Lindert, P. H., *Key Currencies and Gold 1900–1913* (Princeton, 1909).

Livesay, H. C., and Porter, G., 'The Financial Role of Merchants in the Development of US Manufacturing', *Explorations in Economic History*, vol. 9 (1971).

MacGregor, D. H., 'Joint-Stock Companies and the Risk Factor', *Economic Journal*, vol. 39 (1929).

Machlup, F., *The Stock Market, Credit and Capital Formation* (London, 1940).

Martin, H. S., *The New York Stock Exchange* (New York, 1919).

Martins, S. W., *A Great Estate at Work: The Holkam Estate and its Inhabitants in the 19th Century* (Cambridge, 1980).

Matthews, R. C. O., Feinstein, C. H., and Odling-Smee, J. C., *British Economic Growth, 1856–1973* (Oxford, 1982).

McCloskey, D. N., *Enterprise and Trade in Victorian Britain: Essays in Historical Economics* (London, 1981).

McFarlane, L. A., 'British Investment and the Land: Nebraska 1877–1946', *Business History Review*, vol. 57 (1983).

Meeker, J. E., *The Work of the Stock Exchange* (New York, 1930).

Meredith, H. A., *The Drama of Money Making* (London, 1931).

Michie, R. C., 'The Social Web of Investment in the Nineteenth Century', *Revue Internationale d'Histoire de la Banque*, vol. 18 (1979).

Michie, R. C., *Money, Mania and Markets: Investment, Company Formation and the Stock Exchange in Nineteenth-Century Scotland* (Edinburgh, 1981).

Michie, R. C., 'Options, Concessions, Syndicates and the Provision of Venture Capital, 1880–1913', *Business History*, vol. 23 (1981).

Michie, R. C., 'Crisis and Opportunity: The Formation and Operation of the British Assets Trust, 1897–1914', *Business History*, vol. 25 (1983).

Michie, R. C., 'Income, Expenditure and Investment of a Victorian Millionaire: Lord Overstone 1823–83', *Bulletin of the Institute of Historical Research*, vol. 58 (1985).

Michie, R. C., 'The London and New York Stock Exchanges, 1850–1914', *Journal of Economic History*, vol. 46 (1986).

Michie, R. C., 'The Finance of Innovation in late Victorian and Edwardian Britain: A Preliminary Investigation', *Journal of European Economic History* (forthcoming, 1987).

Mitchell, B. R., *Abstract of British Historical Statistics* (Cambridge, 1971).

Mitchell, W. C., *Gold, Prices and Wages under the Greenback Standard* (Berkeley, 1908).

Morgan, E. V., and Thomas, W. A., *The Stock Exchange: Its History and Functions* (London, 1963).

Morris, R. J., 'The Middle Class and the Property Cycle during the Industrial Revolution', in T. C. Smout (ed.), *The Search for Wealth and Stability* (London, 1979).

Munn, C., 'The Emergence of Central Banking in Ireland', *Irish Economic and Social History*, vol. 10 (1983).

Musson, A. E., *The Growth of British Industry* (London, 1978).

Myers, M. G., *The New York Money Market: Origins and Development* (New York, 1931).

Myers, M. G., *Paris as a Financial Centre* (London, 1936).

Myers, M. G., *A Financial History of the United States* (New York, 1970).

Navin, T. R., and Sears, M. V., 'The Rise of a Market for Industrial Securities, 1887–1902', *Business History Review*, vol. 29 (1955).

Newcomen Society, *The Story of the Philadelphia Stock Exchange* (Philadelphia, 1976).

New York Curb Exchange (New York, 1937).

Nishimura, S., *The Decline of Inland Bills of Exchange in the London Money Market, 1855–1913* (Cambridge, 1971).

North, D. C., 'Life Insurance and Investment Banking at the Time of the Armstrong Investigation of 1905/6', *Journal of Economic History*, vol. 14 (1954).

North, D. C., 'International Capital Movements in Historical Perspective', in R. F. Mikesell (ed.), *US Private and Government Investment Abroad* (Eugene, 1962).

Owens, R. N., and Hardy, C. O., *Interest Rates and Stock Speculation: A Study of the Influence of the Money Market on the Stock Market* (New York, 1925).

Paish, F. W., 'The London New Issue Market', *Economica*, vol. 18 (1951).

Paish, F. W., *Long-Term and Short-Term Interest Rates in the United Kingdom* (Manchester, 1966).

Palmade, G. P., *French Capitalism in the Nineteenth Century* (Newton Abbot, 1972).

Parker, W., *The Paris Bourse and French Finance* (New York, 1920).

Paterson, D. G., *British Direct Investment in Canada, 1890–1914* (Toronto, 1976).

Payne, P. L., 'Iron and Steel Manufactures', in D. H. Aldcroft (ed.), *Development of British Industry and Foreign Competition* (London, 1968).

Peake, E. G., *An Academic Study of Some Money Markets and Other Statistics* (London, 1923).

Perry, C. R., 'The British Experience, 1876–1912: The Impact of the Telephone during the Years of Delay', in I. de S. Pool (ed.), *The Social Impact of the Telephone* (Cambridge, Mass., 1977).

The Pittsburgh Stock Exchange, 1894–1929 (Pittsburgh, 1929).

Platt, D. C. M., *Foreign Finance in Continental Europe and the United States, 1815–1870* (London, 1984).

Pollard, S., 'Capital Exports, 1870–1914: Harmful or Beneficial?', *Economic History Review*, vol. 38 (1985).

Powell, E. T., *The Evolution of the Money Market 1385–1915* (London, 1915).

Pressnell, L. S., 'The Sterling System and Financial Crises before 1914', in Kindleberger and Laffarge (eds.), op cit. (1982).

Reader, W., *A House in the City* (London, 1979).

Reed, M. C., 'Railways and the Growth of the Capital Market', in Reed, M. C. (ed.), *Railways in the Victorian Economy* (Newton Abbot, 1969).

Reed, M. C., *A History of James Capel & Co.* (London, 1975).

Rice, W., *The Chicago Stock Exchange: A History* (Chicago, 1923).

Richards, E., 'An Anatomy of the Sutherland Fortune: Income, Consumption, Investments and Returns, 1780–1880', *Business History*, vol. 21 (1979).

Riley, J. C., *International Government Finance and the Amsterdam Capital Market, 1740–1815* (Cambridge, 1980).

Ripley, P., *A Short History of Investment* (London, 1934).

Robertson, D. H., *A Study of Industrial Fluctuations* (London, 1915).

Robson, B. T., *Urban Growth: An Approach* (London, 1973).

Rose, M. B., 'Diversification of Investment by the Greg Family, 1800–1914', *Business History*, vol. 21 (1979).

Rosenbaum, E., and Sherman, A. J., *M. M. Warburg & Co., 1798–1938: Merchant Bankers of Hamburg* (London, 1979).

Rubinstein, W. D., 'The Victorian Middle Classes: Wealth, Occupation and Geography', *Economic History Review*, vol. 30 (1977).

Rubinstein, W. D., 'Wealth, Elites and Class Structures of Modern Britain', *Past and Present*, vol. 76 (1977).

Rubinstein, W. D., *Men of Property: The Very Wealthy in Britain since the Industrial Revolution* (London, 1981).

Rungta, R. S., *Rise of Business Corporations in India 1851–1900* (Cambridge, 1970).

Saul, S. B., 'House Building in England, 1890–1914', *Economic History Review*, vol. 15 (1962–3).

Sayers, R. S., *Gilletts in the London Money Market in 1867–1967* (Oxford, 1968).

Sayers, R. S., *The Bank of England* (Cambridge, 1976).

Scammell, W. M., *The London Discount Market* (London, 1968).

Schluter, W. C., *The Pre-War Business Cycle, 1907 to 1914* (New York, 1923).

Schultz, B. E., *Stock Exchange Procedure* (New York, 1936).

Scott, J., *The Upper Classes: Property and Privilege in Britain* (London, 1982).

Scott, J., and Hughes, M., *The Anatomy of Scottish Capital* (London, 1980).

Sears, M. V., 'The Rise of a Market for Industrial Securities, 1887–1902', *Business History Review*, vol. 29 (1955).

Sears, M. V., 'Gold and the Local Stock Exchanges of the 1860s', *Explorations in Entrepreneurial History*, vol. 6 (1968–9).

Simon, M., 'Pattern of New British Portfolio Foreign Investment, 1865–1914', in A. R. Hall (ed.), *The Export of Capital from Britain, 1870–1914* (London, 1968).

Smiley, G., 'Interest Rate Movement in the United States, 1888–1913', *Journal of Economic History*, vol. 35 (1975).

Sobel, R., *The Big Board: A History of the New York Stock Market* (New York, 1965).

Sobel, R., *The Curbstone Brokers: The Origins of the American Stock Exchange* (New York, 1970).

Spence, C. C., *British Investments and the American Mining Frontier, 1860–1901* (Ithaca, 1958).

Spray, D. E. (ed.), *The Principal Stock Exchanges of the World* (Washington, 1964).

Stancke, B., *The Danish Stock Market, 1750–1840* (Copenhagen, 1971).

Stone, J. M., 'Financial Panics: Their Implications for the Mix of Domestic and Foreign Investments of Great Britain, 1880–1913', *Quarterly Journal of Economics*, vol. 85 (1971).

Stoppard, J. M., 'The Origins of British-Based Multinational Manufacturing Enterprises', *Business History Review*, vol. 48 (1974).

The Story of the Johannesburg Stock Exchange 1887–1947 (Johannesburg, 1948).

Sturrock, J. B., *Peter Brough: A Paisley Philanthropist* (Paisley, 1890).

Sushka, M. E., and Barrett, W. B., 'Banking Structure and the National Capital Market, 1869–1914', *Journal of Economic History*, vol. 44 (1984).

Sylla, R., 'Federal Policy, Banking Market Structure and Capital Mobilization in the United States, 1863–1913', *Journal of Economic History*, vol. 29 (1969).

Sylla, R., 'The United States, 1863–1913', in R. Cameron (ed.), *Banking and Economic Development* (New York, 1972).

Tamaki, N., *The Life Cycle of the Union Bank of Scotland, 1830–1954* (Aberdeen, 1983).

Thomas, W. A., *The Provincial Stock Exchanges* (London, 1973).

Thompson, F. M. L., 'The Land Market in the 19th Century', *Oxford Economic Papers*, vol. 9 (1957).

Tilly, R., *Financial Institutions and Industrialization in the Rhineland, 1815–1870* (Madison, 1966).

Treble, J. H., 'The Pattern of Investment of the Standard Life Assurance Company, 1875–1914', *Business History*, vol. 22 (1980).

Triffin, R., *Our International Monetary System: Yesterday, Today and Tomorrow* (New York, 1968).

US Department of Commerce, *Historical Statistics of the United States* (Washington, 1975).

Utton, M. A., 'Some Features of the Early Merger Movements in British Manufacturing Industry', *Business History*, vol. 14 (1972).

Van Laaner, J. T. M., and Geutzberg, P., *Changing Economy in Indonesia: Money and Banking, 1816–1940* (Amsterdam, 1980).

Wacha, D. E., *A Financial Chapter in the History of Bombay City* (Bombay, 1910).

Ward, J. R., *The Finance of Canal Building in Eighteenth-Century England* (Oxford, 1974).

Weiner, M. J., *English Culture and the Decline of the Industrial Spirit, 1850–1980* (Cambridge, 1981).

Westall, O. M. (ed.), *The Historian and the Business of Insurance* (Manchester, 1984).

White, H. D., *The French International Accounts, 1880–1913* (Cambridge, Mass., 1933).

Whitten, D. O., *The Emergence of Giant Enterprise 1860–1914: American Commercial Enterprise and Extractive Industries* (Westport, 1983).

Williams, B. A., *Investment in Innovation* (London, 1958).

Williams, D., 'The Evolution of the Sterling System', in C. R. Whittlesey and J. S. G. Wilson (eds.), *Essays in Money and Banking* (Oxford, 1968).

Williamson, J. G., *American Growth and the Balance of Payments, 1820–1913* (Chapel Hill, 1964).

Williamson, J. G., *Did British Capitalism Breed Inequality?* (Boston, 1985).

Woolf, E. S., 'The American Market before 1914', *Stock Exchange Journal*, vol. 8 (1963).

Woytinsky, W. S., and E. S., *World Commerce and Governments* (New York, 1955).

Wyckoff, P., *Wall Street and the Stock Markets: A Chronology, 1644–1971* (Philadelphia, 1972).

Young, P., *Power of Speech: A History of Standard Telephones and Cables, 1883–1983* (London, 1983).

Theses

Ayres, G. L., 'Fluctuations in New Capital Issues on the London Money Market, 1899 to 1913' (MSc, London University, 1934).

Cottrell, P. L., 'Investment Banking in England, 1856–1982: Case Study of the International Financial Society' (PhD, Hull University, 1974).

Essex-Crosby, A., 'Joint-Stock Companies in Great Britain, 1890–1930' (M.Com., London University, 1938).

Harrison, A. E., 'Growth, Entrepreneurship and Capital Formation in the United Kingdom's Cycle and Related Industries, 1870–1914' (PhD, University of York, 1977).

Jefferys, J. B., 'Trends in Business Organisation in Great Britain since 1856' (PhD, London University, 1938).

Jones, C. A., 'British Financial Institutions in Argentina' (PhD, Cambridge University, 1973).

Kynaston, D., 'The London Stock Exchange, 1870–1914: An Institutional History' (PhD, London University, 1983).

Lenfant, J., 'British Capital Export, 1900–1913' (PhD, London University, 1949).

Munn, C. W., 'The Scottish Provincial Banking Companies, 1747–1864' (PhD, Glasgow University, 1976).

Naylor, R. T., 'Foreign and Domestic Investment in Canada: Institutions and Policy, 1867–1914' (PhD, Cambridge University, 1979).

Offer, A., 'Property and Politics: A Study of Landed and Urban Property in England between the 1880s and the Great War' (DPhil, Oxford University, 1978).

Springett, R. J. 'The Mechanics of Urban Land Development in Huddersfield' (PhD, Leeds University, 1979).

Weir, R. B., 'The Distilling Industry in Scotland in the Nineteenth and Early Twentieth Centuries' (PhD, Edinburgh University, 1974).

Index

accountants 105, 115, 117
Adamson, Collier & Chadwick 115
Adsit, C.C. 260
advertising 228
agents, foreign ('remisiers') 18, 64, 78,
    85, 88, 90, 106, 115, 117, 152,
    188, 227, 237
agriculture 101, 105, 112–13, 122, 133, 139
    plantations 120, 204, 221, 241
Allegheny Valley Railroad 211
Allen, W.E. 120
Amalgamated Copper 70, 72, 186,
    201, 210
American Bell Telephone Co. 209
American Sugar Refining Co. 186,
    198, 201
American Telephone & Telegraph 212,
    223
American Window Glass 211
Anaconda Copper Company 55, 72
Anglo-American Bank 144
Anglo-American Telegraph Company
    43, 45–6, 70
Anglo-Russian Bank 144
Anspach, Peter 171, 186
Antwerp, W.C. Van, (1913) 260, 272
arbitrage 22, 70–4, Table 3.2, Table
    3.3, 76–9, 82, 85, 91–2, 151,
    154–6, 186–9, 201–2, 204–6,
    256–7, 261
    international security arbitrage 68–9,
    73, 188
arbitrageurs 69, 71, 74, 81, 90, 92,
    155, 186–9, 202
Argentine North-Eastern Railway 55,
    123
Ashurst, Morris & Co. 115
Ashworth, R. 121
assets
    fixed 101, 103, 230
    foreign 112–13
    real 99, 117, 224, 230

Assets Realization Co. 263
Atchison, Topeka & Santa Fe Railroad
    53, 186, 209, 224
Atlantic Mining Co. 178
Austrian
    bonds (1851) 39
    loan (1852) 37

Baker, Mason & Co. 76
Baldwin 167
Bank
    of Commerce 183
    of England 4, 35–6, 143
    of Montreal 240
    of North America 236, 268
    of the United States 170–1; First
        170–1; Second 171
    rate 104
bankers 120, 136, 141–2, 167, 226–8,
    230, 232, 256, 258, 262, 268
bankers' drafts 132
bankers, merchant 64–5
banks xiv, 4–5, Table 2.3, 68, 72, 79,
    87–8, 103–5, 108–9, 116, 119–21,
    135, Table 5.2, 138–40, 142, 144,
    146–8, 151, 153, 167, 170–1, 180,
    183–4, 220–1, 223–4, 228–9,
    232–9, 258, 267–9, 271
    Scottish 4, 7, 136
    Irish 4
banks, merchant 65–7, 78, 87, 114–16,
    123
bankruptcy 107, 155, 236, 268
Banque
    de Paris et des Pays Bas 152
    Française pour le Commerce et
        l'Industrie 152
Baring, crisis of 1890 241
Barings 66, 114, 116
Barnes & Cunningham 187
Barwick, Sir J.S. 120
Battle of Waterloo 36

Bauer, R.M. (1911) 90
Benson, R.H. 66
Bernheimer & Speyer 176
Bethlehem Steel Co. 263
Bills of Exchange 132, 137–41, 146–9, 153–4
Bleecker, James W. 180
Boer War III, 123, 142
bonds 49–50, 53, 56, 79–81, 142, 153, 168, 173, 175, 179, 184, 197–9, 207, 209–11, 214, 220, 222–3, 225–31, 234–6, 238–41, 255, 263
borrower 49, 57, 137–9, 141–2, 182–4, 224, 235–7, 239–40, 273
Bourse 34–7, 39, 41, 45, 55, 58, 69, 88, 90
Braithwaite, J. (1908) 21, 115
British Assets Trust 138
British Vacuum Cleaner Co. 121
Broken Hill Proprietary 55
broker ix, 9, 19–23, 27, 46, 65–6, 68, 76–9, 81, 84, 87, 89, 92, 114–17, 119–20, 137, 140, 142, 150–2, 170–7, 178–81, Table 6.4, 183–5, 186–7, 188, 194–6, 198, 200–8, 210, 220, 229–30, 235–8, 242, 252–6, 258–63, 266, 268–71, 275
  Edinburgh 5, 7
  local 5
  London 4, 7, 19, 21
  money 183
  non-British xiv
  odd-lot 185, 199, 205
  provincial 13–15
  ship 106
Brooks, H.K. (1906) 145
Brough, Peter 120
Building Societies 104–5, 109
Butler, G.P. & A.W. 176, 178
buyers xiii
buying xiv, 4–5, 13–15, 17, 19–22, 35, 38–40, 65–6, 68, 74, 80, 84, 91, 151, 156, 170–1, 174–6, 180–1, 183–8, 196–7, 199–200, 205, 208, 211, 213, 230, 233–4, 238, 240, 257, 259, 261–6, 270, 272–3

cable 71–3, 80–1, 175, 187, 213
  submarine 42–7, 187
Caledonian Railway Stock 8, 10–11, Table 1.1
call money 147–8, 263–4, 267–9

call-over system 17, 184, 263
Canada 239
Canada Cement 124
Canadian Agency 114–16, 124, Table 4.4
Canadian Pacific Railway 54–5, 213, 240
Canals 224
  Scottish 7
Canton Co. 174
Capel, James & Co. 115
capital
  formation 101–2, 105, 110, 112, 117, 226
  market xii, xiii, 3, 34, 37, 99–104, 106–25, 139, 231, 239, 242
Carey, H.S. (1908) 82
carrier pigeons 39
Cazenove & Co. 68
Central Mining Corporation 56
Central Trust Co. 226–7
Central Underground Railway 123
Chaplin, Milne & Grenfell 124
Chase Bank 183
cheques 132, 154–5, 233, 269
Chesapekes 72
Chicago
  Brewing & Malting Co. 57
  Gas Light & Coke Co. 211
  Packing & Provision Co. 57
  Telephone 211
Chick, Samuel 120
Chinnery Bros. 77
Chiozza Money, L.G. (1912) 133
Citizens Traction 211
City Bank 183
City of London 35, 99–100, 114, 123–4, 133
City of New York 177–8
Civil War, USA 184, 187, 196–7, 211, 223–4, 226, 236–7, 254
Clapp & Co. 175
Clarkson & Co. 180
class
  investing 119
  elite 119
  housing, working 102–3
clearing system 269
Clews, Henry & Co. 259
closing prices 7–8, 17–18, 39
Clow, Andrew (1791) 40
Coats, J. & P. 113

Cockram, C.E. 120
Cohen, Lionel (1878) 90
Cohen, L. & Sons 116
collateral 235–6, 273
commercial activities 23, 26, 56, 99,
    105, 108, 110, 124, 143, 171, 198,
    231, 236, 272–3
Commercial and Financial Chronicle
    (1890) 186
Commercial Bank of Scotland 138
Commercial Cable Co. 46, 71
commission (charges) 66,72, 78–80,
    84, 86–8, 100, 142, 187, 196, 200,
    202, 204, 226, 229, 249, 257–62,
    270
    minimum 22, 26, 85, 176, 199, 201,
        203, 212–13, 258, 260–1, 271,
        275
    to brokers 180–1, 183–5
Committee
    for General Purposes (London) 250,
        252
    Governing (N.Y.) 250, 258
    of London Stock Exchange 83–5
    of Trustees and Managers (London)
        250
common stock (USA) 183, 194, 255
communications xii, xv, 5, 7–16,
    19–20, 27, 38–9, 41–6, 64–9, 73,
    77, 81–2, 90, 99, 111, 139, 153–4,
    172–6, 178, 180–81, 186–8, 194,
    200, 202, 204, 208, 213, 222–3,
    251–2, 254, 261, 264, 275
Compania de Massamedes 152
Conant, C.A. (1904) 34; (1914) 156
Consolidated Coal 178
Consolidated Stock and Petroleum
    Exchange 204–8, Table 7.2,
    254–5, 260–1, 273
consols (or *rentes*) 37, 50, 141–3
contacts 15–16, 21, 27, 64–7, 76–7,
    81–2, 90–2, 104, 114–16, 175,
    180–1, 182, 189, 207, 229, 236,
    238, 258–9, 265, 270–1
control, (non-state) 109–10, 232–3,
    249, 251–2, 255, 262
control, (state) 88, 167, 200, 236,
    265–6
    bourse law, 1896, Germany 88
    French, 1893, 1898 88
Cordingley (1893, 1901) 150
cornering operation 266–7, 269

Cornwallis, K. (1879) 167–8
Cory, John 120
coupon-bonds, US 47–8
credit facilities 132, 140, 155–6, 235,
    238, 242, 256, 267, 269
Credit Lyonnais 78, 87
credits 136–40, 149, 150, 181, 221
Crimean War 111, 142
curb market 206–10, 213–14, 254–5,
    273, 275

Davan, Kingsmill (1791) 40
dealers xiv, 17–18, 21, 23, 26, 92,
    150–1, 200, 270
dealing 65, 72, 86, 176, 178, 180, 261,
    264
debentures 137, 139, 143
debits 136
Decker, Howell & Co. 236, 268
Delaware & Hudson Railroad 236
deposits 135, 138, 147, Table 5.5, 221,
    233, 237, 268
Detroit Edison 178
Deutsche Bank 78–9
differential, price, 36, 40–1, 47–8,
    67–9, 141, 145, 171, 180, 183–9,
    201, 227, 234–5, 237, 255, 257,
    261, 265
domestic finance 3
Dominion Coal Co. of Nova Scotia
    209
Doolette, G.P. 120
Drovers' National Bank 211
dual capacity 21–2, 26, 85
Duguid, C. (1913) 47
Duncan, W.J. (1867) 135, 147
Dutch funds 35–6

Eames, F.L. (1894) 188
East India Company 4, 6–7, 35–6
economic performance 3, 49, 100
Economist, The 41, 147
economy,
    domestic (UK) xiv, 100–1, 105, 113,
        118, 133
    domestic (US) 220–42, 249
    national (either) 249
    world xiii, xv, 35, 118, 153, 155, 241
Elliot, Sir Arthur 188
Ellis, A. (1876) 3
Ellis, W.W. (1903) 85
Elsworth & Knighton (1907) 104

equities 143
Escher, F.E. (1911) 155
Estate Agents 103–4, 120

Fenn, C. (1837) 5, Table 1.1, 36
Field, Lindley & Co. 181
Field, Cyrus W. 181
finance, long term 66, 99, 103, 105,
  119, 233–4, 238–40
  funds 65
  source 101, 107
finance, short term 103, 121, 144–8,
  150, 152–3, 233, 237, 239–41, 267,
  269
financial operations xv, 23, Table 2.3,
  100, 154, 176, 226
Financial Review of Reviews (1906) 142
First National Bank 226
Fisk, Harvey & Sons 228
Fitch, Walter & Co. 177
floating debt 237
floor trader 185
flotations 107, 115, 123, 225
fluctuations of market xiv, 4, 7–8,
  10–13, 15, 19, 36, 38, 47–8,
  137–8, 141–3, 145–6, 155–6, 167,
  172, 185–7, 189, 198, Table 7.1,
  240–1, 264–5, 269
foreign exchange 64
Foster & Braithwaite 115
Fourth National Bank of New York
  167
Franco-Prussian War (1870) 34, 49, 69
fraud 107
French Revolution (1789) 36
Friendly Societies 104, 119
function, stock exchange xii–xv, 65,
  81, 84–5, 99, 101, 117, 133, 194,
  203, 213, 238, 241, 249, 266

Gairdner, C. (1888) 132
General Motors 223, 227
General Post Office ix, 9, 14, 43, 82,
  112, 142
German, origin of firms 67, 86–7
  experts 78
gold 120–1, 154–6
Gold & Stock Telegraph Co. 174
Goldman Sachs & Co. 183, 226
Goodhart & Co. 177
government stock
  Bank of England 4

British 6
East India Company 4, 6
foreign 6, 49
South Sea Company 4
UK 6, 7, 24–7, Table 1.3, 34, 37,
  41, 50, Table 2.2, 56, 70, 104,
  114, 118, 119–22, 124, 139,
  142–3
US 171, 173, 183, 196–8, 211, 223,
  226, 230–1, 263, 267, 271, 273
governments, national xiii, 110–11,
  117
Govett & Co. 76
Grand Trunk Railway of Canada 10
Grant, Hooley and O'Hagan 115
Gray, Vivian & Co. 76
Greenwood, W.J. (1911) 34
Grenfell, Arthur (1906–13) 114, 116,
  124
Grey, Earl 68
Griesel & Rogers 183, 236
Groesbeck & Scholey 187
Grohman, W.B. (1880) 112
growth of stock exchange xiii, 3, 48,
  100, 170–81, 194, 203–4, 220, 228,
  237, 250–7
Guarantee Insurance & Investment Co.
  143

Haes & Sons 65
Haight & Freese 175
Hamilton, L.W. (1875) 175
Hamilton & Bishop 176
Hamon, H. 184
Hanover Bank 183, 237
Harris, N.W. 228
Hartfields Wall Street Code 72
Haven, de & Townsend 187, 201
Hayden, Stone & Co. 181, 182, 257
Head, Charles & Co. 178, 187, 201,
  210
Healy, F. & Co. 76
Heaton, J.H. (1908) 43
Hemming, H.G. xii
Heseltine, Powell & Co. 71, 76–7
Hickling, John (1875) 235
Higgins & Clarke 76, 85
Higginson, Lee 226–7
Hill & Kennedy 177
Hirsch, Louis 152
Hirst, F.W. (1910) 57
history, financial xv, 167

Hitchins, C.F. 121
Holden, N.E. 188
housing 102–5, 111, 120, 123, 133, 173, 220–1

Illinois Central Railroad 47
immigrants 87, 92
Imperial Japanese Bonds 143
Imperial Land Company 116
importance
    of London Stock Exchange 3
    of New York Stock Exchange 230, 236–7
industrial companies Table 1.1, 23, 26, 56–7, 76, 99–100, 105, 110, 119–20, 122, 124, 185–6, 198–9, 203–4, 207, 211–12, 222–3, 226
    Nobel Dynamite Trust 56
    United States Steel 56, 70, 231, 234, 259, 263, 272–3
Ingall, F.D. & Co. 69
insurance 180
insurance companies xv, 4–5, Table 2.3, 104–5, 108–9, 119–21, 140, 143–4, Table 5.3, 171, 196–7, 210, 220–1, 223–4, 227–8, 232–4, 237, 239, 271
    Scottish 7
interest rates 57, 72, 141–2, 145, 151–3
intermediaries 66, 99, 101, 114, 123, 137, 141, 143, 151, 154, 180, 184, 220, 225, 228, 237–8
internal history 3
International Power Company (1902) 68
International Pump 236
investment 67, 101–4, 110, 112–14, 119–22, 135, 141, 167, 177, 198, 230–3, 235, 238–41, 253, 265, 273
investor 35–6, 90, 107, 208
    foreign xiv
    N.Y. xiv
investors 4, 19, 23, 37, 41, 53, 57, 80, 89, 104, 108, 110, 114–23, 170, 177, 188, 199, 203, 209, 211–12, 223–6, 228–31, 234, 236, 238–41
Investor's Monthly Manual (1909) 102, 107
Investor's Review (1895) 141
Irving, Richard & Co. 66
issues xiv, 19, 26–7, 35, Table 2.2, 53, 57, 101, 110, 113, Table 4.3, 114,

Table 4.4, 116–17, 123, 141, 143, 171, 181, 194, 197–8, 207, 212, 220, 225–32, 238, 240, 263–4, 272–3
    government 6, 66
    non-government 6–7

Japhet, Saemy & Co. 67, 78–9, 84, 86, 88, 92, 152, 256–7
Java Bank 147
Jay, G.H. & A.M. 92
Jews 86
jobber 15–19, 21–2, 27, 65–6, 77–9, 81, 84–5, 89, 92, 117, 140–1, 150–2, 156, 184, 256, 270–1, 275
    'turn' 15
    jobbing 91
joint-account trading 171, 188, 202, 257, 261
joint-stock 4–5, 7, 18, 23–4, 109–11, 115, 119, 121, 123–4, 142–3, 147, Table 5.6, Table 5.7, 171
    government domination; British and foreign (1840) 4
    Scottish Table 1.1, 7

Karminski, Eugene (1912) 87
Karo, Max 88
Kennedy, H. & Co. 235
Kleinworts 66
Knauth, Macleod & Kuhne 188
Kuhn, Loeb & Co. 183, 226–7

Lake Superior Steel 124
Laurie, H.W. 86
Leicester, Earl of 119
Lester, F.M. (1888) 212
Linlithgow Oil 121
Loans 141, 150, 180–4, Table 6.4, 220–1, 235–40, 250, 259, 267–9
    South American 36
    USA 36
    French indemnity 69
Lockwood, F.M. & Co. 258
Loewenstein 92
Logan & Bryan 183
London Auction Mart (1893) 103–4
London County Council 140
London Joint-Stock Bank 142
loopholes in regulations 22, 85–6, 259
Lorde, Standish 171, 186
Louisville & Nashville Railroad 53

Lowenfeld, H. (1907) 121

Mackibin, Goodrich & Co. 176
Maddison, E.C. (1877) 141
mail 48, 111, 171–2, 175
  mail packet (shipping) 35
management, stock exchange 42, 81–4, 250
manufacturing 101, 104–6, 113, 115, 139, 197–8, 206, 208, 210, 222–3, 225–6, 274–5
  iron & steel 108, 113
  cotton-spinning 108, 113
  cycle 106, 108
  tyre 108
  breweries & distilleries 108, 110, 120
  motor vehicles 106, 110
Mar, Eugene Del 180
  Walter Del 180
Maritime Review (1904) 106
Marjoribanks, Capel & Co. (1830) 5
market
  economy ix
  mechanism xiii, 100, 111, 114, 154–6, 184–5, 229, 237, 241, 263
  over-the-counter (OTC) 208, 210, 213–14, 273
  unlisted 198–9, 203–4, 231
markets, after-hours 73, 78, 80, 83–5, 254
Martin, J.G. (1898) 209
Mayer & Co. 236
Medwin & Lowy 89, 156
membership, stock exchange xiii, 3, 16, 19, 21–2, 27, 34, 41, 79, 81–4, 90, 92, 105, 117, 122, 156, 176–7, 180–1, 186–7, 194–6, 199–207, 213, 225, 229, 249–60, 262, 271–2, 274
  admission 66, 86–8, 251–3
mergers 109, 225, 274
messenger boys 207
Mexican Central Railway 209
Milburn, L.E. 120
Milwaukee & Chicago Brewing & Malting Co. 57
Mincing Lane 78, 92, 253
mining Table 1.1, 23, 26, Table 2.3, 56–7, 76, 105, 108, 115, 120, 123, 133, 143, 196–9, 203–4, Table 7.2, 206–7, 211–12, 222–3, 253, 259, 273

copper 69, 209–10
  gold 120–1
  'mania' 17, 167
  metal 55
  South Africa 55–6, 74, 78–9, 123–4
  US 70
Missouri, Kansas & Pacific Railroad 263
monetary system, international xii
money market xii, xiv, xv, 4–5, 13–15, 19, 21, 67, 73, 132–57, 237–42, 267–9, 275
Montagu, Samuel & Co. 67
Morgan, C.W. & Co. (1900) 50
Morgan, J.P. 56, 226–7
Morrison, H. (1906) 16–17, 26–7
mortgages 103–5, 108, 110, 113, 121, 135, 176, 221
Morton, Bliss & Co. 66
Morton Bros. 76–7
Mount Morgan Mining 55

Nathan & Rosselli 71–2, 86–7, 151–2
National City Bank 226
national debt 4, 7, 24, 26, 37, 53, 69, 99, 111, 122, 141–3
  European governments 36
  world 49–50
  US 70
National Lead Co. 198
negotiation 16
new issues market 181, 187
newspapers 72, 116, 230
New York Central Railroad 47
New York State Assembly 170
New York Tribune (1892) 187; (1914) 185, 189
New York Times (1890) 241
Nobel Dynamite Trust 56, 121
North British Railway 11, Table 1.1
Northern Pacific Railroad 187
Nourse, E.G. (1910) 175

O'Connor, John 180
Oesterreichische Laenderbank 78
offices 4, 13, 19, 46, 133, 177, 181, 187, 230, 260
'open board' (1869) 194, 203, 254
option 40, 140, 148
  'put' 140
  call 147–8, 184, 235–6, 263–4, 267–9
Overstone, Lord (1881) 119

payment 264–9, 275
Peabody, Kidder 226
Pennsylvania Railroad 53, 72, 222
personal services 23, 105, 108, 226
Philadelphia & Reading Railroad Co.
    174
Pittsburgh Brewing 211
Pneumatic Tubes 9, 45, 81
Poley and Gould (1911) 68
Powell, L. & Sons 76
Pratt, S.S. (1903) 34, 80
premises
    of London Stock Exchange 19
    of New York Stock Exchange 250,
        253, 262
prices 142
    fixed 39–40
profit 40, 66–9, 74, 78, 90, 92
promissory notes 108
public debt 223–4
Pynchon, Raymond & Co. 188

quarrying 105, 120
quicksilver mining 263
quotations 109–11, 178, 196, 198–9,
    201, 204, 207, 209–10, 213, 231–2,
    249, 261, 270–5

railroads 170–3, 181, 184–7, 196–7,
    204, Table 7.2, 209–11, 222–4,
    226, 230–3, 235–6, 239–41, 263–4,
    271, 275
    'mania' 253
railways 5–7, Table 1.2, 23, 26, 37,
    39, 50, 54, 56, 70, 76, 80, 99,
    111–13, 115–23, 139, 142–3
    American 47–8, 53–4, 69
    Argentine North-Eastern Railway 123
    Canadian Pacific 54
    French 37, 50
    Grand Trunk Railway of Canada 10
    'railway mania' 11, 18, 41
    Scottish 7–8, 10
Rand Mines 56
Randolph, E. & C. 71–2, 152, 201
Raphael, R. & Sons 65, 67, 76, 116
Raymond, Pynchon & Co. 71
Reading Railroad 72, 185, 186–7, 233
records ix–x
regulations of business 21–3, 26–7,
    81–2, 85–6, 88–90, 178, 194–203,
    249–50, 253–60, 262, 271–2, 274–6

relationships, external 3–27, 35, 37–8,
    41, 64, 66, 68–9, 71, 87, 90, 136,
    146, 153, 156, 175–8, 179, 182–3,
    186–7, 189, 198–214, 237, 240–2,
    260–1, 270, 274–5
relay stations 172
'remisiers' 85, 90
Renton, James Hall (1878) 151
Report into the control of money and credit
    (1913) 168, 273
Rio Tinto 55
Robertson, John & Co. (1833) 5
Robinson, K. (1907) 55
role
    of London Stock Exchange ix,
        xii–xiv, 3, 8, 81, 84, 99, 101,
        105, 116, 132, 156
    of New York Stock Exchange 169,
        208, 220, 225, 229–31, 233,
        236–42, 253, 275
    the Curb 207
Rosenbaum, W.E. (1910) 80
Rothschilds 66, 114, 116
Royal Bank of Scotland 138
Royal Commission (1878) 3
rubber plantation 78, 93, 253, 272
    Malayan 79, 92
Russell, William 142
Rutherford, H. K. 120

Samuel, J.B. & Co. 68
Satterthwaite, E. & Co. 66
savings 101–2, 106, 109, 117–19, 123,
    135, 137, 143–4, 153, 156, 220,
    224, 230, 234, 237–8, 240, 269
Schweder, R.E. & Co. 70
Sears, Roebuck & Co. 223
secondary market 101, 117, 122, 230–1
securities 3–27, Table 2.3, Table 2.4,
    Table 3.1, 76
    domestic 36, 41, 92–3, 104, 109, 143
    government 45
    international 4, 36–8, 41, 47–8, 55,
        64–5, 92
    world 38
securities market
    American xiv–xv, 37, 68, Table 6.2,
        168–89, 194–214, 220–1, 228,
        271, 273, 275
    British xiii, 3–27, 35, 67, 99, 118,
        132, 139, 143, 152, 249
    government 4

securities market (cont'd)
national xiv
not sole 3
provincial 5, 7
Scottish 3, 5, Table 1.1
world xiv, 34–5, 40, 66, Table 4.3,
143, 271
Seligman, Henry 227
sellers xiii
selling xiv, 4–5, 13–15, 17, 19–22, 35,
38–40, 65–6, 68, 74, 80, 84, 91,
151, 156, 170–1, 174–6, 178–81,
183–7, 196–7, 199–200, 205, 208,
211, 213, 230, 233–4, 238, 240,
257, 259, 261–6, 270, 272–3
services 124, 132
expert 179, 185, 189
London Stock Exchange xiv, 7, 35,
122
stock market 122
share certificate 65
shareholders 5, 198, 209, 222–3, 227–8
shares 4, 13, 21, 23, 27, 67–8, 72, 78,
87, 89, 116–17, 119, 122, 139,
141, 178, 181, 186, 233, 250, 252,
255, 259, 263
Shepherd, James & Co. 143
Shepherds & Chase 142
shipping xv, 105–8, 120, 210
Shorter's Court 83, 254
shunters 15–18, 21
London 5
shunting 15–23, 26
solicitors 103–5, 115–16, 120, 226, 256
Simon & Co. 68
Smith, St. Aubyn & Co. 137
Solomon & Co. 90
South Sea Company 4, 36
Spalding (1911) 146
speculation xiii, 232, 242, 265–6, 268
Spencer, Trask & Co. 177
Sperling & Co. 143
Speyers 183
Spicer, E.E. (1908) 154
Spiegel, E. & Co. 123
stamp duty 89
Standard Oil of New Jersey 223, 231
Standard Oil Trust 223
Statist, The 91
steam transport xv, 39, 71, 106
Stedman, E.C. (1905) 206
Steel Company of Scotland 121

sterling 146
Stimson & Sons (1896) 104
stock 113
stock exchanges xiv, 3, Table 1.2, 13,
15–16, 18–22, 24, 26, 39, 167,
171–2, 176–7, Table 6.3, 178, 188,
199–204, 206, 208–13, 261, 271
Aberdeen Table 1.3 (c), 18, 24
Alexandria 74
Amsterdam 34–6, 39, 42–3, 53, 69, 74
Berlin 42, 53, 55–6, 69, 74, 76
Boston 167–8, Table 6.1
Brussels 42, 69
Cairo 56
Cardiff 23
Chicago 57, 167, 169
Colombo 74
Constantinople 56
Dublin 4
Edinburgh 11
Frankfurt 37, 42, 53
Germany 88
Glasgow Table 1.3 (b), 8, 9–11, 14,
17–18, 23, 56
Havana 74
Hamburg 56
Irish 17–18
Johannesburg 56, 74
Liverpool 11, 23
Madrid 56
Manchester 11, 18
Melbourne 55
Moscow 56
Paris 34–5, 37, 39, 41–3, 53, 55–6,
67–9, 74, 88
Philadelphia 167, 170–1
provincial 3
San Francisco 167
Sheffield 23
Vienna 43, 56
stocks 4, 13, 16, 21, 23, 27, 34, 49–50,
53, 56, 67, 77–8, 81, 87, 89, 117,
119, 122, 140–1, 153, 169, 171,
172–4, 177, 178, 184, 194, Table
7.1, 197–9, 207, 210, 212, 214,
220, 222–3, 225–6, 228–31, 233–6,
238–41, 255, 263–5, 269–71
stockholders 55
stockjobbers 184, 270
supply and demand xiii, 8–10, 13, 42,
69, 101, 105, 117, 123–4, 137,
178, 225, 232–4, 242

Sutherland, Duke of 120
Swiss Bankverein 78

taxation 89, 111, 133, 224
telegram 43, 45–6, 82, 173, 175
telegraph ix, xv, 7–11, 15, 19–20, 27, 42–3, 45, Table 2.1, 47, 65–6, 68, 70–1, 73, 77, 79, 81–3, 111, 132, 155, 172–7, 186–7, 189, 199–200, 202, 220, 254
telephone 8, 13–14, 20–2, 44, 47, 77, 79, 81–2, 92, 111–12, 132, 155, 173, 175–6, 187, 189, 199–200, 207–8, 210, 220, 232, 251, 254, 260–1, 270, 273
Tennant, Sir Charles 120
Tharsis Sulphur & Copper 55, 121
Throgmorton Street 83, 254
ticker-tape machine 13, 19–20, 174–5, 200–1, 251, 260–1
Times, The (1845) 41
trading floor 4, 7, 9, 13, 19–21, 71, 77, 81–2, 174–5, 183, 187–8, 200–2, 229, 235–6, 242, 251, 254, 259, 263, 270, 272–3
trading hours, differing 73–4, 79–80, 82–4
trading post system 263–4, 270
transport 105, 197, 208, 211, 222–4, 226–7, 264, 274
trends of market xiii, 27, 38, 48, 133, Table 5.1, 135, 137–8, 141, 154, 156, 185
Trustee Savings Bank 142
turnover 34, 39, 169, Table 6.1, 180, 184, 194–8, 204, 210–12, 231–3, 240–1, 249, 255, 257–8, 263, 265, 274

variety 91, 249, 270
volume 91, 168, 183–4, 189, 194, Table 7.1, 198–9, 202–3, 209, 237, 249, 257, 262, 270

underwriting 117, 226, 228
Union Bank of Scotland 121, 138
Union Pacific & Erie Railroad 185, 186, 210, 232
United Alkali 121
United Exchange 22
U.S. Leather Co. 198
U.S. Steel 56, 70, 185, 186, 223, 237, 240
Urban Utilities x, Table 1.1, Table 2.3, 99, 101, 111–12, 114, 139, 170, 196, 208, 210, 222–4, 271
infrastructure 49, 111–13, 117–18, 123, 223, 239
Scottish 7
U.S. 70
Utah 72

Vermeer & Co. 69

Wagg Helbert & Co. 86
Walker & Watson (1894) 119
Wall St. 175, 228, 232–3
Warren (1908) 17
Weil, M.L. (1908) 207
Western Union 71, 227, 237
Westinghouse Air Brake 211
Williams, J. Covey 68
Wilson, George 76
Wilson, J.C. & Co. 177
Withers, G. (1907) 68, 81; (1910) 148
Woerishoffer, C.F. 188
Woodlock, T.F. (1908) 235

An environmentally friendly book printed and bound in England by www.printondemand-worldwide.com

#0270 - 110612 - C0 - 216/138/17 - PB